always up to date

The law changes, but Nolo is on top of it! We offer several ways to make sure you and your Nolo products are up to date:

1 **Nolo's Legal Updater**
We'll send you an email whenever a new edition of this book is published! Sign up at **www.nolo.com/legalupdater**.

2 **Updates @ Nolo.com**
Check www.nolo.com/update to find recent changes in the law that affect the current edition of your book.

3 **Nolo Customer Service**
To make sure that this edition of the book is the most recent one, call us at **800-728-3555** and ask one of our friendly customer service representatives. Or find out at **www.nolo.com**.

please note

We believe accurate, plain-English legal information should help you solve many of your own legal problems. But this text is not a substitute for personalized advice from a knowledgeable lawyer. If you want the help of a trained professional—and we'll always point out situations in which we think that's a good idea—consult an attorney licensed to practice in your state.

Fourteenth Edition

Legal Research

How to Find & Understand the Law

by Attorneys Stephen Elias and Susan Levinkind

Edited by Richard Stim

FOURTEENTH EDITION	JULY 2007
Editor	RICHARD STIM
Cover Design	SUSAN PUTNEY
Book Design	TERRI HEARSH
Production	SARAH HINMAN
Proofreading	CHRISTINE SINNOTT
Index	THÉRÈSE SHERE
Printing	DELTA PRINTING SOLUTIONS, INC.

International Standard Serial Number (ISSN) 1539-4115

ISBN 1-4133-0693-4

Dedications

To Catherine and Megan
Whose special gifts
Ease these troubled times
And illuminate my future
— SE

To Elana
my heart's companion
And to Andrea, Scott, Sammy and Adam
for immeasurable pleasures
— SL

Acknowledgments

Over the years many wonderful people have contributed to this book in many different ways, including insights into legal research resources and techniques, text editing, error checking and book and cover design. We specifically wish to acknowledge the contributions of Nolo publisher Jake Warner, Mary Randolph, Janet Portman, Jackie Clark Mancuso, Eddie Warner, Stephanie Harolde, Nancy Erb, the late Diana Vincent-Daviss, Shirley Hart-David, Robert Berring, Terri Hearsh, Toni Ihara, Raquel Baker, James Evans, Ella Hirst, Nolen Barrett, Ling Yu and our legal research students.

Table of Contents

5 Getting Some Background Information

6 Constitutions, Statutes, Regulations and Ordinances

7 Understanding Case Law

Appendix
Glossary of Legal Terms

Index

Your Legal Companion

If you're new to legal research and you need to find some legal case or law, you may be apprehensive. Whether you're in front of a computer or in a law library, it feels like you're searching for the proverbial needle in the haystack. After all, there are so many different research resources and so many places to look. How can you efficiently locate the relevant material?

Relax.

With a little practice and some diligence, you'll find everything you need. Legal research may seem like strange unchartered territory, but it's not. This book will serve as your map (or in modern parlance, your GPS locator). Once you research a couple of topics, you will soon find that there's a simple method to this madness.

One key is to dive right in. Opening books and viewing legal websites will make much of this book come alive in a way that our words, no matter how carefully chosen, cannot. You will especially benefit by actually doing—one step at a time—the research exercises set out in some of the chapters, and by completing the research problems provided.

Keep in mind that legal research comes in many forms and that legal researchers have a myriad of faces. So, we have designed this book to be a flexible tool, of use to researchers of various levels of sophistication.

If you are new to legal research, start with Chapter 2 and work your way through the book. Chapter 2 will introduce you to an efficient and sensible method for approaching most any legal research project. Chapter 3 provides an overview of our legal system.

Chapters 4 through 11 show you how to:

- identify your research problem according to recognized legal categories;
- locate books that will give you an overview of the laws that affect your particular issues;
- find and use law resources on the Internet;
- find, read and understand the law itself: statutes (laws passed by legislatures), regulations (rules issued by government agencies) and cases (decisions by courts);
- use the tools found in all law libraries—*Shepard's Citations for Cases* and case digests—that let you find court opinions that address the issues you're interested in; and
- organize the results of your research into a legal memorandum.

Chapter 12 provides real-life examples that put all the steps together and gives you a clear picture of how to solve a legal research problem. And of course, throughout this book, we also provide an overview of how to use and locate the types of resources available on the Internet.

Chapter 11 contains a set of legal research problems and answers that let you test your skills in a law library. Library and Internet exercises that enhance your skills in key areas are also contained in the chapters. Finally, Chapters 2 through 10 have review questions and answers. If you already have some general legal research skills but want guidance on a particular aspect or phase, turn to the appropriate chapters for a thorough explanation of a particular strategy.

If you want a quick refresher on the specific steps involved in a particular research task—for example, how to find a particular state statute you've heard about—use our "Summing Up" feature. These are in colored boxes. A list of summaries directly follows the Table of Contents in the front of the book.

In short, when it comes to finding that legal needle in the haystack, don't fear. If it's out there, we'll help you find it.

We'd Like to Hear From You

The registration form at the back of the book allows us to notify you of current product information and is our way of hearing from our readers about how they liked (or didn't like!) this book. We use your comments when we prepare for new printings and editions. But we have found that people tend to fill the form out right away, before they have used the book and can tell us specifically what worked and what didn't. Please note your thoughts below as you use the book, then complete the form and mail it to us at Stephen Elias/Legal Research Book, Nolo, 950 Parker Street, Berkeley, CA 94710.

Notes:

_____

_____

_____

_____

_____

_____

_____

_____

_____

_____

_____

_____

_____

_____

_____

Quick Legal Research Tips

This book provides the information you need to systematically research the vast written and electronic resources that together make up "the law." But instead of learning legal research techniques, you may just want to find specific items such as statutes, cases, regulations or plain-English overviews of legal topics.

Here are some quick tips on using the Internet to find and read these and other law-related materials. Each quick tip section contains a cross-reference to the part of this book that handles the particular task in more detail.

I want to use Google and other online search engines to perform keyword searches.

See Chapter 4 for more information on using Google as a legal search engine. For more information on using free Westlaw or LexisNexis services in your law library to find legal references, see Chapter 9.

If you want a solid answer to a legal question, you will need to undertake a more systematic search of available legal resources. See Chapter 2 for an overview of the legal research process online and in the law library.

I want to find a federal statute (law enacted by Congress and signed by the president).

The most direct route is to use the FindLaw website (www. findlaw.com/casecode/uscodes/), which permits you to search federal laws (organized in the U.S. Codes) by title, section, or keyword. You can also use the Google search engine. When using Google, provide the literal name or number of the law in quotation marks. If the new law has a lot of words, it usually works to just use the distinctive elements of the phrase. For example, when looking for the Bankruptcy Abuse Prevention and Reform Act of 2005, the phrase "bankruptcy abuse" would be sufficient for the statute's name. Similarly, if the law has a nickname, you can use that phrase. If you can think of key words that identify the law, provide those as well. For instance, if a new law creates an additional procedure for collecting child support, you could likely find it by typing in the terms: "child support" and "collection." If you know the year that the law was passed, add that as well (so that you don't get an out-of-date law by the same name). See Chapter 6 for more detail on searching for federal statutes online and in the law library.

I want to find a state statute (law passed by state legislature).

Our first choice is to use the Cornell Law School site (www.law.cornell.edu/states/listing.html) where you will see a state-by-state index for state laws. If you search instead with Google, type your state's name (so that the search engine won't give you an Illinois law while you are in Texas) and then provide the literal name or number of the law, in quotation marks. If the new law has a lot of words, it usually works to just use the distinctive elements of the phrase. Similarly, if the law has a nickname, you can use that phrase. For example, you can locate California's sex offender registration law (AB 488) by typing: "Megan's Law" California. If you can think of key words that identify the law, provide those as well. For instance, if a new law creates an additional procedure for granting pregnancy leave to employees, you could likely find it by typing in the terms: "pregnancy leave" and "employee." If you know the year that the law was passed, add that as well (so that you don't get an out-of-date law by the same name). See Chapter 6 for more detail on searching for state statutes online and in the law library.

I want to find a state statute (law passed by state legislature) organized by topics.

Again, we recommend the Cornell Law School website (www.law.cornell.edu/topics/state_statutes.html), which has organized state statutes by topic. See Chapter 6 for more detail on searching for state statutes online and in the law library.

I want to find a U.S. Supreme Court case (a published Supreme Court opinion).

Try the Cornell Law School website, which provides a thorough index of Supreme Court decisions (www.law.cornell.edu/supct/index.html). If you are searching for a Supreme Court case using Google, type "Supreme Court" in quotation marks and then add any combination of the following elements:

- Type one or both names of the parties to the case. You can also search with the "v." abbreviation, as well—for example we typed in *Planned Parenthood v. Casey* and retrieved a copy of the 1992 Supreme Court Case.

- Include one or more terms that describe the subject matter of the case. For example, we typed 'Betamax' and 'Supreme Court' and retrieved the 1984 Supreme Court case, *Sony v. Universal*.
- Type the year of the case.

See Chapter 9 for more detail on finding U.S. Supreme Court cases online and in the law library.

I want to find a federal court case (a published judicial opinion).

Start at the Cornell Law School website, which provides a thorough index of federal court decisions (www.law.cornell.edu/federal/opinions.html). If you are searching for a federal case law using Google, type any combination of the following elements:

- Type one or both names of the parties to the case. You can also search with the "v." abbreviation, as well—for example *Planned Parenthood v. Casey*.
- Include one or more terms that describe the subject matter of the case.
- Type the year of the case.
- Type the name of the court that heard and decided the case.

Note that cases decided previous to 1995—that is, before the Internet was used to catalog court cases—usually are only available in private databases that require a subscription for a fee. See Chapter 9 for more detail on finding a federal court case online and in the law library.

I want to find a state court case (published opinions by state courts).

Begin with the Cornell Law School website, which provides a thorough index of state court decisions (www.law.cornell.edu/opinions.html#state). If you are searching for a state case using Google, type the name of the state and any combination of the following elements:

- Type one or both names of the parties to the case. You can also search with the "v." abbreviation, as well—for example *Planned Parenthood v. Casey*.
- Include one or more terms that describe the subject matter of the case.
- Type the year of the case.
- Type the name of the court that heard and decided the case.

Note that cases decided previous to 1995—that is, before the Internet was used to catalog court cases—usually are only available in private databases that require a subscription for a fee. See Chapter 9 for more detail on finding state courts cases online and in the law library.

I want to find a federal regulation (rules issued by federal agencies).

The FindLaw website is a good place to start. FindLaw provides a searching system for the federal code of regulations (www.findlaw.com/casecode/cfr.html). See Chapter 6 for more detail on finding federal regulations online and in the law library.

I want to find a state regulation (rules issued by state agencies).

You'll find many state regs by using FindLaw (www.findlaw.com/casecode/state.html). See Chapter 6 for more detail on finding state regulations online and in the law library.

I want to find an ordinance passed by a particular city or county (local laws).

Your best bet for finding city and county ordinances is FindLaw. Go to the FindLaw link for state laws (www.findlaw.com/casecode/). Scroll down to the list of U.S. State Laws and click the relevant state. The next web page should provide available city and county ordinances for that state. See Chapter 6 for more detail on finding ordinances online and in the law library.

I want to find a plain-English discussion of a particular legal topic.

Two sites provide plain-English legal information. Nolo, the publisher of this book (www.nolo.com), offers a great deal of helpful legal resources. On the homepage, enter the keywords in the search box and choose "Search Entire Site" from the drop-down menu below the search box. FindLaw (www.findlaw.com) also provides helpful legal resources for consumers and for lawyers. As you're also aware, the Google search engine will also help you find legal information.

Type relevant key words into the search box. For instance, if you are looking for articles on the status of medical marijuana law in Colorado, enter these terms in this format: [medical marijuana law Colorado]. See Chapter 5 for more detail on finding plain-English discussions online and in the law library.

I want to find a particular state or federal court form.

The Google search engine (www.google.com) is the easiest method for locating state or federal forms. Try typing any combination of the following elements into the search box:

- the state that issued the form or, if it's a local form, the court where you will use it;
- the title of the form or a few unique terms that would likely be in the title—for example, "Petition Administer Estate" for a "Notice of Petition to Administer Estate;"
- The subject matter of the form in the absence of a specific name—for example "Summons Eviction;"
- It may also help to use the term "form."

See Chapter 5 for more detail on finding federal and state court forms.

I want to find discussions of legal issues in the news.

Using the Google search engine (www.google.com), you can search for news results in two ways. First, you can run a search on Google's main page and then click the "News" link on the top of the search results page. Or, you can direct a search to find only news articles. To perform the latter, go to the Google home page and click "more" and then click "News Search."

Stay on top of breaking legal news stories. If you want to stay abreast of a specific news subject, try "Google News Alerts." You will receive daily (or "as it happens") emails based on your choice of query or topic. Go to www.google.com/alerts and type in the search terms.

An Overview of Legal Research

This chapter provides a basic approach to virtually any legal research task in the law library or on the Internet. This is nothing we invented; rather, it is the almost universal method of experienced legal researchers. Once you understand how this overall approach works, any research task will be greatly simplified. Although some of what we say is fairly conventional (for example, keep accurate notes), much of it isn't. For example, we suggest that achieving the highest quality of legal research requires a commitment to perseverance and patience, and a belief in yourself.

Patience and Perspective

A certain type of attitude and approach are required to efficiently find the information you need among the billions of legal facts and opinions in a law library or on the Internet. Probably the most important quality to cultivate is patience—a willingness to follow the basic legal research method diligently, even though it's a time-consuming process.

Unfortunately, many legal researchers are impatient, preferring to make a quick stab at finding the particular piece of information they think they need. While a quest for immediate gratification is sometimes appropriate when attempted by a master researcher, it most often results in no satisfaction at all when attempted by the less experienced.

Perhaps it will be easier to understand how legal research is best approached if we take an analogy from another field.

Seeking and finding legal information is a lot like learning how to cook a gourmet dish. To cook the dish, you first need to settle on a broad category of cuisine —Japanese, French, Nouvelle California, etc. Next, you find one or two good cookbooks that provide an overview of the techniques common to that specific cuisine. From there you get more specific: You find a recipe to your liking, learn the meaning of unfamiliar cooking terms, and make a list of the ingredients. Finally, you assemble the ingredients and carefully follow the instructions in the recipe.

Legal research also involves identifying a broad category before you search for more specific information. Once you know the general direction in which you're headed, you are prepared to find an appropriate background resource—an encyclopedia, law journal, Internet article, treatise—to educate yourself about the general issues involved in your research. Armed with this overview, you can then delve into the law itself—cases, statutes, regulations—to find definitive answers to your questions. And, when your research is finished, you can pull your work together into a coherent written statement. (Writing up your research is crucial to knowing whether you really are finished.)

Of course, in the legal research process there are lots of opportunities for dead ends, misunderstandings and even mental gridlock. Answers that seemed in your hand five minutes ago evaporate when you read a later case or statutory amendment. Issues that seemed crystal clear become muddy with continued reading. And authoritative experts often contradict each other.

Take heart. Even experienced legal researchers often thrash around some before they get on the right track. And the truth is, most legal issues are confused and confusing— that's what makes them legal issues. Just remember that the main difference between the expert and novice researcher is that the expert has faith that sooner or later the research will pan out, while the novice too easily becomes convinced that the whole thing is hopeless. Fortunately, this book— and many law librarians—are there to help the struggling legal researcher.

How to Find (and Feel at Home in) a Law Library

Before you can do legal research, you need access to good research tools. The best tools are still found primarily in law libraries, although sometimes legal research involves government document and social science collections.

Many law libraries are open to the public and can be found in most federal, state and county courthouses.

Law school libraries in public universities also routinely grant access to members of the public, although hours of access may be somewhat restricted depending on the security needs of the school. It is also often possible to gain access to private law libraries maintained by local bar associations, large law firms, state agencies or large corporations if you know a local attorney or are willing to be persistent in seeking permission from the powers that be.

Law libraries can be intimidating at first. The walls are lined with thick and formally bound books that tend to look exactly alike. Then too, for the layperson and beginning student, it is easy to feel that you are treading on some sacred reserve, especially in courthouse libraries where the average user is a formally-attired lawyer and where, on occasion, a judge is present. You might even

have the secret fear that if it is discovered that you're not a lawyer, you'll either be asked in a loud voice to leave or, at best, be treated as a second-class citizen.

If you remember that public funds (often court filing fees) probably helped buy the books in the library and pay the people running it, any initial unease should disappear. It may also help you to know that most librarians have a sincere interest in helping anyone who desires to use their library. While they won't answer your legal questions for you, they will often put in your hands the materials that will give you a good start on your research or help you get to the next phase.

A good way to deal with any feelings of intimidation is to recall your early experiences with the public library. Remember how the strangeness of all the book shelves, the catalog and the reference desk rather quickly gave way to an easy familiarity with how they all fit together? Your experience with law libraries will similarly pass from fear to mastery in a very short time.

Helping you understand the cataloging, cross-reference and indexing systems law libraries use is one of the most important functions of this book. As you proceed, we hope you will see that learning to break the code of the law library can be fun.

Legal Research on the Internet

When the first edition of this book was published in 1982, the Internet was largely unknown to the American public. Now, "being on the Internet" is pretty much like having a phone, very common if not yet totally universal. And when questions arise in everyday life, we increasingly turn to the Internet for answers. Want to know where the term "redneck" came from? Type the word in one of the search-engine query boxes that accompany every Internet browser and you'll find more information on the subject than you probably care to read.

As with general information, a lot of legal information is accessible "out there" in cyberspace. In Chapter 4, we'll explain how one search engine—Google—has revolutionized many of the common legal research tasks. Unfortunately, much of the information that you want can still only be reached through "closed" databases that aren't picked up by the common search engines. Thanks to some great Internet "catalogs," however, finding the law—statutes, cases, regulations and interpretive materials—is a straightforward task. Throughout this book we explain how

to use these catalogs and do your research in the comfort of your home or office. Also, in Chapter 4 we provide an overview of online searching techniques. We encourage you to familiarize yourself with that chapter before embarking on your Internet legal research journey.

A Basic Approach to Legal Research in the Law Library

The core task in answering any legal question is to determine the likely answer you would get from a judge. To do this, your ultimate goal will be to find published court opinions that answer the question in a factual context that is as close to yours as possible. The diagram depicted below takes you through the typical steps and resources necessary to reach that goal when using a law library.

As you can see, the diagram is shaped a bit like an hourglass. You start with a universe of possibilities, then narrow your search until you find one or two relevant cases. Those cases, in turn—with the assistance of certain cross-reference tools—allow you to rapidly locate many additional relevant cases.

Your most fervent hope when you start a basic legal research task is to find at least one case that perfectly—and favorably—answers your specific research question in an identical factual context. Of course, this goal is seldom, if ever, met in reality. But the more cases you can locate that are relevant to your question, the better your chances of nailing down a firm answer.

The method depicted in the diagram is appropriate for the type of research that involves an open-ended question about the law. However, it may be overkill for someone who has a very specific research need, such as finding a specific case, reading a specific statute, finding out whether a specific case is still good law, and so on. For those tasks, see the chart at the end of the chapter.

Also, we don't intend the diagram as a lockstep approach to legal research. For example, it may be most efficient in certain circumstances to start your research in a *West Digest* (a tool that summarizes cases by the legal topics they address) instead of using a background resource or code for this purpose. It all depends on such variables as the amount of information you already bring to your quest, the time you have to spend and the level of certainty you are after. Your goal, after all, is to arrive at the best possible answer to your question in the least possible time, not to mechanically complete a laborious research process.

Here, then, is the diagram and a discussion of each research step portrayed in it.

Internet note: If you are doing the bulk of your research on the Internet, you may be using a different set of tools in a somewhat different order.

Step 1: Formulate Your Legal Questions

The top box, "your broad legal research topic," represents the first step in legal research: formulating the questions you wish to answer. This is not as easy as you may think. Often we think we have a question in mind but when we try to answer it, we find that we don't quite know what we're looking for. The best bet here is to make sure that your question has a logical answer. For instance, if you have been bitten by a dog and are looking for information about dog bites, break your search down into some specific answerable questions, such as:

- Who is responsible for injury caused by a biting dog?
- What facts do I have to prove to sue and win compensation for the dog bite?
- Is there a statute or ordinance that covers dog bites?
- Does it make any difference if the dog has or has not ever bitten anyone before?

Keep in mind that the first articulation of your research questions will probably change as your research progresses. In this example, you may start out thinking that your issue involves dogs, only to find out that it really involves the duties of landowners to prevent harm from dangerous conditions on their property.

Step 2: Categorize Your Research Questions

The next box down represents the classification stage. Because of the way legal materials are organized, it is usually necessary to place your research topic into a category described by using the three variables shown in this box. Exactly how this is accomplished is the primary subject of Chapter 4.

Also covered in Chapter 4 is the next stage in the chart, when you break down your question into many words and phrases. That enables you to use legal indexes to find a background discussion of your topic.

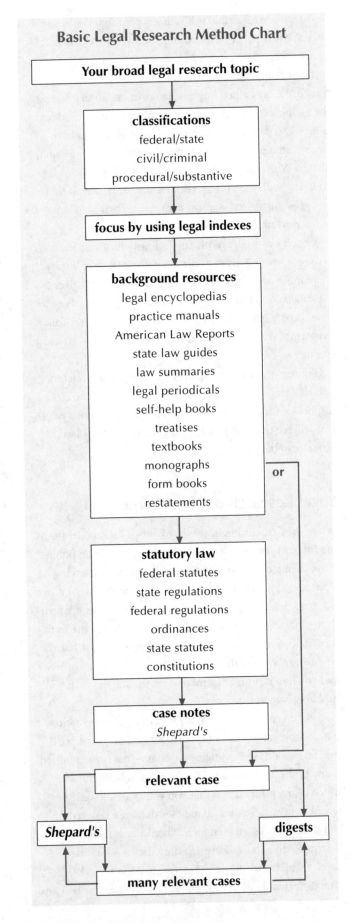

Basic Legal Research Method Chart

Step 3: Find Appropriate Background Resources

When starting a legal research task, you need an overview of the legal issues connected with your questions and an idea of how your questions fit into the larger legal fabric. This background information can normally best be obtained from books and articles, written by experts, that summarize and explain the subject. How to identify and use these background resources is covered in Chapter 5.

Step 4: Look for Statutes

After you review background resources, you will want to proceed to the law itself. Usually, you should hunt for statutory law first. In most instances, an analysis of the law starts with legislative or administrative enactments—statutes and rules—and ends with court decisions that interpret them. You too should usually deal with the statutory material first and the cases second. We show you how to research statutes in Chapter 6.

However, some important areas of the law are developed primarily in the courts—the law of torts (personal injuries) is a good example. If you have a tort problem—and the background resource provides you with appropriate references—you might wish to start with cases first, and then come back and research statutory law if and when it is indicated. This alternative path is shown on the chart by the line that goes directly from "background resources" to "relevant case."

Step 5: Find a Relevant Case

After finding one or more relevant statutes or rules, you will want to see how they have been interpreted by the courts. To pinpoint cases that discuss the statute (or rule, regulation or ordinance) you are interested in, use the tools listed in the next box in the "Basic Legal Research Method Chart": case notes and *Shepard's Citations for Statutes.* These tools are addressed in Chapter 9.

As soon as you find a case that speaks directly to your research question, you are almost home. This is because two major research tools—*Shepard's* and *Case Digests*—cross-reference all cases by the issues decided in them. So if you find one case discussing your question, you can often quickly find a bunch of others discussing the same question.

Step 6: Use *Shepard's* and Digests to Find More Cases

Once you find a relevant case, *Shepard's Citations for Cases* and the West Digest system allow you to rapidly go from that case to any other cases that have some bearing on your precise questions. These tools are covered in detail in Chapter 10.

Step 7: Use *Shepard's* to Update Your Cases

Once you have found cases that pertain to your issue, you need to find out whether the principles stated in these cases are still valid law. To do this, you need to understand the factual context of each case, analyze each case for its value as precedent and use the digests and *Shepard's Citations for Cases* to locate the most recent cases that bear on your issue. We show you how to do all of this in Chapters 7 through 10.

Six Time-Saving Research Tips

The research method just outlined and the techniques explained in the rest of this book work only if you proceed methodically. Otherwise, even though you know how to accomplish many legal research tasks, you are still likely to end up sifting through the law library book by book, spending many hours more than are necessary. In this context, here are six tips for more efficient legal research.

Take Careful Notes

Beginning any legal research effort involves a certain amount of guesswork. You may make several false starts before adopting an approach that works. And what may seem like a wrong approach at first may turn out to be the best one after all. Unfortunately, it is human nature not to keep careful track of your preliminary work, which means that you may find yourself repeating it.

To avoid this, teach yourself to take complete notes from the beginning on all the materials you're using, including the location and substance of any possibly relevant statute, case or comment mentioned in the materials. It may seem like a burden at first, but it will soon become second nature as you see how often it saves you time in the long run. A good article entitled, "How to Look up Law and Write Legal Memoranda Revisited," by F. Trowbridge Vom Baur, provides some still-sound, structured methods for documenting your research.

It appears in a law journal called *The Practical Lawyer* (May 1965) and can be found in most law libraries.

Check Out the Law Library

Law libraries are always organized according to some plan. When first using a law library, it is helpful to take a brief self-guided tour, carefully noting where the major groupings of materials are located, so you'll know where to go for your books instead of repeatedly searching from wall to wall. This book introduces you to legal research materials and tools such as codes, case reports, digests, encyclopedias and *Shepard's Citations*. Knowing where they are before you dig into your research will make your efforts more efficient. Although many libraries have maps at the reference counter that show where materials are located, they don't replace the walk-around method.

Collect Your Materials in Advance

As you check different cases and statutes for relevant material, you may find yourself reading only a few lines in many different books. So it is a good idea to make a list of all the books involved in the next phase of your research task and gather them in one place before you start reading. This allows you to find everything you need at once rather than continually popping up and down. While this advice may seem obvious, apparently it isn't; you can observe the "jump up and scurry" approach to legal research on any visit to the library.

Find Special Tools and Resources Unique to Your State

This book focuses on the legal research resource tools that are common to the 50 states and are found in the great majority of law libraries. We also discuss some of the resources particular to the more populous states. There are, however, a number of special state-specific tools and resources that we don't mention. So in addition to using the major legal research materials and tools discussed here, check with your law librarian about other state-specific materials.

For instance, where we discuss legal encyclopedias in Chapter 5, we provide the titles of the two main national legal encyclopedias and 15 state-specific encyclopedias. If you are interested in the law of one of the states for which we have not specified an encyclopedia, don't turn to one of the national ones without first checking to see whether the subject you are interested in has been dealt with in a resource designed specifically for your state. If you can find such local materials (perhaps a law review article or a state bar publication), you stand a good chance of finding the answer to your question a lot faster than if you use general or national materials.

Get Yourself a Good Law Dictionary

Your legal research will constantly introduce you to new and strange terminology that has developed over hundreds of years. When doing research in the law library, it is extremely helpful to have a good law dictionary at your fingertips.

The most well-known law dictionary is *Black's Law Dictionary*. Unfortunately, many of the entries are hard to decipher and are not sufficiently context-sensitive—that is, they are too abstract to fit real-life situations. More user-friendly dictionaries that should serve you well are:

- *Law Dictionary*, Gifis (5th ed., Barron's, 2003); and
- *Ballentine's Law Dictionary: Legal Assistant Edition*, Handler (Thomson, 1993).

Use the Catalog

Most law libraries will have a catalog that lists by author and subject all of the books and periodicals in the library. These days, the catalog will likely be computerized, although a few may still use the card system. The call number on the upper left-hand portion of the card and on the screen tells where the item is located in that library. If an unaided search seems a bit intimidating at first, the law librarian will be happy to show you where to find your materials.

It is important to remember that many important legal research materials—such as articles, statutes and cases—are collected and published in large books or sets of books. A catalog will tell you where the books are located, but it will not tell you where a specific article, case or statute is. For example, if you want to do your own divorce and there is no good self-help book for your state, you could use the catalog to find such helpful background materials as a law school textbook on divorce law, the *Family Law Reporter* (a loose-leaf publication) and any practice manuals or form books on divorce that have been published for your state. However, you couldn't use it to locate the statutes of your state concerning divorce; nor would the catalog help you find any cases on a particular point. To do that, you will have to use legal indexes and other research tools that we discuss later in the book.

Library Exercise: Paperchase

This Paperchase will lead you to many of the legal research resources that you will be learning to use in this book. Follow the instructions, and when you are finished you will have a profound and witty quotation as well as the knowledge of where things are in your law library.

Here is the quotation, with blanks to be filled in according to the instructions for each word:

"_____ is _____ly
　　　　(1)　　　　　　　　　　　　　　(2)

_____ and _____
　　　(3)　　　　　　　　　　　　　　(4)

_____ ." _____
　　　(5)　　　　　　　　　　　　　　(6)

_____ , _____ – _____
　　　(7)　　　　　　　　(8)　　　　　　(9)
.

A. Find the *United States Code Annotated (U.S.C.A.)*. Find the volumes for Title 42 Public Health and Welfare. Find the volume containing Title 42 §§ 1771-1982. Turn to page 226. Halfway down the page starts the first section of Chapter 16, Section B. What is the number of the §? Write the number in blank (9).

B. Find the *Supreme Court Reporter*. Find Volume 80A and turn to page 900. What is the last name of the plaintiff in the case starting on page 900, Victor Donald _____? Write the name in blank (7).

C. Find *Federal Reporter,* 2d series. Find Volume 939 and turn to page 808. What is the last name of the first named plaintiff in the case starting on page 808, Ruth E. _____? Write the name in blank (6).

D. Find *Federal Supplement*. Find Volume 616 and turn to page 1528. What is the first word of the name of the plaintiff in the case that starts on page 1528, _____ Blue Music, Inc.? Write the word in blank (2).

E. Find the *Federal Practice Digest 4th*. Find the volumes covering Criminal Law. Select Volume 35 and turn to page 725. Find the case in the right-hand column under "C.A. 10 (N.M.) 1985. Eighth Amendment does not apply until after adjudication of guilt." What is the third word in the name of the defendant? Write the word in blank (1). Hint: The Court of Appeals cases are in alphabetical order by name of state, regardless of the circuit they belong to.

F. Find *U.S. Code Congressional and Administrative News*. Find the volumes for 103rd Congress First Session 1993, and select Volume 2. The pages in the first part of the book are numbered 107 STAT 1485, 107 STAT 1486, etc. Go to the act that starts on page 107 STAT 1547 (NATIONAL DEFENSE AUTHORIZATION ACT FOR FISCAL YEAR 1994). Find § 1702 of the act (Consolidation of Chemical and Biological Defense Training Activities). What page is the full text on? 107 STAT ____. Write the page number in blank (8).

G. Find *Corpus Juris Secundum (C.J.S.)* 1966 edition. Find the article on Negligence, and find § 21, which defines *mere accident* or *Act of God*. The definition of *unavoidable accident* starts on page 647. At the end of the first paragraph of this definition is the phrase, "and in this sense the term is held to be equivalent to or synonymous with, 'mere accident or _____ accident.'" Write the left-out word in blank (3). (If your library has a later edition, this won't work.)

H. Find *American Jurisprudence 2d (Am. Jur. 2d)*. Find the article on Interest and Usury. The article begins with "I. In General; § 1. Definitions and distinctions." The second sentence of definitions and distinctions starts with the phrase: "_____ interest is interest computed on the principal only." Write the left-out word in blank (5).

I. Find *Words and Phrases* (the large 40+ volume set). Find the definition for "Neutral Spirits" in Volume 28A. What is the next word defined? Write the word in blank (4).

Answer: "Truth is rarely pure and never simple," Oscar Wilde, 1854-1900.

An Online Search Strategy

When doing legal research, it's pretty easy to get bogged down in an informational swamp. Your search efforts on the Internet will often produce a long list of links to possibly helpful sites, each of which must be visited to know what's in them. While the length of your results list can be cut back with good key word searching techniques, you'll often find the right link or links by sheer trial and error.

Once you've found a relevant link, however, you must face another potential problem. How valuable is this information? Is it accurate? Is it up to date? And if you are researching primary law sources such as statutes, regulations and cases, is the publisher of the materials "official?"

For instance, should you rely on a statute you found online when the site where you found it is not the official publisher of statutes for the state in question? While we can't completely resolve these issues for you, we can make a few suggestions that will help you navigate the law on the Internet to a successful conclusion.

The first step to doing legal research is to understand what type of legal information you are looking for. Legal questions can conveniently be divided into four types:

- Are you searching for general information about a legal subject of interest?
- Are you searching for the law itself (statutes, court opinions, regulations, ordinances)?
- Are you searching for information about current legal events (such as celebrity trials)?
- Are you searching for a reliable answer to a specific legal question?

Here are some suggestions on how to use the Internet to address these legal questions.

General Information About a Legal Subject

Many people want to bone up on a particular subject. They are looking for the same level of information commonly found in a general-purpose encyclopedia. For instance, you might want a general discussion of:

- What laws are involved when selling a business?
- What's the difference between a living trust and a will?
- When is a new idea patentable?
- What effect does divorce have on pensions earned during a marriage?

These types of questions can be answered without regard to your specific circumstances. For instance, the laws involved when selling a business will be the same for everyone. In Chapter 5, we explain how to use legal background materials to address these types of questions, and we show you how to find background materials on the Internet.

It's important to know when you're looking for background information and when you're actually asking for an answer to a particular legal question. If your question can be started with "Can I …?", "What will happen if …?" or "Can they …?", you're asking for specific legal authority that says, in effect, "Yes, you can" or "No, you can't" in the context of your individual circumstances. To get reliable answers to specific questions like these concerning your situation, you need to dig a lot deeper than when you are searching for background information that applies to everyone. See below for an overview of how this type of research can be carried out on the Internet.

The Law Itself

Another category of legal information is the law itself. The law itself is found in what we call "primary law sources." For most people, the most common primary law sources are the pronouncements—issued by local, state and federal legislative bodies—that we call ordinances, statutes and regulations. Lawyers are also familiar with another type of primary law source—court decisions that either interpret a statute, regulation or ordinance or make some law of their own.

There are many reasons why you may want to find a particular primary law source. Two of the most likely reasons are:

- You may have learned about a particular new law or court decision through the media or at your job, and you want to read it for yourself; or
- You may want to know what the law itself says because you are trying to answer a specific legal question.

If you are searching for the law for the first reason, your research will be self-limiting—that is, you will search for the appropriate law source, find the law source and read the law source, period. In Chapters 6 and 9, we provide examples of how to find statutes and cases online.

If you are searching primary law sources for the second reason—that is, you want to answer a legal question—you usually will have to find and read other legal materials as well as the law itself. Again, see below for this type of search.

Current Legal Events

Many people search for information related to a current legal event. Recent examples would be the Anna Nicole Smith custody battle, the Virginia Tech shootings, or the events surrounding the Phil Specter murder trial. Getting information on current legal events involves finding articles and discussions of interest, online and off. We don't address this type of research in this book. An excellent site for keeping abreast of legal developments is CourtTV [www. courttv.com.]

Reliable Answers to Specific Legal Questions

This category of legal research involves a hunt for the answer to a very specific legal question, such as:

- I live in North Carolina. I've been charged with second offense drunk driving. My passenger was injured as a result. What penalties do I face?
- Can I run a home school in North Dakota if I've been convicted of a felony?
- My brother is the executor of our parents' estate. I don't like how he is handling it. What can I do about it?
- I want to open a business typing divorce papers for people who are doing their own divorces. Will I get into trouble with the lawyers if I do this?

These are the types of questions that people ask lawyers. To confidently answer these questions, you usually must turn to a variety of legal resources, including background discussions by experts, statutes, court opinions that interpret the statutes, and court opinions that make laws of their own (the common law). Then, you'll want to use some confirming techniques (like *Shepardizing*) that will assure you that your information is current. In the rest of this section, we provide a brief overview of how you can reliably answer questions online, using the search techniques discussed earlier in this chapter and the step-by-step examples spread throughout the book.

Step 1: Categorize your issue. The first step to doing legal research online is to put your research issue in the correct legal category. Chapter 4 provides a number of suggestions for doing this.

Step 2: Get the lay of the land. As we point out in Chapter 2, before trying to answer a specific legal question it is always a good idea to get a little background information about the legal field that your question concerns. This background information not only alerts you to some of the key issues you'll have to consider, but also gives you a basic vocabulary that will be useful as you continue your research. Also, of course, by reading background materials, you will frequently get directed to the relevant statutes or cases, which you'll have to read if you want a reliable answer to your question.

Step 3: Find relevant statutory authority. After you get the lay of the land, you'll want to zero in on a statute that is as specific to your question as possible. In Chapter 6, we show you how to find federal and state statutes on the Internet. If your background reading has pointed you to a specific statute, then your search should be pretty straightforward. However, if you have to find a statute by performing a category or key word search, then you'll need to be armed with the proper vocabulary. See Chapter 4, where we explain how to come up with words for searching an index. The same exercises apply to preparing for a key word search.

Step 4A: Find a relevant case interpreting the statute. Once you find a relevant statute (or regulation or ordinance), you will want to find out how the courts have interpreted it. In Chapter 9, we show you how to find federal and state court opinions on the Internet. The most comprehensive way to search for interpretations of your relevant statute is to enter the statute citation in the search box along with some appropriate key words describing the issue being researched.

Step 4B: Search for a case. Sometimes there is no relevant statute on a particular subject. Constitutional law, for example, consists primarily of interpretations of the meaning of the Constitution as found in cases decided by the U.S. Supreme Court. If the answer to your question is likely to appear in case law, you can progress directly to your search for relevant cases after reading your background material.

Step 5: Update your case. If you do find a relevant case, your next step is to find out how it has been used in other courts and whether the case remains good law. In Chapter 10, we show you how to do this by using citation systems such as Westlaw *KeyCite* or the Lexis *Shepardize* service.

Step 6: Assess your research results. If you have faithfully taken Steps 1-5, you are likely to have a tentative answer to your legal question. As we suggest in Chapter 11, you would be wise to prepare a brief legal memorandum. Writing down what you've done will help you know whether you've accomplished all that you set out to do. As you do so, ask yourself these questions:

- Can I rely on the source of the background information I used? Was it published by a reputable legal publisher or legal expert? Does it conform to

the other information I discovered while doing my search?

- Was the source of the statutes and cases I found the official source for these items? If not, was the website sponsored in some way by an official source, such as the court or the legislature? If there is no connection between the website and an official source, was the statute or case consistent with what I learned from my background resource?
- Is the way other cases treated the relevant case consistent with your understanding of the case?

If your answers to any of these questions cast some doubt on the reliability or authenticity of your research results, consider paying a visit to your local law library and double checking your search results against the statutes and cases as reported by the official or established publishers described in Chapters 5 through 9.

Understand the Legal Uncertainty Principle

Legal research rarely produces an absolutely certain answer to a complicated question. Indeed, unless you are searching for a simple bit of information such as the maximum jail sentence for arson in Texas, trying to find the definitive answer to a legal issue is often impossible.

There is a reason for this legal "uncertainty principle." Under the American justice system, any dispute that ends up in court is subject to the adversary process, where two or more parties fight it out and a judge or jury decides who wins. Of course, the fact that statutes are constantly cranked out and amended by legislatures and then subjected to judicial definition and redefinition substantially adds to the total confusion.

What all this means is that defining the "law" that governs any set of facts involves predicting how the courts would rule if presented with the question. If a prediction is based on clear statutes and court decisions, the level of uncertainty will be fairly low. However, if the statutes and case law are themselves subject to conflicting interpretations, as many are, then even the best legal research may amount to little more than a sophisticated form of fortune-telling. Put another way, while in some instances you may believe you have found out "what the law is," a person with a different set of preconceptions may arrive at a different result.

We mention the legal uncertainty principle simply to warn you against trying to nail down an absolute answer to most legal questions. Often, the best you can hope for is to understand the legal issues involved in a particular problem well enough to convince those who need to be convinced that your view is correct.

Know When You're Done

Once you understand that your search for the truth will necessarily come up short of absolute certainty, how can you tell when it's time to quit? To answer this question when the time comes, it's essential to develop a good sense of proportion and priorities.

Here are some questions to answer as part of trying to conscientiously answer the big question, "Am I done?"

- **Have you logically answered the question you wanted answered when you began?** To test your answer, buttonhole a friend, pose your question and then answer it on the basis of what your research disclosed. You will soon discover whether your logic holds up.
- **Are the laws and facts in the cases you have found pertinent to the facts of your situation?** To test your answer, decide whether the difference between the facts of your situation and the facts of any cases you've found (or those addressed by the statute you've located) could possibly make a difference in the answer to your question.
- **Do the cases you found refer to (cite) each other?** Cases cite other related cases as authority for their decisions. So each relevant case you find leads you to other cases. On any one issue, you'll eventually develop a list of cited cases; when it ceases to "grow," you'll know you're done.
- **Are the materials you've found to support your answer as up-to-date as you can get?** Because law changes so rapidly, a case or statute that is only a year old may already be obsolete. You haven't finished your research until you've checked all information to be sure it's current.
- **Have you used all major research resources that might improve your understanding or make your answer more certain?** If there are four different resources that might bear on a tax problem (for example, books that interpret Internal Service

Revenue regulations), it is wise to check all four rather than presuming any one to be correct or definitive.

- **Can you explain your reasoning in writing?** If your research is reasonably complete, you should be able to express in writing the question you researched, your answer to it and the basis for your answer. It is common to think you've finished a research task, only to discover when you try to write it up that there are gaping holes. Chapter 11 suggests some guidelines for putting your research results into written form, and the answers to the research problems in Chapter 11 contain sample memoranda as examples.

If your answer to all the questions posed above is a resounding or even a qualified "yes," then you've probably done about as much as makes sense. If you feel, however, that any of these questions deserves an honest "no" or a waffling "maybe," you have more work to do.

Review

Questions

1. Where can law libraries be found?
2. Give six examples of legal research.
3. What is your most fervent hope when you begin a basic legal research task?
4. What are the seven basic steps to legal research?
5. What are some ways to know when you're done with your research?

Answers

1. • Most federal, state and county courthouses.
   • Law schools.
   • Privately maintained law libraries (local bar associations, large law firms, state agencies and large corporations).

2. • A police officer looks in her manual to decide what charges to hold a criminal suspect for.
   • A social security recipient calls up his regional office to ask about the agency's eligibility policies.
   • Looking up a specific statute.
   • Reading a newly decided U.S. Supreme Court case.
   • Studying a new federal regulation published in the *Federal Register*.
   • Obtaining documents from a state or federal government.

3. To find at least one case that perfectly—and favorably—answers your specific research question in an identical factual context.

4. • Formulate your research questions.
   • Categorize your research questions.
   • Find appropriate background resources.
   • Look for statutes.
   • Find a relevant case.
   • Use *Shepard's* and Digests to find more cases.
   • Use *Shepard's* to update your cases.

5. • You have logically answered the question you wanted answered when you began.
   • The laws and facts in the cases you've found are pertinent to the particular facts of your situation.
   • The materials you've found to support your answers are as up-to-date as you can get.
   • You have utilized all major research resources that might improve your understanding or make your answer more certain.

An Overview of the Law

What Is the Law?

In this book, we generally think of "law" as the sum total of the rules governing individual and group behavior that are enforceable in court. Primarily, as you will see, this means state and federal statutes, agency regulations, local ordinances and published court decisions (cases). However, this is not the only possible definition of law.

It's important to view law in a more practical way, focusing not only on the law as it is written down in statutes and casebooks, but also on what happens in the real world. For example, if the Social Security Administration terminates the disability benefits of eligible recipients despite the repeated rulings of federal courts that such terminations violate federal law, the fact that the federal law exists appears of little value to the people affected. Similarly, if police and prosecutors are reluctant to prosecute certain types of crimes, such as those involving domestic violence, law as it exists in the community will be far different than what is written in the books. Finally, suppose a Supreme Court justice votes to reverse a murder conviction on the basis of previous court decisions. If the other eight vote to uphold the conviction, the "law" will appear vastly different to the one justice and the condemned person than to the eight-justice majority.

At the very least, we recommend cross-checking information from library research with what goes on in the particular legal area on a day-to-day basis. Probably the best way is to check your conclusions with lawyers or other people familiar with local court, agency or police practices.

Another important view of law is that our Constitution is ultimately subject to a higher law. Some people believe that this law exists in nature, called "natural law," and applies to everyone whether they ascribe to it or not; others believe that ethics are many sets of rules developed by various philosophers over the ages and either chosen by or imposed on society. When Supreme Court nominees come before the Senate for confirmation, they usually are asked whether they believe that written law—constitution, statutes, cases—is all there is, or whether natural law should be used to "inform" or guide their interpretations of the Constitution.

Changing the Law

A number of groups who feel that the American legal system is no longer designed to produce justice are engaged in an effort to examine and replace many of the system's legal underpinnings. This effort is not dealt with in this book. If you believe things should be different than they are, and you find no support for your view in existing statutory or case law, you may wish to study some of the books you will find cataloged under the heading "jurisprudence" in any good-sized law library. Legal reform, ethics, philosophy and religion are other likely headings.

Foundations of American Law

Because we draw our cultural heritage from so many different traditions, our legal system is a bit like a jigsaw puzzle. There are big pieces of English law (itself drawn from Norman, German, Saxon, Scandinavian and Roman societies) side by side with smaller bits from Spanish, French, Native American and ancient biblical sources. These have all been modified by our peculiar North American experience.

Until the 12th century, law in the western world operated on several primary levels. Collections of written laws such as the *Augustinian Code* or the *Code of Charlemagne* (both traceable to Roman law) created a broad written legal framework. This basic system still prevails in many countries (and in Louisiana in this country) and is known as the "civil" law. In addition, the Catholic Church governed many activities under a large body of ecclesiastical law. Finally, all kinds of rules and regulations, many of which were never written down, were enforced by kings, local lords and courts, both ecclesiastical and secular.

A legal tradition called the "common" law, quite different from that of the civil law, developed in England after the Norman conquest in 1066. At least since the reign of the great legal reformer Henry II in the 1100s, decisions by English grand juries, kings, magistrates and (slightly later) trial juries were written down and eventually catalogued according to the type of case. When the courts were called on to decide similar issues in subsequent cases, they reviewed the earlier decisions and, if one was found that logically covered the contemporary case, they applied the principle of the earlier decision. This doctrine is called *stare*

decisis—Latin for "let the decision stand." The common law thus consists of court opinions in specific disputes that state legal principles and must be followed in subsequent court cases about the same type of dispute.

This does not mean that every judge's decisions stand forever. Courts reflect society's values (however imperfectly), and old case law is rejected as society changes. But the principle of *stare decisis* is a strong one; judges are reluctant to discard well-established rules and take pains to explain (or deny) a significant departure from precedent.

Large areas of law developed in England in this case-by-case common law tradition. Eventually, two basic types of courts evolved: the law courts and special "chancery" courts established by the king to handle types of cases and provide types of relief that tradition did not allow the regular courts to entertain. The principles developed in the law courts were called "legal" or "law," while the principles developed in the king's chancery courts were called "equitable" or "equity." This distinction still exists in modern American law, although now there are not usually two separate kinds of courts.

England also, beginning hesitantly with the Magna Carta in 1215, developed a parliamentary system under which statutes proposed by the king or his ministers were enacted by Parliament. These statutes were gathered together into books not too different from today's civil law codes.

During America's colonial period, most of the English common law tradition and many of the English statutes became firmly entrenched, though modified to some extent in accordance with the religious and cultural beliefs of the colonists. At independence, the basic legal system did not change. For the most part, the new country simply continued to follow English law.

There was, of course, one big difference. The U.S. Constitution was ratified in 1789, and neither the laws of Parliament nor the edicts of King George III had any further power in the new United States. The Constitution became the foundation on which our legal house was built. Both the law inherited from England and that enacted by Congress and state legislatures eventually had to either find support in this foundation or be discarded.

The Increasing Importance of Statutes and Regulations

In the 200-plus years of American history, the English common law (case-by-case) tradition has been modified. Statutes and administrative regulations have become more

important, both to make new law and codify (put into a written, prescriptive form) broad principles developed by the case law. Especially since the New Deal of the 1930s, federal and state agencies have been created at a rapid rate. Most of these agencies have the authority, within certain prescribed limits, to make rules that have the force of statutes passed by Congress and state legislatures. Many of them also have the power to judge disputes that arise under these rules. For example, Congress passed a statute—the Social Security Act of 1935—that created the Social Security Administration (SSA). The Social Security Act also authorizes the SSA to write rules and to set up its own forums to decide disputes arising under the rules.

The Development of American Common Law

Despite the increasing importance of statutes and regulations, many areas of our law still consist almost entirely of court decisions—but now by American courts. Also, the courts of this country are empowered to interpret statutes when a dispute arises as to their meaning. As well as using other interpretative techniques, a judge will look at earlier cases to see how they have interpreted the statute and will apply the prevailing interpretation unless she feels it is wrong or clearly doesn't apply to the current dispute. In other words, court opinions in America, as in England, serve as authority or "precedent," which is often binding and always important to subsequent court decisions.

As a practical matter, the only court opinions that become part of the American common law are those that are contained in recognized publications known as "reports" or "reporters." In most state court systems, the only court opinions that are published in this way are those issued by appellate courts—that is, courts that deal solely with legal issues on appeal from trial courts. In the federal court system, all appellate court decisions are published and many trial court decisions make it into print as well. The higher the court, the more likely it is that the decision will serve as precedent for other courts. For example, a decision by a U.S. District Court judge will carry far less precedent weight than will a U.S. Supreme Court case or Circuit Court of Appeal case on the same issue.

So far we have talked about the United States of America as if it were one political unit. For many reasons, it often seems that this is true. However, it is important to remember that we have a federal system under which 50

sovereign political states have banded together voluntarily and agreed to give the federal government certain powers spelled out in the U.S. Constitution. All powers not expressly granted to the federal government are reserved to the states. The states in turn have divvied up some of their power among counties, cities and special districts.

Where Modern American Law Comes From

Laws are made at three basic levels: federal, state and local. Operating at each of these levels are three sources of law: legislatures, judges and executive officers (usually acting through government agencies). See the list set out below. The next chapter provides some tips on deciding which source of law controls your issue.

Sources of Law

- The U.S. and state constitutions and cases that interpret them produce constitutional law.
- Congress passes laws called "statutes," which constitute federal statutory law.
- Federal courts decide cases and write opinions that constitute federal case law.
- Federal courts decide cases and write opinions about state statutes when the parties before the court are from different states.
- Federal administrative agencies created by Congress and staffed by the executive branch issue regulations that constitute the federal administrative law.
- Sovereign Native American tribes have their own courts and laws, which constitute tribal law.
- State legislatures pass statutes, which constitute state statutory law.
- State courts decide state cases and write opinions, which constitute state case law.
- State administrative agencies (created by state legislatures and staffed by governors' office appointees) write regulations, which constitute state administrative law.
- Local governments pass ordinances that become police codes, building codes, planning codes, health codes, etc.

About Going to Court

When someone new to the law, whether law student, paralegal or citizen interested in her own case, thinks of "going to court," the images that come to mind are often movie-like scenes with argumentative attorneys, stern judges, and courtrooms filled with spectators and the press. The complexity of it all can seem too much to deal with. As one judge put it:

The lay litigant enters a temple of mysteries whose ceremonies are dark, complex and unfathomable. Pretrial procedures are the cabalistic rituals of the lawyers and judges who serve as priests and high priests. The layman knows nothing of their tactical significance. He knows only that his case remains in limbo while the priests and high priests chant their lengthy and arcane pretrial rites (Daley v. County of Butte, 227 Cal. App. 2d 380, 392 (1964)).

In fact, the great majority of court matters are handled in a quite straightforward manner, without fanfare, argument or stress. Typical are cases that ask a judge to appoint a guardian or conservator, approve an adoption or name change, allow the probate of a simple estate, grant an uncontested divorce, discharge certain debts in bankruptcy, or seal a criminal record. On the other hand, criminal cases are usually no picnic, and any case can get messy when a real dispute exists or lawyers have a financial incentive to string the matter out, as can often happen in complicated business disputes for which attorneys bill by the hour.

But whatever the matter, filing a case and pushing it through court always involves carefully following a number of technical court rules. The trick is knowing these procedural rules in minute detail. Among the highest compliments a lawyer can be paid is, "She sure knows her way around the courthouse"—that is, she has mastered the rules of the game. Fortunately, these rules are, for the most part, available to all.

For example, suppose you want court protection against someone in your household who is abusing you. You must understand not only the law that governs such a situation (what protection is available), but also the actual steps that you must follow to get your request properly before a judge. You may have the best case in the world, but a lack of knowledge about court procedures will prevent anyone from hearing it.

Small Claims Court

All states have a small claims court or procedure with simplified rules that are usually fairly easy to follow. Small claims court clerks are usually required by statute to help people with all procedural details. If you can squeeze the amount of your monetary claim within the small claim limits for your state (usually from $2,000 to $5,000), you may find that small claims court is an excellent alternative to the formal legal system. One of the nicest aspects of small claims court is that in many states, litigants are not allowed to be represented by lawyers. By learning to do your own research and writing, you can present a solid case and not run the risk of being overwhelmed by an experienced hired gun on the other side. Unfortunately, most small claims courts are not designed to handle problems other than those where one person has a monetary claim against the other. (For more information, see *Everybody's Guide to Small Claims Court,* by Ralph Warner (National and California editions, Nolo).)

This Is Not a Practice Guide. This section talks in general terms about the steps in civil litigation, and it is not intended as a guide for the aspiring lawyer or paralegal, or for the reader who intends to represent herself in court. To find out in more detail about civil and criminal procedure, start with a good background resource (as discussed in Chapter 5). You can get information about how to represent yourself in a civil court proceeding in *Represent Yourself in Court,* by Paul Bergman and Sara J. Berman-Barrett (Nolo).

How a Court Case Works: Steps in Litigation

Court procedures and rules are substantially similar in all state and federal courts. Details vary, however, and similar procedures are often referred to by different names. For example, an eviction action is called "unlawful detainer" in California and "summary process" in Massachusetts. Yet the proceedings are basically the same.

If your case is uncontested—that is, there's no dispute and it's simply a matter of getting the papers right—a lot of this section won't apply. The discussion here is intended primarily for people who are involved in a civil dispute that the court is being asked to resolve. It looks at how a typical contested case develops and proceeds through the courts.

The Pretrial Process

The first phase of a contested civil case is called the pretrial phase.

The plaintiff files a complaint

A case begins when a document called a "complaint" is filed with the court by the plaintiff (the party who sues).

The Complaint. This document tells what happened and what the plaintiff wants done about it—that is, a monetary award, court order or other remedy. It also tells the court the legal basis for the litigation.

The defendant responds

The defendant (the party who is sued) is served with (given) a copy of the complaint and has a certain time to respond in writing—usually 30 days. If no response is made, a "default" judgment may be obtained by the plaintiff, which means the plaintiff wins without having to fully prove the case.

There are a variety of ways the defendant may respond. The plaintiff's complaint and the defendant's responsive papers, taken together, are commonly referred to as the "pleadings" in the case.

The Answer. Most commonly, the defendant files an "answer," a statement setting out which parts of the complaint the defendant agrees and disagrees with. Under the procedural rules of most states, the defendant's answer must also contain any affirmative defenses (factual statements of the reasons or excuses for the defendant's actions) and counterclaims (claims that the plaintiff in fact owes the defendant money) that the defendant has. The defendant can also state that she doesn't have enough information about the allegations and denies the complaint on that basis.

Motion to Dismiss for Failure to State a Claim. This document—also called a "demurrer" in some states—asks the court to dismiss the suit instead of requiring an answer from the defendant. Usually, the basis for this request boils down to this: Even if the facts in the plaintiff's complaint are true, so what? Or to put the same thing a little more formally, the defendant is saying that the plaintiff has no legal theory (given the facts as the plaintiff has alleged them) upon which to properly base a lawsuit. The defendant is requesting the court to stop the plaintiff from wasting everyone's time and to end the matter then and there.

The court does not decide any facts as part of a hearing on a motion to dismiss. Strictly for the purpose of deciding the motion, the judge assumes that the factual allegations in the complaint are true and then decides whether the law supports the claim for relief. If the judge grants the motion but allows the plaintiff a chance to fix the problem ("granted with leave to amend"), the plaintiff simply rewrites the complaint and the process starts all over again. If the judge grants the motion without leave to amend, the case is ended unless the plaintiff appeals the decision. On the other hand, if the judge overrules (denies) the demurrer, the defendant must file an answer. The defendant can ask the appellate court to review the denial (called asking for a "writ of mandamus"), but this remedy is rarely granted.

Both sides engage in discovery

From the time that the pleadings in a case are filed (and rarely, before), each party has the right to engage in an activity termed "discovery." Discovery involves a number of specific procedures by which the parties seek information from each other both to bolster their own cases and to prevent Perry Mason-type surprises at trial.

Discovery often adds considerably to the time and expense of litigation. Because each side usually attempts to avoid giving information to the other, disputes constantly arise over what information must be turned over. These disputes are resolved by the trial court in "discovery motion" proceedings. If a party does not like the result, it is usually possible to take the matter to a higher court before the underlying case proceeds further. Accordingly, discovery often results in cases going into a holding pattern.

Normally, discovery consists of the following devices:

Depositions. Witnesses or parties are required to go to the office of one of the attorneys and answer questions, under oath, about their knowledge of the dispute. The testimony is taken down by a stenographer or, increasingly, by a tape recorder. Usually the attorney for the side of the case on which the witness will testify is also present.

Interrogatories. One party sends another written questions to be answered under oath by a certain date. Interrogatories are also used to ask the other party to identify the source and validity of documents that may be introduced as evidence at trial.

Admissions of Facts. Factual statements are set out that the other side must admit or deny. Anything that isn't denied is considered admitted.

Production of Documents. One party asks another to produce specified documents. In a complicated case, one side may ask the other for file cabinets full of material. There are often motions (arguments heard by a judge) about how much fishing one side can do in the other's records.

Summary judgment is requested

Once the pleadings are on file, either side may ask the court to rule in their favor without trial. To get a summary judgment, the party must show the absence of a dispute about any important facts in the case (called "triable issues of material fact"). This showing is made in the form of written statements under oath, termed "declarations" or "affidavits." Trials serve to determine facts, so if there are no disputed facts, there's no reason to have a trial. The judge can go ahead and apply the relevant law to the undisputed facts.

Different Sides of the Coin: The Difference Between a Demurrer and Summary Judgment

A demurrer and a motion for summary judgment are both motions that may be made by the defense in an attempt to get rid of the case before it goes further. (The plaintiff may also move for summary judgment, in an attempt to secure a quick victory without the expense of a trial.) A demurrer argues to the judge, "All the factual claims are true, but there's no legal issue here"; a motion for summary judgment says, "In spite of the claims, there's no real factual dispute that would merit a full trial." In federal court, a demurrer is brought as a motion to dismiss.

Example 1: Peter is a woodworker who lives on United States government land (a federal Air Force base) and sells wooden toys to the toy store on the base. His written agreement with the store specifies the price the store will pay for each toy, when Peter is to deliver the toys, and what materials he is to use. The contract says nothing about the store buying a minimum number of toys each month. Peter has increased his production and would like the store to buy his entire line, and he sues them in federal court for breach of contract when they refuse. The toy store files a motion to dismiss, pointing

out that since the contract does not have an "output" clause, they cannot legally be forced to buy all of Peter's toys.

Example 2: Peter's sales to the toy store continue and one of his toys, a rocking horse, is sold to a family with a two-year-old. The child develops a rash that the parents believe is caused by the finish on the rocking horse. Peter discovers that all of the children in the youngster's day care center on the base have identical rashes, which have been traced to the use of a harsh cleanser on the center's furniture. Armed with an affidavit from the center's director, Peter moves for summary judgment. The parents are unable to offer factual support for their theory that the toy's finish caused the rash, so the court grants Peter's motion.

One or more sides files motions

At any time after the pleadings have been filed, but before trial, the plaintiff or defendant may ask the court to order the other side to do something or to refrain from doing something. Sometimes these requests, called motions, are used to preserve the status quo until the case can come to trial. For example, if the circumstances are truly urgent, a party can request the court to issue a "temporary restraining order" (TRO) or "preliminary injunction," stopping the defendant from taking some action before trial. As mentioned, motions may also be filed to enforce discovery (that is, to require a party to answer questions or produce documents when appropriate) or to protect a party against abusive discovery (for example, requiring attendance at a week-long deposition).

One side requests a trial date

In some court systems, a case is never set for trial unless one of the parties requests it. Accordingly, a party who feels adequately prepared can file a document with the court requesting a trial and specifying whether it should be held in front of a jury. These documents are titled differently in different courts, such as "memorandum to set," "at-issue memorandum" and "motion to set for trial." Whatever their titles, they may be opposed by the other party (for a variety of reasons) or agreed to.

A pretrial conference is held

Usually, once a case is set for trial, a pretrial conference between the parties, their lawyers and the judge is scheduled. At the pretrial conference, the judge makes sure that everyone understands what the remaining issues are in the case and gets an idea of how long the trial will take. Many judges use these conferences—often quite successfully—to pressure the parties to settle the case. If no settlement is reached, the trial date is fixed.

The Trial

Most lawsuits never go to trial. The parties settle their dispute or simply drop the case. Often, the outcome of a pretrial motion resolves the case or encourages one of the parties to settle. If a case does go to trial, it's usually because the parties disagree so much about the underlying facts that they need a judge to decide whose version is correct.

Trials involve a set of rituals that are supposed to ferret out the truth. No one trial is like any other—each is a function of who the parties are, what type of legal issues are involved, the personalities of the attorneys and the demeanor of the judge. But the biggest determinant of what happens in a trial is whether it is a trial by jury or a trial by judge. Many of the rules governing trial procedure are aimed at producing an impartial jury and making sure that the jury doesn't receive evidence that is unreliable in some fundamental way. Judges, on the other hand, are presumed to be able to act impartially and tell reliable evidence from unreliable evidence.

Jury trials

Jury trials begin with the selection of the jury. The judge and lawyers for both sides question potential jurors about their knowledge of the case and possible biases relating to their clients and the important issues in the case. This process is called *voir dire.*

Motions in Limine

From the first moment of the trial to the last, one or both parties may want the judge to run some aspect of the trial in a certain way. For instance, the plaintiff may want to prevent the defendant from even trying to prove a certain point, believing that to do so would hopelessly prejudice the jury against the plaintiff. These types of requests are called "motions in limine" (that is, motion on the verge of trial). They are considered by the judge in a meeting outside the hearing of the jury, usually in the judge's office.

Once a jury is selected, the attorneys address the jury in opening statements that outline what they expect to show in the upcoming trial. Then the plaintiff begins, offering testimony from witnesses and information in documents to establish a version of events. The testimony and documents are then subject to challenge by the defendant through a process called "cross-examination."

Once the plaintiff's case is presented, the defendant has the opportunity to present a defense, subject to the plaintiff's cross-examination. Commonly, the plaintiff gets the last shot (called a "rebuttal") in an opportunity to answer the defendant's case.

Trial Talk for Non-Lawyers. *Represent Yourself in Court*, by Paul Bergman and Sara Berman-Barrett (Nolo), is an excellent guide to what goes on in a trial. It is based on the Federal Rules of Civil Procedure, which most states follow as well, and is the best place to start if you are involved in any stage of trial work. *How to Win Your Personal Injury Claim*, by Joseph Matthews (Nolo), provides a straightforward discussion on how to file, process and settle a personal injury claim.

When the parties are through presenting their cases, each side gets to make a closing argument, summarizing what they think they've proved and imploring the jury to see it their way. Then the judge explains to the jurors that it is their job to decide what the facts are in the case and that they should follow certain legal principles in deciding whether those facts warrant a decision for the plaintiff or the defendant. Collectively, these explanations are called "jury instructions."

Although it is the judge's responsibility to give the instructions, the plaintiff and defendant are first invited to give the judge their proposed instructions. Because the jury instructions in a case often determine who will win and who will lose, both sides spend a considerable amount of time drafting instructions that will be most favorable to their side. A meeting between the judge and the parties is held to iron out discrepancies, the judge being the final decision-maker. Then the judge assembles the instructions that are to be given in a final written version and reads from it verbatim.

Researching the Rules of Evidence

Any source of information that a party offers as proof of a fact is called "evidence." There is admissible evidence and inadmissible evidence, and the rules that determine which is which are quite complex. But they almost always revolve around two issues:

- whether a particular source of information is too unreliable to let a jury consider; and
- whether an out-of-court conversation that someone is trying to introduce may be kept out of evidence.

Many of the disputes during a trial revolve around what evidence is admissible and what isn't, and the many bench conferences (when the attorneys and the judge huddle and whisper out of the jury's hearing) that occur during the typical trial involve whether a bit of testimony or a particular document should or should not be allowed "into evidence." Decisions by the judge on these disputes are often the subject of severe Monday-morning quarterbacking in an appeal by the losing party.

The rules of evidence for each state are usually published as part of that state's statutes. Most states also have background resources that devote themselves to analyzing the rules of evidence in excruciating detail. Although evidence is clearly related to court procedure, it is often considered a "substantive law" field of its own. (See Chapter 5.)

Researching Jury Instructions

Compilations of acceptable jury instructions are available in most states for common types of cases—for instance, auto accident cases. In California, civil jury instructions are published in *B.A.J.I.* (*Book of Approved Jury Instructions*) and criminal instructions are in *CALJIC-Crim* (West Group). Federal jury instructions can be found in *Modern Federal Jury Instructions,* by Leonard Sand (Matthew Bender).

If the losing party appeals, the instructions that were offered by that party but rejected by the judge often form an important part of the appeal, since the decision by the judge is considered a "legal decision" that is an appropriate subject for an appeals court. (See "Appeals," below.)

Once the jury has heard the instructions, they retire to a room to decide the case. In civil cases the plaintiff must prove its case by a "preponderance of evidence"—that is, it must be more probable than not that the plaintiff is right. The jury need not be unanimous; the normal requirement is a 3/4 vote in favor of either party. Most civil juries consist of twelve jurors, but some states are experimenting with six-member juries.

When the members of the jury have reached a verdict, they report it to the judge, who announces it in open court with the parties present.

Any party who is dissatisfied with the verdict can ask the judge to set it aside or modify it. But usually the judge upholds the verdict and issues a judgment for the winner.

Judge trials

Judge trials are a lot easier than jury trials. There are far fewer squabbles about evidence, since there is no jury to be concerned about, and no jury instructions to prepare. When all the evidence is in and parties have made final arguments to the judge, the judge decides the case and issues a judgment, usually accompanied by a document termed, "Findings of Facts and Conclusions of Law." This document lets the parties know why the judge reached the decision and gives them a basis for deciding whether or not to appeal.

Appeals

Any party who is dissatisfied with the judgment may appeal the issue to a higher court. Appeals are almost always about the legal decisions made in a pretrial motion or a trial—in jury trials decisions about evidence and the jury instructions, and in judge trials decisions about the judge's conclusions of law. They are seldom about the decision by the judge or jury as to whether certain facts were true or false. However, some appeals successfully argue that the judge's or jury's decision was not properly based on the evidence introduced in the case.

Appeals are usually allowed from final decisions in a case, such as a judgment of dismissal, summary judgment or judgment after trial. However, sometimes decisions by the court before final judgment is entered can be reviewed by an appellate court before the trial continues. These are termed "interlocutory appeals."

For example, as discussed in "How a Court Case Works: Steps in Litigation," above, parties are usually subjected to a pretrial process called "discovery." This requires each side to disclose to the other the evidence and testimony that will be presented at trial so that the element of surprise is reduced. Should one party refuse to disclose information, the other party can seek an order from the court requiring disclosure. If the non-disclosing party wants to contest the court order, an appellate court can be asked to immediately step in and decide whether the order was improper. These interim interlocutory appeals are the exception to the rule; appellate courts much prefer to refrain from reviewing lower court decisions until the trial is over and they can decide all questions at once.

In some states, seeking help from a higher court in these situations is termed an appeal, while in others it is termed a request for a "writ of mandate" or "writ of prohibition." Writs are orders directed at officials by courts, or at lower courts by higher ones. When immediate relief from a higher court is necessary, the relief often involves a "petition for a writ" rather than the "filing of an appeal."

As mentioned, sometimes the basis of an appeal is a disagreement with the trial court's determination of the facts. This might happen, for instance, when there is clear and overwhelming evidence on behalf of one party, but the judge or jury ignores the evidence and finds for the other side. Generally speaking, however, appellate courts don't disturb a trial court's determination of the facts unless it was completely unsupported by the evidence.

In an appeal, "briefs"—typewritten statements of the parties' views of the facts and law—are submitted to the appellate court. The appellate court also has a copy of the entire written "record" of the trial court. This record usually consists of all documents submitted by the parties to the trial court, exhibits and documents introduced in the trial, a transcript of exactly what was said at the trial (produced by a court reporter or a tape recorder) and all judgments and orders entered by the trial court.

In addition to considering the briefs and the trial court record, the appellate court usually hears oral arguments from the attorneys on each side. After the oral arguments, the justices (judges on courts of appeal are usually called "justices") discuss the case and arrive at a decision. A justice representing the majority (sometimes the justices who hear the case will not agree on how it should be decided) is assigned to write the opinion.

If a party disagrees with the outcome of an appeal in the appellate court, another appeal can usually be made—to a state supreme court or the U.S. Supreme Court. (See Chapter 7 for which courts appeals are filed in.) That requires filing a "Petition for Hearing" in a state court, or a

"Petition for Writ of Certiorari"—or, as it is usually called, "Petition for Cert"—asking the Supreme Court to consider the case. If the court grants a hearing or issues a Writ of Certiorari to the court that decided the case being appealed, it will consider the case. If it denies a hearing or "cert," then it won't.

Supreme courts grant hearings or cert only in a very small percentage of cases presented to them. They usually choose cases that present interesting or important questions of law or an issue that two or more lower appellate courts have disagreed on. For example, if the federal Court of Appeals for the 6th Circuit decides that the military registration system is unconstitutional because it doesn't include women, and the Court of Appeals for the 7th Circuit decides that the system is constitutional, the U.S. Supreme Court might grant cert in these cases and resolve the conflict.

Filing Cases Directly in Appellate and Supreme Courts

Occasionally, cases can be brought directly in the intermediate appellate courts or supreme courts, but only when there are extremely important issues of law in the case and little factual dispute. Also, under federal and state constitutions, certain types of disputes go directly to the supreme courts; this is called "original jurisdiction," as opposed to their usual appellate jurisdiction. For example, if one state sues another, the suit is brought in the U.S. Supreme Court, not a U.S. district court.

When the U.S. Supreme Court or a state's highest court decides a case, it almost always issues a published opinion. U.S. Supreme Court cases serve as precedent and binding authority for all courts, and cases from a state's highest court serve as precedent and authority for all courts in that state. Supreme Court decisions are very important sources of law. (See Chapter 7 for more on precedent and authority.)

Introduction to Reported Cases

Decisions by appellate courts, federal trial courts, and specialty courts (such as bankruptcy) are printed in books called "Reporters." Each set of reporters contains opinions from a particular court or group of courts. For example, there are regional reporters (these contain opinions from the appellate courts of a group of neighboring states), state reporters (these contain only one state's appellate decisions) and subject matter reporters (these contain decisions affecting a certain area of law). For instance, "P." (which stands for Pacific) is the reporter series that collects the appellate decisions from the western states, Hawaii and Alaska; "Cal. App." contains appellate (but not Supreme Court) cases from California; and "B.R." contains federal bankruptcy opinions. In addition, federal cases are reported in their own sets, one for trial level decisions (called "F. Supp.") and one for appellate opinions from the Circuit courts of appeals (abbreviated as "F."). When the editors of the Reporters decide that their sets have become too long, they begin a new series and identify the new one as "2d" or "3d," and so on. In Chapter 9, we provide more information on how to use and interpret case citations.

Library Exercise: Using Citations to Find Cases

A case citation is like a street address: It tells you where you can find the case among the many sets of reported cases (called "Reporters") in the library. For example, the citation "26 F.2d 234" tells you that the case is found in the "Federal 2d" set of reporters, in volume 26, on page 234. Most citations end with information in parentheses, which tells you what court decided the case and the year of the decision; but you do not need to use that information when you are simply trying to locate a case in the library.

Questions

1. Find the case at 766 F. Supp. 662. What is the name of the case? What opinions are contained in the reporter series?

2. Find the case at 792 P.2d 18. What is the name of the case? What opinions are collected in the reporter abbreviated "P."?

3. Find the case at 830 F.2d 11. What is the name of the case, and what is contained in the reporter series that printed it?

4. Find the case at 461 N.W.2d 884. What is the name of the case? What decisions are included in the "N.W." reporters?

5. Find the case at 476 A.2d 1236. What is the name of the case, and which reporter series contains it?

Answers

1. The case is *Johnson v. Johnson*. "F. Supp." contains trial level cases from the federal district courts.

2. The case is *Petersen v. Bruen*. The *Pacific Reporter* contains appellate and supreme court decisions from the western states, Hawaii and Alaska.

3. The case is *Smith v. Smith*. All of the decisions from the federal Circuit courts are printed in the "F." series of reporters, which has gone beyond 2nd and now is in its 3rd series.

4. The case is *People v. Jamieson*. The "N.W." (Northwest) reporter is in its second series, and contains opinions from the appellate and supreme courts of the northwest states.

5. The case is called *State v. Rockhilt*. The "A." (Atlantic) reporter, second series, contains opinions from the appellate and supreme courts of the Atlantic states.

Review

Questions

1. What is the "law" that people research in the law library?
2. What does the common law consist of?
3. What does *stare decisis* mean?
4. How is power shared between the federal, state and local governments?
5. What are the three major phases in civil litigation?
6. What are pleadings?
7. What is summary judgment?
8. What is the difference between summary judgment and a trial?
9. What aspects of a trial court's decision are reviewable on appeal?

Answers

1. The "law" is the sum total of the rules governing individual and group behavior that are enforceable in court. Primarily, as you will see, this means state and federal statutes, agency regulations, local ordinances and court decisions.
2. The common law consists of court opinions in specific disputes that state legal principles and must be followed in subsequent court cases about the same type of dispute.
3. *Stare decisis* is Latin for "let the decision stand." When courts are called on to decide similar issues in subsequent cases, they review the earlier decisions. If one is found that logically covers the contemporary case, the courts apply the principle of the earlier decision. This is how the common law develops.
4. Fifty sovereign political entities (states) have banded together in a union and agreed to give the federal government certain defined powers spelled out in the U.S. Constitution. All powers not expressly granted to the federal government are reserved to the states. The states in turn have divided up some of their power among counties, cities and special districts.
5. Pretrial, trial and appellate.
6. Together, the plaintiff's complaint and the defendant's responsive papers are referred to as the "pleadings" in the case. Pleadings articulate the issues in the case—the actual dispute between plaintiff and defendant.
7. To get a summary judgment, the party must show the absence of a dispute about any important facts in the case (called "triable issues of material fact"). This showing is made in the form of written statements under oath, termed "declarations" or "affidavits." If these statements show a lack of basic factual disagreement between the parties, as is often the case, the judge will then proceed to apply the law to the facts and decide the case.
8. Trials are held to determine the facts when they are disputed by the parties and involve a formal procedure designed to control just which evidence will be considered. Summary judgment is premised on the idea that there are no factual disputes, and therefore no need for a trial. The judge can go ahead and apply the relevant law to the undisputed facts.
9. Normally, appellate courts only are interested in whether the law was correctly followed and won't disturb a trial court's determination of the facts—unless it was completely unsupported by the evidence.

Putting Your Questions Into Legal Categories

This chapter helps you accomplish Step 2 of the legal research method (described in Chapter 2). First, it shows how to organize your legal question into the conceptual categories used by publishers of law books and websites, a necessary and preliminary step to finding appropriate background resources (which are covered in the next chapter). Second, this chapter introduces you to some techniques for using legal indexes. Legal indexes are most commonly used to find:

- relevant discussions in the background resources you select;
- statutes in annotated codes (Chapter 6); and
- cases through the case digest system (Chapter 9).

When doing Internet research you will be using search techniques that are similar to those used in searching indexes. These techniques are introduced below.

The Land of the Law

GUARD: *Sir, we have interrogated the prisoner for three hours but can't get any information.*

SUPERVISOR: *Does the prisoner refuse to speak?*

GUARD: *Oh no, sir, he talks constantly, it's just that we can't understand a word of it.*

SUPERVISOR: *Oh, what nationality is he?*

GUARD: *Lawyer.* [*]

If "lawyer" is a nationality, the judicial system itself is certainly a country complete with its own rules, logic, customs, values, benefits, penalties and linguistic peculiarities. Fortunately, the gulf between the "land of the law" and the "land of normal life," which seems extremely broad at times, can be bridged without great difficulty.

Two basic facts, once firmly understood, will greatly help you cope when you visit the Land of the Law. The first is obvious: The Land of the Law is run almost exclusively by lawyers. Laws are drafted by lawyers for legislatures, which are also often heavily influenced by or made up of lawyers. Laws are interpreted by lawyers who have become judges. Laws are enforced by lawyers who are district attorneys and attorneys general. Disputes are commonly arbitrated and decided by lawyers acting as referees. Agency regulations are drafted by the agency's legal department. Presidents, governors and corporate executives all have lawyers at their sides. In short, lawyers are in firm control of the law business.

The second important fact is that lawyers tend to think very much alike. It is no wonder. Lawyers gain entrance to their profession by going to law school, where they are taught by law professors who are lawyers. As part of this training, law students are taught subtly and not so subtly to think like lawyers, act like lawyers, talk like lawyers, dress like lawyers and breathe like lawyers. In addition:

- Most law schools teach the same subjects.
- Most law schools use the same teaching method.
- Most law schools attempt to produce the same type of product.
- Most law schools succeed.

How does this uniformity help you find your way around the Land of the Law? It simply means that you need come to terms with only one dialect and culture. A lawyer from California can speak to a lawyer in North Dakota using one set of terms and concepts, and you can too once you learn the lingo.

Obviously, you won't be able to do this all at once, but if you spend any amount of time in the Land of the Law, you'll be surprised at how fast your vocabulary grows. Indeed, you'll soon realize that what seemed like a complex language is really only a collection of terms (jargon) containing very few verbs, and most of the nouns are only new terms for concepts you already know. (This is why we advise you to arm yourself with a good law dictionary.)

That lawyers think as well as talk alike is extremely helpful to the lay legal researcher. Lawyers are great reductionists. The system they use to classify legal knowledge involves carving it all into successively smaller categories. If you think of a set of nesting boxes, which always seem to have yet another smaller box inside, you will have a pretty good idea of how this works.

The background materials you will use in your research also are organized this way, dividing their contents into smaller and smaller subject categories. As a first step in performing effective legal research, then, you need to be able to think of your problem in terms of these categories. Then you'll be able to find relevant background materials and really get going on your legal research. Below we introduce you to the main legal classifications and suggest how to go about applying them to your problem.

* This is a paraphrase of the words that accompanied a cartoon in the popular "Crock" cartoon series.

Find the Broad Legal Category for Your Problem

Assume that you seek a lawyer's advice because you injured your back when you slipped on a banana peel at the supermarket. An experienced lawyer will go through a thought process that, if verbalized, might sound something like this:

"Ah, let's see, this person slipped, fell and injured herself, possibly badly. Back injuries cause a lot of pain—that means high damages. Definitely it is a personal injury case, a civil matter, negligence. Let's see, in order to recover for negligence, some action or inaction on the part of the supermarket must have been wrongful. In this situation it probably wasn't an intentional tort, but more likely carelessness, or negligence. Hmm, whether the market was negligent probably depends on how long employees let the peel remain on the floor before the accident. Hmm, wonder if there were any prior occurrences like this?"

This exercise in stream-of-consciousness writing demonstrates how lawyers reduce problems to smaller parts and classify the parts according to familiar—to them—legal jargon. While this process may seem a little intimidating if you are unfamiliar with the law, don't worry. Anybody can learn to break big questions down into little ones and to cast a legal research problem into its appropriate topics and subtopics. And as we mentioned, once you are able to hang the proper labels on various factual situations, your ability to perform meaningful legal research will be almost assured. You may be surprised at how easy the classification game really is.

There are four main questions to answer when classifying your legal question:

- Does it involve federal law, state law or both?
- Does it involve criminal law or civil law?
- Does it involve the substance of the law or legal procedure?
- What legal category does it belong in?

When you have answered each of these questions, you will find it much easier to choose the background resources to look in first. If your question involves the substance of the federal criminal law, you will be interested in one group of books; if it involves state civil law, you will be looking for others. Narrowing your search further, placing your question in the right category will tell you which specific books—and parts of the books—you need. For instance, if your federal law problem involves the federal drug laws, you will probably use a different book than if it involves securities fraud.

Does the Situation Involve Federal Law or State Law?

Probably the single-most important classification is whether your issue involves state law, federal law or both. This is important because discussions of state law and federal law are commonly found in completely different books. The chart below lists topics usually covered by state law, federal law or both.

State Law

For constitutional and historical reasons, most legal research involves state rather than federal law. The U.S. Constitution restricts Congress' power to regulate to a few specific areas and leaves most lawmaking power to state governments.

Federal Law

For most of our country's history, federal law was limited to court interpretations of the U.S. Constitution and the Bill of Rights, as well as the topics that Congress is specifically authorized to address under the Constitution, such as the regulation of commerce and immigration. Social welfare was not high on the government's agenda. Now, however, federal law commonly affects a broad range of social welfare, health and environmental issues.

Both State and Federal Law

A large number of legal areas now involve both state and federal law. Federal and state governments both are concerned about such topics as environmental law, consumer protection and the enforcement of child support statutes, and both have written laws on these subjects. A good general rule is that whenever federal funds are involved, at least one element of federal law is involved.

One reason for the increasing overlap of federal and state law is that Congress is authorized by the Constitution to spend money for the general welfare, and it creates programs under which federal funds are offered to state governments under certain conditions. Typically, the state must match the funds in whole or in part and administer

the program in strict conformity with requirements established by Congress. While no state must participate in this type of program, few states are able to resist. Since the 1930s (the New Deal), hundreds of these cost-sharing programs have been created and continue to operate.

When states participate in these programs, typically they are given some latitude by the federal laws in how the program is conducted. This means that state statutes and regulations must be passed to govern the state operation. And courts end up interpreting these statutes and regulations when disputes arise under them. In short, federal cost-sharing programs created by federal law stimulate the creation of state law as well.

If you have a problem that is affected by both federal and state law, you may have to look to both state and federal law background resources to get a firm handle on your problem.

A Partial Listing of Federal, State and Mixed Categories

State Law. Child custody, conservatorships, contracts, corporations, crimes (in most cases), divorce, durable powers of attorney for health care and financial management, guardianships, landlord-tenant relationships, licensing (businesses and professions), living wills, motor vehicles, partnerships, paternity, personal injuries, probate, property taxation, real estate, trusts, wills, worker's compensation and zoning.

Federal Law. Admiralty, agriculture, bankruptcy, cases that interpret and reinterpret the U.S. Constitution and civil rights laws, copyright, crimes involving the movement of people or substances across state lines for illegal purposes, customs, federal tax, food and drug regulation, immigration, interstate commerce, maritime, Native Americans, patent, postal, Social Security and trademark.

Both State and Federal Law. Consumer protection, employment, environmental protection, health law, labor law, occupational safety, subsidized housing, transportation, unemployment insurance, veterans' benefits and welfare law.

Does the Situation Involve Criminal Law or Civil Law?

Another important classification to make before beginning your research is whether you are dealing with "criminal" or "civil" law. This classification is also necessary to determine which background resources to use first.

Criminal Law

Generally, if a certain type of behavior is punishable by imprisonment, then criminal law is involved. For example, legislatures have generally chosen to treat shoplifting as a crime, and convicted shoplifters can end up in jail. On the other hand, most legislatures have chosen not to criminalize shady business practices. Instead they have designated them as matters for which victims can sue for monetary compensation—that is, civil offenses.

Criminal charges are usually initiated in court by a government prosecutor, though some states allow minor criminal charges to be brought by a victim. The government is always involved, however, because crimes are considered "offenses against the people." Accordingly, if you are involved in a legal dispute with a non-governmental individual or corporation, then the matter is not criminal. But because both the state and federal governments are often involved in civil as well as criminal matters, it is impossible to tell whether you are dealing with a criminal or civil situation based solely on the fact that a government entity is one of the parties.

Civil Law

All legal questions that don't involve crimes are matters of the civil law. When a suit is filed in court over a broken contract, deliberate or negligent injury, withheld government benefit, failed marriage (divorce) or any other dispute, a civil action has been brought and civil law is involved. In a civil action, the court may be asked to issue orders, award monetary damages or dissolve a marriage, but imprisonment is almost never a possibility. An exception is when a court orders a parent to pay child support and the parent willfully refuses.

Is the Problem Substantive or Procedural?

Primarily for legal analysis and classification, the law has been divided into two large subgroups. One of these includes all law that establishes the rights we enjoy and the duties we owe to the government and to other people and entities. This type of law is often referred to as the "substantive law." The other major subgroup includes all law that governs the way the justice system works. This law is termed "procedural." Once you pigeonhole your issue into one of these two categories, you are much closer to jumping into your research. To see how this classification works, let's apply it to the criminal and civil areas of the law.

Criminal Law

"Criminal law" and "criminal procedure" are treated separately by most legal resources.

The Difference Between Criminal Law and Criminal Procedure

The difference between substantive criminal law and criminal procedure is well-illustrated in cases where a person is found guilty of a particular crime but escapes punishment because the proper procedures weren't used and her rights were violated. For example, if the police search a house without a search warrant and they find an illegal drug, the possessor of the drug may go free because there was no warrant. The fact that the possession of the drug is defined as a crime is a substantive criminal law matter, while the results of engaging in a warrantless search is a matter of criminal procedure.

Substantive Criminal Law. Substantive criminal law concerns the definition and punishment of crimes. For example, the substantive criminal law tells us the difference between burglary (breaking and entering into the premises of another with the intent to commit a theft or felony) and larceny (taking personal property rightfully in the possession of another with intent to steal). It also specifies how each of these crimes is to be punished. Below is a list of common criminal substantive law categories.

Criminal Law Substantive Categories

Assault and battery	Malicious mischief
Breaking and entering	Marijuana cultivation
Burglary	Murder
Conspiracy	Rape
Disorderly conduct	Robbery
Drug and narcotics offenses	Shoplifting
Drunk driving	Smuggling
Juvenile offenses	Tax evasion
Kidnapping	Trespass
Larceny	Weapons offenses
Lewd and lascivious behavior	

Criminal Procedure. Criminal procedure concerns the way people accused of crimes are treated by the criminal justice system. For example, criminal procedure involves such things as what kinds of evidence can be used in a criminal trial, when an accused must be brought to trial, when a person can be released on bail and so on. Below is a list of common criminal procedure categories.

Criminal Procedure Topics

Arraignments	Pleas
Arrests	Preliminary hearings
Confessions	Probation
Cross-examination	Probation reports
Extradition	Right to counsel
Grand jury	Search and seizure
Indictments	Sentencing
Jury selection	Speedy trial
Jury verdicts	Suppression of evidence
Miranda warnings	Trials
Plea bargaining	Witnesses

Civil Law

Substantive Civil Law. Substantive civil law consists of numerous sets of principles that determine the rights, duties and obligations that exist between individuals and institutions such as corporations and governments. Each set of principles is covered by a separate civil law category,

developed by the courts and legislatures over a long time. For example, when a car accident damages property and injures people, a set of principles labeled "tort law" that has been formulated over a 600-year period determines who is liable to whom and for what.

Most legal research involves the substantive civil law. To help you fit your problem into the correct category, we have provided a large list of categories with definitions for each. These are found in "Substantive Civil Law Categories," below.

Civil Procedure. The rules that govern how our civil justice system works are often termed "rules of civil procedure." They control such matters as which courts have authority to decide different kinds of lawsuits, what papers need to be filed, when they need to filed, who can be sued, what kinds of proof can be offered in court and how to appeal.

In the past, civil procedure varied considerably from state to state and court to court. Now, many states have procedures that are very similar to the Federal Rules of Civil Procedure that are used in all federal courts. However, although the trend is definitely toward national uniformity, courts' procedures still vary from one location to the next.

Rather than provide a list of civil procedure categories here, we refer you back to Chapter 3 for a close reading of court procedures. That material will provide some categories to start your research. Also, see Chapter 6 for pointers on researching procedure.

Substantive Civil Law Categories

The list set out below contains some of the more common substantive civil law categories utilized by the law books. Some of these areas overlap and may be used interchangeably by book titles and indexes. If you can assign one or more of the categories to your problem, it will be much easier for you to find what you're looking for. If you can't get your problem to fit within one of these categories, don't despair. Go on to the discussion later in this chapter on how to use legal indexes, and then proceed with your research.

Administrative Law: the law governing how administrative agencies function, including the procedures used by agencies when they issue regulations, the way agencies conduct hearings, the scope of authority granted agencies by the legislature and how agencies enforce their policies, decisions and regulations.

Bankruptcy: who can use the bankruptcy courts and under what circumstances, the rules and procedures used by the bankruptcy courts when a person or business files a bankruptcy petition to cancel debts or restructure them so as to continue operations, which debts are subject to cancellation or restructuring, and how any remaining assets of the person declaring bankruptcy are distributed. Bankruptcy is governed by federal law but also involves the interpretation of state property exemption rules.

Business and Professions Law: restrictions and license requirements placed on professionals (for example, doctors and lawyers) and other occupational groups, such as building contractors and undertakers.

Business Entity Law: state statutes dealing with how to create business entities such as corporations, limited liability companies and partnerships; state and federal statutes and cases that deal with how the various types of business entities are to be operated and taxed; the rights of shareholders, the rights and duties of the entity's officers and directors, the relationship between an entity and side parties who commercially interact with it; procedures for elections of officers; and how evidence of ownership in the entity (stock, shares) is issued.

Civil Rights Law: statutes and constitutional provisions that apply to discrimination on the basis of such legally-recognized characteristics as race, sex, ethnic or national background or color. (See also Housing Law and Prison Law.)

Commercial Law: the federal and state regulations governing commercial relations between borrowers and lenders, banks and their customers, wholesalers and retailers and mortgagors and mortgagees. Generally, this area involves disputes between businesspeople rather than between a businessperson and a consumer. (See also Consumer Law.)

Computer Law: the various issues that are especially relevant to the manufacture, use and sale of computers and computer software. This area includes such topics as copyrighting and patenting of computer software, warranties connected with computer sales, use of computer-generated documents in court, access to computerized files, privacy in connection with computer databases, computer-related crimes and trade secret protection in the computer industry.

Constitutional Law: all situations where the constitutionality of governmental action is called into question. A few representative examples of constitutional law issues are: state laws that conflict with federal laws, the imposition

of prison discipline on prisoners without adequate regard for fairness, federal laws that give Congress veto power over subsequent administrative regulations and a school board permitting prayer to occur in its schools. There are hundreds of other constitutional law questions. Many of these are also found under the other substantive law labels, such as housing law, civil rights law, prison law and media law.

Consumer Law: federal and state statutory requirements governing transactions between a seller and a buyer of personal property in a commercial setting. This field typically involves situations where persons buy items on time—such as cars, household furniture or electronic equipment—and a dispute arises as to whether the transaction was fair, whether the buyer was provided with sufficient notice of what the transaction actually involved or, if the goods didn't work, whether the seller is responsible under a warranty or guarantee.

Contracts: written and oral agreements, when such agreements are enforceable, when they may be broken, and what happens if they're broken or cancelled. Contract law is primarily concerned with general questions of contract law rather than with specific types of contracts. For specific types of contracts, see Consumer Law, Commercial Law, Insurance Law, Property Law, Landlord-Tenant Law, Intellectual Property Law and Labor Law.

Corporation Law: how corporations are formed, the requirements for corporate structure, the rights of shareholders, the rights and duties of corporate officers and directors, the relationship between a corporation and outside parties who commercially interact with it, procedures for elections of officers, how stock is issued, and similar matters.

Creditor/Debtor Law: how debts are collected, restrictions on collection practices, harassment by collectors, credit and credit card issues, how personal and business debts may cancelled or reorganized in bankruptcy, enforcement of judgments, wage garnishments, levies on personal property, and foreclosures.

Cyberlaw: how the Internet affects copyright, trademark, libel, pornography, contracts, privacy and court jurisdiction.

Education Law: the rights of students and the restrictions placed on them by schools, school funding formulas, educational standards, home schooling, competency testing, remedial programs for the developmentally disabled and educationally handicapped, financial assistance to students, student political affairs, teachers' rights and responsibilities, business and labor matters peculiar to schools (for example, teachers' unions, tenure, placement) and similar matters.

Elder Law: Social Security, Medicare, Medicaid, nursing homes, and Special Needs Trusts.

Employment Law: the rights of employees and the restrictions placed on employers by law. This area is also concerned with employment discrimination against minorities (see also Civil Rights), wrongful discharge of employees (see also Torts), and management-labor relations (see also Labor Law).

Energy Law: the state and federal laws governing the production, distribution and utilization of coal, natural gas, oil, electrical and nuclear power, and with such alternative sources of energy as solar power, wind power and co-generation; also covers what rates energy companies are entitled to charge consumers, the process for obtaining rate changes, the licensing of energy production plants and consumer service requirements.

Environmental Law: the numerous state and federal statutes, regulations and cases that govern the uses of the environment by business, government and individuals. Covers issues of air and water pollution, the environmental impact of new projects, the uses of national forests and parks, the preservation of endangered species, toxic and nuclear wastes, and similar matters.

Estate Planning: how people arrange for the distribution of their property after they die, and how they can avoid paying taxes and probate fees by taking certain actions while they're alive; includes such subjects as living trusts, joint tenancies, wills, testamentary trusts and gifts.

Evidence: what kinds of items and testimony can be introduced as proof in a trial or hearing, the methods used to introduce such proof, who has the responsibility to introduce what types of proof on what types of issues, and how much weight the trier of fact (judge or jury) should give different types of proof.

Family Law, Divorce Law, Domestic Relations Law: all matters relating to annulment, marriage, separation, divorce, taxation upon divorce, child support, child custody, child visitation, marital property, community property, guardianships, adoptions and durable powers of attorney; also, the principles governing living-together situations are taken from this area of the law. (See also Juvenile Law.)

Health Law: the type and quality of medical treatment received from hospitals, health facility regulation and planning, occupational health and safety requirements, rural and neighborhood health clinics, the management of epidemics, the control of pesticide use, and other issues related to health.

Housing Law: numerous programs financed in whole or in part by the federal government that involve housing subsidies for construction and rental assistance, public housing, state and local planning requirements related to the type and amount of housing in different areas, and discriminatory housing practices. (See also Civil Rights Law.)

Insurance Law: problems arising under any kind of insurance contract, such as life insurance, car insurance, homeowners' insurance, fire insurance and disability insurance. (See Unemployment Insurance Law for a separate treatment of that topic.) This area is also concerned with the duty of insurance companies to exercise good faith when dealing with insureds and beneficiaries. (See also Tort Law.)

Intellectual Property Law: the laws and procedures governing copyrights, trademarks, trade secrets and patents.

Juvenile Law: juvenile delinquency (when a child commits an act that would be a crime if he were an adult), child neglect and abuse by parents, juvenile-status offenses (acts that are not crimes but that are juvenile offenses, like running away from home or being truant from school), and juvenile court procedures.

Labor Law: issues surrounding unionization, union actions and actions by employers towards workers, whether organized or not, that are considered unfair labor practices; collective bargaining agreements, strikes, labor negotiations and arbitration under a collective bargaining agreement.

Landlord/Tenant Law: concerned with all issues arising out of the landlord-tenant relationship, such as evictions, responsibility for repairs, cleaning deposits, leases and rental agreements, inspections, entries by the landlord, liability for injuries, rent control and similar matters.

Media Law: the laws and requirements that pertain to the print and broadcast media, include such items as libel, privacy, censorship, open meeting laws, access to government information and court records, licensing of radio and television stations, and restrictions on television and radio programming.

Military Law: all matters under the authority (jurisdiction) of the military, including discharges, enlistment contracts, mandatory registration laws, court martials, pay and pension benefits.

Multimedia Law: legal issues created by the development of multimedia products, including copyright, patent, trademark, fair use, permissions, licensing, privacy, libel, import, export, trade secrets, nondisclosure agreements, site licenses and shrinkwrap licenses.

Municipal Law: zoning, ordinances, land-use planning, condemnation of property, incorporation of cities, contracting for public improvements, and other matters of local concern.

Prison Law: prison conditions, prison disciplinary procedures, parole, constitutional rights of prisoners and adequate access to legal information and medical treatment. (These issues are also often found under the Civil Rights, Civil Procedure, Criminal Procedure and Constitutional Law categories.)

Property Law: the purchase, maintenance and sale of real estate, easements, adverse possession, landowner's liability, mortgages and deeds of trust, homesteads, subdivision and construction requirements, and issues arising from land use regulation. (See also Municipal Law.)

Public Benefits Law: federal and state statutes and cases dealing with federal benefits such as TANF (temporary assistance for needy families), Social Security (SSA), Social Security Disability (SSDI), Supplemental Security Income (SSI), food stamps, school lunches, foster homes, Medicaid, Medicare and state disability. See also Elder Law and Unemployment Insurance.

Public Utilities Law: the duties, responsibilities and rights of public utilities that provide water, telephone service, sewage, and garbage disposal and gas and electricity.

Tax Law: all issues related to federal and state taxation of such items as income, property left in an estate, personal property, business profits, real estate, and sales transactions.

Tort Law (Personal Injury Law): any injury to a person or business that is directly caused by the intentional or negligent actions of another. Examples of commonly known intentional torts, where the person intends the act and knew or should have known that it would result in someone being injured, are:

- assault (putting another in reasonable fear of being struck);
- battery (the objectionable touching of another without his or her consent);
- intentional infliction of emotional distress (outrageous actions affecting another person that the actor knows or should know will result in extreme emotional discomfort);
- libel and slander (a false statement made to someone about a third person that has the capacity to harm the third person's reputation or business);
- trespass (entering onto another's property without consent or legal justification);

- false imprisonment (restricting a person's freedom of movement without legal justification);
- invasion of privacy (substantially interfering with the right of a person to be left alone);
- malicious prosecution (suing a person without just cause for ulterior motives);
- wrongful discharge from employment (under certain circumstances, terminating an employee for improper reasons); and
- breach of covenant of good faith and fair dealing (the bad faith refusal of a party to a contract to perform its obligations under the contract, usually under circumstances where the other party is left personally vulnerable, as in insurance and employment situations).

The most common tort of all is called "negligence." This involves behavior that is considered unreasonably careless under the circumstances and that directly results in injury to another. In deciding whether a given activity is unreasonably careless, the courts must determine whether it was reasonably foreseeable that the kind of injury suffered by the plaintiff would result from the act alleged to be negligent. Medical malpractice, legal malpractice and most automobile accidents are examples of negligence.

Finally, some persons are held liable under tort law for acts that weren't intentional or negligent. Usually some kind of inherently dangerous activity is involved. The legal classifications are:

- Strict liability (holding certain classes of service providers, such as common carriers or persons who operate dangerous businesses, including explosives manufacturers, liable for injuries to persons partaking of the services regardless of whether negligence can be proven).
- Product liability (a kind of strict liability that holds a manufacturer liable for injuries caused by unsafe products).

Trust Law: statutes and cases dealing with how various types of trusts can be created to provide management over property or to preserve a person' assets while he or she is alive and pass these assets to others upon his or her death. Trust law includes such issues as: a) when a trust is revocable (the person creating it can revoke or amend it at will) or irrevocable (can only be changed or revoked by court order); b) how and when the assets in the trust are subject to state and federal taxation; and c) what duties the person managing the trust assets (the trustee) has

under state prudent investor rules and general rules for fiduciaries. See Estate Planning and Elder Law.

Unemployment Insurance: all matters relating to unemployment insurance benefits.

Vehicle Law: all matters related to the registration, use and transfer of motor vehicles, drivers' licenses and noncriminal traffic offenses (legally most traffic offenses are "infractions," not crimes; however, driving while intoxicated, reckless driving and hit-and-run are usually considered crimes).

Veterans' Law: the treatment of veterans under various federal programs dealing with education, health, disability and insurance benefits. Also concerned with the upgrading of less-than-honorable discharges.

Warranties: the obligations of sellers of goods and services to stand behind their products. The law of warranties comes from state and federal statutes and from common law contract principles. (See also Contract Law and Consumer Law.)

Wills: how wills are interpreted and the requirements for making a valid will that effectively allow a person to carry out her desires after her death in respect to her property, her family and any other person or institution to whom she wishes to leave property. (See also Estate Planning.)

Workers' Compensation: rights of workers who are injured or killed in work-related accidents.

Classification Overview

If you have roughly classified your problem as suggested above, you will have one of the following types of problems:

- Federal—Criminal—Substantive
- Federal—Criminal—Procedural
- Federal—Civil—Substantive
- Federal—Civil—Procedural
- State—Criminal—Substantive
- State—Criminal—Procedural
- State—Civil—Substantive
- State—Civil—Procedural

Once you categorize your research question in this manner, you will be prepared to find the most appropriate background resource to start your research. The next chapter shows you how to find a good source of background information. First, however, we introduce you to legal indexes. Whether you are using background resources, looking for statutes, or finding cases in a legal digest, you will be well-served by the information in the following section.

Identify Specific Terms for Your Problem

Most law books contain indexes organized by subject. These indexes are usually quite specific, and you almost always have to use them to strike pay dirt in your legal research. You have gotten off to a good start by putting your problem into a broad legal category. Now you must get more specific.

There are no hard and fast rules for how indexes are set up and what headings are used. How well an individual index is organized depends so much upon the knowledge and thoroughness of the person making it that indexing is recognized as an art form. One index might refer to divorces under the "domestic relations" category, while another might use the term "family law" to designate the broad category. Still a third index might use only the word "divorce."

Most people—especially those unfamiliar with the law—experience difficulty when first faced with a legal index. This, of course, is because the indexes themselves often use legal jargon. For instance, the law on the subject of whether more than one person can be sued in one lawsuit is typically indexed under "Joinder of Parties." Who would think of looking there unless he was already familiar with the term?

Also, indexes can be quite unpredictable when it comes to more specific matters. For example, suppose you want to find out who is responsible for the back injury that resulted from your slip and fall at the supermarket. After some cross-referencing by using the list of civil topics in this chapter, you might figure out that you were dealing with a "tort." Where would you go next, however? Under this general category, would you look under "slip," "fall," "back injury," "liability," "carelessness," "negligence" or "supermarket"? Unfortunately, there is no clear answer to this question.

You must be prepared to use all of these words, as well as a number of others, to get to the specific material you desire. The trick in using an index well mostly involves being able to come up with many alternative words that describe or relate to your research topic. Simply put, the more words you can think of, the better your chances of finding what you're looking for.

If you're feeling a bit overwhelmed at this point, here's some good news. Many legal indexes use ordinary as well as legal words for their headings, and contain elaborate cross-indexing systems so that even if you don't choose the right word to begin with, you will finally get to it through cross-reference entries. Good indexes cross-reference every significant term, so that if the primary information is carried under "family law," for example, the word "divorce" would have "see family law" under it.

Several legal research experts have constructed methods for breaking a legal research problem down into words and phrases that can be looked up in a legal index. Probably the most complete method is that employed by law professor William Statsky.

The Statsky "Cartwheel" Approach

The Statsky approach uses a diagram—called a Cartwheel—which prompts the reader for different categories of words.

For example, suppose that the research problem involved, among other things, who is authorized to perform a wedding and what ceremony, if any, need be conducted. The structure of the Cartwheel is shown below:

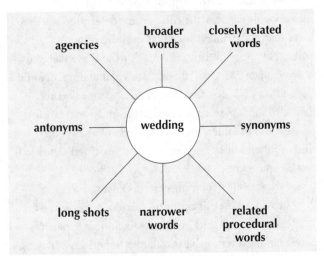

Reproduced by permission from *Domestic Relations*, by William P. Statsky, copyright © 1978 by West Publishing Company (out of print). All Rights Reserved.

The first step in using the index and table of contents in any law book is to look up the key word—"wedding" in this case—in that index and table. If that's not successful, either because the word is not in the index or table or because the page or section references after the word in the index and table do not lead to relevant material in the book, the next step is to think of as many different phrasings and contexts of the word "wedding" as possible.

The Cartwheel method has 18 steps to help you come up with terms to look up in an index or table of contents. It is, in effect, a word association game that should become second nature to you with practice.

MORTGAGES

MORTGAGES—Cont'd

Statute of limitations. Limitation of actions, generally, ante

Title derived under judgment or process, 2A:16–5

Trustees,
 Parties to foreclosure action,
  Against trustee, 2A:50–15
  By trustee, 2A:50–13
  Validation, sales, 2A:50–14

Validation,
 Prior judgments by confession, 2A:50–12
 Sheriff's deed, misnomer of defendants, 2A:50–20

Waiver,
 Rights or privileges by mortgagor, invalidity, 2A:50–2.2

Warrant, entry of satisfaction judgment for foreclosure and sale, 2A:50–32

MOTELS

Hotels and Motels, generally, this index

MOTION PICTURES

Moving Pictures, generally, this index

MOTIONS

Delinquent Children, this index

Discharge of idiot or lunatic arrested or imprisoned in civil action, 2A:41–1

Newsperson information disclosure privilege, criminal proceedings, 2A:84A–21.1 et seq.

Struck jury, 2A:75–1

MOTOR HOTELS

Hotels and Motels, generally, this index

MOTOR VEHICLE CERTIFICATE OF OWNERSHIP LAW

Motor Vehicles, this index

MOTOR VEHICLES

See, also, Traffic Regulations, generally, this index

Accidents. Traffic Accidents, generally, this index

Attachment proceedings, county district court, 2A:18–62

Certificates of ownership,
 Evidence,
  Crimes and offenses, 2A:82–10.1

Certificates of registration. License and registration, post

County District Courts, this index

County Traffic Court, generally, this index

Crimes and offenses,
 Certified copy of certificate, evidence of ownership, 2A:82–10.1
 Disorderly persons, generally, post

MOTOR VEHICLES—Cont'd

Crimes and offenses—Cont'd
 Evidence, ownership, 2A:82–10.1

Dealers,
 Defined,
  Buying, selling, etc., vehicles on Sunday, 2A:171–1.2

Defined,
 Buying, selling, etc., of vehicles on Sunday, 2A:171–1.2
 Sunday sales, 2A:171–1.2

Delinquent children, drivers licenses and registration certificates, postponement, revocation, or suspension, 2A:4A–43

Disorderly persons,
 Imprisonment for buying, selling, etc., motor vehicles on Sunday, 2A:171–1.1

Drivers Licenses, generally, this index

Emergency squads, tort liability, 2A:53A–12

Evidence,
 Certificate of ownership, crimes and offenses, 2A:82–10.1
 Copies of motor vehicle records, 2A:82–10

Financing statements, secured transactions, termination and removal from files, commercial code, 2A:37A–1

First aid squads,
 Tort liability, 2A:53A–12

Garage Keepers' and Automobile Repairmen's Liens, generally, this index

Lanes, generally, this index

Law of the road. Traffic Regulations, generally, this index

License and registration,
 Certificates of registration,
  Delinquent children, postponement, revocation, or suspension, 2A:4A–43
  Delinquent children, postponement, revocation, or suspension, 2A:4A–43
 Drivers Licenses, generally, this index
 Postponement, delinquent children, 2A:4A–43
 Shortwave radios, installation, 2A:127–4
 Suspension or revocation,
  Delinquent children, 2A:4A–43
  Sunday sales of vehicles, 2A:171–1.1

Liens and incumbrances. Garage Keepers' and Automobile Repairmen's Liens, generally, this index

Municipal Courts, this index

National ski patrol system, torts, immunities, 2A:53A–12

New motor vehicle, defined, 2A:171–1.2

1. Identify all the major words from the facts of the research problem. Place each word or small set of words in the center of the Cartwheel.
2. In the index and table of contents, look up all of these words.
3. Identify the broader categories of these major words.
4. In the index and the table of contents, look up all of these broader categories.
5. Identify the narrower categories of these words.
6. In the index and table of contents, look up all of the narrower categories.
7. Identify all the synonyms of the words.
8. In the index and table of contents, look up all of these synonyms.
9. Identify all the antonyms of these words.
10. In the index and table of contents, look up all of these antonyms.
11. Identify all closely-related words.
12. In the index and table of contents, look up all of these closely-related words.
13. Identify all procedural terms related to these words.
14. In the index and table of contents, look up all of these procedural terms.
15. Identify all agencies, if any, which might have some connection to these words.
16. In the index and table of contents, look up all of these agencies.
17. Identify all long shots.
18. In the index and table of contents, look up all of these long shots.

If we were to apply these 18 steps of the Cartwheel to the word "wedding," here are some of the words and phrases that you would check in the index and table of contents of every law book that deals with family law.

Broader Words: celebration, ceremony, rite, ritual, formality, festivity

Narrower Words: civil wedding, church wedding, proxy wedding, sham wedding, shotgun marriage

Synonyms: marriage, nuptial

Antonyms: alienation, annulment, dissolution, divorce, separation

Loosely Related Words: matrimony, marital, domestic, husband, wife, bride, anniversary, custom, children, blood test, premarital, spouse, relationship, family, home, consummation, cohabitation, sexual relations, betrothal, minister, wedlock, oath, contract, name change, domicile, residence

Procedural Terms: application, petition, authorization

Agencies: Bureau of Vital Statistics, County Clerk, License Bureau, Secretary of State, Justice of the Peace

Long Shots: dowry, common law, single, blood relationship, fraud, religion, license, illegitimate, remarriage, antenuptial, alimony, bigamy, pregnancy, gifts, chastity, community property, impotence, incest, virginity, support, custody, consent, paternity

Perhaps you might think that some of the word selections in the above categories are a bit farfetched. But you simply will not know for sure whether or not a word will be fruitful until you try it. To be successful, you must be imaginative.

An excellent aid for coming up with lots of related legal words is *West's Legal Thesaurus/Dictionary* by William Statsky (Thomson, 1995). By simply finding one related term or phrase, you will open up a cornucopia of additional leads. Also, a regular thesaurus can be helpful in stimulating your imagination. Although the legal thesaurus/dictionary is over twenty years old, it still is quite serviceable for most research projects, and used copies are available on Amazon.com for between $18 (paperback) and $60 (hardcover).

Understanding Index Jargon

Indexes themselves use jargon that may be quite confusing if you're not used to it. Here are definitions of some of the more commonly used indexing terms:

Generally, this index. When a term is followed by a "Generally, this index," it means that the term can be located as a main entry in its alphabetical place in the index. For instance, if you find "child support" under the larger heading of "Minors," and it is followed by "Generally, this index," look for it as a main entry.

See also. The terms following the "see also" may produce related subject matter.

See. The material you are seeking will be found directly under the term following the "see" rather than under the original term.

See ___ infra. The entry is found under the same main entry but further down alphabetically. Basically, it's Latin for "below."

See ___ supra. The entry is found under the same main entry, but further up alphabetically. Latin for "above."

An Informal Approach

If you don't want to follow the Cartwheel method, there are other ways to approach legal indexes. The one that we use most of the time has six steps:

Step 1: Select several key plain-English terms that define the research problem, and several alternatives to these terms.

Step 2: Use these words to select one or more probable legal categories.

Step 3: Search the index for a main entry relevant to your problem and be prepared to follow up cross-references.

Step 4: Search for relevant subentries under the main entry.

Step 5: Bounce back to another main entry if your first choice doesn't pan out.

Step 6: Once you find a good main entry and subentry, think even smaller and more detailed.

For instance, suppose your research question is whether a drunk driving conviction results in the loss of a driver's license. The first step is to determine some key terms. You might start with drunk driving and such variations as "operating a motor vehicle under the influence of intoxicating beverages" or "driving while intoxicated." The same process would hold true for "driver's license." Possible alternative terms for driver's license are "operator's permit" or "operator's license."

The second step is to determine whether these terms logically fit under one of the general civil or criminal law substantive categories. Vehicle law would be the most appropriate category, so you would probably start with vehicles.

The third step is to search the index and be prepared to follow up cross-references. For instance, in this example, if you started with vehicles, you would probably be referred to "motor vehicles."

The fourth step is to search for subentries under an appropriate main entry. For instance, if you looked for drunk driving under motor vehicles, you might find an alternative term, such as "operating under the influence."

The fifth step is to go back to another main entry if your first choice doesn't pan out. For example, if you found no reference to drunk driving or its equivalent under motor vehicles, consider looking under "alcohol," "traffic offenses," "alcoholic beverages" or "automobiles." You also might come up with some more variations of your specific terms.

The sixth step is to conceptualize even more detailed entries that are likely to refer you to material on your specific question. For instance, once you find an entry that covers drunk driving under the main entry "motor vehicles," you might consider looking for such specific terms as "license," "suspension," "revocation," "restriction" and "forfeiture."

If you run up against a brick wall, take a deep breath and start over. Reconceptualize your question, come up with new terms, and find a different substantive category. We can't emphasize strongly enough that the reason most research fails is that the researcher runs out of patience at the index-searching stage.

Below are three examples from index listings for this example to demonstrate the different ways indexes can be organized. The one thing they all have in common is that they are organized from general terms in the main entry to specific subentries. The samples show the different ways that indexes can treat the topic of license revocation for drunk driving.

Legal Indexes on the Internet

Law materials on the Internet frequently are not accompanied by an index. Rather, you are expected to find specific material by using one or more of these tools:

- **Menus.** The typical menu approach works like a nested table of contents. Click on the largest category and get a list of sub-categories. Click on a sub-category for a third level of entries. This can go on for any number of levels—depending on the material—until you find a link that is appropriately specific.
- **Key Words.** The key word approach lets you search for materials that contain the words you enter in a search or "query" box. By asking for materials that contain some words and not others, you can often obtain highly specific results.
- **Key word menus.** This method presents you with a drop-down menu of key words. Once you select a key word, you will be taken to materials that have been associated with the key word by the publisher of the material.

Although none of these tools works exactly like a print index, you should keep the same principles in mind when using them. If you don't find what you are looking for at first, keep trying. If your initial key words don't produce anything helpful, change them. If your choice of terms in a drop-down menu doesn't work, select some new ones. We discuss searching by key word and menu in much more detail below.

287   **MOTOR VEHICLES**

MOTOR VEHICLES—Continued
Horns and warning devices—Continued
    Necessity of flags where explosives transported, 75 § 409.
    Penalty for violation of regulations concerning, 75 §§ 401, 405.
    Repair or emergency vehicles, warning devices, 75 § 352.
    Requirement of, 75 § 401.
    Siren, bell, compression or sparkplug whistle, attachment to, purpose, 75
      § 401.
    Use of flag in connection with towing other vehicles, 75 § 452.
Hunting from,
    Permit, 34 § 1311.401.
      Disabled veteran, 34 § 1311.418a.
    Prohibited, 34 § 1311.704.
      Penalty for, 34 § 1311.731.
Hydrants, parking near prohibited, 75 § 612.
Incorporated towns, enforcement of Vehicle Code by officials, 75 § 731.
Infants, see Minors, post this head.
Information,
    Supplied by secretary of revenue, 75 § 787.
    To be shown in record, etc., 69 § 612.
    Violation of,
      Speed laws, 75 § 501.
      Vehicle Code, time of filing, 75 § 731.
Inspection of equipment,
    Exemption from fee for inspection certificate, 75 § 331.
    Fee for certificate, 75 § 306.1.
    Official, 75 § 431.
    Penalty for violation of regulations as to, 75 § 431.
Insurance, see Insurance and Insurance Companies.
Intersections,
    Acquisition of land by township of first class to afford unobstructed view, 53
      § 57040.
    Center, 75 § 546.
    Definition, Vehicle Code, 75 § 2.
    Duty to keep to right in crossing, 75 § 522.
    Grade crossings, generally, see Grade Crossings.
    Interpretation of traffic signals at intersections, 75 § 635.
    Keeping to right in crossing, 75 § 522.
    Parking near intersection prohibited, 75 § 612.
    Parking prohibited within, 75 § 612.
    Pocono Mountain Memorial Parkway, restrictions. 36 § 655.2.
    Right of way, 75 § 573.
      Pedestrians, 75 § 572.
    Rim Parkway, restrictions, 36 § 655.2.
    Rules at intersections,
      Center of intersection, 75 § 546.
      Right of way, 75 § 572.
      Right to turn and manner of making turn, 75 § 546.
    Speed on approaching or traversing, 75 § 501.
    State highways, see State Highways.
    Stopping before entering or crossing, 75 §§ 591, 712.
    Through highways, establishment, 75 § 712.
    Traffic signals, duty to obey and interpretation thereof, 75 § 635.
    Turn by vehicles and manner of making turn, 75 § 546.
Interstate bridges, driving on with excessive weight, 75 §§ 1231, 1232.
Interstate commerce,
    Size, weight or construction of vehicles, violation of federal statute or regula-
      tion, 75 § 457.
    Violation of federal statute or regulation, 75 § 435.
Intoxicating liquor,
    Operating while under the influence of as unlawful, 75 § 231.
    Revocation of license of vehicles used in violating law, 47 § 6—604.
➤   Revocation of operator's privilege for driving while under influence, 75 § 191.
Jobber defined, 75 § 2.
Judgments for damages,
    Certified copies forwarded to secretary of revenue, 75 § 1265.
    Failure to forward certified copy to secretary of revenue, penalties, 75
      § 1265.

MOTOR VEHICLES

TRAFFIC

Searching by Subject Matter Categories on the Internet

Looking for your answer by trying to place it within a website's categories and subcategories is called "topical" or category searching. It works best when you want background information, but it can also be useful for more specific legal questions.

Topical Categories and Subcategories

Topical categories and subcategories reflect the thinking of people who organize the law according to its subject matter. For instance, in most lawyers' minds, all materials having to do with how to control what happens to your property after you die should be grouped under the topical category known as Estate Planning, while materials on wills will be grouped under the "Wills" subcategory, and so on.

To find relevant material under this approach, all you need to know is under what category your subject of interest fits. All of the law collections on the Internet use similar classification systems. To get a better handle on what categories your research might fit under, revisit earlier sections in this chapter. There we help you fit your legal questions into the proper legal categories. Once you go through that exercise, you'll be able to use the categories employed by most online search engines and law libraries.

Use Nolo's Online Law Centers

A good starting place for understanding where your legal question might fit within traditional legal categories is to use one of the Nolo.com Law Centers [www.nolo.com]. The Centers explain many common legal issues in plain English in articles written by Nolo authors and editors. The material is reviewed every few months to make sure it's up to date. For example, let's say you want some information about living wills, which are documents directing the kind of healthcare you receive if you become comatose or are close to death and can't speak for yourself. If you selected the Wills and Estate Planning link from the list of Law Centers on the Nolo.com home page, you would end up with the following list of subcategories:

Main Topics

Wills

Getting Organized for Your Family

Living Trusts and Avoiding Probate

Power of Attorney

Estate Taxes

Life Insurance

Executors & Probate Court

Related Topics

Health Care & Elder Care

Social Security & Retirement

Now what? As it turns out, none of these Main or Related Topics mentions the phrase "living wills." This brings us face-to-face with a basic rule of topical legal research: If the category you have used for your search doesn't match up with a category that your electronic library uses, you'll need to be flexible. Either come up with a different general description or category for your topic, or see if any of the categories that are used appear to describe your research topic in different words.

In our hypothetical case, you are looking for information about a document that speaks for you about your healthcare preferences if you're unable to do so at the time. And so, from the list on the page, the subcategory most likely to address your concern is "Health Care." Clicking on this link produces a new list of Main Topics and Related Topics.

One of the Related Topics is living wills. Clicking that topic pulls up a series of articles about living wills and related topics.

Okay, we know that if you had done this search without our help you might have experienced some frustration, since your chosen search term (living will) didn't match up with how Nolo organizes its first level of topics on this subject. If you get yourself in this situation and keep running into blind alleys, consider searching by key word.

Key Word Searching on the Internet

Finding materials according to the words used in them is an accomplishment unique to the electronic law library. Only a computer can keep track of all the words in all the materials stored in it and, upon your request, give you a list of the materials that contain certain words and not others. Now it's true that some collections of printed materials—federal and state statutory codes and West's Case Digests come to mind—have very detailed key word indexes that help you locate materials. But only the computer lets you devise your own "key words." And only a computer can actually search the materials themselves and give you exactly what you ask for, no more and no less.

Not surprisingly, most legal researchers working in electronic law libraries rely on key word searching. That's because a key word search, done properly, is like a heat-seeking missile and will take you directly to your target. To do a good key word search you need to:

- learn the limits of the search engine you are using and the options specific to that search engine;
- anticipate the probable words used by the materials you are searching; and
- choose words that are most likely to retrieve only relevant materials.

Let's discuss each of these important aspects of key word searching.

Understanding Search Engines

Search engines are software programs that facilitate a search for relevant materials on the Internet. The most common type of search engine is based on an index of all the words in all the indexed documents on the Internet. Stop for a moment and think about the size of this index —can you imagine what the index in this book alone would look like if it gave you a page reference for every word in the text? Luckily, the search engine itself, in ways too techy to explain, does this for the user.

Still, the enormity of the project has resulted in some corner-cutting. Common words like "and" and "the" aren't indexed. (Instead, some common words like "and," "or" and "not" are used to find other words in a Boolean search, which is described in "Fancy Key Word Searches: Boolean Searches," below.) Some search engines don't do their own indexing, but rely on website providers to register their sites and furnish key indexing terms that they feel will best facilitate the searching of their material. The people who tend the search engines fold these terms into the master index.

The master index in each electronic law library (and on every site that features a key word search) is run by an automated program that constantly combs the Internet for newly posted and updated documents and new websites. Then, when you tell the search engine what words you want to search for, the search engine consults its index and reports back, on a "results" or "hit" list, with all the instances where those words are found on the Internet. The engine also creates a link for each hit, so you can go to the page on the Internet where the words have popped up.

The good part of automatic indexes is that they are thorough. Alas, this is also their bad side. Often, these search engines will produce a huge amount of entries for you, and although most search engines try to rank their results according to how relevant they are likely to be, this ranking is very unpredictable. For example, one automatic search engine may put exactly what you are looking for at the top of a list of 200 entries, while another automatic search engine may put it far down the list or even at the bottom.

It would be nice if you knew exactly how the search engine does its ranking, since you could then try to tailor your search in light of that information. Unfortunately, the search engine companies consider that information to be highly proprietary. After all, the better job a search engine does of interpreting the search request and listing the most relevant documents at the top, the more likely it is that the search engine will be used. And since all search engine companies rely on advertising to keep going, the amount of usage is paramount.

Another bad side to automatic search engines is that they operate like the infamous Roach Motel: it's easy for words to find their way into the search engine's index, but the dead ones don't get out. In other words, a hit may refer you to a website that is no longer there or has changed. When this happens, you'll often get a message (known in techno-talk as an "Error 404" message) that the item cannot be found. Some sites give you an email address so you can write to the site and alert them to the dead link, which in reality is more helpful to the site provider than to the frustrated legal researcher.

To help avoid some of the problems that are inherent with automatic search engines, Yahoo and several other search engines build their search indexes by asking website providers to give them an assortment of key words that will tend to lead a searcher to the site and its materials. The website providers also attach these words (called meta-tags) to their own site to facilitate the search. By involving the website provider in the process of reaching out to potential users, these search engines strengthen the relationship between the search terms that the users are likely to use and the materials that they are, in fact, searching for.

This type of search engine may not be as comprehensive as those based on automatic indexing, but your chance of efficiently finding what you're looking for may be greater.

Co-evolution Between Search Engines and Websites

Co-evolution is a process in which organisms adapt to each other in a never-ending dance for survival. For instance, if a plant evolves a poison to deter harmful insects, you can bet that at least some of the insects will evolve an immunity, which causes the plant to evolve a new poison for those evolved insects, and so on.

In much the same way, as search engines evolve more sophisticated ways to retrieve the most relevant documents, so do businesses evolve ways to make sure that the maximum possible searches land on their website. For instance, many search engines give special weight to the number of times a search term appears in the header or title of a document. So, any business that wants to maximize the number of visits to a document on its website will maximize the number of obvious search terms in that document's title. Needless to say, this practice has great potential for rewarding the clever Internet entrepreneur at the expense of overall relevancy of key word searches. But then, of course, the search engines are improved to take into account obviously bogus attempts to fool the searcher.

This problem was recently brought home to the authors, who have provided several examples of key word searching throughout this book. The results that our key word searches produced for the examples are no longer the same. However, when deciding whether to redo the examples to produce more current results, we realized that the problem would reoccur weeks or months later, and that the book would always be behind the co-evolutionary curve that seems intrinsic to the Internet. So, if you try to produce our results using our suggested search terms, you will most likely come up with something completely different. At least you will have the chance to be creative and come up with search terms of your own.

Confining Key Word Searches

When you do legal research in the law library, you obviously don't look in every book for the answer to your question, no matter how narrow and specific your query. Instead, you figure out where your answer is likely to be, and then consult the materials. For example, if you want to know how much time a landlord has before he must account for or return a security deposit, you head for the state codes, look in the master index and make your way to the particular Civil Code that has the answer.

When you're online, you need to adopt the same narrowing strategy. Using a search engine to search the entire Internet for an answer to the question posed above is like looking in every book in the library. The more you focus the field of the search by category before using your search engine to do a key word search, the better. This is because the narrower the collection of materials the search engine must cover, the more likely it is that your search results will produce what you are seeking.

So, if you were looking for the California statute concerning residential security deposits, you would probably take these steps before typing in a key word search:

1. Locate the California statutes online, and
2. Locate the collection of statutes governing landlords and tenants (the category under which you are likely to find the statute you are looking for).

Then you would use a search engine to locate the specific statute on security deposits contained in the civil code. To see how this works for a child support issue, see the Internet Exercise: Finding a State Statute on the Internet, in Chapter 6.

Search Engines Are Tricky

Our explanation on using search engines has just scratched the surface. There are so many of them, each with unique features, that to fully explain the advantages and disadvantages of each would take a book of its own. Because search engines are so powerful in terms of the information they can retrieve from all parts of the world, your best search strategy is to start with a topical search by category and stick with that method as long as it seems to taking you in the right direction. Use a search engine when there is no other reasonable alternative to locating the specific material you seek.

Choosing Your Key Words

A well-thought-out query is one designed to net just the right amount of relevant materials. This requires the same type of word-finding skill as we discussed above, when we talked about using legal indexes. Only here, instead of accessing information according to its type or kind, you must figure out what actual words are likely to be used in the particular document you need (for example, a case, statute or law review article) and then call it up by these words.

For example, suppose you own a restaurant that specializes in pecan pie made from a recipe developed by your great-great-great-grandmother. One day your baker quits and takes up employment down the street, where she starts producing the same pecan pie that you've always considered your proprietary secret. You want to find out whether you have a right to prevent your competitor from selling pies made from your recipe. If you were using conventional legal research techniques, you would find a legal encyclopedia or book specializing in "intellectual property" or "trade secrets" (see Chapter 5 for more on background resources in the law library) and look in the index under "employees," "injunctions," "recipes" and so on. With a little effort, you would soon find some relevant material.

To be sure, if you are searching for background material on the Internet, you can use these same key words. For example, see our background Internet search in Chapter 5. However, if you are looking for primary law that governs your issue (a case, a statute, or a regulation), then these concept words won't work unless they happen to appear in the actual primary law source. Simply put, you probably won't get very far using " trade secret" and "recipe" as your key words. Instead, you have to anticipate what words the source itself is likely to use.

To explain a little bit more, suppose you did search for cases using the terms "trade secret" and "recipes." You would only get cases that use both those exact terms. But there may be other cases about your subject that use different terms, such as "proprietary," "business know-how" and "culinary information." You'll greatly increase your chances of finding a case on point if your request requires the search engine to search for cases containing any of these alternate terms (and more if you can think of them). Of course, if you give the search engine too many words that individually will produce a reference, then you'll get more material than you can reasonably use. Again, the trick to using a search engine is to pull up just the right amount of relevant material.

Fancy Key Word Searches: Boolean Searches

While we don't generally recommend a thoughtless, scattered technique when doing a key word search, the fact is that lots of people never sharpen their search skills beyond this rather rudimentary approach. And, in fact, some search engines encourage you to enter a large number of key words in no particular order. The search engine then uses your terms to figure out, from how the terms are used in the materials being searched, which of those materials are most likely to be the ones that will call forth the most useful results.

The advantage to this blunt searching style is that you don't have to think very hard about what words should be included in the materials identified in the search results list. Unless the search engine page tells you differently, you are free to take this "throw in a bunch of words" approach with just about any search engine. If it works for you, great. Truth be told, sometimes this unsophisticated approach works fine for us, too. Search engines are getting very good at guessing what material is most likely to be relevant.

It's important, however, to realize that the simplicity of this approach has its price. You'll often get a ton of entries on your search results list. And you are pretty much dependent on the "intelligence" of the particular search engine being used—which in our experience is highly unpredictable.

People who spend a lot of time doing online searches have a low tolerance for enormous results lists and a dim view of the default intelligence of search engines. These pros assume that they understand the materials they're after better than a search engine. And they want more control over what items end up on the search results list. To achieve this control, searchers use a method that goes by the mysterious-sounding name of "Boolean logic." Don't be put off by the name. It's really quite simple, as we'll explain.

Be Demanding: Tell the Engine You Want It All

Above, when we explained key word searches, we encountered the most common and simplest Boolean command: the *and* command. If you enter two words in your search engine query box and separate them with an *and*, you are telling the search engine to pull up all documents that contain both words. For example, the query "box and container" produces every document that has both the word box and the word container. That is, it doesn't produce any document that doesn't have both words.

As we've noted, you can stick with *and* and hope that your search terms are both numerous and specific enough to net you a reasonably short list of results. But the problem with the *and* operator is that it can produce too few results and may well exclude many relevant documents. For example, suppose you are searching for a Tennessee case that describes when the police may search closed containers found during a search of an automobile. By asking for "container" and "box," your search may fail to produce some of the Tennessee cases that in fact dealt with this very issue. Why? Because it's quite possible that some of the relevant cases don't use the word "box," and your query in effect tells the search engine to not bother with those cases. Fortunately, Boolean logic lets you get around this problem, as described next.

Hedge Your Bets: Tell the Engine It Has a Choice

Sometimes you're not sure which of two descriptive terms fits the object of your search. In that situation, you can use the command *or* instead of *and*. Using an *or* command is also useful if you aren't sure which term is the correct one. To continue with our box and container example, if your search used *or* instead of *and*, you'd get documents that use the word box, documents that use the word container and documents that use both terms. (To exclude documents that have both terms, you'll need to use a variation on *or*, as explained in " tThe *xor* Logical Operator," below.)

If the database being searched has only a few documents, or the words are unusual, using *or* might be a perfectly reasonable search. For example, suppose you are searching for California Supreme Court cases decided in 1998, and you know that the name of one of the parties is either Moriarty or Morrissey. By using the *or* logical operator, "Moriarty or Morrissey," your chances are great that you'll pull up exactly the case you need. But if you used this same search for any U.S. Supreme Court case decided in the last two hundred years that contained either of these names, you might pull up a long list of cases.

Narrow the Field: Tell the Engine What You *Don't* Want

Now, with the help of *or* you are able to craft a more flexible search. But since *or* can produce an unreasonable number of results, we need more "logical operators" to help us zero in on our answer. Welcome to *and not*.

Variations on the "And" Logical Operator

Many search engines on the Internet use variations on the "and" logical operator. Before you start your Boolean search, it is wise to read the "Help" page that accompanies the search engine so you can become familiar with its peculiarities. Here are the most common variations:

- Some search engines require you to put a plus sign (+) in front of any word that you want to be in the materials you are searching. This has the same effect as typing in the word "and" between the terms to be searched.
- Some search engines allow you to use the logical operator *near* instead of *and* to indicate that the words should have some logical proximity to each other (in the same sentence or paragraph). Usually these search engines also let you specify how many words should separate the two key words. For instance, the logical operator *near/3* means the key words must not be separated by more than three words in either direction if they are to appear on the search results list.
- Some search engines allow you to use the logical operator *adj* to require that the key words separated by this logical operator must appear next to each other in the order you enter them. For instance, the search query "dangerous adj beauty" means that the documents must have the phrase "dangerous beauty" to end up on the search results list.
- Some search engines allow you to use the *adj* logical operator in connection with a specification of how close the key words should be. For instance, "adj/3" means that the key words must appear in the order they are entered in the search engine query box and not be separated by more than three words.

To write a more useful search, you need to specify not only what words the materials being searched should have, but also which ones they should *not* have. You'll isolate the object of your search by describing it both positively and negatively. In theory, if the search has enough of these descriptions, the object should become evident.

To continue with our car search example, think about the fact that since you are looking for cases involving a police search, you don't want to bother with opinions that came from civil, rather than criminal, proceedings. To eliminate opinions from civil lawsuits, you can specify that the results *not* contain the word "plaintiff," which describes a party to a civil, but not a criminal, lawsuit. Typing in "and not plaintiff" would eliminate many irrelevant hits: You'll get cases with box and cases with container, but you'll see no cases with one of those terms and the term plaintiff.

Phrase Searches

Often you will want to search a document for an exact phrase, whether it consists of two words (as in "free speech") or many words ("free speech protected by the First Amendment to the U.S. Constitution"). These are sometimes referred to as "string searches," because they involve a specific string of alphanumeric characters (letters and numbers). How can you do this with the rudimentary commands of *and, or, adj* and *and not* that we've encountered so far?

As you might expect, when you begin "talking" to the search engine with phrases that sound like real English (instead of throwing phrases at it that sound like the Morse code gone haywire), you're complicating things greatly. If you're lucky, the search engine you're using will interpret words that are entered without a logical operator (such as *and* or *adj*) as a phrase that must appear verbatim in a document for it to make the search results list. In other words, if you type in "free speech," the search engine will look for that phrase. If the search engine you're using makes this leap, you're fortunate, and need not interject any other commands.

Other search engines are not so friendly. You must tell the engine that you're looking for a phrase by enclosing the phrase in double or single quotation marks. For instance, the words and punctuation "protected under the first amendment" or 'protected under the first amendment' (the punctuation depends on the search engine) entered into a search engine query box will be interpreted to mean that every word in the phrase must be in the document in the exact order entered in the box. To find out which format the search engine requires for string searches, click on the help or options feature usually located next to the box where you enter your query. Or, just find out by trial and error.

The *xor* Logical Operator

The *xor* logical operator is a subtle variation on the *or* operator. Not every search engine offers it (another reason to read each site's "Help" page). The *xor* logical operator allows you to pull up documents that have either of the words separated by the operator but not documents that have both terms in them. This should be compared with the *or* logical operator, which will pull up documents that have either term or both terms.

Combining Logical Operators

So far our discussion has pretty much focused on queries that only use one logical operator at a time (except for the *and not* logical operator). However, there will be times when you want to combine logical operators. For instance, you may want to search for a document that must have one word but may have either of two other terms.

For example, assume you are looking for information about the circumstances that trigger driver's license suspensions. You would want documents that contain both "license" and "suspend." But each of these documents should also have either the word "driver" or the word "operator" (since you don't know which of these two words will be used in the materials you are searching for.). A query that would accomplish this search would look like this: license and suspend and (driver or operator).

Let's take a moment to understand how a search engine would interpret this query. If you think back to your days in high school algebra (it's a stretch for us, too), you'll remember that the first step in simplifying a complicated equation is to deal with the stuff in the parentheses. Search engines work this way too—they start with the parenthetical phrase and then move backwards from right to left. So, the search engine will look for documents with the word operator or the word driver. Once it has identified this group, it will choose only those documents that also have the word suspend and the word license. You'll end up with documents having the words operator, license and suspend; and a second batch having the words driver, license and suspend.

The ability to properly combine logical operators in one search request to produce a precision search is what the art of key word searching is all about. It definitely involves a learning curve.

Study Online Boolean Searching Tutorials

Virtually every search engine comes with a search tutorial that explains how to perform the different types of key word searches supported by that search engine. One of our favorite Boolean tutorials can be found on the VersusLaw website [www.versuslaw. com]. But there are many others. Our suggestion is to use these free tutorials to bone up on your Boolean search techniques whenever you plan to do serious online searching.

Guided Boolean Searches

Knowing that lots of folks don't read the instruction manual before they use the appliance, some search engines recognize that some searchers, too, aren't accomplished query writers or won't read the help page before writing their search. So these engines walk you through a Boolean search by asking you questions whose answers generate the query. For instance, the engine will ask you to enter two key words and ask whether you want both words to appear in every document or just one word (in other words, is the logical operator to be *and* or *or)*. It will then ask you whether there are any words you don't want to include (or, is there an *and not* feature to your search). These structured search utilities can be handy if you don't want to bother learning Boolean logic, but they typically are not as flexible as a straight Boolean search, because they don't allow you to combine logical operators, as explained in "Combining Logical Operators," above.

Using Wildcard Characters

Our foray into Boolean logic has so far only involved logical operators—those powerful little words that you use to combine words in a way that is best calculated to produce relevant search results. But there is another important tool that you should become comfortable with. Part of the art of writing a good query is knowing when and how to use what are known as "wildcard" characters, which are tags you affix to search terms. When the search engine sees the tag, it knows to look for variations on the term. As with logical operators, different search engines use different characters, or tags, for different purposes. But the principle is the same.

Let's take the asterisk (*) first. For most Internet search engines, the asterisk serves as a word (or part of a word) extender. By placing an asterisk at the end of a string of letters (known as the root), you are asking the search engine to search for any word that starts with the letters preceding the asterisk. For instance, in an earlier example we used the word driver in a search request dealing with the suspension of a driver's license. Because computers are so literal, if we simply put the word driver into the query, the search engine would skip over documents that use closely related words such as drivers, driver's, drivers' or driving. And the document with one of these variations on driver might be just the one you want.

To solve this problem, we use an asterisk at the end of the root of driver, like this: driv*. This search term tells the search engine to report back documents with any word that begins with driv. Once you become familiar with the asterisk wildcard, you will automatically enter the shortest form of a word that would pull in all related words—but don't forget to add the asterisk! For example, the term manag* would pick up manage, management, manager and managers.

Another common wildcard is the place holder. Typically either a question mark (?) or an exclamation point (!) is used. This character serves a function similar to that of a wildcard in poker. When you insert it in a word in a query, it stands for any character occupying that position in the word. Suppose, for example, your search involves women's rights. You would want to include the term women in your search query, but would also want to capture cases that use the term woman. If you only listed "women," you might miss some important cases. By using a place holder for the "e" and the "a" in these two terms (like this: wom?n), you can have the computer search for any case containing either term. This would produce cases using the term women, or the term woman, or both terms.

Be Willing to Modify Your Query

It is unusual for even experienced researchers to get their queries right the first time around. Instead, their initial selection of words either produces too many cases or too few. For example, if you asked to see all federal cases with the terms "environmental" and "impact," your search would produce many hundreds of cases, too many for you to reasonably review. You would need to modify your search so that it would provide fewer, but all relevant, cases. If your situation involves a nuclear power plant, you would modify your search to only include federal cases that use environmental and impact and nuclear and power plant.

On the other hand, if your initial query is too restrictive, you may have to drop a term or two to produce any relevant documents. As a general rule, the more words that must be in a case as requested (for example, every case with the words "drunk" and "intoxicated" and "under the influence"), the fewer cases will be found, since any case that doesn't have all the required terms would not be produced. Conversely, the fewer and more general the words that must be in a case to retrieve it (for example, every case with the word "eviction"), the more cases will be produced.

Searching With Google

Throughout this book, we have described numerous ways to access law, cases, and related research materials using time-tested law library techniques and resources. The old-fashioned methods aren't always the most rewarding, however. For example, one of the authors of this book recently attempted to assist a law library patron seeking a California "substitution of attorney" form—the form to use when you change attorneys or when you want to handle your own case after an attorney has appeared in it. After exhausting traditional print resources, the author opened the Google search engine and entered the following terms: California substitution of attorney form. The first result in the list was just what the customer wanted.

The lesson is pretty clear: Google isn't a tool of last resort in legal research, nor is it a second-rate option for non-lawyers. Rather, it is often a source of instant gratification. This section will guide you through the quick and often profitable ways of getting what you want from Google. Although you're probably already familiar with the Google search system, we've decided to review some search techniques and tools that can help you locate cases, forms, and relevant articles.

Google Tools

Google is more than a search engine, it's a collection of search tools that perform many different functions. Before we begin our explanation of search techniques, let's take a look at what's behind the Google home page. Click the word "more" at the top. You'll see some varied and interesting offerings.

The Google Toolbar

If you use Google regularly—and we recommend that you do—download the Google Toolbar. Doing so will add a Google search box to your browser's window, and you will no longer have to type www.google.com every time you want to enter a search. To get the Google Toolbar, go to www.google.com and click the link marked "More," or type "Google Toolbar" in your search engine.

The toolbar does more than save you the extra step of going to the Google site. By clicking the drop-down menu next to the "Search Web" button, you can select where you want Google to perform its search. For example, if you choose "Current Site," you'll limit your search to the site you're at. If you're at the U.S. Patent and Trademark office site, for instance, and are looking for information about provisional patent applications, you can quickly locate all of the pages within the site dealing with this subject.

The "highlight" button on the Toolbar is particularly handy. If you click the "highlight" button (the icon looks like a felt-tipped marker), your search terms will be highlighted—each term in a different color—throughout the selected Web page of each result. You'll be able to quickly zero in on your results on a text-heavy site.

News Searches

Often you may need timely information on a newsworthy subject. Because Google's search priorities are often based on the popularity of a site—statistics that accrue over time—current information may be buried at the end of search results. Google compensates for this by allowing you to perform a news search in which the search engine looks for timely media reports on the searched terms. It also organizes the news results by providing most current first. For example, to obtain the latest information about the number of Firefox Browser users we performed a news search for the terms: Mozilla Firefox. We retrieved a series of news articles including one that documented the number of program downloads. We also retrieved articles regarding the safety of the program for Internet use as well as a growing business preference for the browser.

You can search for news results in two ways. First, you can run a search on Google's main page but then click the "News" link on the top of the search results page. Or, you can direct a search to find only news articles. To perform the latter, go to www.google.com and click "more" and then click "News Search."

Stay on top of breaking legal news stories. If you want to stay abreast of a specific news subject, try "Google News Alerts." You will receive daily (or "as it happens") emails based on your choice of query or topic. Go to www.google.com/alerts and type in the search terms.

Scholar Searches

If you'd like to limit your Google search to locate scholarly papers, try Google's "Scholar Search" feature. Go to www.google.com and click "more" and then click "Scholar." Your search will be limited to scholarly literature, including peer-reviewed papers, theses, books, preprints, abstracts, and technical reports from the broad areas of research that are available on the Web. For example, when we researched alternative energy systems and typed the term "fuel cell microgrid" into Scholar Search, we were rewarded with several academic papers explaining the subject.

News Groups

When you perform a Google search, Google will also—if you choose—search results from hundreds of Google discussion groups (also known as news groups) on the Web. These discussion groups may help and can lead to other resources, but don't rely solely on them. It's often very difficult to separate the wheat from the chaff.

If you're familiar with discussion groups, then you're already aware that these sites often post a wide range of commentary—from crackpots to experts. For example, we typed "work for hire" and some of the results were accurate and directly on target—especially those from the "misc.legal.moderated" group. However, others were less reliable and a few were inaccurate.

To view hits that include discussion groups only, run your search on the main Google page, then click the "Groups" link on the top of the search results page. Or, if you're using the Google Toolbar, click the word Google on the left and choose Google Links, Google Groups, then type your search into the query box.

Google Answers

Google Answers provides an inventive approach to research. You can post your question and the amount you are prepared to pay for the answer—usually between $10 and $50. Researchers who troll this site looking for work can accept your offer, then provide an answer. For example, we needed to determine the geographic reach of the various law enforcement officials in the town of Mill Valley, California. We offered $10 and posted the following question: "If a person were arrested for burglary or a similar felony in Mill Valley, California, what police force would arrest the perpetrator and where (that is, what police station or jail) would the perpetrator be taken for purposes of arraignment or further questioning?"

Within one hour we received a response, a portion of which is excerpted below:

"Mill Valley has two jurisdictions: The city limits are serviced by the Police Department, and the Sheriff's Department services the unincorporated areas. If your street signs are brown with white lettering, you are within the city limits. If your street signs are blue with white lettering, you are in the unincorporated area."

The remainder of the response indicated where felons were taken after arrest and the procedures for contacting arrested persons in each jurisdiction along with supporting links that provided more documentation.

You will need to register to use Google Answers. Go to the Google home page, click "More," and then click "Google Answers."

Quick Definitions

Looking for a quick legal definition? Of course you could use Nolo's online dictionary (www.nolo.com). But you could also type "define:" followed by a space and the word to be defined in your Google search box. For example, we typed "define: estoppel" into the Google search engine and received several legal explanations of the term, such as, "A person's own act, or acceptance of facts, which preclude his or her later making claims to the contrary."

Interested in new Google technologies? Google is constantly testing new research products. For example, as this book went to press, Google was testing a system for finding the real-time location of taxis in certain cities (Google Ride Finder). If you'd like to see and test what Google is currently cooking up, check out Google Labs. Go to the Google home page, click "more," and then click "Labs."

Google Preferences

Do you want more than ten search results per page? If you want 20, 30, 50, or 100 search results per page, you can specify the number, as well as numerous other preferences.

For example, you can have search results open on a separate Web page. To access these options, click the "Preferences" button on the toolbar or the Preferences link on the Google Search Page.

Local Searching

Are you trying to locate a business in a specific location? Try using Google's Local search. Go the Google home page and click "Local." Type a search term in the "What" box, then enter the location in the "Where" box. For example, we needed to locate a hypnotherapist in San Francisco. We typed "hypnotherapy" into the What search box, and San Francisco into the Where box and received ten results, along with references, maps, and phone numbers.

Google Calculators

The Google search box is also a calculator. Right in the box on the home page, you can perform quick calculations by using the plus sign ("+"), the multiplication sign ("*") the division symbol ("/") or any other common spreadsheet or calculator terminology. For example, we typed the calculation ((234+56)*12)/6. Google can even translate from metric to nonmetric and vice versa—for example, type "400 feet in meters" and Google will respond with 121.92 meters.

Searching Books

Google is in the midst of cataloging books into one massive bibliographic search system, known as the Google Print Index. You can use Google's Book Search feature to access this database and to locate books on specific topics. Whenever books contain content that matches your search terms, you'll see links to those books under Book Results at the top of your Book Search results page. If you click any book's title, you'll see the page in that book that contains your search terms, as well as other information about the title. (Amazon.com has a similar technology at work at its website). Though this tool shows great promise, we had mixed results with the current version, probably because Google is in the early stages of scanning books. To access this tool, click "More" on the Google home page. Then click "Web Search Features" and "Book Search."

Google Images

Though it's not a high priority for most legal researchers, there may be occasions when you need an image of a person, place, or thing. For example, when we wanted a current picture of Justice Sandra Day O'Connor, we typed her name in the search engine and clicked "Images." This search feature is not foolproof. Our search also turned up pictures of book covers and other Supreme Court justices. You can also use the imagine-finding feature by clicking the "Images" link on the top of the search results page.

Google's Numerology

The people at Google have designed their search engine to enable you to track many items indexed by number—for example, you can look for numbered FedEx and UPS parcels, patents, vehicle IDs (VINs), area codes, zip codes, UPC Codes, and even FAA registration numbers (that's the number of an airplane, typically printed on its tail). Just type the number into the search box. Try typing your telephone number with area code—it won't work for unlisted numbers—and see what happens. (If you're looking for patents, you'll have to type the word patent and leave a space before the number.)

Google Basic and Advanced Search Modes

Like virtually all general-purpose search engines, Google offers two modes of search: Basic, and Advanced. If you're using the Google Toolbar, you can access the Advanced Search mode by clicking the word Google and choosing Google Links, Advanced Search from the drop-down menu. If you're on the Google search page, click Advanced Search.

The Advanced Search mode relies on the same "Boolean" approach to key word searches described earlier in this chapter. As a general rule, you'll do a better search if you use the Advanced Mode than the basic mode. However, because we want to give you a search methodology that doesn't require much of a learning curve, we'll use the Google Basic Search mode for most of this section.

When performing searches with Google, here are some tips and tricks to keep in mind:

- **Google ignores many common words and characters.** Google disregards words such as where, the, how, why, and some single digits and letters. (Google believes these slow down your search without improving the results.) You can see which words are ignored on the search results page—for example, if you type this search. "Who is the Chief Justice?" Google will let you know "The following words are very common and were not included in your search: who is the." If you want the search to include the common word, put a "+" sign in front of it—for example, Americans +with Disabilities Act. (Be sure to include a space before the "+" sign.)

- **You can make Google search for synonyms.** If you want to search not only for your search term but also for its synonyms, place the tilde sign ("~") immediately in front of the search term.

- **You can search for a range of numbers.** If you want to obtain results within a numerical range—for example, copyright law results between 1980 and 1990, just include the two numbers, separated by two periods, with no spaces, into the search box along with your search terms. For example, type, "copyright law 1980..1990."

- **Use quotation marks for phrases.** Often you'll want only results that include an exact phrase or name, such as "Bankruptcy Abuse and Prevention Act." In this case, simply put quotation marks around your search terms. If you are researching a person, particularly one whose name includes a word that's also a noun (like James Woods or Tom Cruise), putting the name in quotation marks may narrow your search results.

- **Get rid of multi-meaning terminology.** If your search term has more than one meaning, you can focus your search by putting a minus sign ("–") in front of words related to the meaning you want to avoid. (Be sure to include a space before the minus sign.) For example, let's say you're researching marijuana laws. You searched using the word marijuana, but now want articles using the word "pot." Obviously, you don't want results concerning cooking pots, coffee pots, or melting pots. You would type "pot –cooking –coffee –melting" and it would eliminate many of the unnecessary common results.

Using "I'm Feeling Lucky"

You've probably noticed the "I'm Feeling Lucky" button as a Google searching choice. This feature takes you to the most relevant website that Google found for your query. You won't see the search results page at all.

Using Google to Find Laws

Most states have a system of posting new laws on the Internet shortly after they are enacted. Congress takes a little longer, but special interest groups often fill the void at their websites. For instance, groups tracking the Bankruptcy Abuse and Prevention Act of 2005 will probably post the new law before the official legislative website (Thomas.gov) gets around to it. Using Google may be the fastest way to find the law.

If you are searching for a new law, try using any combination of the following elements:

- If you're after a state law, type your state's name (so that the search engine won't give you an Illinois law while you are in Texas).

- If possible, provide the literal name or number of the law, in quotation marks. If the new law has a lot of words, it usually works to just use the distinctive elements of the phrase. Similarly, if the law has a nickname, you can use that phrase. For example, you can locate California's sex offender registration law (AB 488) by typing: "Megan's Law" California.

- If you can think of key words that identify the law, provide those as well. For instance, if a new law creates an additional procedure for collecting child support, you could likely find it by typing in the terms: "child support" and "collection."

- If you know the year that the law was passed, add that as well (so that you don't get an out-of-date law by the same name).

Using Google to Find Court Cases

In Chapters 7 through 9, we go into detail about researching court cases and we explain that state and federal appellate courts (courts that decide appeals from trial courts) publish their opinions in order to provide guidance on the law. Most of these state and federal appellate courts publish their new opinions on the Internet. Also, one or more organizations that are interested in the subject matter of newsworthy cases maintain their own websites. If you are searching for a new law, try any combination of the following elements:

- Type one or both names of the parties to the case. You can also search with the "v." abbreviation, as well.
- Include one or more terms that describe the subject matter of the case.
- Type the year of the case.
- Type the name of the court that heard and decided the case.

Note that cases decided previous to 1995—that is, before the Internet was used to catalog court cases—usually are only available in private databases that require a subscription for a fee. U.S. Supreme Court cases are an exception and can be searched back into the late 19th century.

Using Google to Find Forms

Courts and lawyers are highly dependent on forms, and Google is great for finding the right one. Many websites offer both free forms and forms for a small price. A Google search for a particular form usually uncovers many sites to choose from. If you are searching for a form, try any combination of the following elements:

- Type in the state that issued the form or, if it's a local form, the court where you will use it;
- Use the title of the form or include a few unique terms that would likely be in the title—for example, "Petition Administer Estate" for a "Notice of Petition to Administer Estate;"
- Include the subject matter of the form in the absence of a specific name—for example "Summons Eviction;"
- It may also help to use the term "form."

Keep in mind that some forms are not issued by the federal, state, or local government. Instead, you may be looking for a document that looks and acts like a form, but is really just a legal document. For example, a living will includes common clauses and directions concerning a person's wishes in the event of catastrophic illness or injury. Usually, all you need to do is fill in some names, date the document, and sign it. Consequently, hospitals, lawyers (and Nolo!) have written living wills with fill-in-the-blanks portions. You can still find forms like these through Google by following the principles outlined in this section.

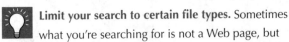 **Limit your search to certain file types.** Sometimes what you're searching for is not a Web page, but a specific document that is stored on the Web in PDF, Microsoft Office, or other format. For example, most government forms are stored in PDF format. You can narrow your search in this manner by typing "filetype:[name of file type]. "For example, when looking for a specific tax form, we typed Schedule C "filetype:pdf" and our first search result was the downloadable PDF version of the IRS form.

Review

Questions

1. Why is it necessary to fit your research problem within certain legal categories?

2. What are the four main questions to answer when categorizing your legal question?

3. What are some legal categories that usually are a matter of state law?

4. What are some legal categories that involve federal law?

5. What are some categories that involve both state and federal law?

6. What's the main way you can tell whether a research issue involves criminal or civil law?

7. What's the difference between civil substantive law and civil procedure?

8. What's the first step to using the informal index-searching method?

Answers

1. The books with which you start your research are organized according to these categories.

2. Does it involve federal law, state law or both?
   Does it involve criminal law, civil law or both?
   Does it involve the substance of the law, or legal procedure?
   If it involves the substance of the law, what is its appropriate subtopic?

3. Real estate, zoning, divorce, guardianship, paternity, child custody, conservatorships, living wills, durable powers of attorney for health care and financial management, contracts, testamentary wills, probate, personal injuries, trusts, the licensing of businesses and professions, landlord-tenant relationships, partnerships and small corporations, motor vehicles and most, but not all, crimes.

4. Admiralty, agriculture, bankruptcy, copyright, federal tax, food and drug regulation, immigration, interstate commerce, maritime, patent, postal, trademark, customs, Native Americans and crimes involving the movement of people or substances across state lines for illegal purposes. Also a matter of federal law are the many cases that interpret and reinterpret the U.S. Constitution and the civil rights laws that have been passed by Congress since 1964.

5. Environmental protection, labor law, consumer protection, veterans' benefits, health law, welfare law, occupational safety, subsidized housing, transportation, employment, unemployment insurance, child support enforcement.

6. If the research issue involves behavior that is punishable by imprisonment, then criminal law is involved. Civil law is involved in cases of a broken contract, personal injury, withheld government benefit, divorce or other dispute where the court is asked to issue orders, award money damages or dissolve a marriage.

7. Substantive civil law consists of numerous sets of principles that determine the rights, duties and obligations that exist between individuals and institutions such as corporations and governments. Civil procedure involves how our civil justice system works—that is, such matters as which courts are appropriate for which kinds of lawsuits, what papers need to be filed, when they need to be filed, who can be sued, what kinds of proof can be offered in court and how to appeal.

8. Select several key plain-English terms that define the research problem, and several alternatives to these terms.

5

Getting Some Background Information

Once you've tentatively classified your problem and settled on the terms and keywords that define your issue (Chapter 4), you are well on your way. You have squeezed your issue (often a somewhat square peg) into its proper legal niche (the proverbial round hole) and are now ready to find some answers. First you will find the appropriate resources to answer your questions. Then you will use your legal index skills to find helpful discussions within the resources themselves.

How Background Resources Can Help

Especially if you're unfamiliar with the area of law you're going to be researching, it makes great sense to start with broader introductory materials rather than plunging directly into the primary sources of the law (statutes, cases and regulations). Fortunately, nearly every major area of the law has been discussed and summarized by experts, in many different kinds of books and periodicals.

Starting with background materials (often called "secondary sources") is the same technique you used when you did research for high school or college papers. For example, if you wanted to teach yourself something about cloning, you would probably start by reading a broad introduction to genetic engineering such as that found in many new encyclopedias. This might lead to a book that presented more detail. Next you would probably be ready to dive into materials dealing with the specific areas you were interested in, perhaps gene-splicing, DNA analysis or monoclonal antibodies.

Getting a general understanding of an area before looking for the answer to a narrow question is particularly important when it comes to legal research. The answers to almost all specific legal questions depend on a number of variables to which the background resource can alert you. Then, when you go on to read the actual laws—statutes, cases and regulations—you'll know what to look for.

For instance, consider this question: Can an unmarried tenant be evicted for having overnight guests? The answer depends on such variables as:

- What does the lease or rental agreement say?
- How long do the guests stay?
- Are the guests lovers, and is this a factor in the landlord's decision to evict?
- Does the state or city have a statute or ordinance making it illegal to discriminate in the renting of housing against people based on their marital status or sexual orientation?
- Is overcrowding a factor?
- Does the city or county have a rent control ordinance?
- Is the eviction really for some other reason not permitted by law?

Reading a background resource's discussion of guests and eviction would tell you that these are the questions you need to answer to resolve your original question.

Legal background materials are usually directed at a particular audience: non-lawyer, law student or lawyer. But don't let these labels scare you off—non-lawyers often find useful information in materials that were written with lawyers in mind, and vice versa. Many books, articles and, increasingly, computer software and databases can be of immense help to all users.

 An Encyclopedia of Background Resources: West's Legal Desk Reference. *West's Legal Desk Reference,* by Statsky, Hussey, Diamond and Nakamura, lists background (secondary) resources both by state and by legal topic. For instance, if you are in Illinois, this resource tells you what background materials have been published specifically for that state. And if your research question involves drunk driving, you can find many pertinent articles, books and encyclopedia entries under "Alcohol." Additionally, *West's Legal Desk Reference* provides key words and phrases that will help you use the indexes to other resources that you encounter in the course of your research. Although some of these books may no longer be in print, many libraries will continue to stock the latest editions.

Self-Help Law Resources

In recent years many law books aimed at nonlawyers have been published. Some of these books impart an overall understanding of one or more legal topics; others are more in the "how to do it" spirit. The publisher of this book, Nolo, has the longest list. Nolo has titles ranging from *How to File for Bankruptcy* and *How to Form a Nonprofit Corporation* (both nationwide) to *Patent Pending in 24 Hours.* A complete list of Nolo publications is available at its website at www.nolo.com. You can also receive a catalog by sending in the registration card at the back of this book.

Another popular series of books written for non-lawyers is sponsored by the American Civil Liberties Union and published by Bantam Books. A partial list of titles includes:

Norwick, *The Rights of Authors, Artists and Other Creative People*

Stark and Goldstein, *The Rights of Crime Victims*

Outten, *The Rights of Employees*

Hunter, Michelson and Stoddard, *The Rights of Lesbians & Gay Men*

Pevar, *The Rights of Indians and Tribes*

Rudovsky, et al., *The Rights of Prisoners*

Bernard, *The Rights of Single People*

Rubin, *The Rights of Teachers*

Ross, et al., *The Rights of Women*

Guggenheim, et al., *The Rights of Families*

Marwick, *Our Right to Government Information.*

For a complete listing of ACLU's *Rights* series, visit the store on their website at www.aclu.org.

Look first for self-help law materials in a law library or large public library. Many of them carry complete sets of Nolo books as well as self-help books by other publishers. If you want to buy a self-help book, check out the business, reference or law sections of a larger bookstore (or call Nolo or visit its website at www.nolo.com).

We suggest that before buying a book or computer program, you look through it to see whether the language is understandable and the concepts useful and specific. And if you are planning on using the book to accomplish a legal task—rather than simply to obtain a general overview of the subject—check whether the material actually leads you step by step through the entire process, gives you the necessary forms for doing it yourself, and is sufficiently sensitive to differences in state laws. Otherwise the book or program may turn out to be useless for your purpose.

Self-Help Law on the Internet. Nolo is an excellent place to start when looking for background resources on the Web. Nolo's site features a series of law centers on dozens of topics of common interest to the nonlawyer, including Small Business, Wills and Estate Planning, Employment (Workplace Rights and Independent Contractors), Consumer (Travel, Insurance and Legal Malpractice), Patent, Copyright & Trademark, Debt and Credit (Bankruptcy, Credit Repair and More), Courts and Mediation (Small Claims and Trial Tactics), Tax Problems (Audits, Tax Bills and More), Real Estate (Renting, Buying and Neighbors), Parents & Children (Custody, Adoption and More), Immigration, Spouses and Partners (Divorce, Living Together and More), Older Americans (Social Security and Retirement) and an Update Service on all topics.

Although Nolo is the leading publisher of self-help law materials, the Internet has spawned many websites that also offer general legal materials geared for the non-lawyer, for example, www.findlaw.com (click "The Public" at the top of the page).

A Bibliography of Self-Help Law Publications. *Do-It-Yourself Law: HALT's Guide to Self-Help Books, Kits & Software,* by James C. Turner, Theresa Meehan Rudy and Edward J. Tannouse (HALT 2006). A good survey of self-help law books in various fields has been put together by an organization known as HALT. You can order the book directly from HALT's website at www.halt.org.

Law Textbooks

Many books published as textbooks for law students (sometimes called "hornbooks") offer an excellent point of departure for legal research. Most of these textbooks are published by the West Group or Foundation Press. These books, which are conceptual in nature, are excellent if you want a basic understanding of the variables in any specific area of concern. However, they are not very helpful when it comes to finding specific answers to specific questions or providing accurate, up-to-date information about the state of the law when you need it.

You can find most of these books in any law bookstore (usually near law schools) or law library. For a catalog of materials published by the West Group, write to P.O. Box 64833, St. Paul, MN 55164-0833, or visit its website at www.westgroup.com. The University Textbook series is published by Foundation Press, www.foundation-press.com. Below is a partial list of some commonly used legal textbooks.

Other good background resources are the concise law summaries intended primarily as study guides for law students. Titles such as *Gilbert's Law Summaries, Black Letter Series, Emmanuel Law Outlines, Legalines* and *Law in a Nutshell* can be found in legal bookstores and law libraries. All provide an up-to-date framework or overview

of a legal subject area, making it easier to understand the law you are researching. Look through a few first to see which best meets your research needs; some will be more useful than others. They are often written in a dense conceptual shorthand and are more helpful as a review once you already have a grasp of a particular area.

Online Law School Sites. Many law schools have online sites that offer well-organized catalogs of online legal resources. You can often call up and download a full text version of whatever catalog-listed resource you wish to read in more detail. But sometimes the material you seek—even though referred to in an online catalog—hasn't yet been put into computer-readable form and posted. In that event, you'll need to track the resource down in a regular law library.

Law schools with websites frequently provide their own lists of other law schools with sites. The best way to learn how these law school sites work is to browse one or more of them. Below, we list a few of our favorites to get you started:

- Georgetown: www.ll.georgetown.edu
- Cornell: www.law.cornell.edu/index.html
- Emory: www.law.emory.edu/LAW/refdesk/toc.html.

Legal Encyclopedias

As of August 2007, the legal encyclopedias we describe here are only available in law libraries, or, in some cases, in large legal databases, such as Westlaw and LexisNexis, that charge steep fees for incidental users. Similarly, the law library is where you will find the bulk of the materials we describe later in this chapter. For example, an encyclopedia called *American Jurisprudence* can be found on Westlaw. You may be able to subscribe to that product by using your credit card, but the fee will be steep. Your law library may have a subscription to Westlaw that allows you access to that product for free. Even then, however, you may still prefer to use the law library for that product, since hardcover encyclopedias are often easier to use than the online versions. If you are doing your research exclusively online, and the law library doesn't have a subscription to the legal database that contains the background resource you want to use, skip to the section, "Background Resources on the Internet."

There are lots of books designed to educate lawyers about the ins and outs of various legal subjects. They are usually very specific—sometimes to a fault—and usually provide a truckload of references (citations) to the primary law sources (cases, statutes and regulations) on which the discussion is based. Simply put, these background resources provide not only a conceptual overview of your research problem, but also an excellent bridge from your background reading to the next phase of your research— the law itself. The most common of these background resources are legal encyclopedias.

Legal encyclopedias contain detailed discussions of virtually every area of the law. These encyclopedias are organized alphabetically by subject matter like regular encyclopedias, but with broader main entries and a lot more subentries. In addition, they contain thorough indexes at the end of the entire set of volumes and detailed tables of contents at the beginning of each topic. The discussions are footnoted with references to cases and statutes that provide the primary-law foundation for the statements in the text. Keep in mind that legal encyclopedia articles discuss and describe the law—they aren't part of the law. Judges and legislatures write "the law," as discussed in Chapter 3.

Legal encyclopedias are often a good place to start your research. Because they cover the entire range of law and their entries are broken into small segments, you are very likely to find material relevant to your research problem. Each entry provides a solid treatment of the particular topic, gives you a good idea of the all-important variables associated with your issue, and refers you to specific statutes and cases (the stuff the law is made of) to help you get to the next research phase.

Also, most law libraries—even small ones—have encyclopedias, but may not have some of the other resources described in this chapter.

National Legal Encyclopedias

Two encyclopedias, *American Jurisprudence* and *Corpus Juris*, provide a national overview of American law. The entries are generalized and don't necessarily provide state-specific information. However, they do contain footnoted references to court decisions from many different states and from federal courts, where relevant. *American Jurisprudence* is commonly known as *Am. Jur.* The current edition

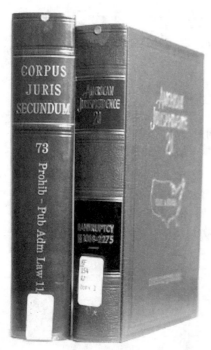

Corpus Juris Secundum and **American Jurisprudence**

of *American Jurisprudence* is abbreviated *Am. Jur. 2d*. The current edition of *Corpus Juris* is abbreviated *C.J.S.* (*Corpus Juris Secundum*—they love Latin). Always use the most recent series—law libraries usually shelve only the most recent—unless you are looking for something that you believe was carried in the earlier series but dropped in the later.

To give you an idea of how these books are set up, the table of contents and discussion employed by *Am. Jur.* on the law concerning firearms are shown below.

Which legal encyclopedia should you use if your law library has both? Many researchers favor *Am. Jur. 2d* over *C.J.S.* because they feel that *C.J.S.* tends to have too much unnecessary information.

However, to fully answer this question, it is necessary to make a brief detour into the world of law book publishing. Bear with us, please; you'll find this information valuable in other phases of your legal research.

There are two primary publishers of American law library resources and tools: West Group and LexisNexis. West publishes *C.J.S.* while LexisNexis publishes *Am Jur.2d*. Each publisher also produces a great many other legal titles. More important, each publisher has attempted to structure its family of books into a complete, internally cross-referenced research system. Thus it is often possible to complete a legal research task by using only West publications. The same is somewhat less true for LexisNexis resources.

If you prefer the West system of research (called the "key number system," discussed in detail in Chapter 10), you may want to use *C.J.S.*, which uses this system by providing cross-references after each article, even though you might feel that *Am Jur.2d* has some advantages. Likewise, if you are a LexisNexis fan, *Am Jur.2d* may be your cup of tea despite the fact that *C.J.S* has some excellent features.

State Encyclopedias

In addition to national encyclopedias, there are at least 15 state-specific encyclopedias. State-specific encyclopedias are organized the same way as the national ones. When researching a question that deals with the law of your particular state, it is almost always best to start with the state-specific encyclopedia, if one exists. That way you can avoid sifting through a discussion on the law in all the states to find the law of your state.

WEAPONS AND FIREARMS   79 Am Jur 2d

I. IN GENERAL

II. POWER TO REGULATE

III. PUBLIC REGULATION

A. CARRYING OR POSSESSING WEAPONS

1. IN GENERAL

2. CONCEALED OR DANGEROUS WEAPONS

2

Am. Jur. 2d, Part of Table of Contents for Topic "Weapons and Firearms"

79 Am Jur 2d   WEAPONS AND FIREARMS   § 3

§ 3. —Unloaded firearm.

Generally, it is held that an unloaded gun, used as a firearm and not as bludgeon, is not a dangerous weapon within the contemplation of statutes punishing assaults made with dangerous or deadly weapons, although there is substantial authority to the contrary.[36] It is generally, but not universally, considered to be a matter of defense to show that the weapon was unloaded, rather than a substantive part of the state's case to aver and prove that it was loaded.[37] There also is authority that an unloaded revolver or gun merely pointed at the person is not a dangerous weapon within the meaning of statutes defining assault and robbery while armed with a dangerous weapon, although many courts hold that an unloaded gun or pistol is a dangerous weapon within the meaning of such statutes;[38] and generally, an unloaded pistol or revolver is regarded as within the meaning of statutes against carrying concealed "dangerous or deadly weapons"[39] or denouncing the carrying "of any concealed and dangerous weapon."[40] It has been held that a statute prohibiting the carrying of a weapon capable of inflicting bodily harm, concealed on or about the person, did not apply to an unloaded pistol found in the glove compartment of the defendant's automobile, no ammunition having been found on or about the defendant's person or in the vehicle.[41] In a few cases the courts have recognized that if the gun was unloaded, that fact would have a bearing on the determination as to whether it was carried as a weapon.[42]

Generally an unloaded gun or pistol used to strike with is not necessarily a dangerous weapon, but is such, or not, according to its size, weight, and the manner of using it.[43] Accordingly, to resolve the factual question whether a

---

36. See 6 Am Jur 2d, ASSAULT AND BATTERY § 54.

As to whether a simple criminal assault may be committed with an unloaded firearm, see 6 Am Jur 2d, ASSAULT AND BATTERY § 34.

As to civil action for damages for an assault by pointing unloaded firearm, see 6 Am Jur 2d, ASSAULT AND BATTERY §§ 109, 123.

37. See 6 Am Jur 2d, ASSAULT AND BATTERY § 93.

As to presumption as to whether gun was loaded, see 6 Am Jur 2d, ASSAULT AND BATTERY § 94.

38. See 67 Am Jur 2d, ROBBERY § 5.

39. Asocar v State, 252 **Ind** 326, 247 NE2d 679; Mularkey v State, 201 **Wis** 429, 230 NW 76.

Annotation: 79 ALR2d 1430, § 8.

40. Mularkey v State, 201 **Wis** 429, 230 NW 76.

A pistol mechanically capable of being fired is a deadly weapon within the meaning of the statute prohibiting the carrying of a concealed "deadly weapon," even though it was unloaded and no ammunition was on the carrier's person or was readily available. Commonwealth v Harris **(Ky)** 344 SW2d 820.

41. State v Haugabrook, 31 **Ohio** Misc 157, 57 Ohio Ops 2d 322, 272 NE2d 213.

42. State v Larkin, 24 **Mo** App 410.

Annotation: 79 ALR2d 1432, § 8.

In Carr v State, 34 **Ark** 448, in reversing a conviction under a statute making it a misdemeanor to wear any pistol concealed as a weapon unless upon a journey, the evidence being that defendant was carrying two unloaded pistols, the court said that it must be shown that the pistols were carried as weapons, for the purpose of convenience in a fight, and that in the instant case the pistols were useless for that purpose.

43. State v Mays, 7 **Ariz** App 90, 436 P2d 482; State v Jaramillo (App) 82 **NM** 548, 484 P2d 768; Hilliard v State, 87 **Tex** Crim 15, 218 SW 1052, 8 ALR 1316.

Annotation: 79 ALR2d 1423, § 6[a]; 8 ALR 1319.

Library Exercise: Using *Am. Jur.*

You are on a team researching the question of whether a parent in Michigan may educate her children at home because she believes she can do a better job of educating them than can the teachers in the local school. The school district superintendent has demanded that the children enroll in school. If home schooling is an option in Michigan, what is the standard by which the quality of the home education is measured?

You are assigned to use *American Jurisprudence 2d (Am. Jur. 2d)* to find Michigan home schooling cases. Give the full citation, including the date, for each case. Do not go beyond *Am. Jur.* except to obtain information needed for full citations.

Questions

1. Go first to the General Index to *Am. Jur. 2d.* What will you look under? Think of at least two subject headings to try.

2. Look under these headings. What do you find regarding home schooling?

3. Is there a statement in the article regarding the parent's inquiry? What is the law in Michigan? What citations to cases do you find?

4. Don't give up! Case citations are in the footnotes. Be sure to check the pocket parts. Do you find any cases there from Michigan?

5. From your research thus far, what can you tell the parent?

Answers

1. Probable headings might be: Home Schooling, Education, Schools.

2. Using the March 2000 Index, the entry under Home Schools tells you to use "Schools and Education." Under Education it also sends you to "Schools and Education." Under Schools and Education there are two subheadings: "Home Instruction" telling you to go to "Correspondence Course or Schools" (not what we are looking for) and "Home Schooling" which sends you to an article in Schools, sections 255-257.

3. In section 256 we are told that a state may reasonably regulate home education, including imposing teacher certification and curricular requirements. No cases are cited in the text and nothing is there specifically about Michigan.

4. Yes. In footnote 14, we are referred to *People v. Bennett* (1993) 501 N.W.2d 106. This case amplifies discussion in section 256, especially as they apply in Michigan.

5. Michigan does allow home schooling, but subject to requirements such as teacher certification and specific curriculum. We will have to read *Bennett* in order to tell her exactly what is required in Michigan.

State-Specific Legal Encyclopedias (Alphabetized by State)

California Jurisprudence 3d (West Group)

Florida Jurisprudence 2d (West Group)

Illinois Jurisprudence (Lexis Publishing)

Indiana Law Encyclopedia (West Group)

Michigan Law and Practice (Lexis Publishing)

Strong's *North Carolina Index 3d* (West Group)

Ohio Jurisprudence 4th (West Group)

Pennsylvania Law Encyclopedia (Lexis Publishing)

Tennessee Jurisprudence (Lexis Publishing)

Michie's *Jurisprudence of Virginia and West Virginia* (Lexis Publishing)

American Law Reports

This series of books has two titles: *American Law Reports (A.L.R.)* and *American Law Reports, Federal (A.L.R. Fed.).* A.L.R. covers issues primarily arising under state statutes and in state cases, as well as federally oriented issues that arose before 1969, the year A.L.R. Fed. was first published. A.L.R. Fed. covers issues that arise primarily under federal statutes or in federal cases. Either one of these titles is an excellent place to begin.

Both publications are multi-volume sets that contain discussions of narrow issues that have been suggested by newly-decided court cases. Each discussion comments

on the case itself and then discusses other cases that have considered the same or similar issues.

A.L.R. and *A.L.R. Fed.* are different from the legal encyclopedias described earlier in that they don't attempt to cover every subject. This, of course, means some bad news and some good. You may not find what you're looking for, but if you do you'll be well rewarded. Fortunately, *A.L.R.* has an excellent index that allows you to find out very quickly whether the news is good or bad for you.

American Law Reports

Examples of the Kinds of Issues Covered by *A.L.R.*

- Circumstances justifying grant or denial of a petition to change an adult's name
- Visitation rights of the father of a child born out of wedlock
- Whether a public utility is responsible for damages for interruption, failure or inadequacy of electric power.

A.L.R. comes in five series (*A.L.R., A.L.R. 2d, A.L.R. 3d, A.L.R. 4th* and *A.L.R. 5th*) according to the date of the articles. Unlike the legal encyclopedias, the newest series does not replace previous ones. *A.L.R. 5th* may contain an almost entirely new set of topics not covered in *A.L.R. 4th*, for example. The older series are kept up to date with "pocket parts" (inserts in the back of each hardcover volume) and hardbound volumes called the Later Case Service. *A.L.R. Federal* is still in its first series.

Phone Updates. The publisher of *A.L.R.* now offers a telephone hotline that provides up-to-date information about cases that have been decided but not yet published. The number is 800-225-7488.

Examples of What the *A.L.R. Fed.* Series Covers

- What constitutes violation of § 134 of the Consumer Credit Protection Act prohibiting fraudulent use of credit cards
- The seizure and forfeiture under 19 U.S.C.S. ¶ 1526(e) of imported merchandise bearing a counterfeit trademark
- Employer's right under § 8(a)(1) of the National Labor Relations Act to ask an employee whether the employee intends to participate in a strike.

Form Books

Form books are pretty much what their name suggests: collections of legal documents. Practicing attorneys copy and use the forms, so they don't have to reinvent the wheel every time they need a new document.

Form books can be of great help if your research question involves either state or federal procedure, whether civil or criminal. Judicial and administrative procedures inevitably involve the preparation and filing of forms; there are forms for almost every possible legal action, from petitioning for a divorce to changing your name, to evicting a tenant to petitioning the United States Supreme Court. Court rules invariably require specific documents to be filed in very specific formats, depending on the type of case. You can copy the format from the examples.

The documents are usually presented in a fill-in-the-blanks format. To accomplish a specific procedural task, the user need only choose the correct document, modify the language a little to fit the needs of the particular case, fill in the information where indicated, and file the finished document in court.

Leaving nothing to chance, form books usually discuss the procedural rules that are relevant to the use of each form. In other words, when you find the form you need, chances are you'll also find an overview of the procedure itself and instructions on how to make the most common modifications.

It's important to understand that these form books may not contain certain forms required by state law. For instance, many California court procedures require forms prepared by the California Judicial Council. These California forms can be obtained free or at a nominal price from the courts that use them, and also are collected in a special book called the *California Judicial Council Forms Manual*, published by a publisher called the Continuing Education of the Bar (CEB) and available in most law libraries.

The California Judicial Council Forms are also available for download at www.courtinfo.ca.gov (click "Self-Help" in the upper left corner, then click "Forms & Instructions") and at www.accesslaw.com (click "California Resources" on the homepage).

A typical form book entry, taken from *American Jurisprudence Legal Forms, Second Series,* is shown below. We show the form as well as the accompanying material provided about the law governing the procedure. Pay attention to the paragraph labeled "Annotation References,"

which is taken directly from the book's pocket part (update).

The forms in *Am. Jur. Legal Forms* are national in scope and often lack the specificity found in a form book prepared specifically for your state. When looking for an appropriate form or the procedure that goes with it, it is best to start with a publication that is specific to your state or topic, if there is one. As in the case of state encyclopedias, state form books have been published only in the more populous states.

Form Books

Finding Forms. The following is a partial list of form books and their publishers. After each title is an abbreviation that conforms to the classification system set out in Chapter 4. For example, *California Practice With Forms* carries the code S/C/P for State/Civil/Procedural. The entire list of abbreviations follows the list of form books.

If your state is not represented in the list, ask your law librarian to help you find a form book for your state. Also, read the next section on Practice Manuals; you might find some help there.

NAME

§ 182:52

of ___18____, State of ___19____, and since such time has resided with her husband at the above address.

4. Applicant desires to change her name to ___20____, her maiden surname, for the following reasons: ___21____ *[specify reasons, such as to continue her professional or business use of her maiden name or to avoid confusion between her professional or business relations with those of her husband or to assert her equal partnership with her husband in the marital relation or to assert her ethnic heritage, of which she is proud, or other legally permissible reason].*

5. ___22____ *[State information as to publication of notice of intent to change name, if required by statute.]*

Dated: ___23____, 19_24__.

[Signature]

[Jurat]

☑ **Notes on Use:**

See also Notes on Use following § 182:43.

Annotations: Right of married woman to use maiden surname. 67 ALR3d 1266.

Circumstance justifying grant or denial of petition to change adult's name. 79 ALR3d 562.

Cross references: For other change of name forms, see § 182:54 et seq.

V. CHANGE OF NAME

§ 182:51 Scope of division

Material in this division consists of forms related to change of name. Included are such matters as application to a court of record for change of name and relevant affidavits and notices.

§ 182:52 Introductory comments

Unless applicable statutes provide otherwise, a person may change such person's name at will, without any legal proceedings, merely by adopting another name. In most states, however, statutes set forth specific procedures and requirements for change of name; such procedure usually includes filing a petition or application with a court of record. The court hearing a petition or application for change of name has discretion to either grant or deny it, the general rule being that there must exist some substantial reason for the change.[8]

8. *Text references:* Change of name, generally. 57 AM JUR 2d, Name §§ 10–16.

Annotations: Circumstances justifying grant or denial of petition to change adult's name. 79 ALR3d 562.

(For Tax Notes and Notes on use, see end of form)

Form and Explanation From *Am. Jur. Legal Forms, 2nd Series*

§ 182:53 Annotation references

ALR annotations treating the subject of change of name by an individual are set forth below.

ALR annotations:

Circumstance justifying grant or denial of petition to change adult's name. 79 ALR3d 562.

Change of child's name in adoption proceeding. 53 ALR2d 927.

§ 182:54 Application for change of name

To: __1_____ [court of record]

APPLICATION FOR CHANGE OF NAME

Applicant states:

1. Applicant resides at __2_____ [address], City of __3_____, County of __4_____, State of __5_____, __6_____ [ZIP], and has resided there for more than __7__ [number of months or years] prior to filing this application.

2. Applicant was born __8_____ [in the City of __9_____, County of __10_____, State of __11_____ or set forth foreign address] on __12_____, 19__13__. Applicant was named __14_____ and has always been known by that name.

3. The name of applicant's father is __15_____, and the name of applicant's mother is __16_____. They reside at __17_____ [__18_____ (address), City of __19_____, County of __20_____, State of __21_____, __22_____ (ZIP) or set forth foreign address].

4. Applicant __23_____ [is or is not] married. __24_____ [If married, give information as to date and place of marriage, spouse's name, and date and place of spouse's birth.]

5. Applicant desires to change applicant's name to __25_____ for the following reasons: __26_____.

6. __27_____ [State information as to publication of notice of intent to change name, if required by statute.]

7. __28_____ [State information required by statute as to financial matters, any criminal records, and pending actions or other proceedings in which the applicant may be a party.]

Dated: __29_____, 19__30__.

[Jurat]

[Signature]

☑ **Notes on Use:**

Text references: Statutory regulation of change of name, generally. 57 AM JUR 2d, Name §§ 11–16.

(For Tax Notes and Notes on use, see end of form)

Form Books (Partial List)

S = State

F = Federal

C = Civil

Cr = Criminal

Su = Substantive

P = Procedural

Bender's Forms of Pleading (Matthew Bender) S/C/P

California Forms of Pleading and Practice (Matthew Bender) S/C/P

California Practice With Forms (West Group) S/C/P

California Forms: Legal and Business (West Group) S/C/Su

Federal Procedural Forms, L. Ed. (West Group) F/C/Cr/P

Florida Jur. Forms: Legal and Business (West Group) S/C/Su

Florida Criminal Procedure (West Group) S/Cr/P

Florida Pleading and Practice Forms (West Group) S/C/P

Illinois Forms: Legal and Business (West Group) S/C/Su

Indiana Forms of Pleading and Practice (Matthew Bender) S/C/P

Massachusetts Pleading and Practice: Forms & Commentary (Matthew Bender) S/C/P

New Jersey Forms—Legal and Business (West Group) S/C/Su

New Jersey Criminal Procedure (West Group) S/Cr/P

New York Forms—Legal and Business (West Group) S/C/Su

Bender's Forms for the Consolidated Laws of New York (Matthew Bender) S/C/Su/P

Carmody-Wait: Cyclopedia of New York Practice With Forms 2d (West Group) S/C/Su/P

Ohio Forms—Legal and Business (West Group) S/C/Su

Ohio Forms of Pleading and Practice (Matthew Bender) S/C/P

Standard Pennsylvania Practice 2d (West Group) S/C/Cr/Su

Texas Criminal Practice Guide (Matthew Bender) S/Cr/Su/P

Texas Forms—Legal and Business (West Group) S/C/Su

Texas Litigation Guide (Matthew Bender) S/C/Su/P

Texas Jurisprudence Pleading & Practice Forms 2d (West Group) S/C/P

Most states and individual courts have websites that contain or link to all the forms required to file claims. You can also obtain many federal court forms at www. uscourtforms.com.

Practice Manuals

Practice manuals, like form books, contain lots of forms and instructions for how to use them. However, form books tend to cover the entire spectrum of legal practice; practice manuals usually cover a specialized area of practice.

For example, a publication called *Defense of Drunk Driving Cases*, by Richard Erwin and Marilyn Minzer, tells you everything you need to know when handling a drunk driving offense. For attorneys who frequently handle this type of case, this book is the bible. There are practice manuals for torts, contracts, family law, real estate transactions, search and seizure questions and a myriad of other issues. Some are state-specific while others are national in scope.

Many of these books are well-written and -organized. They can give you a good understanding of the procedural and substantive law, as well as the hands-on instructions necessary to file and prosecute or defend your own case. These resources are generally available in law libraries. You can find them by looking up your subject in the library card catalog or by asking the librarian. Below is a partial list to get you started.

Practice Manuals (Partial List)

Bender's Forms of Discovery (Matthew Bender)

Connecticut Estates Practice (West Group)

Defense of Drunk Driving Cases (Matthew Bender)

Defense of Narcotics Cases (Matthew Bender)

Florida Corporations (West Group)

Georgia Divorce (West Group)

Georgia Probate (West Group)

Handling Accident Cases (Matthew Bender)

Illinois Tort Law and Practice (West Group)

Immigration and Procedure Law (Matthew Bender)

Kentucky Probate (West Group)

Law and the Family New York (West Group)

Massachusetts Corporations (West Group)

Michigan Probate (West Group)

Minnesota Dissolution of Marriage (West Group)

Minnesota Probate (West Group)

New York Estates Practice Guide, 4th Ed. (West Group)

New York Law and Practice of Real Property, 2d Ed. (West Group)

New York Zoning Law and Practice (West Group)

Ohio Corporations (West Group)

Ohio Probate (West Group)

Ohio Real Estate Law and Practice (Banks-Baldwin)

Pennsylvania Estates Practice (West Group)

Prosecution and Defense of Criminal Conspiracy Cases (Matthew Bender)

Settlement of Estates and Fiduciary Law in Massachusetts, 4th Ed. (West Group)

Tennessee Corporations (West Group)

Tennessee Probate (West Group)

Texas Family Law Service (West Group)

Trademark Registration Practice (West Group)

Wisconsin Corporations (West Group)

Wisconsin Real Estate Practice (Dearborn Finan)

Continuing Legal Education Publications

Some publishers are dedicated to providing practicing lawyers with continuing education. Two of these—the Continuing Education of the Bar (CEB) and the Rutter Group—direct their materials towards California lawyers and one, the Practising Law Institute (PLI), focuses on New York lawyers. Publishers in some other states produce analogous resources, often called "CLE" (Continuing Legal Education) books.

Continuing legal education publishers produce detailed practice guidelines, instructions and forms for many different areas of law and practice, both state and federal. They also publish written materials used in continuing legal education seminars that they sponsor. Continuing education materials are usually available in the law libraries in the states for which they are published.

CEB (Partial List): *Advising California Employers, Advising California Partnerships, Debt Collection Practice in California, California Eviction Defense Manual, California Zoning Practice, California Tort Guide, California Administrative Hearing Practice.* See their website for a complete list of publications: www.ceb.com.

Rutter Group (Partial List): *Civil Procedure Before Trial, Personal Injury, Family Law, Landlord-Tenant.* Go to the Rutter website for a complete list of publications: www.ruttergroup.com.

PLI (Partial List): *Evidence in Negligence Cases, A Guide for Legal Assistants, Henn on Copyright Law: A Practitioner's Guide, Advertising Compliance Handbook, Friedman on Leases, Bankruptcy Deskbook, How to Prepare an Initial Public Offering, Litigating Copyright, Trademark and Unfair Competition Cases, Understanding the Securities Laws.* Go to the PLI website for a complete list of publications: www.pli.edu.

West Group (Partial list): *Farm and Ranch Real Estate Law.* See the West website for a complete list of publications: http://west.thomson.com.

Law Reviews and Other Legal Periodicals

Because the law is always developing and changing, legal professionals are constantly analyzing its evolution. You can find articles about new legislation, current legal theories and viewpoints, and important cases in law journals published by law schools, commercial publishers, and professional legal societies, such as bar associations.

The articles in journals produced by law schools are written by law students, professors and even practicing attorneys, and sometimes present a whole new view of an area of the law. They tend to focus on where the law is going as opposed to where it is or where it's been, although they may provide some history to set the stage for the discussion.

On the other hand, journals produced by bar associations and other professional groups tend to be much more practical, with an emphasis on recent developments. Many law reviews and journals are general, covering subjects across the legal spectrum. But increasingly, legal periodicals are starting to specialize in such fields as taxation, environmental law, labor, entertainment and communications and women's studies.

Law reviews and journals are almost always published in paperback pamphlets, usually on a quarterly basis. At the end of the year, libraries bind the issues into a hardcover volume.

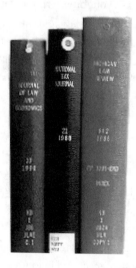

Even if articles are more academic than practical, they still may contain valuable descriptions of the state of the law in the specific area being discussed, and can provide you with research leads.

Examples of Topics Covered by Legal Periodicals

- A father going through a divorce wants to find up-to-date information on how child support is handled in joint custody situations.
- A gay person wants to find out his remedies for employment discrimination.
- A computer programmer wants to find out the extent of patent protection for software.
- An estate planner wants to find out the trends in state legislation affecting revocable living trusts.
- A surrogate parent wants to know how the courts are handling custody and visitation requests.

Below is the cover of an issue of the *Harvard Journal on Legislation.*

KB
H339
HJL
v. 28
no. 1
LOAN
Copy 1

HARVARD JOURNAL
on
LEGISLATION

ARTICLES

LIMITATIONS OF ACTION UNDER THE FTCA: A SYNTHESIS AND
PROPOSAL .... *Kent Sinclair and Charles A. Szypszak*
SCHOLARSHIPS AND THE FEDERAL INCOME
TAX BASE .... *Charlotte Crane*

STATUTE

LEASES OF PERSONAL PROPERTY: A PROJECT FOR CONSUMER
PROTECTION .... *John J.A. Burke and John M. Cannel*

NOTE

JUDICIAL PROTECTION OF BALLOT-ACCESS RIGHTS: THIRD PARTIES
NEED NOT APPLY .... *Bradley A. Smith*

COMMENT

BUDGETARY TREATMENT OF FEDERAL CREDIT
PROGRAMS .... *J. Edmund Colloton, Jr.*

RECENT DEVELOPMENTS AND LEGISLATION

RECENT PUBLICATIONS

LAW LIBRARY

FEB 21 1991

UNIVERSITY OF CALIFORNIA
BERKELEY

Volume 28, Number 1   Winter 1991

Copyright © 1991 by the
PRESIDENT AND FELLOWS OF HARVARD COLLEGE   ISSN 0017-808x

Harvard Journal on Legislation

Most law libraries contain the more influential of these journals and law reviews, and some libraries (especially in large law schools) have virtually a complete set. You can find articles by using an electronic index, called LEGALTRAC, or either of two printed indexes, the *Index to Legal Periodicals* (tan cover) or the *Current Law Index* (red and black cover).

Index to Legal Periodicals* and *Current Law Index

All indexes are organized by subject, author and title, and contain an abbreviated reference to the review or journal in which the article is located. The printed indexes contain numerous volumes, which are organized according to the years in which the contents were published. The electronic index provides a cumulative listing and is thus easier to use than the printed indexes. Below is an excerpt from the *Index to Legal Periodicals* that lists, by subject, the article titled, "Leases of Personal Property: A Project for Consumer Protection," which appears in the issue of the *Harvard Journal on Legislation* shown above.

"*Harv. J. on Legis.*" is an abbreviation for *Harvard Journal on Legislation*. The numbers indicate that the article is in Volume 28, pages 115-166, and that Volume 28 was published in the winter of 1991.

If you look at some other listings, you will see other strange abbreviations for law reviews, like *Ky. L. J.* and *Ark. J.* You are not expected to magically guess what these abbreviations mean. Lawyers don't carry this information around with them either. When you become mystified by an entry, simply consult the table of abbreviations at the front of the volume. An excerpt from the table is shown below.

The *Current Law Index* is used in the same way; you go from the index to the table of abbreviations to the actual article.

The LEGALTRAC computerized index to legal periodicals is part of a larger database called INFOTRAC, which contains information on a number of additional resources such as business and general periodicals. Larger law libraries may offer the complete INFOTRAC database. Most, however, have only the LEGALTRAC index. Instructions for using LEGALTRAC are shown on the screen and are very easy to follow. If you get confused, ask a law librarian for help. Incidentally, LEGALTRAC may be connected to a printer so that you can print out the information instead of copying it longhand.

How to Find Law Review Articles on the Internet.

One good way to locate articles in general law reviews and law journals is to use the FindLaw law review references at http://stu.findlaw.com/journals/. This website also refers you to a searchable index and list of law reviews found by clicking the Law Review Project link (or entering www.lawreview.org in your browser). You can browse the alphabetical list of online law journals and select one. Depending on the law review you end up with, you may:

- view full text articles in the most recent issues;
- view abstracts of the articles in the most recent issues; or
- order a full issue by email for a nominal fee.

Another good way to search for law review articles on the Internet is through the University of Southern California's site at http://lawweb.usc.edu/library/resources/journals.html or via the Hieros Gamos website at www.hg.org/journals.html#v.

Unfortunately, nothing like the LEGALTRAC index is currently available on the Internet. This means that you'll need to browse for a relevant article journal by journal. Also, most of the journals post only recent articles, going back just a year or two.

Listings in the *Index to Legal Periodicals*

ABBREVIATIONS OF PERIODICALS INDEXED

For full information consult the list of Periodicals Indexed

A

A.B.A. J. — American Bar Association Journal
A.F.L. Rev. — The Air Force Law Review
Adel. L. Rev. — Adelaide Law Review
Adelphia L.J. — The Adelphia Law Journal
Admin. L.J. — Administrative Law Journal (Washington, D.C.)
Admin. L. Rev. — Administrative Law Review
Advoc. Q. — The Advocates' Quarterly
AIPLA Q.J. — AIPLA Quarterly Journal
Akron L. Rev. — Akron Law Review
Akron Tax J. — Akron Tax Journal
Ala. L. Rev. — Alabama Law Review
Ala. Law. — The Alabama Lawyer
Alaska L. Rev. — Alaska Law Review
Alb. L. Rev. — Albany Law Review
Alta. L. Rev. — Alberta Law Review
Am. Bankr. L.J. — The American Bankruptcy Law Journal
Am. Bus. L.J. — American Business Law Journal
Am. Crim. L. Rev. — American Criminal Law Review
Am. Indian L. Rev. — American Indian Law Review
Am. J. Comp. L. — The American Journal of Comparative Law
Am. J. Crim. L. — American Journal of Criminal Law
Am. J. Fam. L. — American Journal of Family Law
Am. J. Int'l L. — American Journal of International Law
Am. J. Juris. — The American Journal of Jurisprudence
Am. J.L. & Med. — American Journal of Law & Medicine
Am. J. Legal Hist. — The American Journal of Legal History
Am. J. Tax Pol'y — The American Journal of Tax Policy
Am. J. Trial Advoc. — The American Journal of Trial Advocacy
Am. Soc'y Int'l L. Proc. — American Society of International Law Proceedings
Am. U.J. Int'l L. & Pol'y — The American University Journal of International Law and Policy
Am. U.L. Rev. — The American University Law Review
Anglo-Am. L. Rev. — The Anglo-American Law Review
Ann. Conf. on Intell. Prop. — Annual Conference on Intellectual Property
Ann. Rev. Banking L. — Annual Review of Banking Law
Ann. Surv. Am. L. — Annual Survey of American Law
Ann. Surv. Austl. L. — Annual Survey of Australian Law
Annals Air & Space L. — Annals of Air and Space Law
Antitrust Bull. — The Antitrust Bulletin
Antitrust L.J. — Antitrust Law Journal
Arb. J. — The Arbitration Journal
Ariz. J. Int'l & Comp. L. — Arizona Journal of International and Comparative Law
Ariz. L. Rev. — Arizona Law Review
Ariz. St. L.J. — Arizona State Law Journal
Ark. L. Notes — Arkansas Law Notes
Ark. L. Rev. — Arkansas Law Review
Army Law. — The Army Lawyer
Auckland U.L. Rev. — Auckland University Law Review
Austl. B. Rev. — Australian Bar Review
Austl. Bus. L. Rev. — Australian Business Law Review
Austl. J. Fam. L. — Australian Journal of Family Law
Austl. J.L. & Soc'y — Australian Journal of Law and Society
Austl. J. Lab. L. — Australian Journal of Labour Law
Austl. L.J. — Australian Law Journal
Austl. Tax Rev. — Australian Tax Review
Austl. Y.B. Int'l L. — Australian Yearbook of International Law

B

B.C. Envtl. Aff. L. Rev. — Boston College Environmental Affairs Law Review
B.C. Int'l & Comp. L. Rev. — Boston College International and Comparative Law Review
B.C.L. Rev. — Boston College Law Review
B.C. Third World L.J. — Boston College Third World Law Journal
B.U. Int'l L.J. — Boston University International Law Journal
B.U.J. Tax L. — Boston University Journal of Tax Law
B.U.L. Rev. — Boston University Law Review
B.Y.U. J. Pub. L. — BYU Journal of Public Law
B.Y.U. L. Rev. — Brigham Young University Law Review
Banking L.J. — The Banking Law Journal
Bankr. Dev. J. — Bankruptcy Developments Journal
Baylor L. Rev. — Baylor Law Review
Berkeley Women's L.J. — Berkeley Women's Law Journal
Bldg. & Constr. L. — Building and Construction Law
Bond L. Rev. — Bond Law Review
Bracton L.J. — Bracton Law Journal
Brit. Tax Rev. — British Tax Review
Brit. Y.B. Int'l L. — The British Year Book of International Law
Brooklyn J. Int'l L. — Brooklyn Journal of International Law
Brooklyn L. Rev. — Brooklyn Law Review
Buffalo L. Rev. — Buffalo Law Review
Bus. Law. — The Business Lawyer

C

C. de D. — Les Cahiers de Droit
Cal. Law. — California Lawyer
Cal. Real Prop. J. — California Real Property Journal
Cal. W. Int'l L.J. — California Western International Law Journal
Cal. W.L. Rev. — California Western Law Review
Calif. L. Rev. — California Law Review
Cambrian L. Rev. — The Cambrian Law Review
Cambridge L.J. — The Cambridge Law Journal
Campbell L. Rev. — Campbell Law Review
Can. B. Rev. — The Canadian Bar Review
Can. Bus. L.J. — Canadian Business Law Journal
Can. J. Fam. L. — Canadian Journal of Family Law
Can. J.L. Juris. — Canadian Journal of Law and Jurisprudence
Can. J. Women & L. — Canadian Journal of Women and the Law
Can. Tax J. — Canadian Tax Journal
Can.-U.S. L.J. — Canada-United States Law Journal
Can. Y.B. Int'l L. — The Canadian Yearbook of International Law
Canterbury L. Rev. — The Canterbury Law Review
Cap. U.L. Rev. — Capital University Law Review
Cardozo Arts & Ent. L.J. — Cardozo Arts & Entertainment Law Journal
Cardozo L. Rev. — Cardozo Law Review
Cardozo Stud. L. & Lit. — Cardozo Studies in Law and Literature
Case W. Res. J. Int'l L. — Case Western Reserve Journal of International Law
Case W. Res. L. Rev. — Case Western Reserve Law Review
Cath. Law. — The Catholic Lawyer
Cath. U.L. Rev. — Catholic University Law Review
Chi.-Kent L. Rev. — Chicago Kent Law Review
China L. Rep. — China Law Reporter
Civ. Just. Q. — Civil Justice Quarterly
Clearinghouse Rev. — Clearinghouse Review
Clev. St. L. Rev. — Cleveland State Law Review
Colo. Law. — The Colorado Lawyer
Colum. Bus. L. Rev. — Columbia Business Law Review
Colum. Hum. Rts. L. Rev. — Columbia Human Rights Law Review
Colum. J. Envtl. L. — Columbia Journal of Environmental Law
Colum. J.L. & Soc. Probs. — Columbia Journal of Law and Social Problems

Library Exercise: Finding Law Reviews: Exercise One

You have a friend who was sexually abused as a child. She had apparently repressed the memory completely until a recent incident, when she was 35 years old, brought floods of vivid and painful memories. Your friend asks you to help her do some legal research on whether she can sue the abuser after all this time. You want to learn how courts have dealt with the statute of limitations in such cases. You have gathered a research team to search the literature for relevant law review articles, and you have volunteered to find articles published in 1995.

Questions

1. What is the most direct way to find law review articles on a specific subject?

2. What subject headings could you look under? Think of three.

3a. Find six to ten relevant articles in the indexes for your time frame, and locate two or three of the articles. (When scanning lists of articles in the indexes, look for catchwords such as childhood, incest, sexual abuse. Don't select articles about statutes of limitation in general, or on related issues.) Which years of the indexes should you look in?

3b. What did you find under the topics you consulted in *Current Law Index*?

3c. What did you find under the topics you consulted in *ILP*?

4. What 1995 articles did you find?

5. It is also possible to do online research of this topic. Check with your librarian to see what services, if any, are available to you.

Answers

1. Use the two major printed indexes to law reviews. They are the *Current Law Index* and the *Index to Legal Periodicals*.

2. Statute of Limitations; Child abuse; Sexual abuse.

3a. You are looking for articles published in 1995. Because these might not be in the index until the year after publication, use *Current Law Index* 1995 and 1996 (Subject Indexes) and *Index to Legal Periodicals* 94-95 and 90-91.

3b. In *Current Law Index*, under Statutes of Repose, it says "see Limitation of Actions." Under Child Abuse,

there were several subtopics, and among them, Abused Children. Under Abused Children, it says "see also Adult Child Abuse Victims and see also Sexually Abused Children." Therefore, the topics to look under are: Limitation of Actions and Adult Child Abuse Victims.

3c. In the *Index to Legal Periodicals,* following what we found in the *Current Law Index,* look under Limitation of Action. The *Index to Legal Periodicals* uses this heading also. Under Child Abuse, it says "see also Child Sexual Abuse." Note: *Index to Legal Periodicals* does not use the same headings as the *Current Law Index.* For example, the topic Adult Child Abuse Victim appears only in the *Current Law Index.*

4. The following articles were listed:
   - *Permissive Statute of Limitation Policies.* 36 Catholic Lawyer 83-9 (1995).
   - *Memory Repression in Sexual Abuse Cases as a Basis for Tolling the Statute of Limitations (Recent Developments in Utah Case Law).* Utah Law Review, 344-350 (Winter 1995).
   - *Recovered Memories of Childhood Sexual Abuse: the Admissibility Question.* 68 Temple Law Review 249-280 (Spring 1995).
   - *The Discovery Rule: Allowing Adult Survivors of Childhood Sexual Abuse the Opportunity for Redress.* Brooklyn Law Review 199-233 (Spring 1995).
   - *The Delayed Discovery Rule and Roe v. Archdiocese.* Law and Inequality: A Journal of Theory and Practice 253-270 (June 1995).

   (If you found others, congratulations!)

5. INFOTRAC, a general periodical online indexing service, is subscribed to by many public libraries (as well as county law libraries). LEGALTRAC, a service within INFOTRAC, indexes legal periodicals. If your library has INFOTRAC, it may also have purchased LEGALTRAC. On LEGALTRAC, you could find *The Ohio Supreme Court Sets the Statute of Limitations and Adopts the Discovery Rule for Childhood Sexual Abuse Actions: Now it is Time for Legislative Action!* Cleveland State Law Review, 499-528 (Summer 1995).

Library Exercise: Finding Law Reviews: Exercise Two

You are on a team researching the question of whether a parent in Indiana may educate her children at home, over the objections of the school district, because she believes she can do a better job of educating them than can the teachers in her local school. You are assigned to use *American Jurisprudence 2d (Am. Jur. 2d)* to find references to law review articles on the topic.

Questions

1. Look in the five-volume softback set of the *Am. Jur. 2d* General Index under "Schools." Do you find an appropriate subheading?

2. Find the section on schools in Volume 68 ("Sales and Use Taxes" to "Searches and Seizures"). What citations to law review articles do you find?

Answers

1. Yes. In the 2004 edition under Schools and Education, there is a subheading "Home Schools," which sends you to the article entitled *Schools,* sections 255-257.

2. Lisa M. Lukasik, *"The Latest Home Education Challenge: The Relationship Between Home Schools and Public Schools,"* 74 N.C. L. Rev. 1913 (1996).

Specialized Loose-Leaf Materials

Most practicing lawyers and many others who work in the legal system, such as teachers, paralegals, legal research specialists and even some law librarians, find it necessary to specialize. There's just too much information generated by the courts and legislatures to keep up with everything. Specialization typically means not only mastering a particular body of knowledge—for example, tax, zoning, bankruptcy or personal injury—but diligently keeping on top of it.

Several publications cater to this need by offering an exhaustive loose-leaf compilation of recent developments in a certain field and weekly or monthly loose-leaf supplements. These materials provide information about new laws, regulations and judicial and administrative decisions that might affect the field of law covered by the publication.

For anyone who must maintain an up-to-the-minute grasp on what's going on in a particular legal area, these services can prove invaluable. However, they may be too specialized for your purposes unless your research topic falls squarely within one of these special categories. If it does, locate the appropriate service, read the instructions on how to use it at the front of the first volume, and check the index. You might solve your problem almost immediately. All the loose-leaf services listed here can be found in a good law library.

Selected Loose-Leaf Services

Commerce Clearing House (CCH)
- Bankruptcy Law Reports
- Consumer Credit Guide Reports
- Employment Safety and Health Guide
- Labor Law Reports
- Medicare and Medicaid Guide
- Standard Federal Tax Reports
- State Tax Guide
- Unemployment Insurance Reports
- Worker's Compensation

Bureau of National Affairs (BNA)
- Environment Reporter
- Fair Employment Practices
- The Family Law Reporter
- Labor Relations Reporter
- Occupational Safety and Health Reporter
- Product Safety & Liability Reporter
- United States Law Week (U.S. Supreme Court decisions)

West Group
- Social Security Law and Practice

Library Exercise: Using a Loose-Leaf Service

You are researching the issue of whether an author's royalties constitute "self-employment earnings" and are thus subject to the self-employment tax. You have been assigned to find cases on this issue in *CCH Standard Federal Tax Reporter*, a loose-leaf service.

Questions

1. Find the volumes entitled *CCH Standard Federal Tax Reporter*. (Do not confuse them with the look-alike *State Tax Reporter* or the *Tax Court Reporter*.) What volume do you choose?

2. To find information by its topic (or subject), in which section of the Index volume do you look?

3. Under which tab heading do you look?

4. Is there an entry and subheading regarding the issue?

5. To what does the "32,588.124" refer?

6. How do you find "¶ 32,588.124"?

7. When you go to that volume and find ¶ 32,588.124 (¶ numbers are at the bottom of each page), what do you find?

8. What is the name and citation of one of the three cases?

9. Where would you look to find out what the abbreviations in the citations [TCM, TC Memo, Dec.] mean?

Answers

1. The most recent Index volume located right before Volume One (instead of after the last volume as in other publications).

2. Topical Index, which is marked by a red flag in the 2004 edition.

3. Behind the tab, "Topical Index," we look for the top "Authors."

4. Yes. Under "Authors," there is a subheading entitled "Self Employment Tax … 32,588.124."

5. At the top of each page in the Topical Index it says, "references are to Paragraph (¶) numbers."

6. Each volume of the 19-or-so-volume set shows the code sections and ¶ numbers included in it. Volume 13 includes capital gains, S corporations and self-employment tax at ¶¶ 30,351-32,680.

7. Short descriptions of the facts and holdings of three cases about authors, royalties and self-employment tax. The citation we want is behind the last tab of the volume.

8. *P.P. Irwin*, 72 TCM 1148, Dec. 51,629(M), TC Memo 1996-490; *R.L. Hittleman*, 59 TCM 1028, Dec. 46,683 (M), TC Memo 1990-325; *W.R. Langford*, 55 TCM 1267, Dec. 44,891(M) TC Memo 1988-300. Descriptions are on page 56,605 of Volume 13 (2004).

9. The Index volume begins with a red-tabbed section entitled "About This Publication." At the end of this section is a list entitled "ABBREVIATIONS AND REFERENCES."

Treatises and Monographs

Like experts in every field, legal experts publish books. When a book attempts to cover an entire area of the law, it is called a treatise. Typically, law treatises have titles like *Prosser on Torts*, *Powell on Real Property* and *Corbin on Contracts*. When a book covers just a small portion of a general legal field, or introduces a new concept into the legal realm, it is called a monograph. Whatever they are called, hundreds of these books can be found in the stacks of the normal law library, and can often be very helpful in providing an overview of a subject.

There is a big difference between these resources and the textbooks discussed earlier in this chapter. While textbooks cover entire legal topics with the intent to teach, treatises and monographs exist to provide in-depth reference materials. Generally, they delve much deeper into an area than you would care to go. They also become dated more quickly despite periodic supplementation. However, if you really want to amass expertise on a topic and have the patience to put up with the ultimate in hairsplitting, give these resources a try. Some of the more useful and up-to-date ones are listed below.

Treatises (Partial List)

Anderson, *American Law of Zoning* (3rd Ed. West Group)

Business Organizations With Tax Planning (Matthew Bender)

Collier on Bankruptcy (Matthew Bender)

Rohan, *Condominium Law and Practice—Forms* (Matthew Bender)

Rohan, *Cooperative Housing Law and Practice Forms* (Matthew Bender)

Couch on Insurance (Clark Boardman)

Larson, *Employment Discrimination* (Matthew Bender)

Gorden and Mailman, *Immigration Law and Procedure* (Matthew Bender)

Kheel, *Business Organizations* (Matthew Bender)

Long, *Law of Liability Insurance* (Matthew Bender)

Antieau, *Local Government Law* (Matthew Bender)

Nimmer on Copyrights (Matthew Bender)

Rohrlich, *Organizing Corporate and Other Business Enterprises* (Matthew Bender)

Rosenberg, *Patent Law Fundamentals* (West Group)

Powell on Real Property (Matthew Bender)

Frumer, *Products Liability* (Matthew Bender)

Securities and Federal Corporate Law (West Group)

Pattishall, *Trademarks and Unfair Competition* (2d Ed. West Group)

Feller, *U.S. Customs and International Trade Guide* (Matthew Bender)

Williston on Contracts (4th Ed. West Group)

Larson, *Workers' Compensation Law* (Matthew Bender)

Library Exercise: Using Treatises

You are on a team researching the issue of whether a person who was arrested on a charge of selling drugs to an undercover police officer may use the defense of entrapment. The officers supplied the drugs to the person they eventually arrested, and also purchased them from him. You are assigned to find helpful treatises.

You have used the *A.L.R.* index to find a recent *A.L.R.* article on the specific situation of the defendant's arrest: *Entrapment as a Defense to a Charge of Supplying Narcotics Where Government Agents Supplied the Narcotics to Defendant and Purchased Narcotics From Defendant*, 9 A.L.R. 5th 464.

Questions

1. Find the *A.L.R.* article and find one of the two treatises listed under "Sources" at the beginning of the Research article. What are the two treatises?

2. In one of these two treatises, find the 1987 New Mexico case which said that "where the government was both the supplier and the purchaser of the contraband, and the defendant was recruited as a 'mere conduit,'" the defendant may claim entrapment as a defense. If you use Bailey and Rothblatt, read the pocket part.

Answers

1. Bailey and Rothblatt, *Handling Narcotic and Drug Cases*, 1972, Lawyers Coop; and 1 LaFave and Israel, *Criminal Procedure*.

2. *Baca v. State*, 106 N.M. 338, 742 P.2d 1043 (1987).

Restatements of the Law

Legal scholars are always trying to pinpoint exactly what the law "is" on a particular subject. In some cases, groups of scholars have convened under the auspices of an organization called the American Law Institute (ALI) for the purpose of putting into writing definitive statements of the law in various areas. These statements are termed "Restatements of the Law" and have been produced for such topics as contracts, torts and property.

While these tomes cover their subjects exhaustively, they do not in any way constitute the law itself (although they may prove persuasive to courts considering a particular issue). They are usually of little help to the beginning researcher looking for a good background resource. To begin with, they are not in a narrative form, but rather consist of very terse summations of legal principles and longer comments explaining them. The language in these comments is generally arcane, and the various restatements are not well indexed or organized for efficient retrieval of information. Because these publications are trying to reconcile often unreconcilable contradictions in the law, they tend to produce more confusion than enlightenment. For example, in one case where one of the authors represented a group of people in a court action for nuisance damages against an airport for excessive noise, both the author's side and the airport relied on the same passages of the Restatement of Torts in arguing their clearly opposite positions.

You are most likely to encounter a Restatement when a case refers to a particular section or speaks of adopting the "Restatement view" on some issue. After you read the section and accompanying comments, you can see how other courts have interpreted it by using a book called *Restatement in the Courts*, found with the other volumes of the *Restatement*.

Background Resources on the Internet

When you need to find general background information in the law library, you head for the shelves containing the legal encyclopedias, practice manuals, legal periodicals and legal treatises. For example, if you're beginning a research project on the duty of an insurance company to cover a property loss, you might look in the *A.L.R.* Index under "Insurance" and go from there.

But if your quest for background information takes you towards the computer, don't expect to be able to pull up *A.L.R.* or any of the other materials mentioned above, unless you are willing to pay a hefty fee. See "Using Fee-Based Publishers on the Web" for more on these services.

Using Fee-Based Publishers on the Web. West Group, LexisNexis and Matthew Bender all publish background materials on the Internet. There are a number of pricing options depending on whether you want access over a period of time or are willing to pay "by the slice." The subscriptions typically run into the many hundreds of dollars,

and the slices typically cost between $5 and $35 each, depending on how much information you get.

These services are relatively slow, and you need to wade through a number of informational screens to figure out how to get what you're looking for. However, if legal research plays an important part in your life, you should visit these sites to see what they offer. For background materials, we recommend the Matthew Bender site as the most likely to deliver on your search. Their site is located at www.bender.com. Check out their "Authority on Demand" feature. West is located at www.westlaw.com. Lexis is located at www.lexis.com.

Fortunately, the Internet also provides free background materials that can be extremely helpful, especially to the novice or casual legal researcher. These materials have been collected by attorneys, law schools and law libraries and consist primarily of FAQs (Frequently Asked Questions), articles written by lawyers for online publication, electronic law journals and online legal encyclopedias like the one published by Nolo on its website.

This "Justia" In

Justia.com (www.justia.com) is an all-purpose legal website that compiles and collects legal web resources. Created by one of the founders of Findlaw, this site is a good place to start any legal research project.

Finding Background Materials on the Internet

Many sites on the Internet provide one-stop shopping for statutes, important cases, regulations and commentary on a particular legal area. Because of the resources they contain, these sites are the equivalent of practice guides. But they differ from their hardcopy cousins in an important respect: hardcopy practice guides tend to be logically organized, following the typical course of a lawsuit or the chronology of a problem. The online sites, on the other hand, are haphazard collections of related resources and leave it to the user to figure out how they fit together, if at all.

You can go far by using an online search engine, such as FindLaw's LawCrawler [http://lawcrawler.lp.findlaw.com], The Meta-Index for U.S. Legal Research [http://gsulaw.gsu.edu/metaindex] or Yahoo [www.yahoo.com/law]. As we saw

in Chapter 4, search engines allow you to use key words to generate lists of specific topical materials, one or more of which may be just the background information you seek.

Probably the best place to start for online background materials is the Cornell University Law Site:

- Go to www.law.cornell.edu.
- Click the "Law About…" button on the left side of the page. This will produce a menu of large legal categories and a link to an alphabetical list of more detailed topics.
- Find the area of your research on the alphabetical list.
- Click the appropriate link.

You will find a brief overview of the topic on the left side of the page and a list of resources on the right side of the page. For most topics the list of resources follows the same pattern. Federal legislative and case law materials come first, then state legislative and case materials, and finally, after you scroll down a bit, a list of links to other sites related to that topic. It is this list of resource links that will lead you to the background materials you seek. (In Chapter 6 we explain how to use the Cornell site to find state statutes on particular topics.)

As with other types of Internet searching, you'll need to check out each link to see whether the background information it presents will be helpful to you. Obviously there are no guarantees, but this approach is as likely to yield helpful materials as any we can think of.

Here are some of our favorite topic-specific sites:

Bankruptcy. The Bankruptcy LawTrove [www.lawtrove .com/bankruptcy]. This site provides an extensive list of online bankruptcy-related materials, including other online bankruptcy sites.

American Bankruptcy Institute Consumer Commons [www.abiworld.org]. This is a consumer-friendly site with laws, news, a consumer education center, and links to courts.

Bankruptcy Legislation and Reform News. [http:// bankruptcymedia.com/bkfinder/bankruptcyreformnews .html]. This site helps you keep up to date on new bankruptcy legislation, including the Bankruptcy Abuse Prevention and Consumer Protection Act of 2005.

Copyright. The U.S. Copyright Office [www.copyright.gov]. This site offers regulations, guidelines, forms and links to other helpful copyright sites.

Stanford University's Copyright and Fair Use site [http:// fairuse.stanford.edu].

Intellectual Property Mall at Franklin Pierce Law Center [www.ipmall.fplc.edu]. An excellent general intellectual property site.

The Jeffrey R. Kuester Law Firm [www.kuesterlaw. com]. This law firm site provides an online reference service that will lead you to other copyright resources on the Web.

Corporate Law. The Securities and Exchange Commission [www.sec.gov]. It has all the investment statutes and regulations, current litigation, opinions and staff legal bulletins.

Business Law Lounge from the 'Lectric Law Library [www.lectlaw.com/bus.html].

Criminal Law and Criminal Justice. Nolo's Criminal Law Center [www.nolo.com]. This is a great place to start for questions about criminal procedure. Choose "Rights and Disputes."

Buffalo Criminal Law Center [http://wings.buffalo.edu/ law/bclc]. This has links to the criminal law and procedure statutes of all 50 states.

Divorce. (See also Family Law.) DivorceNet [www .divorcenet.com]. A site with excellent legal resources.

DivorceSource [www.divorcesource.com]. In addition to background materials on virtually all divorce issues, this site provides a comprehensive series of links to state divorce statutes.

Elder Law. The Senior Law Home Page (www.seniorlaw. com) provides links to articles about guardianships, conservatorships, Medicare and Medicaid, living wills, physician's directives, durable powers of attorney, senior abuse, and other issues that commonly affect seniors. The Kansas Elder Law Network (www.neln.org) is another good springboard for researching elder law issues. The National Academy of Elder Law Attorneys (www.naela.com/naela/ hotlinks.htm) also provides information and links to elder law resources.

Family Law. American Bar Association's Family Law Section [www.abanet.org/family/famsites.html]. This site provides numerous links to family law materials available on the Internet.

Cornell's Legal Information Institute [www.law. cornell.edu]. This is a great site for family law, with links to uniform laws, cases and additional Internet resources.

Adoption.com: Where Families Come Together [www. adoption.com]. This site provides information about adoption agencies, international adoption and many other adoption issues.

Domestic Violence: [www.womenslaw.org] provides state-by-state legal information about domestic violence

and how to obtain a restraining order, with downloadable forms and links to local resources.

First Amendment/Free Speech. First Amendment Cyber-Tribune [http://fact.trib.com].

Electronic Frontier Foundation [www.eff.org]. This site focuses on free speech law and policy issues in the online environment.

Healthcare. American Health Lawyers Association [www.healthlawyers.org]. This site has an extensive set of links to healthcare and health law sites.

Center for Health Law Studies at St. Louis University School of Law [http://law.slu.edu/healthlaw/research/links/topical.html]. This site has links to health law resources arranged by topic.

Human Rights. The Human Rights Library [www.umn.edu/humanrts].

Landlord-Tenant Law. Rentlaw.com [www.rentlaw.com]. This site has good summaries of relevant state laws.

TenantNet [www.tenant.net]. This site provides information about landlord-tenant law, with a focus on tenants' rights. TenantNet is designed primarily for tenants in New York City, but the site offers links to similar sites in many other states as well as the text of the federal fair housing law.

Lesbian and Gay Issues. Queer Legal Resources [http://qrd.tcp.com/qrd/www/legal]. This site provides information about lesbian and gay rights, including issues affecting couples.

American Civil Liberties Union's Lesbian and Gay Rights page [www.aclu.org/issues/gay/hmgl.html].

Patents. The U.S. Patent and Trademark Office [www.uspto.gov]. This is the place to go for recent policy and statutory changes and transcripts of hearings on patent law issues.

Delphion [www.delphion.com]. This site offers simultaneous searching in U.S. and European patent databases, access to Derwent patent data, and IP licensing search capabilities.

For current information on what's being patented, check out FreshPatents.com [www.freshpatents.com]. You can also stay on top of current events in patent law at Phosita, an intellectual property law blog [www.okpatents.com/phosita]. For a critical (sometimes caustic) look at patent news and events, check out Greg Aharonian's Internet Patent News Service. To subscribe, send the message "NEWS" to the email address, "patnews@patenting-art.com."

Small Business. Small Business Development Center National Information Clearinghouse [http://sbdcnet.utsa.edu].

The Small Business Administration [www.sba.gov]. This free site provides information about starting, financing and expanding your small business.

Tax Law. American Bar Association's Tax Section [www.abanet.org/tax]. This site provides numerous links to tax-related materials available on the Internet.

The Internal Revenue Service [www.irs.gov]. This site has tax information, publications and forms that you can download.

AccountantsWorld [www.accountantsworld.com].

Federation of Tax Administrators [www.taxadmin.org]. This is a complete, reliable site for state tax information.

Tax and Accounting Sites Directory [www.taxsites.com]. This is a monster site.

Trademarks. U.S. Patent and Trademark Office [www.uspto.gov]. This is the website of choice for trademark searching, trademark registration, papers issued by the USPTO on various trademark and domain name issues, and general information about the trademark laws. Also available through this site are the rules used by the trademark examiners and descriptions of goods and services deemed acceptable for trademark registration applications.

GGMark [www.ggmark.com]. This is a great general-purpose trademark site. It provides background information on virtually every aspect of trademark law and a comprehensive set of links to various trademark-related sites.

ICANN [www.icann.org]. This website is the starting place for researching domain name disputes and the rules that apply to them.

Wills and Estate Planning. The Kansas Elder Law Network [www.neln.org]. This is a great site for the whole country—not just Kansas. It contains background materials on all aspects of estate planning, as well as links to other sites.

National Academy of Elder Law Attorneys [www.naela.com/naela/hotlinks.htm].

Workplace Rights. Equal Employment Opportunity Commission [www.eeoc.gov]. The EEOC has resources both for employers and employees. Everything you need to know for compliance is here.

National Labor Relations Board [www.nlrb.gov]. The NLRB publishes decisions here.

Cornell's Legal Information Institute [www.law.cornell.edu]. This site offers links to a variety of sites related to such employment law issues as wages and hours

regulations, collective bargaining, employment discrimination, unemployment, pensions, workplace safety and workers' compensation.

Jackson Library at the University of North Carolina [http://library.uncg.edu/depts/docs/us/harass.html]. This site has an exhaustive set of sexual harassment resources.

Your Money. Debt Counselors of America [www.dca.org or www.myvesta.org]. This is a nonprofit online resource dedicated to helping people get out of debt. You'll find free publications, recommended books, a forum for posting your debt questions and special programs to assist you.

National Consumer Law Center [www.nclc.org or www. consumerlaw.org]. This site offers information and advice on low-income consumer issues.

Consumer.gov [www.consumer.gov/yourmoney.htm]. The government offers consumer money advice at this site.

The Better Business Bureau [www.bbb.org/complaint.asp]. This site allows you to file consumer complaints online.

Review

Questions

1. What is the primary reason for using background resources to start your research?
2. What are some tips to remember when purchasing a self-help law book?
3. What are law student study texts (hornbooks) most useful for?
4. What are the advantages of starting your legal research in a legal encyclopedia?
5. What are the names of the two major national encyclopedias?
6. What are the publishing philosophies for each encyclopedia?
7. For what types of research issues is *American Law Reports* a good background resource to use to start your research?
8. When can legal periodicals be of most help in legal research?
9. How can you find articles of interest in legal periodicals?

Answers

1. To get a general understanding of the relevant legal area before looking for the specific answer to a narrow question. The answers to almost all specific legal questions depend on a number of variables to which the background resource can alert you.
2. Do a little reading to see whether the language is understandable and the concepts useful and specific. Check whether the material actually leads you step-by-step through the entire process. Check whether the book gives you the necessary forms for doing it yourself. Check whether the book pays attention to differences in state laws.
3. These books, which are conceptual in nature, are excellent if you want a basic understanding of the variables in any specific area of concern.
4. Legal encyclopedias cover the entire range of law. Their entries are broken into small segments, and you are very likely to find material relevant to your research problem. Each entry provides a solid treatment of the particular topic, gives you a good idea of the all-important variables associated with your issue, and refers you to specific statutes and cases (the stuff the law is made of) to help you get to the next research phase.
5. *Corpus Juris Secundum (C.J.S.)* and *American Jurisprudence (Am. Jur)*.
6. As a general rule, the West publishing philosophy is to provide all the information and let you, the researcher, choose what you wish to use. The LexisNexis philosophy is to exercise a little editorial discretion and present you only with what it thinks is most important to researchers.
7. *A.L.R.* is an excellent place to begin when you have determined that your problem falls within the state/civil/substantive or federal/civil/substantive categories.
8. When you are interested in new legislation, current and innovative legal theories and the meaning of important cases.
9. There are three subject indexes to legal periodicals: LEGALTRAC, an electronic index, and two printed indexes—the *Index to Legal Periodicals* (tan cover) and the *Current Law Index* (red and black cover).

6

Constitutions, Statutes, Regulations and Ordinances

When people speak of "the law," they usually mean statutes—enactments by Congress and state legislatures. Statutes set out the rules that we all must live by. Reflecting this, most of this chapter tells you how to find and understand statutes.

We also address two other important research tasks: how to research constitutional issues and how to locate regulations issued by government agencies. Constitutions are important because they set the guidelines within which legislatures must operate when passing statutes. And agency regulations are important because they are the rules used to implement statutes in the real world.

Constitutional Research

The U.S. Constitution is the supreme law of the land. All laws, state and federal, must comply with it. Both state and federal courts use the U.S. Constitution to decide whether a statute or regulation is proper and enforceable. Especially in areas dealing with civil rights and civil liberties, court decisions that interpret the U.S. Constitution affect everybody throughout the United States.

There are also state constitutions. These documents provide the same guidance at the state level that the U.S. Constitution does at the federal level. However, state constitutions are subject to the provisions of the U.S. Constitution in certain areas and even must bow to federal statutes in some contexts. As a general rule, state constitutions can add to a state citizen's rights but can't take rights away that are provided for in the U.S. Constitution. In other areas, conflicts between a state constitution and the U.S. Constitution are generally resolved in favor of the latter. And decisions by state courts that interpret state constitutions affect only the citizens of those states.

Most research into what the law is on a particular topic does not involve constitutional research. This is because statutes and regulations define the law in most instances. However, you may find yourself doing constitutional research if you suspect a statute or regulation is unconstitutional. For example, if a state statute barred anyone but a lawyer from holding estate planning seminars, nonlawyer estate planners would probably want to know whether this law violated the First Amendment's freedom of speech provision.

Constitutional research can be very time-consuming. Most constitutions use extremely broad language that creates the possibility of differing interpretations. And even if the language appears precise, many judges are willing to reach beyond the literal words to figure out what the constitution's framers really intended. These factors mean that you can't understand how a constitutional provision might affect your situation unless:

- you are already familiar with the Constitution and how it has been applied to similar fact situations; or
- you engage in some first-class constitutional research.

Below we provide some guidelines for doing constitutional research. An example of how this type of research proceeds is in Chapter 12.

The U.S. Constitution in the Law Library

Most constitutional research involves the U.S. Constitution. There are several basic steps to doing sound constitutional research.

Step 1: Find a good constitutional law textbook. The federal Constitution and most state constitutions have been around a long time, and to really zero in on what the constitution will mean in your situation, you have to be aware of how each word and phrase in the relevant provision has been interpreted by the courts over the years (and centuries). There is nothing like a good textbook to bring you up to speed. See, for example, *Constitutional Law: Principles and Policies* (Introduction to Law Series) by Erwin Chemerinsky, or *American Constitutional Law 2d* by Laurence H. Tribe.

Skim the table of contents until you find some subject listings that speak to your general issue. If that doesn't work, use the index. (Chapter 4 explains how to come up with a list of terms to look up in a legal index.)

Most people undertaking constitutional research are concerned with the Bill of Rights (the first ten amendments). The Fourteenth Amendment is also a frequent subject of research, since it prohibits the states from denying their citizens due process of law and the equal protection of the law.

The Bill of Rights

First Amendment: freedom of speech, freedom of religion, freedom of association, separation of church and state

Second Amendment: right to bear arms

Third Amendment: right not to have soldiers quartered in homes

Fourth Amendment: right of privacy, right against unreasonable searches and seizures, right to confront adverse witnesses

Fifth Amendment: right to trial by jury, right to due process of law (life, liberty, property), right against self-incrimination, freedom from double jeopardy

Sixth Amendment: speedy and public trial, right to representation by counsel, right to confront witnesses (cross-examination), right to subpoena witnesses

Seventh Amendment: right to trial in civil cases

Eighth Amendment: right to reasonable bail, ban on cruel and unusual punishment

Ninth Amendment: people retain rights in addition to those granted in the Constitution

Tenth Amendment: everything not prohibited is allowed

Step 2: Find a good case. When using a textbook to research constitutional issues, remember that—like most textbooks—constitutional textbooks are only intended to lay out some general principles and then pass you on to the actual court cases that have done the interpreting. So, when you read the textbook, be on the lookout for a citation to a case that might be relevant.

If the textbook doesn't do the job, use the subject indexes to the *Supreme Court Digest* or *Federal Practice Digest.* We tell you how to do this in Chapter 9.

If neither the textbook nor the digests get you started on the right track, use one of the annotated federal codes (discussed below) to locate the actual constitutional provision. Then, use the case notes to locate one or more relevant cases. (See Chapter 9, where we explain how to do this.)

Step 3: Find other relevant cases. Once you find a case that appears to address your precise issues, you are in luck. You can use the techniques we describe in Chapter 10 for skipping from that case to other similar cases until you find one or more that really nails down the answer you're seeking.

Two words of advice about federal constitutional research:

1. Judges often interpret a constitutional provision to achieve the result they want, not the result that might seem to naturally flow from past decisions or the plain language of the Constitution. Be prepared to encounter cases that contradict one another, that are shockingly illogical and that are flat-out wrong. But remember, if it's the U.S. Supreme Court speaking, the case is the law of the land until another Supreme Court case says it isn't.

2. Constitutional research often is the art of getting around a case that appears to be squarely against your position. Even if you find one or a number of cases that seem to apply to your situation, there are almost always ways to argue that your situation is different and not governed by the cases. As an example, see the research story in Chapter 12, where we suggest some ways to get around a particular Supreme Court issue.

Constitutional Research

In 1994 we were asked a question that involved us in a constitutional research project. If you were asked the same question today, your conclusion might be different (depending on the current state of the law), but you could use the same approach that we did. This is what we were asked:

"One of the states has a law from the 1940s that prohibits the handling of poisonous snakes except by trained and licensed medical personnel. May this law be applied to a religious sect that has recently established a presence in the state and would like to use snakes as part of their ritualistic religious practices?"

The process we followed started with a background resource, *American Constitutional Law 2d* by Laurence H. Tribe, which laid out the history of free exercise of religion claims and analyzed current Supreme Court cases. Tribe led us to read *United States v. Lee*, 455 U.S. 252 (1982), the first case to diminish the requirement of earlier cases that the government show a *compelling* interest in order to justify an encroachment on the free exercise of religion. In *Lee*, the Court held that the government only has to show that its rule is *important* in order to be allowed to apply it to the claimant, although it limits or prohibits the claimant's religious practice (such as snake handling). This isn't good news for the snake handlers, but there are a few lines of inquiry that could help us "make a case" for them.

By Shepardizing *Lee*, we found a later important free exercise case, *Employment Division v. Smith*, 110 S. Ct. 1595 (1990), where the claimants were fired and then denied unemployment insurance after they were arrested for using peyote in a religious ceremony in violation of Oregon's anti-drug laws. *Smith* says that a free exercise claim (one that asks that I be exempted from a law of general application, such as drug laws or school attendance laws, because forcing me to comply limits or prohibits my freedom to practice my religion) can only succeed if I can show that another constitutional right is also infringed, such as freedom of speech.

So, one avenue for us to explore was: What other right of the snake handlers besides freedom of religion is infringed by the prohibition? Freedom of speech is another First Amendment right, so we started looking for Supreme Court cases on the issue of freedom of speech to find factual circumstances and statements of law in the opinions that could help us characterize the snake handlers' activities as "speech." Cases could be found through background resources and the digests *(Supreme Court Digest* or *Federal Practice Digest)*. We started with Tribe, and learned that speech doesn't have to be actual words in order to be constitutionally protected, but can also be an act that expresses an idea. In *Stromberg v. California*, 283 U.S. 359 (1931), state law prohibited the display of any red flag as a symbolic act of opposing organized government, and the Court found it to be an unconstitutional restriction of freedom of speech. This prominent case was a good place to start, because once we found one good free speech case, we could find others by Shepardizing it or by using the West topic and key numbers assigned to its headnotes to get into the digests.

Another avenue of inquiry is that of questioning whether the statute is really one of "general application," or whether it was passed specifically in order to prohibit religious snake handling. And, even if it was directed specifically at the religious practice, is there any Constitutional prohibition against the government doing that? Initial research in background sources (Tribe and the *Nutshell on Constitutional Law*) yielded two cases that would be a good place to start: *Lemon v. Kurtzman*, 403 U.S. 602 (1971) and *United States v. O'Brien*, 391 U.S. 367 (1968).

Another case, *Church of the Lukimi Babalo Aye, Inc. v. City of Hialeah*, 113 S. Ct. 2217 (1993), is relevant but not directly on point. In that case the law was struck down because the statute had been passed specifically to prohibit the religious practice. In our situation, however, the law was passed decades before the snake handlers had moved to the state. Of course, the church's lawyer would argue that the original motivation for the law was anti-religious, but that might be hard to prove so long after the fact.

For more ideas, information and insights, we searched for snake handling cases and law review articles. Tribe

Constitutional Research (continued)

cited one snake-handling case, *Swann v. Pack*, 527 S.W.2d 99 (1975). We Shepardized *Swann* and all the snake cases cited in *Swann*. In the end, it turned out that *Swann* was the latest snake-handling case and had cited all the others: *Harden v. State,* 188 Tenn. 17, 216 S.W.2d 708 (1949), *Hill v. State*, 38 Ala. App. 404, 88 So. 880 (1956), *Kirk v. Commonwealth*, 186 Va. 836, 44 S.E.2d 409 (1947), *Lawson v. Commonwealth*, 291 Ky. 437, 164 S.W. 972 (1942), *State v. Massey*, 229 N.C. 734, 51 S.E.2d 179 (1949).

Law review articles can be very helpful in constitutional research because they cite all the primary and secondary sources they can find (saving you a lot of research), and they usually have a point of view that can help you get ideas on how to approach your case.

To find law review articles about snake cases, we searched the *Index to Legal Periodicals* for the few years following *Swann*. In the 1973–1976 volume, under Freedom of Religion, our search through a long list of titles came up with "Religious Snake Handling Abated...," Vand. L. Rev. 29:495-513 (March 1976). Law reviews usually take awhile to respond to cases, so the 1976-1979 volume yielded more articles in: Wash. U. L. Q. 1976:353-67 (Spring 1976); Ky. L. J. 65:195-219 (1976-1977; and Kan. L. Rev. 25: 585-93 (Summer 1977).

These are just the beginning of several roads of inquiry that you could follow to build an argument that has logic and reason within the context of Supreme Court opinions.

• provide links from the discussion to the text of the cases that are referenced.

The Library of Congress maintains sites that will help you in your constitutional research:

- The Constitution and Bill of Rights: [http://lcweb2. loc.gov/const/const.html]
- The Bill of Rights: [http://lcweb2.loc.gov/const/bor.html].

The National Archives also maintains helpful sites:

- The Constitution: [www.archives.gov and select "100 Milestone Documents."]
- Bill of Rights: [www.archives.gov].

State Constitutions in the Law Library

State constitutions are a little easier to research than the U.S. Constitution, because they haven't gotten nearly as much judicial play over the years as the U.S. Constitution. However, as the U.S. Supreme Court continues to experience profound changes in its personnel, many advocacy groups may begin turning to state constitutions as a source of individual rights and liberties.

The best approach to researching your state's constitution is to find a state-specific encyclopedia (see the selected list in Chapter 5) and read a background discussion of the provision that relates to your situation. Then locate the actual constitutional provision and read the case notes that follow it. (We tell you how to do this in Chapter 9.)

State Constitutions on the Internet

The best way to find a state constitution is to use an online catalog that lets you view all Internet legal resources on a state-by-state basis. Our favorite site for researching this is the Cornell State Index (www.law.cornell.edu/states/listing. html) that provides lists of state-specific resources.

Introduction to Federal Statutes

Federal statutes are enactments by Congress, either signed by the president or passed over a veto. They are organized by subject, indexed and published under a specific title number in a series of books called the *United States Code*. We describe the *United States Code* in more detail in the next section.

But sometimes the statute you are looking for will not be in the code. It may have been passed too recently, or it may have been repealed and taken out of the code. Finding

The U.S. Constitution on the Internet

There are two good sources for starting your U.S. Constitutional research: the annotated Constitution maintained by FindLaw [www.findlaw.com/casecode/constitution] and the U.S. government website for the U.S. Constitution [www.gpoaccess.gov/constitution/browse. html]. These sites:

- organize the U.S. Constitution by article and amendment;
- include a discussion of each article and amendment according to the U.S. Supreme Court cases that have interpreted them; and

recent statutes and finding repealed statutes are both covered later in this chapter.

Federal statutes start out as "bills" introduced in a session of Congress. They are assigned labels and numbers depending on which house of Congress they originate in. For example, a bill introduced in the U.S. Senate might be referred to as Senate Bill 2 (S. 2). A bill that originated in the U.S. House of Representatives might be known as House of Representatives Bill 250 (H.R. 250).

Few of the many bills introduced in Congress become law. To do so they have to be passed by both houses and signed by the President, or passed over his veto. Once a bill becomes law, it is called a statute, assigned a new label and given a new number. The basic label is Public Law (Pub. L.). Following the Pub. L., the statute will have one number that corresponds with the number of the Congress (for example, 94th) that passed it, followed by a second number that is simply the number assigned to that specific bill by the Congress. So Pub. L. No. 94-586, for example, refers to Public Law 586 passed by the 94th Congress.

The bill drafters are aware that their handiwork will end up in codes and accordingly assign code numbers to the separate bill provisions. Sometimes these code numbers add new material to existing statutory schemes, while other times they amend existing statutes. So, when you research a Bill or Public Law, you will know where, in the existing statutes, the new legislation is intended to go.

How to Find Statutes in the United States Code

The U.S. Code is the starting place for most federal statutory research. It consists of 50 separate numbered titles. Each title covers a specific subject matter. For instance, Title 35 contains the statutes governing patent law, Title 11 contains the bankruptcy statutes and Title 18 contains most of the statutes governing federal crimes. Some titles are published in only one book—for instance, Title 17, which covers the law of copyright. Others have many volumes—Title 26, the tax code, currently has 16 hardcover volumes and a separate paperback index.

Two versions of the U.S. Code are published in annotated form: The *United States Code Annotated,* or *U.S.C.A.* (West Group), and the *United States Code Service,* or *U.S.C.S.* (Lexis Publishing). Most law libraries carry both, but smaller libraries may only have one (usually the *U.S.C.A.*).

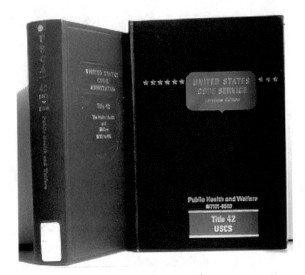

United States Code

In addition to all the current federal statutes, these extremely useful sets of annotated books contain information pertaining to each statute, including:

- one-sentence summaries of court cases that have interpreted the statute (discussed in Chapter 9*);
- notes about the statute's history (such as amendments);
- cross-references to other relevant statutes;
- cross-references to administrative regulations that may be helpful in interpreting the statute;
- citations to the legislative history of the statute; and
- research guides (references to relevant materials by the same publisher).

Because of all this helpful information, these annotated codes are almost always used in place of the bare *U.S. Code* when doing research on federal statutes. Throughout this book, when we refer to "the federal code" or to the *U.S.C. (United States Code),* we mean an annotated edition (*U.S.C.A.* or *U.S.C.S.*).

Getting Started

There are several approaches to finding statutes in the annotated U.S. codes:

- If you know the citation to the statute, select either *U.S.C.A.* or *U.S.C.S.,* find the title number given in the citation and turn to the indicated section. (See "Using Citations to Find Federal Statutes," below.)
- If you know the common or popular name of the statute but don't have the citation, consult the *Shepard's* or *U.S.C.A. Popular Names Index.* (See "Using Popular Name Indexes to Find a Federal Statute," below.)

- If you don't know the citation and don't know what the statute is called, but can figure out from its subject which title the statute will be found in, consult the subject index for the specific title, found in the last volume of the title. (See "Using Annotated Code Indexes to Find a Federal Statute," below.)

- If you don't find what you're looking for in the specific title index, or you don't know what title to start with, consult the general subject index at the end of the entire series. (See "Using Annotated Code Indexes to Find a Federal Statute," below.)

 When You Search for a Statute It Is Crucial to Get the Most Current Version. Although the annotated codes are published in hardcover, each book has a paper supplement—called a pocket part—inserted in the back of the book. The pocket part updates the hardcover book annually. Always search the pocket part when you are trying to find a statute. See "Using the Pocket Part to Get the Latest Version," below, for more on this.

Finding the U.S. Code on the Internet. You can find a non-annotated version of the code for free on the Internet in at least two places:

- Office of the Law Revision Council: [http://uscode.house.gov/lawrevisioncouncil.php]
- Cornell Legal Information Institute: [www4.law.cornell.edu].

Using Citations to Find Federal Statutes

The reference to any primary law source—including federal statutes—is termed a "citation." The citation, which is always written in a standard form, tells you precisely where the law is located. Citations to federal statutes contain the title of the U.S. Code where the statute is found and the section number.

Example: The citation for the Civil Rights Act of 1964 is:

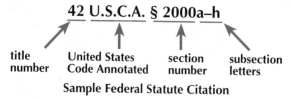

42 U.S.C.A. § 2000a–h

title number | United States Code Annotated | section number | subsection letters

Sample Federal Statute Citation

Finding this statute in the law library is easy. Locate the set of books labeled *U.S.C.A.* (maroon) or *U.S.C.S.* (black and blue). Look at the spine of the volumes marked 42 to find the one that includes § 2000a-h.

Library Exercise: Finding a Statute From Its Citation: Exercise One

You are reading a case about embezzlement of pension funds and the opinion refers to "Title 18 U.S.C. § 1961 et seq." The judge has overturned the defendant's conviction because the evidence showed that he stole only once. You decide to read the statute.

Questions

1. Where do you look to find the statute?
2. Find the volumes covering Title 18. Select the volume covering §§ 1761 through 1962. Open the volume and find § 1961. What sections are included in this statutory scheme?
3. What is the title of this statutory scheme?
4. Read § 1961 (1) Definitions. Is embezzlement from pension and welfare funds indictable under the RICO statute?
5. Would one act of embezzlement of pension or welfare funds constitute a violation of the RICO statute?

Answers

1. It will be found in the sets of *United States Code Annotated* or in *United States Code Service*. Use *U.S.C.A.*, where the titles and section numbers are on the books' spines.
2. Title 18 §§ 1961-1968.
3. "Racketeer Influenced and Corrupt Organizations," also known as "RICO."
4. Yes, in Section (1)(B) we are told that "'racketeering activity' … means any act which is indictable under any of the following provisions of title 18, United States Code: … § 664 (relating to embezzlement from pension and welfare funds)."
5. No, Section (5) of the statute specifies that there must be "a pattern of racketeering activity" (at least two acts).

Library Exercise: Finding a Statute From Its Citation: Exercise Two

You are reading a case in which the court upheld the expulsion of a public high school student for an entire year for bringing a realistic looking but non-functional solid wood "gun" to school, pointing it at other students and saying "bang." The judge cited 20 *U.S.C.A.* § 7151. You would like to know if the cited statute requires or permits such a long-term expulsion.

Questions

1. How do you find the statute?
2. In *U.S.C.A.* or *U.S.C.S.*, look at the volumes that cover Title 20 and choose the one that will have § 7151. Don't forget to look in the pocket part for sections that were added since the printing of the hardbound edition. Turn to the section. What is the name of the Act?
3. Does the statute allow expulsion of a student for a whole year?
4. How does the statute define "weapon"?
5. How do you find section 921 of title 18?
6. Does the term "weapon" prohibited in 20 *U.S.C.A.* § 7151(b)(3) include a non-functional solid wood "gun"?
7. What conclusion might you draw from your reading of the statute and the case?

Answers

1. Use the sets of *U.S.C.A.* or *U.S.C.S.*
2. "Gun-Free Schools Act."
3. Yes. § 8921(b)(1) requires a school to expel a student for a least a year, who brings a weapon to school.
4. § 7151(b)(3) says a firearm has the same meaning as in section 921 of title 18.
5. In *U.S.C.A.* or *U.S.C.S.*, look at the volumes that cover title 18 and choose the one that contains section 921.
6. Probably not. Title 18 § 921(a)(3) says the term "firearm" means (A) any weapon which will or is designed to or may readily be converted to expel a projectile by the action of an explosive; (B) the frame or receiver of any such weapon; (C) any firearm muffler or firearm silencer; or (D) any destructive device. Because the solid wood "gun" cannot expel any projectile and definitely cannot do so by the use of an explosive and is not a destructive device, it does not fit the definition of a weapon according to § 7151(b)(3).
7. 20 *U.S.C.A.* § 7151 seems not to apply to the case. There might be some other statute prohibiting such an act, but it probably wouldn't require a one-year expulsion.

Using Popular Name Indexes to Find a Federal Statute

You may hear a federal statute referred to by its popular name—for example, the Civil Rights Act, the Taft-Hartley Act or the Marine Mammal Protection Act. You can find such a statute by using:

- the "popular names index" that accompanies the *United States Code Annotated* (*U.S.C.A.*);
- the "popular names table" volume that accompanies the *United States Code Service, Lawyer's Edition* (*U.S.C.S.*); or
- *Shepard's Acts and Cases by Popular Names: Federal and State.* This publication is particularly useful

for finding both state and federal statutes and cases through their popular names. Not all libraries carry it, however.

The *U.S.C.A. Popular Names Index* is included with the *U.S.C.A.* set of books, directly following it on the shelves. This index gives a citation that refers you to the correct title and section (for example, Title 20 § 607) of the named statute. Below are the popular names index entries for two of the three acts mentioned above. As you can see, the Civil Rights Act of 1964 is contained in Titles 28 and 42, and the Marine Mammal Protection Act is found in Title 16 of the federal code. "Using Citations to Find Federal Statutes," above, explains how to find the actual statute once you've found a citation.

POPULAR NAME TABLE

832

Civil Rights Act of 1957
Pub. L. 85–315, Sept. 9, 1957, 71 Stat. 634 (See Title 5, § 5315(19); Title 28, §§ 1343, 1861; Title 42, §§ 1971, 1975, 1975a, 1975b, 1975c, 1975d, 1975e, 1995)
Pub. L. 86–383, title IV, § 401, Sept. 28, 1959, 73 Stat. 724 (Title 42, § 1975c)
Pub. L. 86–449, May 6, 1960, title IV, title VI, 74 Stat. 89 (Title 42, §§ 1971, 1975d)
Pub. L. 87–264, title IV, Sept. 21, 1961, 75 Stat. 559 (Title 42, § 1975c)
Pub. L. 88–152, § 2, Oct. 17, 1963, 77 Stat. 271 (Title 42, § 1975c)
Pub. L. 88–352, title V, July 2, 1964, 78 Stat. 249 (Title 42, §§ 1975a–1975d)
Pub. L. 90–198, § 1, Dec. 14, 1967, 81 Stat. 582 (Title 42, §§ 1975c, 1975e)
Pub. L. 91–521, §§ 1–4, Nov. 25, 1970, 84 Stat. 1356, 1357 (Title 42, §§ 1975a, 1975b, 1975d, 1975e)
Pub. L. 92–64, Aug. 4, 1971, 85 Stat. 166 (Title 42, § 1975e)
Pub. L. 92–496, Oct. 14, 1972, 86 Stat. 913 (Title 42, §§ 1975a–1975e)
Pub. L. 94–292, § 2, May 27, 1976, 90 Stat. 524 (Title 42, § 1975e)
Pub. L. 95–132, § 2, Oct. 13, 1977, 91 Stat. 1157 (Title 42, § 1975e)
Pub. L. 95–444, §§ 2–7, Oct. 10, 1978, 92 Stat. 1067, 1068 (Title 42, §§ 1975b, 1975c, 1975d, 1975e)
Pub. L. 96–81, §§ 2, 3, Oct. 6, 1979, 93 Stat. 642 (Title 42, §§ 1975c, 1975e)
Pub. L. 96–447, § 2, Oct. 13, 1980, 94 Stat. 1894 (Title 42, § 1975e)

Civil Rights Act of 1960
Pub. L. 86–449, May 6, 1960, 74 Stat. 86 (Title 18, §§ 837, 1074, 1509; Title 20, §§ 241, 640; Title 42, §§ 1971, 1974–1974e, 1975d)

→ Civil Rights Act of 1964
Pub. L. 88–352, July 2, 1964, 78 Stat. 241 (Title ㉘ § 1447; Title 42, §§ 1971, 1975a–1975d, 2000a–2000h–6)
Pub. L. 92–261, §§ 2–8, 10, 11, 13, Mar. 24, 1972, 86 Stat. 103–113 (Title ㊷ §§ 2000e, 2000e–1 to 2000e–6, 2000e–8, 2000e–9, 2000e–13 to 2000e–17)

● ●

Manpower Development and Training Amendments of 1966
Pub. L. 89–792, Nov. 7, 1966, 80 Stat. 1434 (Title 42, §§ 2572b, 2572c, 2582, 2583, 2601, 2603, 2610b, 2611, 2614)

Marihuana and Health Reporting Act
Pub. L. 91–296 title V, June 30, 1970, 84 Stat. 352 (Title 42, § 242 note)
Pub. L. 95–461, § 3(a), Oct. 14, 1978, 92 Stat. 1268 (Title 42, § 242 note)

Marihuana Tax Act of 1937
Aug. 2, 1937, ch. 553, 50 Stat. 551

Marine Corps Personnel Act
May 29, 1934, ch. 367, 48 Stat. 809

Marine Insurance Act (District of Columbia)
Mar. 4, 1922, ch. 93, 42 Stat. 401

→ Marine Mammal Protection Act of 1972
Pub. L. 92–522, Oct. 21, 1972, 86 Stat. 1027 (Title ⑯ §§ 1361, 1362, 1371–1384, 1401–1407)
Pub. L. 93–205, § 13(e), Dec. 28, 1973, 87 Stat. 902 (Title 16, §§ 1362, 1371, 1372, 1402)
Pub. L. 94–265, title IV, § 404(a), Apr. 13, 1976, 90 Stat. 360 (Title 16, § 1362)
Pub. L. 95–136, §§ 1–4, Oct. 18, 1977, 91 Stat. 1167 (Title 16, §§ 1372, 1380, 1384, 1407)
Pub. L. 95–316, §§ 1–4, July 10, 1978, 92 Stat. 380, 381 (Title 16, §§ 1379, 1380, 1384, 1407)

Library Exercise: Finding Statutes by Their Popular Names

This exercise asks you to find citations to several statutes known only by their popular names. Additional research exercises that include these and other skills are in Chapter 11.

Questions

1. (State Statutes) You are researching the limitations placed by different states on the importation of plants from another state. You come across a reference to a New Mexico law, the "Harmful Plant Act." You want to find the citation to this statute.
   a. What nationally-applicable index can be used to locate the citation to a state statute by its popular name?
   b. Using that resource, what is the citation for the Harmful Plant Act?

2. (Federal Statutes) While researching the historic relationship between the United States and the countries of the Middle East, you read about something called the Middle East Peace and Stability Act. Where in the *U.S. Code Annotated (U.S.C.A.)* can you find the citation for this act?

3. (Federal Statutes) You are researching the legal aspects of the introduction of oleomargarine into American culture, and find a mention of the Oleomargarine Acts passed in the early part of the 20th century.
   a. What resource provided by *U.S.C.S.* can you use to find the citation to these Acts? (You want the Oleomargarine Acts specifically, not any other statutes that may affect oleomargarine.)
   b. Find the statute in *U.S.C.S.* Use the material following the statute (which includes sections titled "Cross References," "Research Guide" and "Interpretive Notes and Decisions"). Two references mention colored oleomargarine. What are they?

4. (Federal Statutes) While researching laws that protect the environment and wildlife, you come across a reference to the Congaree Swamp National Monument Expansion and Wilderness Act, with a notation that it was passed in the 1988 100th Congress. Use the *U.S. Code Congressional and Administrative News* to find this statute.

Answers

1. a. *Shepard's Acts and Cases by Popular Names: Federal and State.* (If you had access to New Mexico statutes, you could find the citation in the popular name index to that annotated code; but *Shepard's* has citations to cases and statutes from all the states.)
   b. By looking in the volume subtitled "ACTS G-Q," under Harmful Plant Act, you find that the citation to the Act is New Mexico Statutes, 1978, §§ 76-7A-1 et seq.

2. By looking in the Popular Name Table at the end (after Z) of the index volumes to the *United States Code Annotated,* you find that the citation to the Act is Title 22, §§ 1961-1965.

3. a. The *United States Code Service* has a Table of Acts by Popular Names in one of the Tables volumes at the end of the set. The Oleomargarine Acts were enacted May 9, 1902, and are now designated as Title 21, § 25. The "ch. 784" means that the Acts were designated as chapter 784 in the Statutes at Large in 1902.
   b. (1) Colored oleomargarine, intrastate sales of, 21 *U.S.C.S.* § 347 et seq.
      (2) "States may ... prohibit manufacture of oleomargarine artificially colored." *McCray v. United States,* 195 U.S. 27, 49 L. Ed. 78, 24 S. Ct. 769 (1904).

4. There are several volumes for each session of Congress: one set for 1988, for example, and a set for 1989. The last volume for each year contains Tables and Indexes. Look at the Table of Contents in the front of that volume in the 1988 set, and you will see that the Popular Name Acts is Table 10 on page 416. In Table 10, you find The Congaree Swamp ... Act, and are referred to page 2606. On the spine of each volume for 1988, the included pages are listed. Volume 2 includes page 2606, where you find the Act.

Finding Statutes by Chapter, Section or Title Number

Sometimes statutes are commonly known by a title, chapter or section number that refers to how the statute itself is organized, not to the book in which it can be found. For instance, many people may have heard of Title VII, the statutes that address discrimination in the workplace. However, this Title VII has nothing to do with Title 7 of the *United States Code*. Instead, it is the Congressional designation for a group of statutes within the Civil Rights Act of 1964. In fact, the Title VII statutes are located in Title 42 of the *United States Code*.

Where did the "Title VII" come from? When bills are written, they are assigned internal organizing labels for legislative purposes. A bill isn't assigned to a Title of the federal code until it actually passes and becomes a law.

If you are researching a statute that you know only by one of its internal organizing designations—such as Title VII, Chapter 7 (Bankruptcy Code) or Section 8 (Low Income Housing Assistance)—first see whether it is listed that way in a popular names index. If not, focus on the subject of the statute—for instance "civil rights" or "job discrimination"—and use one of the Code indexes discussed below.

Using Annotated Code Indexes to Find a Federal Statute

If you think a federal statute may apply to your situation, but you don't know the name or citation of the statute, start with the index. Each title of the annotated codes has a separate index located at the back of the last book of the title. There is also a general index for all the titles as a whole. If you know what title your statute is in—or likely to be in—start with the index for that title. If you aren't sure which title your statute is in, use the general index.

For example, suppose you are interested in federal statutory restrictions on the use of federal education funds by state schools. If you happen to know that such restrictions are found in Title 20, you can use the index

to that title. If you didn't know in advance that Title 20 contains the education statutes, however, you would use the general index at the end of the entire code.

Some titles contain a variety of subject matter. For instance, Title 42 contains statutes relating to water resources, water planning, voting rights, civil rights and the National Science Foundation in addition to its general topic of public health and welfare.

If you are using the *U.S.C.S.* and don't find what you're looking for in either the title index or the general index, try the *U.S.C.A.* index, or vice versa. The second one you try may have one of the terms you look up. Once you find the correct citation, you can use whichever annotated code suits you best.

Using One Citation to Research Statutory Schemes

It is usually insufficient to just locate one statute when seeking an answer to a legal question. Statutes tend to come in bunches. For instance, if you are doing research to find out whether a particular person is entitled to inherit from a person who died without a will, it might be necessary to skim five or six separate statutes before you would fully understand what the law is on this subject. A group of related statutes is termed a statutory scheme. Fortunately, statutes that form part of a statutory scheme usually are all located together, so it's only a question of reading from one to another. Sometimes, however, a statutory scheme is bound together by a bewildering set of cross-references.

Sometimes an index will alert you to the existence of a statutory scheme. You know you have to look at more than one statute if an index entry to a statute has an "et seq." at the end. ("Et seq." means "and following.")

To better understand the concept of statutory schemes, let's look at the federal Civil Rights Act of 1964, which contains a large number of individual statutes dealing with discrimination in such matters as housing, public accommodations and employment. Some of the statutes prohibit discriminatory acts on the basis of race, creed, national origin, color or sex. Other statutes provide remedies for violations—that is, penalties for discrimination and procedures for enforcement of the law.

Library Exercise: Finding Federal Statutes by Using the Index to the U.S. Codes

The students at Gallaudet University, a university created by federal statute to "provide education and training to deaf individuals and otherwise to further the education of the deaf," are outraged because the Board of Trustees of the University has not even one trustee who is deaf.

You are assigned to research federal statutes to find out how the Board is selected/elected. Find the statute about the University, determine how the Board members are selected/elected and advise the concerned students.

Questions

1. Where in *U.S.C.A.* or *U.S.C.S.* do you look?
2. What words or phrases in the General Index do you look under?
3. What do you find under that entry?
4. Take down the *U.S.C.A.* or *U.S.C.S.* volume for Title 20 that will include § 4301, et seq. Turn to the Act and look at the Table of Contents for the Act. Where will you find information about the Board of Trustees?
5. Turn to those sections (don't forget the pocket parts) and read them. If a member of the Board other than a public member dies or retires, how is the vacancy filled?
6. Does the code section address the issue of deaf members?
7. Is there anything in subsection (a)(1)(B) that suggests your inquiry might not be finished?

Answers

1. In the General Index to either annotated code, *U.S.C.A* or *U.S.C.S.*
2. Try the most specific: Gallaudet University.
3. Using *U.S.C.A.*, the first of the many entries says, "Text of Act, 20 U.S.C. § 4301, et seq." Using *U.S.C.S.*, the subheading Board of Trustees says, "§ 4303…"
4. Section 4303(a) and (b) address the composition and powers of the Board.
5. By vote of the remaining members of the Board of Trustees.
6. No.
7. Yes, subsection (a)(1)(B) provides that, of the 18 non-public members, "one of whom shall be elected pursuant to the Regulations of the Board of Trustees …." We will need to read the regulations to see whether the Board's own rules require at least one deaf member. If they don't, it might be useful for the students to know how regulations are proposed and passed, in case they want to press for a rule requiring at least one deaf member.

Library Exercise: Using Annotated Code Index to Find a Federal Statutory Scheme

You are on a research team working on a Native American reservation. One of the elementary school teachers has asked you whether a traditional children's game played with cards and sticks (where pennies are won and lost) would be considered illegal gambling. He is worried about a law called something like the "Indian Gambling Regulation Act." You have gone to the library and are looking for the Act by using the Popular Name Table in the United States Codes.

Questions

1. Where in *United States Code Annotated (U.S.C.A.)* and *United States Code Service (U.S.C.S.)* is the Popular Name Index?

2. Using what the teacher told you about the name of the statute, what do you find in the Popular Name Table?

3. There are five notations under the Indian Gaming Regulation Act, showing that Congress established the Act in 1988 and amended it four times (in 1991, 1992 and twice in 1997). Where in the U.S. Code can the Act be found?

4. You are looking for a "statutory scheme," which will probably involve a group of Code sections. Title 25 U.S.C. §§ 2701–2721 looks like the most likely candidate. Check Title 18 U.S.C. §§ 1166 and 1168 just in case. What is the subject matter of the Title 18 statutes? (Remember to check the pocket part.)

5. Now turn to Title 25 §§ 2701–2721. At the beginning of the scheme, in a part entitled "Chapter 29–Indian Gaming Regulations," is a Table of Contents. Look through the Table of Contents to find the section that will define different gaming activities.

6. Read § 2703. In what category (I, II or III) would the children's game most likely fall?

7. Go back to the Table of Contents and look for an entry regarding the regulation of Class I gaming. Do you find one?

8. Read § 2710(a). What sovereign (the federal, state or Native American government) regulates Class I gaming?

9. How will you answer the teacher's question?

Answers

1. In the *U.S.C.A.*, it is in the last volume of the soft-backed multi-volume General Index, after Z. In the *U.S.C.S.*, it is in one of the books of tables at the end of the set.

2. There is an entry for "Indian Gaming Regulatory Act."

3. In Title 18 U.S.C. § 1166–1168; and in Title 25 §§ 2701–2721.

4. Title 18 U.S.C. § 1166 deals with the application of State gambling laws to gaming activities on Native American reservations except those activities covered by the Indian Gaming Regulatory Act. Section 1168 describes the punishment for stealing from a gaming establishment licensed by the National Indian Gaming Commission.

5. Section 2703 is entitled "Definitions."

6. Section 2703(6) defines "Class I gaming" as including, among other activities, social games for prizes of minimal value. The teacher's game would fit within this definition. The 2003 pocket part has no relevant updates.

7. Yes, § 2710(a) deals with "Exclusive jurisdiction of Class I and Class II gaming activity."

8. The section states that Class I gaming on Native American lands is within the exclusive jurisdiction of the Indian tribes and is not subject to the provisions of the Indian Gaming Regulation Act.

9. As long as the game remains a social one played for minimal prizes, it will not be considered "gambling," and the teacher need not apply for permission from the National Indian Gaming Commission.

The basic Civil Rights Act, of which these various statutes form a part, was originally passed by Congress in 1964. Both the original statutes, and some that were added later, have since been amended from time to time. The statutes together constitute a statutory scheme, passed by a number of different sessions of Congress.

The part of the Civil Rights Act of 1964 that deals with employment discrimination is commonly known as Title VII. You may hear it said that somebody has filed a Title VII complaint about a discriminatory employment practice.

In fact, Title VII is itself a collection of statutes and can be termed a statutory scheme in its own right. If you believe you have been discriminated against and want to read the law, you will need to read the separate statutes that cover (1) what must be alleged in the complaint, (2) what defenses are available to the employer, (3) what kinds of remedies the court is authorized to grant, (4) whether attorneys' fees should be paid, and so on.

Using the Pocket Part to Get the Latest Version

Federal statutes often are amended or replaced by subsequent sessions of Congress. Indeed, many laws are totally changed by amendment and deletion in just a few years. This continuous change has required a method for keeping hardcover federal annotated codes up-to-date. The primary method for doing this, in virtually universal use for all collections of annotated statutes, both state and federal, is called the "pocket part system."

Pocket parts are paper supplements that fit inside each hardcover volume, usually at the back. They are published once a year and contain any statutory changes occurring in the interim. When the pocket parts get too bulky because of legislative changes, either a new hardcover volume is published that incorporates all of the changes since the last hardcover volume was published, or a separate paperback volume is published that sits on the shelf next to the hardcover book.

Always check the pocket part to see if a statute you're reading has been amended or repealed. If you don't, you may find that the statute you discovered in the hardcover volume has long since been amended or even repealed.

⚠ If the book you are using does not have a pocket part or a separate paperback pamphlet next to the hardcover volume on the bookshelf, and the book was not published in the year you are doing your research, inform the law librarian and ask if there is a current pocket part available. Never rely on out-of-date codes when doing statutory research unless you know that the statute being sought has not been amended since the publication of the book.

The pocket parts for *U.S.C.A.* reprint the sections of any statutes in the hardcover version that have been amended. Sections of the statute that have not been amended are not reproduced in the pocket part; instead, you are referred to the hardcover volume for the text. The example set out below first shows the portion of the statute as found in the hardcover volume and then shows how amendments appear in the pocket part. Note how the pocket part refers the reader back to the hardcover volume for sections that have not been changed.

The United States Code Service (U.S.C.S.) handles its pocket part in exactly the same way.

⚠ When you know the approximate date a statute was passed, you should first check the publication date of the hardcover volume. If this date is prior to your statute, then go right to the pocket part. In fact, many researchers prefer to start with the pocket part and then work backwards to the hardcover. Either way is fine so long as you never, ever, forget to check the pocket part.

⚠ Pocket parts are published only once a year. If you suspect that a statute was passed or amended recently enough to not be included in the current pocket part, use the techniques discussed below.

Using the Internet to Find a Federal Statute

Here we'll show you how to find a federal statute on the Internet. As we point out in this chapter, the federal statutes have been codified in a collection called the United States Code. The full text of the United States Code is available on the World Wide Web. This Internet exercise demonstrates two ways to find a federal statute—by doing a key word search or by browsing the statutes by subject matter headings until you find a relevant statute.

Internet Exercise: Finding a Federal Statute on the Internet

You are a computer engineer. Although you landed a high-paying job right out of college, you also unfortunately engaged in a high-spending lifestyle and now find yourself deep in debt and contemplating bankruptcy. In addition to your credit card debts and debts owed for medical and legal services (you've been divorced twice), you also owe $35,000 on student loans.

You've decided that filing for bankruptcy only makes sense if you can get out from under those loans, but you've heard that student loans are hard to get rid of in bankruptcy. It's time to read the law for yourself. After reading Chapter 4, you learn that bankruptcy is mostly a matter of federal law. You'll need a website that has the federal bankruptcy statutes.

We began our search using the Cornell Legal Information Institute, one of our favorite sites for legal research.

The Cornell Legal Information Institute (LII) offers a great site for searching the U.S. Code:

Go to www.law.cornell.edu.

- Place your mouse pointer on the "Constitutions and Codes" button on the left. This produces a pop up menu that lists codes and constitutions for various jurisdictions.

- Select the U.S. Codes link. This takes you to the main search page.
- Decide how you want to conduct your search.

As shown on the right side of the page, "Ways to Access Material," there are a number of ways to search for the statute, including:

- By key word search (search engine);
- By table of contents of the various titles in the U.S. Code (which can be browsed for specific statutes);
- By use of a form for entering statutory citations if you happen to have them; and
- By popular names of statutes, such as the "Bankruptcy Anti-Abuse and Consumer Protection Act."

Although it's possible to search the entire code by key word, this will likely provide a lot of irrelevant material. It's far more efficient to use the Table of Contents feature to first determine the U.S. code title in which the statute is likely included and then use the key word search for that specific title.

How to Find a Recent or Pending Federal Statute Online

Previous editions of this book provided extensive information about researching recent or pending federal statutes in the law library. Prior to the Internet, such searching invariably required hardcopy materials. Now, however, a website maintained by the Library of Congress called Thomas (after Thomas Jefferson) makes it so easy to find recent or pending federal legislation that we have dropped the hardcopy information and focus exclusively on the use of Thomas (http://thomas.loc.gov).

On the Thomas home page, top and center, you see a box with the heading "Legislation in Current Congress" where you can search for a pending bill by:

- sponsor (the senator or congressperson responsible for introducing the bill);
- a word or phrase contained in the bill; or
- the bill number.

Above the current legislation box you can click the "Explore New Features" link and also search current legislation by topic/subtopic and by use of a drop-down list for congresspersons and senators.

The list your search produces briefly describes the bill and its current status (in committee, passed from the Senate to the House, Engrossed, Enrolled, and so on).

If you want to search for a previous bill that has recently become law, you would take these steps:

- click the "Find More Legislation" box;
- enter a bill number if you know it, or key words if you don't;
- check the number of the last couple of congresses (you can check for a bill introduced back in 1991-1992 if you wish);
- check the box for enrolled bills sent to the president (because only enrolled bills can go on to become law); and
- click Search.

You will be presented with a list of bills that meet your search criteria.

Thomas allows a number of other searches for both current and previous legislation, such as Committee Reports (which help you interpret the bill), Congressional Record entries related to the bill, and searches by Public Law Number.

At the bottom of the box at the left-hand screen, the help link will provide excellent guidance on how to use this site. We are confident that once you become familiar with Thomas, you will never want to go back to the hardcopy method of researching previous or pending federal legislation.

Now that you've had a brief introduction to Thomas, here's a word of advice. As we've shown, there are many ways to crack the congressional legislative database. And the site is being constantly upgraded and improved. If you find a variance between our example and the Thomas you encounter, it's because nothing on the Web stays the same way for very long. See Chapter 13 for more on the dynamic nature of the Internet.

Finding Out-of-Date Federal Statutes in the Law Library

If you are looking for a specific statute that has been amended or deleted and no longer appears in the United States Code, you can find it in two publications:

- the *Statutes at Large*, and
- the *U.S. Code Congressional and Administrative News*.

The *Statutes at Large* series contains statutes organized by their public law numbers instead of their federal code citations. The *U.S. Code Congressional and Administrative News* publication also carries statutes by their public law

number, but is annotated and generally an easier resource to use.

For example, suppose a significant income tax reform bill wins passage in 1992 and is signed by the president. If a new volume of the *United States Code* is published in 1993, the laws for the tax years before passage of the tax reform measure will no longer appear in the code. The annotated codes show the statutes as they currently stand.

If, however, the IRS decides to audit you in 1993 and a dispute arises over your tax return for 1991, you may want to locate the law in effect for that tax year, even though it no longer currently applies. The statutes at large permit you to do this.

First, examine the current version of the statute. Directly beneath it, in parentheses, are listed the citations to every public law that affected the statute. You can use these citations to reconstruct the statutory language that was in effect during the period you are interested in. Here is how.

Assume that in 1993 you want to know what the law on a particular point was in tax year 1991. Your research in the *United States Code* shows you that the latest amendment occurred in 1992. The citation for this amendment is shown as Pub. L. No. 107-678. The next most recent amendment occurred in 1990. The citation for that amendment is Pub. L. No. 104-1289. That is the statute you would want to find to see what the law was before the most recent amendment. To find Pub. L. No. 104-1289 in *Statutes at Large* or the *U.S. Code Congressional and Administrative News*, find the volume that contains the statutes for the 104th Congress (this information appears on the spine), turn to where Pub. L. No. 104-1289 appears—it will be in numerical order within the volume—and *voila*, you have your statute.

Library Exercise: Finding Statutes by Pub. L. No.

This exercise asks you to use the *U.S. Code Congressional and Administrative News* to find a statute known only by its Public Law number. Additional research exercises that include these and other skills are in Chapter 11.

Question

You are researching federal disaster assistance acts, and find a reference to Pub. L. No. 101-82. Using *U.S. Code Congressional and Administrative News* only, find the statute and any clues as to where to find its legislative history.

Answer

The 101 means the statute was passed by the 101st Congress. On the spine of Volume 1 of 101st Congress 1st session 1989, it says Laws Pub. L. No. 101–1 to 101–189.

The statutes are more or less in order by their public law number, and Public Law No. 101-82 is found on page 103 Stat. 564 (Stat. = *Statutes at Large*). The title is Disaster Assistance Act of 1989. Right under the title it says "For Legislative History of Act, see p. 514."

Finding State Statutes in the Law Library and on the Internet

Many of the principles that apply to researching federal statutes can be used when dealing with state statutes. However, there are some differences in federal and state legislative processes and in the resources that you use to find and interpret state statutes.

Overview of Annotated Collections of State Statutes

State statutes are organized by subject and published in two formats:

- annotated volumes that contain explanatory information about each statute and references to court decisions that have interpreted the statutes; and
- non-annotated volumes, which contain only the text of the statutes.

Intensive legal research almost always is done with the annotated volumes. However, many people, lawyers and non-lawyers alike, use the non-annotated version of certain statutes (say, the criminal statutes, or those relating to probate) as a handy desk reference.

Some states organize their statutes into codes according to subject. California, for example, has a separate code for each legal area—the Penal Code for criminal statutes, the Education Code for education statutes, and so on. New York organizes its statutes in a similar fashion, except that instead of the word "code," the word "law" is used. In New York you find education statutes in the volume called Education Law, the criminal statutes in the volumes labeled Penal Law, and so on.

In a number of other states, statutes are collected into annotated volumes organized by title number or by "chapter." In Vermont, for instance, the *Vermont Statutes Annotated (Vt. Stat. Ann.)* consists of Title 1 through Title 33, each Title covering a particular subject matter area.

Finally, in still other states, the statutes are simply numbered sequentially without regard to their subject matter and published in collections with such names as *Massachusetts General Laws Annotated (Mass. Gen. Laws Ann.), Michigan Compiled Laws Annotated (Mich. Comp. Laws Ann.)* and *Maine Revised Statutes Annotated (Me. Rev. Stat. Ann.).*

Using State Statute Indexes

Many collections of state statutes have indexes for each subject (that is, for each title, code or chapter) and for the collection of laws as a whole. In California, a separate index called *Larmac*, published by Lexis Publishing, also provides a detailed subject index to California statutes.

If your state's statutes are found in two or more publications, feel free to use either index. For example, the California statutes are published both in *West's Annotated Codes* and in *Deering's Annotated Codes* (Lexis Publishing). If you can't find what you're looking for in the West index, use the Deering index. Since both publications index the same statutes and use the same citations, a citation you find in the Deering index can be looked up in the West code,

and vice versa. (For assistance in using legal indexes, see Chapter 4.)

Understanding State Statutory Citations

Citations to state statutes normally refer to the title (or volume) and section numbers. The three examples shown below are typical.

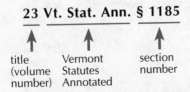
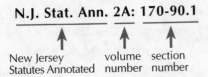
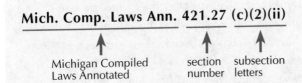

Sample State Statute Citations

In the states that have codes, like New York and California, citations look like those shown below.

Sample California and New York Citations

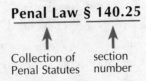

Using Citations to Find Statutes

To read a particular statute, first locate the volumes containing your state's statutes. Then find the correct volume or title (the first number of the citation). Finally, turn to the correct section number. Once you have read the statute, make sure you have the current version. We tell you how to do this in "Using Pocket Parts to Get the Latest Version," below.

Reading All Relevant Statutes

State statutes are organized in clumps called "statutory schemes." If you are interested in a particular area of the law (small claims court, for example) be sure to read all relevant statutes on that subject. You may find that you can sue for up to $2,000 in one statute and then learn in another one that a lower limit has been set for cases involving evictions.

Using Pocket Parts to Get the Latest Version

In many states, legislatures have a severe case of hyperactivity, continually passing new statutes and amending old ones. It is very important to get the very latest version of the statute you are interested in.

Hardcover volumes of state statutes should have current "pocket parts," paper supplements that fit inside the back cover of each hardbound volume. These update the hardcover portion on an annual basis (unless the hardcover volume you are using has just been published or the legislature only meets every other year). Always check the pocket part to see if a statute you're reading has been amended or repealed. If the pocket part is not current (say you are using the book in 2008 and the pocket part says 2006), ask the law librarian if there is a newer version.

There are two ways that pocket parts show updates. In most states, the part of the statute that has been amended is shown in the pocket part, with additions underlined and deletions marked by asterisks. For example, a California statute in its original form as it appeared in the hardcover volume, and the amended version as it appeared in the pocket part, are both shown below. As you can see, words that have been added to the statute are underlined and words that have been taken out are represented by asterisks.

---

§ 1942.   Repairs by lessee; rent deduction; limit

If within a reasonable time after notice to the lessor, of dilapidations which he ought to repair, he neglects to do so, the lessee may repair the same himself, where the cost of such repairs do not require an expenditure greater than one month's rent of the premises, and deduct the expenses of such repairs from the rent, or the lessee may vacate the premises, in which case he shall be discharged from further payment of rent, or performance of other conditions. (Enacted 1872. As amended Code Am.1873–74, c. 612, p. 246, § 206.)

Main Volume Statute

---

§ 1942. Repairs by tenant; rent deduction or vacation of premises; presumption; limit; nonavailability of remedy; additional remedy

(a) If within a reasonable time after <u>written or oral</u> notice to the * * * <u>landlord or his agent, as defined in subdivision (a) of Section 1962,</u> of dilapidations <u>rendering the premises untenantable</u> which * * * <u>the landlord</u> ought to repair, * * * <u>the landlord</u> neglects to do so, the * * * <u>tenant</u> may repair the same himself where the cost of such repairs does not require an expenditure * * * <u>more</u> than one month's rent of the premises and deduct the expenses of such repairs from the rent <u>when due,</u> or the * * * <u>tenant</u> may vacate the premises, in which case * * * <u>the tenant</u> shall be discharged from further payment of rent, or performance of other conditions <u>as of the date of vacating the premises.</u>

Pocket Part Statute

In some states, the pocket parts reprint the sections of any statutes that have been amended. Sections of the statute that have not been amended are not reproduced in the pocket part; instead, you are referred to the hardcover volume for the text. Note how the pocket part refers the reader back to the hardcover volume for sections that have not been changed.

Finding State Statutes and Legislation on the Internet

Every state now maintains its statutes on the Internet. Sometimes the state itself runs the site, while in other states the job may be contracted out. The websites vary in their format, but almost all of them allow you to search for statutes by topic, by key word searches and by specific code numbers. If you do a lot of searching of your state's legislation, you'll undoubtedly become familiar with where that information is located. However, if you search now and then, you may forget where to go. If that happens, your best bet is to visit Nolo's site (www.nolo.com) and use the Nolo legal research tools to locate your state's legislative materials (see the following exercise). You also can start your research with the Findlaw state law resources site (www.findlaw.com/casecode/#statelaw). Simply click your state and you will be taken to a page with links to your state's constitution and statutes. Finally, the Cornell Legal Information Institute [www.law.cornell.edu] is another incredibly helpful site that also offers links to state resources. It lets you search for statutes by topic of interest as well as by popular name. The topic of interest feature is under the "Law by Source or Jurisdiction" section of the Cornell website. See www.law.cornell.edu/states/listing.html.

The Cornell LII Index Is Not Exhaustive. Sometimes statutes within a particular category are found in different parts of a code and even in different codes. The LII topical index may get you to some of the statutes you seek but may miss other relevant statutes. Make sure you browse the statutes surrounding the particular statute pulled up in this topical search. Also, when possible, do a key word search of the entire code to pull up any additional statutes appearing in other parts.

Be aware that if you do a similar search for a state other than the one we use in our Exercise, the websites you encounter may operate a little differently than the ones we visited. But you'll be well prepared after you've gone through our example, since it teaches you all you need to know to navigate slightly different waters.

Internet Exercise: Finding a State Statute on the Internet

You live in a rural Minnesota town and depend on your car to drive to your job in St. Paul. You are the divorced father of three children and are obligated to pay child support. Two years ago you had a medical emergency and couldn't meet your support obligations for six months.

Your ex recently served you with a written demand to pay the arrearage. The demand letter warns you that, if you don't pay in full, your ex may cause your driver's license to be suspended until you do. You want to find the statute that authorizes a license suspension for failure to pay back child support.

1. **Start your research** at Nolo.com. Go to the Nolo home page [www.nolo.com]. In the search box at the top right of the page, enter "child support." On the drop-down menu below the search box, choose Search Entire Site. Then choose Child Support Resource Center, and scroll down to Tools and Resources. Choose Research: State Law. Click on Minnesota. This produces the home page for Minnesota Statutes, Session Laws and Rules.

2. **Under the Minnesota Statutes** grouping, you'll see five options for searching:
   - Table of contents
   - Index
   - Search by key words or phrases
   - Retrieve a section, and
   - Retrieve an entire chapter.

   Let's use the Search by key words or phrases link. That takes you to a search template.

3. **Type "child support"** into the text box. Use the drop-down menu to specify "contains the phrase." Our first search query uses a phrase rather than individual key words because child support is a unitary concept, whereas the words child and support are two different concepts that would bring in a lot of irrelevant documents.

4. **When you hit the search button,** you'll get a long list of statute sections dealing with child support. By scrolling down the list (and advancing to the next page), you find an entry for suspension of a driver's license for failure to pay child support. Click on the entry (171.186), and you'll pull up the statute you are searching for.

5. **There is a downside** to using a simple, broad key word search as we did in Step 3: While it may be the first (and maybe the only) way you think to ask for the information you want, it will almost always yield a long string of answers, which you'll have to wade through to hopefully find your answer. To avoid being buried with results, narrow your search.

6. **To narrow the search** in our exercise, you could enter more words in the search box and specify that the documents retrieved by the computer must contain all of them (in other words, ask for all the words, not a phrase). When we added the phrase "Driver's License" to the phrase "child support," we got four entries, including the statute we were aiming for.

   By adding the extra words to your search, you have narrowed it considerably. But beware—any time you narrow your search, you may get too narrow and miss the statute being sought.

Finding Recently-Enacted or Pending State Statutes

Recently-Enacted State Legislation

If your research involves a statute that is newly passed, repealed or amended, the changes may not yet be reflected in the pocket parts, which come out only once a year. Fortunately, most states have arranged for newly-passed statutes to be published prior to their inclusion in the pocket parts. These legislative update publications have different names in different states. Some examples are *McKinney's Session Law News of New York*, *Vernon's Texas Session Law Services* and *Washington Legislative Services*.

Whatever their names, these publications are organized in pretty much the same way, and there are several ways to get to the statutes you seek. First, the statutes appear in numerical order according to the number given them by the state legislature. In many states, statutes appear according to their "chapter" number. (See the example below.) In others they are listed by "session law" number. If you already know which number statute you're looking for, you can get to it directly.

Another way to use the advance legislative service is by the annotated code or collection citation. If you know, for example, that Labor Code § 560.5 has been amended, a table at the front or back of each legislative service volume will convert your "code" citation to the appropriate chapter number.

Finally, all advance legislative services have a detailed alphabetical table of contents in the front and a cumulative subject index in the back. The examples below show the subject index of a Texas advance legislative service for 1991.

Advance legislative update services are usually located next to the annotated state statutes. If you can't find them, ask the law librarian.

How to Find Pending State Legislation on the Internet

In most states, you can use the Internet to read the text of pending state legislation and check on its status. (See the Internet exercise, Finding Pending State Legislation.)

Summing Up

How to Use the Law Library to Find a State Statute or Amendment Passed Within the Past Year

✔ If you have the annotated code citation for the statute, check the pocket part of your state's annotated code.

✔ If the new statute or amendment is not in the pocket part, go to the most recent volume of the advance legislative service for your state's annotated code.

✔ If you already have the chapter or session law number, look it up starting with the most recent advance legislative service volume. If the statute is not there, work backwards through all volumes dated subsequent to the time the statute or amendment was passed.

✔ If you don't know the chapter or session law number, find the table that converts the annotated code citations into chapter or session law numbers. Then look up that number in the advance legislative service.

✔ If you don't have a citation to the statute or amendment, check the date on any pocket part in your state's annotated code. If the date is after the date the statute or amendment was passed, use the pocket part to the subject index for your state's annotated code.

✔ If the date on the pocket part is earlier than the date the statute or amendment was passed, use the cumulative subject index for the most recent advance legislative service update volume.

Internet Exercise: Finding Pending State Legislation

You live in Missouri and applied for life insurance in November 2000. To your dismay you were refused on account of credit problems you had in 1999. The evening news has just run a segment announcing that Missouri State Senator Luetkenhaus introduced a bill that might affect you. It would require the insurer to inform the applicant if credit history will be used as an underwriting factor. You'd like to read the bill.

1. **An excellent place to begin** looking for pending state legislation is the FindLaw website, which is a catalog of legal resources on the Web. Enter FindLaw's URL in your browser's address box [www.findlaw.com].

2. **On this page, FindLaw offers** a number of links to legal resources. You could start with Legal Subjects, where you might find interesting material about the regulation of insurance companies. But remember that your goal is to read the verbatim text of a newly introduced Missouri bill. To do that, you will want to visit Missouri's legislative site. The most direct way to get there is to click on the "U.S. Law: ... States" link on the Findlaw home page, under the "For Legal Professionals" heading. This will take you to a page that lists all the states. Select Missouri.

3. **Like other FindLaw pages,** the one you see now offers several options as to where to go next. As we explained in Chapter 5, primary materials are rules issued by the government in statutes (called codes when they are organized by subject), court cases and administrative agencies. Secondary sources are books written about the law. Even if you don't remember the lessons of Chapter 5, FindLaw gives you a hint: the primary materials link has the word "codes" after it.

4. **Here again, you are given** a choice of many paths to Missouri legal information. In the middle of the list you will see Bill Information. As you know from reading this chapter, bills are pending state legislation (legislation that has been introduced but has not yet become law). If you click on Bill Information, you will produce a screen that provides three ways to find pending legislation: you can do a key word search, bill number search or sponsor/co-sponsor search.

5. **Because you know the name** of the sponsor (Senator Luetkenhaus), you can enter his name in the search box, choose 2002 Basic in the year/criterion box and click on "Go." This will produce a results screen. You will need to scroll down to find a reference to the pending bill (HB 1502). Alternatively, you can locate this information by starting at the State of Missouri home page [www.state.mo.us]. Click the drop-down menu showing "Gov't Offices" and click "Legislative." Then choose Missouri House. That takes you to the Missouri House of Representatives home page where there is a search feature for House and Senate Bill Tracking. Choose "Past Session Information" from the list on the left, then 2002 Regular Session, then joint bills tracking search, choose 2002 Basic in the year/criterion box and type in Luetkenhaus; you will find a list of bills, including HB 1502. You can download an Adobe Acrobat version of the bill to read.

Pending State Legislation

As shown above, searching for pending state legislation is a piece of cake on the Internet. However, if for some reason you want to find hardcopy text of pending state legislation, here are some tips.

If you want to examine a piece of legislation that is currently before your state legislature, probably the best way is to call your local elected representative's office and ask for a copy of the bill. If you know what the bill concerns and, if possible, the legislator who is sponsoring it, you probably won't need to know the number of the bill. However, if you want to use your local law library (or your public library if it is large enough to carry state legislative materials), follow these steps:

- Determine the number of the bill—for example, Assembly Bill 27 or Senate Bill 538.
- If you don't know the bill's number, find out whether the legislature prints a subject index to current legislation. If so, use the index. If not, call your elected representative's office and ask for the number.

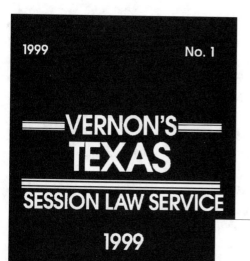

1999   **No. 1**

VERNON'S TEXAS

SESSION LAW SERVICE

1999

SEVENTY-SIXTH LEGISLATURE

**Regular Session
Chapters 1 to 61**

In This Issue

LAWS APPROVED TO May 10, 1999

Summary of current legislation, see Legislative
Highlights, page I.

Proposed Constitutional Amendments

Appendix—Court Rules

Tables and Index

WESTLAW Legislative Database: TX-LEGIS
See Preface for further information

INDEX

I-1

Vernon's Texas Session Law Service

- Ask the reference librarian whether your legislature publishes a daily or weekly journal summarizing current legislative activity. If it does, locate the listing for the bill by its number and determine its status. (For instance, is it still in committee, or has it passed both houses?) If there is no journal, ask your elected representative or the bill's sponsor to find out the bill's status.
- Find out whether your local law library receives copies of the bills (called "slip laws") as they are produced and amended. If so, locate the latest version of the bill and read it.

How to Read Statutes

Most legal research projects involve finding out what the law "is" in a particular circumstance. This usually involves finding a statute and then deciding how a court would interpret it given the facts in your situation. Courts consider it their responsibility to carry out the legislature's will as expressed in its statutes. If a statute is unclear—and many are—the court will try to figure out what the legislature intended. Only if the legislature exceeded its powers or intended something unconstitutional will courts ignore the dictates of a statute—and that doesn't happen very often.

Trying to determine what the legislature intended is often like trying to predict the roll of dice. Sometimes it seems that statutes are deliberately written to be incomprehensible. Certainly, many of them are almost impenetrable. One simple reason for this is that the lawyers who draft them have often not mastered basic English and disguise the fact by relying on "wherefores," "therefores," "pursuants," and so on.

Also, and perhaps more important, from the time a proposed statute is drafted until it emerges from the legislature in final form, legislators compromise, delete words and add more words in an attempt to get enough votes to pass the bill. What may have begun as straightforward and clear language often becomes so riddled with exceptions and conditions that the result presents serious difficulties to anyone who wants to understand what was intended. In the words of one frustrated judge:

I concur in the opinion of the majority because its construction of Code of Civil Procedure Section 660 seems plausible and hence probably correct, although— given the cosmic incomprehensibility of the section—one can never be absolutely sure.

It occurs to me that Section 660 illustrates poignantly the maxim so useful in statutory construction—that if the Legislature had known what it meant, it would have said so.

It seems to me shameful, however, that large sums of money should change hands depending upon one's view of what this dismal, opaque statute means.

(Bunton v. Arizona Pacific Tanklines, 141 Cal. App. 3d 210, 190 Cal. Rptr. 295 (1983).)

When searching for the meaning of a statutory provision, courts employ a number of rules of interpretation that have been developed over the years. These "rules" are often imprecise and sometimes contradictory, but if you are aware of them you should arrive at a more accurate interpretation than if you use only your common sense. Below we provide some guidelines that reflect the approach used by the courts for reading and understanding statutes.

Rule 1: Read the statute at least three times, then read it again.

Often a different and hopefully more accurate meaning will emerge from each reading. Never feel that somehow you are inadequate because despite a number of readings you aren't sure what a particular statute means. A great many lawsuits result from the fact that lawyers disagree about confusing statutory language.

Rule 2: Pay close attention to "ands" and "ors."

Many statutes have lots of "ands" and "ors" tucked into different clauses, and the thrust of the statute often depends on which clauses are joined by an "and" and which by an "or." When clauses are joined by an "or," it means that the conditions in at least one of the clauses must be present, but not in all. When clauses are joined by an "and," the conditions in all the clauses must be met.

Interpreting "Ands" and "Ors"

Consider the following provision taken from 42 *U.S.C.A.* § 416:

"An applicant who is the son or daughter of a fully or currently insured individual, but who is not (and is not deemed to be) the child of such insured individual under paragraph (2) of this subsection, shall nevertheless be deemed to be the child of such insured individual if:

"(A) in the case of an insured individual entitled to old-age insurance benefits (who was not, in the month preceding such entitlement, entitled to disability insurance benefits)—

"(i) such insured individual—

(I) has acknowledged in writing that the applicant is his or her son or daughter

(II) has been decreed by a court to be the mother or father of the applicant, **or**

(III) has been ordered by a court to contribute to the support of the applicant because the applicant is his or her son or daughter,

"**and** such acknowledgment, court decree, or court order was made not less than one year before such insured individual became entitled to old-age insurance benefits or attained retirement age (as defined in subsection (l) of this section), whichever is earlier…"

Interpretation: To be considered a child of an insured individual, a person must satisfy at least one of the three conditions under section (A)(i)—because of the use of the word "or"—and the condition must be met within one year of when the insured individual became entitled to old-age insurance benefits or attained retirement age, because of the "and."

Rule 3: Assume all words and punctuation in the statute have meaning.

Often, statutes seem to be internally inconsistent or redundant. Sometimes they are. However, courts presume that every word and comma in a statute means something, and you should do the same. If you're unsure about what a word or phrase means, look it up in a law dictionary or a multi-volume publication titled *Words and Phrases*.

Rule 4: Interpret a statute so that it is consistent with all other related statutes, if possible.

Sometimes it appears that a statute is totally inconsistent with other statutes in the same statutory scheme. It may be, but a judge who examines the statutes will make an attempt to reconcile the meanings so that no conflict exists. It is wise, therefore, to ask yourself whether any interpretation of the statute can be made that will make it consistent rather than inconsistent with other statutes.

Rule 5: Interpret criminal statutes strictly.

Over the centuries the courts have applied a doctrine called "strict interpretation" to the criminal law. This reflects the policy that no person should be held accountable for a crime without adequate notice that his behavior was criminal. The only way to provide this type of notice is to insist that criminal laws be interpreted literally. And the defendant must be afforded the benefit of any ambiguities in the language. For example, to convict somebody of "breaking and entering a building belonging to another with the intent to commit theft or a felony therein" (a common definition of burglary), a prosecutor has to prove each element of the crime—that the person broke and entered and intended to commit a felony inside.

Example: A young man in Vermont was charged with breaking and entering into the county courthouse, a felony. He had been found in the morning passed out under the judge's desk with some rare coins in his pocket that had been taken from the desk.

At his trial, the young man testified that he thought the courthouse was a church and that he simply broke in to get some sleep. However, once inside, he decided to look around and ended up stealing the coins. He didn't remember passing out. The trial judge (not the coin collector, but a more disinterested jurist) instructed the jury that unless they found beyond a reasonable doubt that the young man actually intended to commit a felony or the theft at the time he entered the courthouse, they could not convict him of breaking and entering. He was acquitted.

Rule 6: Interpret ambiguities in statutes in ways that seem to best further the purpose of the legislation.

Much legislation is designed to either protect the public from ills or to provide various benefits. When ambiguities exist in these types of statutes—commonly called social welfare legislation—the courts tend to interpret them so that the protection or benefit will be provided, rather than the other way around.

Example: A statute allows welfare recipients to "earn" up to $100 a month without losing any benefits. The purpose of the statute is to provide an incentive for those on welfare to find work. Tom's father gives him $100 a month to stop drinking. Tom reports this to the welfare department, which promptly reduces Tom's monthly grant by $100. Tom goes to court, arguing that he is "earning" the money by not drinking and is therefore entitled to the $100 exemption. The welfare department contends that since the statute was intended to stimulate employment, the term "earns" means income from employment. The welfare department's argument will probably win, since its interpretation is more consistent with the statute's underlying objective.

Rule 7: Interpret the statute so that it makes sense and does not lead to absurd or improbable results.

Courts are sometimes called on to interpret statutes that, if taken literally, would lead to a result that the legislature could not (in the court's opinion) have intended. In such an instance, a court will strain to interpret the statute so that it does make sense or lead to a logical result.

Example: A California statute literally imposed a $100 daily penalty on landlords who interfered with a tenant's utilities with an intent to evict the tenant. The California Supreme Court ruled that the legislature could not have intended this harsh result, and instead interpreted the statute as allowing a penalty of up to $100 per day.

This rule of interpretation is especially important for non-lawyers to understand. Lawyers are used to the inherent paradoxes and uncertainties in statutory interpretation (indeed, they create them). However, few things are harder for a layperson to take than when the judge rejects a literal interpretation of a statute because "the legislature couldn't have intended it." The moral? When reading a statute, ask whether your interpretation is grounded in common sense and in the way the law was probably intended to work.

Rule 8: Track down all cross-references to other statutes and sections.

People who draft statutes are very fond of including references to other statutes and sections of the same statute. When faced with such a statute, the human tendency is to ignore the cross-references and hope that they don't pertain to your situation. Our advice, quite simply, is to track down each and every cross-reference and make sure you understand how it relates to the main body of the statute you are analyzing. If you don't, you could overlook something crucial. An example of what we're talking about is shown below.

§703.520.   Making of Claim of Exemption.

(a) The claimant may make a claim of exemption by filing with the levying officer a claim of exemption together with a copy thereof. The claim shall be made within 10 days after the date the notice of levy on the property claimed to be exempt was served on the judgment debtor.

(b) The claim of exemption shall be executed under oath and shall include all of the following:

(1) The name of the claimant and the mailing address where service of a notice of opposition to the claim may be made upon the claimant.

(2) The name and last known address of the judgment debtor if the claimant is not the judgment debtor.

(3) A description of the property claimed to be exempt. If an exemption is claimed pursuant to Section 704.010 or 704.060, the claimant shall describe all other property of the same type (including exempt proceeds of property of the same type) owned by the judgment debtor alone or in combination with others on the date of levy and identify the property, whether or not levied upon. to which the exemption is to be applied. If an exemption is claimed pursuant to subdivision (b) of Section 704.100, the claimant shall state the nature and amount of all other property of the same type owned by the judgment debtor or the spouse of the judgment debtor alone or in combination with others on the date of levy.

(4) A financial statement if required by Section 703.530.

(5) A citation of the provision of this chapter or other statute upon which the claim is based.

(6) A statement of the facts necessary to support the claim. **Leg.H.** 1982 ch. 1364, operative July 1, 1983.

Ref.: Cal. Fms Pl. & Pr., "Attachment," "Executions and Enforcement (Pt I)," "Homesteads," "Judgments."

Statute Containing Cross-References

The Importance of Cases That Interpret Statutes

It would be nice if research into the meaning of statutes began and ended with reading the statutes themselves. Unfortunately, statutes are subject to varying interpretations no matter how clearly they are worded or how closely they are studied. Lawyers are paid large sums of money to argue that the word "may" really means "shall," and vice versa. The ability of lawyers to interpret the meanings of common words in new (and often absurd) ways is sometimes breathtaking and often bizarre.

For example, a Nolo author was receiving more than his share of parking tickets as a result of a San Mateo, California, ordinance banning overnight parking and his close friendship with a San Mateo resident, whose many wonderful attributes didn't include a driveway. Afraid that the tickets he inevitably received would eventually sour his romance, the author went to court to overturn the ordinance. He argued that the state statute authorizing cities to ban overnight parking on "certain city streets" didn't mean a city could ban such parking on "all" streets, which was how San Mateo interpreted it when it passed the ordinance. Briefs were written and arguments held on the question of whether "certain" could be read to mean "all" or had to mean "less than all." The judges hearing the case on appeal eventually concluded that certain meant "less than all," so the author's romance was saved.

As this story illustrates, the judiciary is charged with the task of interpreting statutes when a dispute over their meaning is presented in a lawsuit. Court interpretations of statutes are every bit as much a part of the statute as the words themselves.

For example, the California statute mentioned earlier provided that landlords were liable to tenants in the amount of $100 for each day the utilities were shut off by the landlord for the purpose of evicting the tenants. When a landlord appealed a judgment against him under this statute, the California Supreme Court decided that it would be unconstitutional to penalize a landlord $100 per day regardless of circumstances (*Hale v. Morgan*, 22 Cal. 3d 388, 149 Cal. Rptr. 375, 584 P.2d 512 (1978)). The Court interpreted the statute to allow a penalty of up to $100 per day, depending on circumstances. Immediately after this court decision, the law of utility shutoffs in California could only be determined by reading the statute and the court case together. The California legislature later amended the statute to comply with the Court's ruling.

There are two primary ways to find out what the courts have had to say about a particular statute:

- case notes that accompany the statutes in annotated codes, and
- a series of books called *Shepard's Citations for Statutes.*

These methods (and others) are covered in Chapter 9.

What *Shepard's Citations* for Statutes Does

Shepard's Citations for Statutes tells you each time a case has mentioned a particular statute and provides a reference (citation) to the case. In addition, *Shepard's* provides references to amendments that have been made to the statute and instances when attorney general opinions and law review articles have mentioned the statute. Serious statute researchers will want to learn how to use this resource.

Using *Words and Phrases* to Interpret Statutes

"When I use a word," Humpty Dumpty said, in a rather scornful tone, "it means just what I choose it to mean—no more, no less." "The question is," said Alice, "whether you can make words mean so many different things." "The question is," said Humpty Dumpty, "which is to be master—that's all."
—*Alice in Wonderland,* Lewis Carroll

In the Land of the Law, judges are master. To properly interpret a statute, you usually need to know how courts have interpreted one or more of the specialized words and phrases it contains. One tool to help you do this is a multi-volume set called *Words and Phrases* (West Group). It contains one-sentence interpretations of common words and phrases that have been pulled from cases and organized alphabetically. This publication allows you to find out whether courts have interpreted or used any particular word or phrase you are interested in and, if so, how.

In a real sense, *Words and Phrases* is a kind of dictionary that offers contextual definitions instead of the abstract and disconnected entries found in most law dictionaries. Below is part of the *Words and Phrases* entry for "Landlord and Tenant."

As with other hardbound legal resources, don't forget to check the pocket part in the back of each book for the newest entries.

LANDLORD AND TENANT

In general—p. 334
Bailor and bailee—p. 336
Easements—p. 336
Estate for years—p. 336
Farming contracts—p. 336
Innkeeper and guest—p. 338
Joint enterprise—p. 339
Lease by life tenant—p. 339
Lessor and lessee synonymous—p. 339
Locker rooms—p. 339
Lodging house keeper and lodger distinguished—p. 339
Master and servant—p. 339
Occupancy required by employer—p. 340
Oil and gas lease—p. 340
Possession in subordination to another—p. 340
Principal and agent—p. 341
Proprietors and lodgers—p. 341
Purchaser and sub-tenant—p. 341
Rent—p. 341
Safe deposit box—p. 342
Sale—p. 342
Tenancy at will—p. 343
Vender and purchaser—p. 343

In general

The relation of "landlord and tenant" depends upon agreement. Estes v. Gatliff, 163 S.W.2d 273, 275, 291 Ky. 93.

A "landlord and tenant relationship" will be implied from occupancy of premises with owner's consent. Crawford v. Jerry, 11 A.2d 210, 211, 111 Vt. 120.

The relation of "landlord and tenant" arises only where one in possession of land recognizes another as his landlord. Hoffmann v. Chapman, Tex.Civ.App., 170 S.W.2d 496, 498.

A contract establishing "landlord and tenant relationship" does not include principal and agent or master and servant relationships. Butler v. Maney, 200 So. 226, 228, 146 Fla. 33.

The relation of "landlord and tenant" may arise by express or implied contract and on slight evidence. Delay v. Douglas, Mo. App., 164 S.W.2d 154, 156.

Words and Phrases

Library Exercise: Using *Words and Phrases*

Find the dark blue multi-volume set of West's *Words and Phrases.*

Questions

1a. In which book of the set would you look to find a definition of USURER?

1b. There are two definitions under Usurer, from two different courts: Arkansas and New York. By what standard does each state measure usury?

2a. Now use the pocket part to find a more recent definition of USURIOUS from a court in Florida. What are the names of the two cases?

2b. According to the definition, for a transaction to be considered usurious under Florida law, is it enough that the interest exceeds the rate allowed by law?

Answers

1a. In volume 43A ("Unless" to "Vale"), on page 426.

1b. In the Arkansas case, the court says that a usurer is one who lends money at a rate greater than the limit set by law. In the New York case, a usurer is defined as one who lends money at an *excessive or inordinate rate*. The Arkansas case uses an objective standard, whereas the New York case uses a subjective one.

2a. *In re Tammey Jewels, Inc.,* Bankruptcy M.D. Fla., 116 B.R. 290, 292; and *Kraft v. Mason,* 688 So. 2d 679, 684 (1996).

2b. No, several conditions must be met: there must be an express or implied loan, an understanding between the parties that the loan is to be repaid, and a corrupt intent to charge more than the legal rate of interest. The *Kraft* case states that, in order to be guilty of usury, the lender must be aware of the true rate of interest and expect to get paid. The lender in *Kraft* was found not to have usurious intent because she was unsophisticated, didn't realize the true rate of interest and knew her chance of getting repaid was speculative since it depended on the borrower winning a lawsuit.

While *Words and Phrases* can be helpful in understanding statutory language, it isn't a substitute for a court's interpretation of the specific statute with which you are concerned. If the statute has been interpreted by a court, that interpretation will prevail over another court's interpretation of the same language in a different statute under different facts.

Using Attorney General Opinions to Interpret Statutes

Attorneys general, the highest legal officers in government, are often asked by government agencies to interpret the meaning of statutes. When they do, it is often in the form of a written opinion. These attorney general opinions are not binding on the courts, but they have influence, especially when there is no precedent to the contrary. And they can be very helpful in deciphering an otherwise hopelessly complicated statute.

Finding Attorney General Opinions

Attorney general opinions are collected in publications usually called something like *Opinions of the Attorney General of the State of …* A separate set exists for each state and for the federal government. If a statute is the subject of an attorney general's opinion, the citation to the opinion citing the statute will appear after the case citations in *Shepard's Citations for Statutes.* (See Chapter 9 for how to use this valuable tool.) Also, see later in this chapter for an example of how to use the Internet to find state attorney general opinions.

Finding Attorney General Opinions on the Internet

Many states have put their attorney general opinions up on the Internet. You can find them by visiting the National Association of Attorneys General (NAAG) website [www.naag.org]. This site provides links to each state

attorney general's website, as well as bios and phone numbers.

Findlaw is also a good starting place for finding Attorney General Opinions. See the Internet Exercise: Finding an Attorney General Opinion. You can also link to your state AG's office from your individual state's website. The basic URL for all states is www.state.<your state's postal code abbreviation>.us; for example, California's website is at www.state.ca.us.

The exercise shown below walks you through finding an attorney general's opinion on FindLaw. We use Texas as an example, but the techniques outlined here would apply to any other state, with minor variations.

Internet Exercise: Finding an Attorney General Opinion

You are moving to Texas and would like to open a trademark search service. Your business would search the database maintained by the Patent and Trademark Office for possible conflicts between your customers' proposed mark and existing marks that have already been federally registered. You've heard that Texas law is very strict about non-lawyers engaging in any activity that might be considered the practice of law, so to play it safe you decide to talk to a lawyer before starting your new business.

The lawyer gives you some general information about the Texas law. However, much to your surprise, she won't advise you as to whether your business would be legal in Texas. Why? Because of a recent opinion by the Texas Attorney General that says, in effect, that only the courts are qualified to decide whether an activity constitutes the practice of law; and that no attorney can say in advance how the courts would rule in a particular case. Flabbergasted, you ask the lawyer where you can find this opinion. The lawyer doesn't know, but suggests that you look on the Internet.

For this example, begin your search with FindLaw and enter FindLaw's address in your browser [www.findlaw.com].

Because you are searching for a specific document issued by the Texas Attorney General, you will get the best results by choosing the U.S. State Resources link under Search Cases and Codes (under the "Legal Professional" tab).

Browse by Jurisdiction (you are looking for Texas), then choose Attorney General Opinions. This takes you to the home page of the Texas Attorney General. Move your cursor over Opinions (on the left) and choose Search Opinions.

Once you choose "Search Opinions," enter the phrase "unauthorized practice of law" in the box. You will get a list of opinions that are relevant to your search request. By opening and briefly examining each opinion, you will find the "Morales" opinion, which states that the attorney general is unable to give an opinion because only the courts have authority to define what constitutes the unauthorized practice of law.

Using Legislative History to Interpret Statutes

You may be uncertain about the meaning of a statute no matter how much you study it. For instance, many statutes provide that certain government employees are entitled to an administrative hearing if they lose their jobs. What such statutes often don't say is whether the hearing must be provided before the discharge or after it.

If you are unable to find a court decision on the question, how should you proceed? One common way (and in many cases the only way) is to find out what the legislators intended at the time they passed the statute. Their intent can be inferred from legislative committee reports, hearings and floor debates—what is called the statute's "legislative history." The general idea for researching legislative history is simple: Legislators are presumed to know what they're doing and why.

When you investigate legislative history, keep a couple of points firmly in mind. As mentioned earlier, what the legislature intended in a statute is supposed to be gleaned from the "plain words" of the statute itself. So if a judge believes the words of a statute are reasonably clear, no inquiry into the legislative intent will be considered.

The second point is a bit more cosmic. Legislative intent can be seen as a kind of mass delusion that the judicial community buys into when it doesn't know how to interpret a statute any other way. Why a delusion? Because most of the time there is no one clear legislative intent. Typically, a few legislators know what's intended by the words of any particular statute, while the great majority who haven't even read it vote for or against the bill for reasons unrelated to how it's worded. For that reason, some judges stick to the words of the statute, no matter how difficult it is to understand.

Finding Federal Legislative History

Conducting a full investigation of legislative history for a federal statute can be an exhausting and often inconclusive task. You will probably be glad to know that most of the time it is also unnecessary. Normally, locating the more important federal committee reports is all the legislative history research you need to do.

---

16 § 831s   **CONSERVATION   Ch. 12A**

§ 831s. Possession by Government in time of war; damages to contract holders

The Government of the United States hereby reserves the right, in case of war or national emergency declared by Congress, to take possession of all or any part of the property described or referred to in this chapter for the purpose of manufacturing explosives or for other war purposes; but, if this right is exercised by the Government, it shall pay the reasonable and fair damages that may be suffered by any party whose contract for the purchase of electric power or fixed nitrogen or fertilizer ingredients is hereby violated, after the amount of the damages has been fixed by the United States Claims Court in proceedings instituted and conducted for that purpose under rules prescribed by the court.

(May 18, 1933, c. 32, § 20, 48 Stat. 68; Apr. 2, 1982, Pub.L. 97–164, Title I, § 161(2), 96 Stat. 49.)

Historical Note

1982 Amendment. Pub.L. 97–164 substituted "Claims Court" for "Court of Claims".

Effective Date of 1982 Amendment. Amendment by Pub.L. 97–164 effective Oct. 1, 1982, see section 402 of Pub.L. 97–164, set out as an Effective Date of 1982 Amendment note under section 171 of Title 28, Judiciary and Judicial Procedure.

Termination of War and Emergencies. Joint Res. July 25, 1947, c. 327, § 3, 61 Stat. 451, provided that in the interpretation of this section, the date July 25, 1947, shall be deemed to be the date of termination of any state of war theretofore declared by Congress and of the national emergencies proclaimed by the President on September 8, 1939, and May 27, 1941.

Legislative History. For legislative history and purpose of Pub.L. 97–164, see 1982 U.S. Code Cong. and Adm.News, p. 11.

Federal Statute Showing Legislative History Reference

Most statutes in the annotated federal codes (*U.S.C.A.* and *U.S.C.S.*) are followed by a reference to the *U.S. Code Congressional and Administrative News*, which contains federal legislative history. An example of how this works is shown in the federal statute set out above. Examine the small print following the statute. The last paragraph sets out where the legislative history for the original statute and the 1982 amendment can be located in the *U.S. Code Congressional and Administrative News*.

If the federal statute you are investigating does not have a citation to its legislative history, you can check the subject index, popular names table and statutory reference table in each volume of the *U.S. Code Congressional and Administrative News*. There is one major limitation to the value of these indexes and tables, however: They are not cumulative. In other words, they index only materials from the legislative session covered by that volume.

Suppose, for example, that you are dealing with a statute passed in 1984 but don't know its public law number or its *U.S. Code* citation. You can use the subject index for the *U.S. Code Congressional and Administrative News* for that year to find the legislative history.

If, however, you already have the public law number of a statute, find the volume containing the public laws for the Congress indicated in the public law number. For instance, if the number is 94-584, find the volume containing

material for the 94th Congress. Then use the statutory reference table to locate the committee reports.

If you don't know the public law number, the *U.S. Code* citation, or the approximate year the statute was passed, you will have difficulty finding the appropriate committee reports; your best bet is to search for the *U.S. Code* citation.

It is important to remember that the typical statute is amended many times over its lifespan. Each amendment has its own committee reports. The legislative history of a statute, therefore, generally refers to a collection of legislative histories. Each of these legislative histories must be separately researched, because any given volume of the *U.S. Code Congressional and Administrative News* contains only the committee reports for the session covered by that volume.

In the federal statute set out above, the legislative history of the original statute is contained in an earlier *U.S. Code Congressional and Administrative News*, while the history of the 1982 amendment is in the 1982 *U.S. Code Congressional and Administrative News*. You would need to read both to glean a full legislative history of the statute.

Library Exercise: Finding the Legislative History of Federal Statutes

This exercise asks you to locate the legislative history of a federal statute.

Your research involves the custody of Native American children. You are asked to find the legislative history of Title 25, §§ 1911 and 1912—part of the federal Indian Child Welfare Act of 1978.

Questions

1. Find the statutes in the *United States Code Annotated (U.S.C.A.)*. What does the material directly following them tell you about their legislative history?

2. Look for the legislative history and describe the documents you find.

Answers

1. In the "Historical Note" following both sections, it says, "For legislative history and purpose of Pub. L. 95-608, see 1978 *U.S. Code Cong. and Adm. News*, p. 7530."

2. First find the volumes of the 1978 *U.S. Code Congressional and Administrative News* that contain legislative history (shown on the spine). Select the volume that includes page 7530; this is Volume 6. On pages 7530 and following, you find House Report No. 95-1386, Analysis of the Report, Cost Estimate from the U.S. Budget Office and statements from various cabinet officers, legislators and agencies.

Library Exercise: Using *U.S. Code Congressional and Administrative News*

Until 1990, the United States Supreme Court had held that the First Amendment Freedom of Religion protects individuals from penalty or prosecution when the individuals' actions are part of their religion.

In 1990, the Supreme Court upheld the states' right to enforce drug laws against Native Americans whose religious practice included ceremonies in which peyote is used.

Your office wants to defend a client in a similar situation and has heard that the U.S. Congress passed a statute overturning the 1990 decision (*Employment Division v. Smith*, 110 S. Ct. 1595 (1990)).

You are assigned to go to *U.S.C.A.* (not *U.S.C.S.*) and *U.S. Code Congressional and Administrative News* and try to find the statute's text and legislative history. It's called something like "Religious Freedom Act 1993."

Questions

1. Where in *U.S.C.A.* do you start?
2. What do you find under Religious Freedom?
3. Where in *U.S.C.A.* is the "Popular Name Table?"
4. Look up the Religious Freedom Restoration Act in the Popular Name table. What information are you given?
5. Now that you know the Act's Public Law number, where is the best place to find the federal law by its public law number, along with legislative history?
6. How do you find the book with the legislative history in it?
7. Open Volume 3. The headings on the right-hand pages list the Acts in bold type and the Public Law numbers directly below. The Religious Freedom Restoration Act of 1993 begins on page 1892. The first words under the title tell you to "see page 107 Stat. 1488." Where is that page, and what's there?
8. Now, go back to Volume 3. When the Senate Committee on the Judiciary voted on whether to report the bill to the full Senate, how many voted for reporting, and how many against? Where did you find this information?

Answers

1. The General Index for *U.S.C.A.* is the set of softbound volumes at the end of the entire set. "Religious Freedom" would be in the Volume P–R.
2. There is an entry entitled, "Religious Freedom Restoration Act of 1993." Under the entry is the notation, "Text of Act. See Popular Name Table."
3. The last volume of the General Index (U to Z) also includes the Popular Name Table (after Z), which is noted on the spine of the book.
4. We are given its public law number, the date of enactment and the statute number: Pub.L. 103-141, Nov. 16, 1993, 107 Stat. 1488.
5. In the *U.S. Code Congressional and Administrative News.*
6. *U.S. Code Congressional and Administrative News* is arranged by year, with several volumes making up each year. We know that the Act was passed in 1993, so we consult the 1993 volumes. On the bottom of the spine of the third volume ("103rd Congress FIRST SESSION 1993") is the information "LEGISLATIVE HISTORY [P.L. 103–66 con't to 103–160]." The bottom line of information gives the volume's page numbers. Since we are looking for Pub. L. 103–141, we know we have the right book.
7. At the bottom of the spine of Volume 2 of 103rd Congress First Session 1993, the page numbers are 1–662. Page 107 is within those pages. We could also have gone directly to 107 Stat. 1488 when we found the entry in the Popular Name Table (see Question 4).
8. On page 1892, there is a Table of Contents for the Senate Report, showing page numbers of the original report. These page numbers appear in brackets ("[page 2]") at page breaks throughout the Report. Entry VI in the Table of Contents is "Vote of the Committee … 14." [Page 14] begins on page 1903 of our Volume. The vote of each member of the Committee is recorded in that section, and 15 voted for it, 1 against.

Finding Federal Legislative History on the Internet

Most legislative history for federal statutes is reported in committee reports. You can use the Thomas website to find legislative history for the last several sessions of Congress. You also can pick up various helpful items by meticulously reading the *Congressional Record*. Go to http://thomas.loc.gov.

Finding State Legislative History

State legislative history is usually more difficult to uncover than federal legislative history. However, many states have legislative analysts (lawyers who work for the legislature) whose comments on legislation are considered by the state legislators in the same way as committee reports are considered by Congress. These comments are sometimes published in the advance legislative update services as an introduction to the new statute.

Statutes and accompanying comments that are printed in these advance legislative services are later bound and retained in volumes called *Session Laws*, according to the year they were passed. It is sometimes possible to discover the legislative history of an older state statute by finding these legislative analysts' comments with the statute in the bound *Session Laws*. To find a statute in the *Session Laws*, you need the chapter number assigned it by the legislature. That number appears directly after the text of the statute as printed in a code.

It is also common for legislative committees to have their own staff lawyers draft memoranda to guide them in their deliberations. These memoranda are normally not available in law libraries, but they may be kept on file with the legislature. Legislative procedures vary greatly from state to state. In Oregon, for example, committees keep microfilmed minutes of their hearings and records of all exhibits introduced at the hearings. Many other states don't keep such records. The best course for a researcher is probably to ask a law librarian what kinds of legislative history for state laws are available in that state.

⚠ Don't Get Too Carried Away Researching Legislative History. It is often possible, and usually preferable, to determine the meaning of a statute without resorting to the legislative history. Most statutory provisions have been interpreted by courts, and courts tend not to use legislative history unless an important ambiguity really exists.

Using Uniform Law Histories to Interpret Statutes

There is currently an effort to make a number of substantive areas of the law uniform among the states. A group of lawyers, judges and law professors called the National Conference of Commissioners on Uniform State Laws (National Conference) drafts legislation covering certain areas of law and then tries to get as many states as possible to adopt the "uniform" legislation.

The packages drafted by the National Conference are not law and have no effect on our legal system until they are adopted by one or more state legislatures. And the fact that the package is adopted in one or more states does not make it law in any other state that has not adopted it.

This approach to making law uniform has been highly successful in many legal areas. In other areas, the National Conference has met with less success.

Uniform Laws Adopted by Many States

Uniform Commercial Code
Uniform Controlled Substances Act
Uniform Gifts to Minors Act
Uniform Transfers to Minors Act
Uniform Partnership Act
Uniform Child Custody Jurisdiction Act

If the statute you are researching was a uniform law adopted by your state, you can get some help interpreting its meaning by looking at a series of books called the *Uniform Laws Annotated (U.L.A.)*, published by West. It contains all of the uniform laws, the original comments accompanying them, a listing of the states that have adopted them, notations of how states have altered each provision in the course of adopting it, summaries of case opinions that have interpreted each statute, and references to pertinent law review discussions. The *U.L.A.* gives you excellent insight into what any particular part of a uniform law package was originally intended to accomplish and how the states and courts have treated it.

Unfortunately, the *U.L.A.* has neither an overall index nor an overall table of contents. However, the volumes are grouped according to general subject matter. For example, some of the volumes contain uniform laws treating "Estate, Probate and Related Laws," while others contain laws pertaining to "Civil Procedural and Remedial Laws." In addition, each uniform law package carries its own index. So, if you have the reference for a uniform law package, you can find the volume containing this package and use the specific index to find the particular part you are interested in.

How can you tell whether a state statute you are interested in interpreting originally came from a uniform law package? If your annotated state statutes are published by West Group (almost all are), the annotation following the statute will tell you. In addition, the annotation will reproduce the National Conference comment that accompanied the statute as it was originally proposed, and will also contain comments about how the state version of the statute differs from the original.

States seldom adopt uniform law packages lock, stock and barrel. Usually they change or delete some of the statutes in the package. Also, in many cases, new sections are added. So by the time uniform laws have been adopted by the various states, they are no longer, strictly speaking, "uniform." Still, for the most part, if you have an overall understanding of the package as it was produced by the National Conference, you will have a good grasp of the final result in any given adopting state.

On the Internet, the Cornell Legal Information Institute provides links to state statutes that implement various uniform laws as well as provides the actual text of the uniform law for each state. You can find this information at www.law.cornell.edu/states/index.html. Click the "Update Uniform Law Locations" link at the left.

Regulations

Legislatures often pass laws that need active enforcement. For example, a complex series of federal statutes provide for the collection of the federal income tax. However, the federal government wouldn't be solvent very long if it relied on everyone to voluntarily line up and empty their pockets. Accordingly, Congress created the Internal Revenue Service (IRS) to:

- resolve specific questions that arise with respect to how the tax laws should be interpreted;

- provide specific guidelines that enable millions to prepare their own tax returns every year; and
- keep a close watch on us all to make sure we pay our fair (or unfair) share.

The IRS is but one of many of the "administrative agencies" created by Congress over the years to implement its programs. State legislatures have created a similar alphabet soup of agencies to carry out their programs.

Legislatures give such agencies the power to make rules and guidelines to carry out the goals of the statutes that authorized the creation of the agency and the programs over which it has authority. These rules and guidelines are collectively termed "regulations." Some are directed at the general public, some at business entities and some at the agency itself. If they are consistent with the parent legislation, they have the force and effect of law. This is a fancy way of saying that regulations are just as binding and enforceable as statutes. Therefore, when regulations are at issue in a dispute, it is often crucial to first determine whether they are valid under the terms of the statutes that govern the agency's activities—and thus have the force and effect of law.

Courts are willing to overturn agency regulations when they conclude that the agency misinterpreted the law or issued a regulation when it didn't have the authority to do so. For example, the U.S. Supreme Court struck down Federal Occupational Safety and Health Administration (OSHA) regulations that allowed industries to balance worker safety against the cost of implementing safeguards.

Finding Federal Regulations

Most federal regulations are published in the *Code of Federal Regulations (C.F.R.)*, a multi-volume and well-indexed paperbound set organized by subject.

The *Code of Federal Regulations* (C.F.R.)

The *C.F.R.* is organized into 50 separate titles. Each title covers a general subject. For instance, Title 7 contains

regulations concerning agriculture, Title 10 contains energy regulations and so on. *C.F.R.* titles often, but not always, correspond to the *U.S.C.* titles in terms of their subject matter. For example, Title 7 of the United States Code covers statutes relating to agriculture, while Title 7 of the *C.F.R.* contains agriculture regulations. But Title 42 of *U.S.C.* contains statutes on the Medicaid program, while the Medicaid regulations are found in Title 45 of the *C.F.R.*

Along with each regulation, the *C.F.R.* provides a reference to the statute that authorizes it and a reference to where (and when) the regulation was published in the *Federal Register*. (All regulations are supposed to be published first in the *Federal Register*, discussed below.) Below is an example of the information provided along with each regulation in the *C.F.R.*

The best way to find a federal regulation published in the *C.F.R.* if you don't already have the correct citation is to start with the general subject index that comes with this series. If you already know which Title your regulation is likely to be in, use the Table of Contents at the end of each individual Title.

Once you've found a regulation, you need to be sure it's still current. A new edition of the *C.F.R.* is published each year on a staggered quarterly basis. Titles 1-16 are published on January 1, Titles 17-27 are published on April 1, titles 28-41 are published on July 1 and titles 42-50 are published on October 1. Each year the *C.F.R.* covers change colors.

When a new annual edition is published, the regulations in it are current as of that date. However, what if the *C.F.R.* volume that contains the regulation you are interested in was published January 1, 2000, and you are doing your research in July 2001? How can you make sure you are up-to-date? Simple. First, consult the latest monthly pamphlet called *C.F.R.-L.S.A.*, which stands for "List of *C.F.R.* Sections Affected." Find the title and section number of the regulation you are interested in. Then see if there have been any changes between the last published *C.F.R.* volume (January 1 in our example) and the date of the pamphlet (July 2001). Below is a typical page from *C.F.R.-L.S.A.*

Suppose now that you are doing your research on July 15, 2001, and the July version of the *C.F.R.-L.S.A.* has not yet hit the library shelf. You would first use the *C.F.R.-L.S.A.* for June. Then you can use a publication called the *Federal Register*, where all new federal regulations are originally published. The *Federal Register* also contains proposed

regulations, schedules of government agency meetings, presidential documents and lists of bills that have been enacted.

The *Federal Register* can be hard to use because it contains many pages of very small type on newsprint. It is published daily, and a cumulative monthly index is available to help you find the regulation you're after. However, this index is generally organized according to the agency that initiated the action, so unless you know which agency you're dealing with, it's of little help.

If you have a *C.F.R.* citation to the new regulation, or you want to bring your *C.F.R.* search completely up to date (see above), you can consult the *C.F.R.* sections affected list in the latest issue of the *Federal Register*. This will give you a listing of all *C.F.R.* sections that have been affected during the current month of the *Federal Register*.

Summing Up
How to Find Federal Regulations

✔ Consult either the general subject index to the *Code of Federal Regulations (C.F.R.)*, or the *Index to the Code of Federal Regulations* (commercially published by the Congressional Information Service).

✔ After you find the regulation, read the latest monthly issue of the *List of C.F.R. Sections Affected (C.F.R.-L.S.A.)* to see whether changes in the regulation have been made since the *C.F.R.* volume was published.

✔ Consult the *List of C.F.R. Sections Affected* in the latest daily issue of the *Federal Register* for the most current status of a regulation.

✔ For regulations that have been issued since the latest *C.F.R.* volume was published, consult the cumulative index to the *Federal Register* under the appropriate agency.

Finding Federal Regulations on the Internet

The entire *Code of Federal Regulations (C.F.R.)* is available on the Internet. Also, many of the special law collections that are put together for research on the Internet (see Chapter 5) contain the federal regulations that are relevant to the collection's specific topics.

92   **LSA—LIST OF CFR SECTIONS AFFECTED**

CHANGES APRIL 1, 1991 THROUGH NOVEMBER 29, 1991

TITLE 19 Chapter I—Con.   Page

171.33 (b)(1) and (d) heading
     revised.. 40780
     (b)(1) and (d) corrected............. 48823
172.22 (e) added............................40780
     (e) corrected............................. 48823
172.33 (b)(1) revised.................... 40780
177 Interpretive rule.................... 46372
177.22 (b) introductory text
     amended................................46115
178.2 Table amended..................32087
191.10 (e)(1)(i) amended............. 46115
191.21 (c) and (d) amended......... 46115
191.27 (c) amended...................... 46115

Chapter II—United States International Trade Commission (Parts 200—299)

200 Authority citation re-
     vised.......................................36726
200.735-102 (g) removed.............36726
200.735-103 (a) and (c) intro-
     ductory text amended; (b)
     and (c)(2) revised.....................36726
200.735-114 Nomenclature
     change....................................36726
200.735-115 Nomenclature
     change....................................36726
200.735-116 (b) revised................ 36726
200.735-121 Nomenclature
     change....................................36726

Chapter III—International Trade Administration, Department of Commerce (Parts 300—399)

356 Revised..................................37804

Title 19—*Proposed Rules:*

4..............................40283, 48448, 51762
10....................................48448, 51762
19....................................22833, 33733
24...31576
101...21111,
     22369, 55102, 56179
102....................................48448, 51762
113....................................22833, 33733
118...33734
134....................................48448, 51762
142...42568
141...56608
142...56608
144....................................22833, 33733
162...25363
177..............................46134, 48448, 51762

Note: **Boldface entries indicate November changes.**

TITLE 20—EMPLOYEES' BENEFITS

Chapter I—Office of Workers' Compensation Programs, Department of Labor (Parts 1—199)

                                   Page
10.305 Revised..................... 47675
10.306 (a) revised.................47675
10.311 (c) revised................. 47675

Chapter II—Railroad Retirement Board (Parts 200—399)

200.8 (b) amended; (d)(1), (2),
     (3), (f), (g) and (h) redesig-
     nated as (d)(2), (3), (4), (g),
     (h) and (i); (d)(1), (f) and (j)
     added............................... 50247
216 Revised............................ 28692
236 Removed...........................55073
240 Removed...........................55073
323 Added...............................26328
330 Revised............................ 28702
367 Added...............................46375

Chapter III—Social Security Administration, Department of Health and Human Services (Parts 400—499)

404.362 (b)(1) revised; (b)(2) re-
     moved; (b)(3) redesignated
     as (b)(2)......................... 24000
404.367 Introductory text and
     (b) revised....................... 35999
404.401—404.499 (Subpart E)
     Authority citation revised...... 41789
404.401 (d) revised........................ 41789
     Technical correction................. 50157
404.402 (d)(1) revised................. 41789
     Technical correction................. 50157
404.469 Added............................41789
     Technical correction................. 50157
404.501—404.515 (Subpart F)
     Authority citation revised...... 52468
404.520 Added............................52468
404.521 Added............................52468
404.522 Added............................52469
404.523 Added............................52469
404.524 Added............................52469
404.525 Added............................52469
404.526 Added............................52469
404.621 (a)(2)(i) and (ii) re-
     moved; (a)(2)(iii) and (iv)
     redesignated as (a)(2)(i) and
     (ii)................................... 58846

Library Exercise: Finding Federal Regulations

You are a graphic artist making a new package for Sun Dew Margarine. You are searching for federal regulations that regulate how big the word "margarine" must be on the box.

Questions

1. What indexes can you use to find a federal regulation?
2. What words can you look under to find out how big the word "margarine" must be on the box?
3. What does it say under these entries?
4. What does "21 *C.F.R.* 166" mean?
5. Find 21 *C.F.R.* 166. What subsection is titled "Labeling of Margarine"?
6. Find all subsections under 166.40 that deal with how tall the letters must be.
7. What is the smallest the letters can be?
8. Where do you look first to see if there have been any changes to the regulation you are using?
9. Do you find any changes to your regulation listed in that publication?
10. Do you need to read about the changes to 21 *C.F.R.* 166?
11. Do you have to look in each daily issue of that resource?
12. Are there any changes?

Answers

1. The *Index to the Code of Federal Regulations*, the *U.S.C.S. Index and Finding Aids to Code of Federal Regulations* or Martindale-Hubbell's *Code of Federal Regulations Index*.
2. Oleomargarine or Margarine or Food labeling.
3. In the *C.F.R.* index or the *U.S.C.S.* Index: Under Oleomargarine it says: see Margarine. Under Margarine it says: Food grades and standards 21 C.F.R. 166. Under Food labeling it says: Margarine standards 21 C.F.R. 166.

   In the Martindale-Hubbell index: In the Contents at the beginning of volume 1, you see that there are two indexes to Food and Drug regulations; in volume 1, there is an index to Title 21 (Food and Drugs), and in the Topical Index there is a category for Food and Drugs, in volume 3 pages FD-1 to FD-174. On page FD-1 is a list of major subject headings for that category; margarine is listed there, and when you go into the index you find: Margarine 21 C.F.R. 166.40, 116.110. Looking under Food labeling, margarine will get you the same citation to 21 C.F.R. 166.40.

4. *Code of Federal Regulations* Title 21, Section or Part 166.
5. § 166.40.
6. § 166.40(c)(1); § 166.40(h).
7. 20 points or 20/72 of 1 inch.
8. *L.S.A.* starting with the month after the date on the front of the volume you are using. The *L.S.A.*s are usually located near the index volume.
9. No.
10. 21 *C.F.R.* 166.40 is the subsection concerned with letter size. The changes to the legislation do not deal with that subsection, but they should still be read in case they deal with an important related issue.
11. No; the last day of each month includes all changes recorded that month; each day is cumulative for that month as well (July 15 includes all changes recorded July 1-15).
12. When we looked at this regulation in March 2004, the last changes had been made on July 27, 1982.

There are at least a couple places to find the Federal Regulations online. First, you can try the Cornell Legal Information Institute [www.law.cornell.edu]. You'll find the CFR under the Constitutions and Code heading. You can browse by topic, search the section headings by key word or search by citation (if you have one).

You can also access federal regulations at: National Archives [www.access.gpo.gov/nara/cfr/cfr-table-search.html], or you go directly to the specific regulatory agency's website. [www.<agency acronym>.gov; for example, www.fcc.gov].

Another option is to start with Findlaw.com. Let's see how this works.

Internet Exercise: Finding a Federal Regulation

You live in a small town in the U.S.A. You use a wheelchair to get around and also have some weakness in your hands. The small, private business school in your area, Success College, offers a notary public course that you'd like to take. In response to your inquiry about accessibility, the school sends you a letter stating that the Americans with Disabilities Act requires compliance only from public agencies. As a private school, Success claims it doesn't need to accommodate people with disabilities. It's time to research the federal regulations that define who must accommodate people with disabilities and what accommodations they must make.

Go to Findlaw.com. Go to Findlaw's home page by entering the URL in your browser [www.findlaw. com]. Click Laws: Cases & Codes (under the "Legal Professional" tab). Under Federal Laws, choose Code of Federal Regulations (CFR).

The search box under the words, "Code of Federal Regulations," with the search button next to it, offers you the opportunity to search all the regulations for references to the Americans with Disabilities Act. Type "Americans with Disabilities Act" in the box and click on search.

By typing all the words without any "ands" between them, you tell the searching tool that the words are a phrase to be searched for in the exact order you wrote them. When we did this search, we obtained 200 "hits" (references to regulations that mention the Americans with Disabilities Act). By scrolling down the list of these hits, we found some promising entries.

Select one of the listed items. Item 5 ([2002] 28CFR36—PART 36—NONDISCRIMINATION ON THE BASIS OF DISABILITY BY PUBLIC ACCOMMODATIONS AND IN COMMERCIAL FACILITIES) looks promising. There are three ways to view this regulation (28 CFR 36):

- TXT shows you its text online,
- PDF downloads the regulation onto your hard drive, and
- SUM shows you a summary of the listed item, which is useful to know before you make one of the other choices.

SUM is often the most efficient choice, but when you choose it here you'll only see the table of contents of part 36. So, click on the TXT button for item 5 and see if it contains the information you want.

As you read the beginning sections of the regulations, you see that the Americans with Disabilities Act applies to private as well as public facilities. If you scroll down quite a bit further to section 36.309, you'll find that private examinations and courses must also comply. The regulations specify how they must do so.

Finding State Regulations

State regulations are usually more difficult to locate than federal regulations. While at least 30 states have an administrative code containing a portion of the state's regulations, a common practice is for each agency's regulations to be kept in loose-leaf manuals published by the individual agency. This means it is often necessary to know which state agency is responsible for writing a particular regulation before you can find it. Some larger law libraries carry all or most of the regulations for their state, but more often you'll have to call or visit the agency itself to get regulations.

Regulations are constantly being changed by the agencies that issue them, and it is important to always check to make sure that the regulation that you've found is up-to-date. This can be done by checking with the agency, where you might discover someone who will help you find everything you need.

How to Find State Regulations on the Internet

There are many ways to find a state's regulations on the Internet. Many of the sites we list for finding state statutes online will also provide links to state regulations. Your state's website will provide links to state agencies and regulations. Again, the basic address for a state's website is www.state.<state postal abbreviation>.us. In the exercise set out below, we walk you through finding a state regulation with FindLaw.

How to Read and Understand Regulations

The general rules of statutory interpretation also apply to interpreting regulations. But there are some additional factors to consider in the interpretation of regulations. The most important are that:

- Agency interpretations of a regulation should either be followed or argued against, but not ignored. Because regulations are often written to implement a general statutory scheme, they tend to be both wordy and hard to understand, even more so than statutes.

Increasingly, however, regulations are written so that they can be more clearly understood.

- Regulations should be interpreted in a way that best fulfills the intent of the authorizing statute.

Summing Up
How to Find State Regulations in the Law Library

✔ If your state's regulations have been collected and published in an "Administrative Code," use the subject index. If there is no index, find the place in the publication that covers the agency issuing the regulations and check the table of contents.

✔ If there is no administrative code or analogous publication, find out what agency issued the regulations. Then ask the law librarian whether the library carries that agency's regulations.

✔ If the regulations cannot be found in the law library, check with the nearest large public library.

✔ If the regulations aren't kept there, contact the agency issuing the regulations and ask how you can get a copy of them.

A typical regulation consists of the actual rule that is being put forth and a paragraph or two of agency interpretation. Sometimes examples are given on how the regulation is supposed to apply to a specific set of facts. Only the rule part of the regulation acts like a law. The interpretation and examples are designed only to explain its application.

Internet Exercise: Finding a State Regulation

Assume that you've bought a cabin in the Michigan woods, complete with running water and two sinks—but no toilet. An outhouse is the answer. The town clerk told you that there are state regulations concerning outhouses issued by the Department of Environmental Quality (DOEQ). She doesn't have a copy of the regs and told you to find them on the Internet.

1. **Go to FindLaw** [www.findlaw.com]. On the home page, under the "Legal Professional" tab, you'll encounter a number of links to different resources. Click on the word "States" under U.S. Law ... Cases & Codes ... States (since we are looking for state regulations). This takes you to a list of states. Click on Michigan. You will then encounter a list of many resources organized in three main groups. The first set of resources presented includes various heads of statutes (laws, codes). Which to choose?

2. **Take a moment to recall** just what you're looking for: pronouncements from your state government on the proper use of outhouses. Directives like these are among what we identified in Chapter 5 as primary materials—rules issued by the government in statutes (called codes when they are organized by subject), court cases and administrative agencies (like the Department of Environmental Quality). Secondary sources are books that experts write about the law. Even if you don't remember the lessons of Chapter 5, FindLaw gives you a hint: the Primary Materials link has the word "regulations" after it.

3. **On the Michigan Primary Resources** page, you are given the choice of many types of Michigan cases, codes and regulations. Which to choose? "Administrative Code" in the first group is what you are looking for. In many states, the Code of Regulations is called the Administrative Code,

because regulations are promulgated (issued) by administrative agencies.

4. **When you click on Administrative Code** searchable resource, you will produce several choices. You may search the code by numbered sections or search by department index. Because you know the name of the department that issued the outhouse regulations (the Department of Environmental Quality), it is worth trying the Department Index.

5. **Choosing the Department Search Path** illustrates a method of Internet searching that will make your efforts on the Net yield faster, more focused results: Whenever you can properly fit your quest into a narrow, rather than a broad search category, you are more likely to get relevant results.

6. **The list of departments is alphabetical.** Near the middle of the page is Environmental Quality, the department you are looking for. When you click on that department, you will encounter a page that alphabetically lists the various divisions within the Environmental Quality Department.

7. **As you scroll down the page,** you'll see that the Department of Environmental Quality has decided to present their information according to the divisions within the department, which are alphabetized and printed in boldface (such as **Air Quality Division** and **Bureau of Environmental Protection**).

8. **Under Drinking Water and Radiological Protection**, you'll see a listing for Outhouses. Clicking on Outhouses, you will see the state of Michigan's basic rules and standards for constructing a legal outhouse. Your public library may have a book about outhouses, with pictures, diagrams, and artistic designs for ventilation holes.

Procedural Statutes and Rules

If your research involves procedural issues—such as getting the case into court and keeping it there—there are several types of laws to which you need to pay special attention, all of which can usually be found in a law library with the help of the law librarian.

Rules of Civil Procedure

Rules of Civil Procedure are usually statutes passed by a legislature or rules issued by a state's highest court. They govern such matters as:

- who can sue whom, for what kinds of wrongs and in which courts;
- which kinds of documents must be filed with the court to initiate a lawsuit and respond to it;
- time limits for filing various court papers;
- what court papers must say to be effective;
- what ways each side to a lawsuit can find out necessary facts from the other side and from third-party witnesses (discovery);
- how a case is actually brought to trial;
- to what kind of trial you are entitled (that is, by judge or jury);
- to what kind of judgment and relief you are entitled if you win;
- what happens to you if you lose;
- how you can enforce a judgment;
- how you can appeal a judgment if you lose; and
- what kind of appeal is available if the court does not comply with the laws in the pre-trial stage of the case.

You must follow these rules exactly. While some procedural mistakes can be fixed, especially if this is done very promptly, many violations mean that your case is lost, just as surely as if you went to trial and the court or jury found against you.

Rules of Civil Procedure for the federal courts are found in Title 28 of *U.S.C.A.*; Rules of Civil Procedure for state courts are usually found among the other state statutes in a code, title or chapter entitled "Civil Procedure" or "Court Rules."

Rules of Court (if any)

Your state may have an additional publication called Rules of Court or something similar. If so, it will contain rules issued by the state's highest court and specify in more detail the procedures that must be followed. For example, a statute might specify that a certain document must be filed with the court, but the Rule of Court would specify the precise form the document must follow.

Local Rules (if any)

Many courts have their own local rules that get even more detailed. A local rule might specify the size of the paper that must be used or where an attorney's name must be placed on the page. Although these housekeeping matters may not seem as important as the accuracy of the facts and law in your papers, many lawyers have learned the hard way that you ignore them at your peril. Some judges and clerks love to use deviations from local rules as the basis for returning your papers or even denying your motion.

Finding Court Rules on the Internet

Like other government entities, trial courts are beginning to conduct their daily business on the Internet. Some courts simply post a brief description of the court—what it does and where it's located—while others provide virtually the same information you could get if you walked into the clerk's office, including the daily court calendar, personnel and filing information, recent court rulings and the local court rules.

A good list of court websites can be found at the National Center for State Courts [www.ncsonline.org]. Scroll down and click the court websites link.

 Desk References. It is no secret that legal secretaries and paralegals often know more about the actual techniques involved in getting the right papers to the right courts on time than lawyers do. These details are commonly put into a step-by-step form and published in handbooks and "desk references." You can find information about filing fees, service of process, statutes of limitation, time limits, common motions and similar nitty-gritty matters in these publications, which exist in most larger states. For example, in California you can use *California Paralegal's Guide 5th,* by Mack (Lexis Publishing). Ask a legal secretary, paralegal or law librarian if this sort of resource is published in your state.

Local Law—Ordinances

Counties, cities and special districts (for example, school districts or sanitation districts) have a good deal of power over day-to-day life. The amount of rule-making authority that is afforded these local entities is usually set out in the state constitution and statutes. Subject to these higher forms of law, cities commonly have authority to:

- divide their domain into zones of activity (called "zoning power");
- set requirements for new buildings and for the refurbishing of old buildings;
- pass and enforce local parking and driving rules;
- set minimum standards for health and safety in rental properties; and
- promulgate fire and police regulations.

Local laws are usually called "ordinances." Ordinances are like statutes and regulations in that they have the force and effect of law, assuming they are within the local government's lawful authority. Special districts are usually empowered to pass regulations that are also binding law.

Finding Ordinances and Local Laws in the Law Library

Because of the many different forms of local government, it is difficult to specify the exact way in which you might research these ordinances or specialized regulations. Here are some general suggestions:

- Ordinances are often divided into local codes such as the "traffic code," "planning code," "building code" and the like. These codes are usually available in your local public library or law library, and can also be obtained from the pertinent city office for free or a small sum to cover reproduction costs.
- City and county agencies keep collections of ordinances that pertain to their agency.
- Special districts usually publish their regulations in paperbound pamphlets that can be obtained free or for a low price.

Ordinances, like statutes, are occasionally interpreted by the courts. If you want to find out whether or not an ordinance you're interested in has been considered by a court, use either *Shepard's Citations for Statutes* or a special volume called *Shepard's Ordinance Law Annotations*. This latter tool (not found in many law libraries) is organized by subject and provides references with respect to ordinances from all different parts of the country. (For instructions on how to Shepardize statutes or ordinances, see Chapter 9.)

Finding Local Laws on the Internet

State and Local Government on the Net [www.statelocalgov .net] is a great site for finding municipal codes. The Municipal Code Corporation [www.municode.com] also has a helpful site at www.municode.com/resources/ online%20Library.asp. If you draw a blank, you may also be able to find your codes or ordinances at a city or county website. Most cities' and counties' websites follow these formats:

- county: www.co.<county name>.<state postal code>.us
  Example: www.co.alameda.ca.us
- city: www.ci.<city name>.<state postal code>.us
  Example: www.ci.berkeley.ca.us.

Your state website also may have links to its cities and counties.

Review

Questions

1. What's the first step when doing constitutional research?

2. What does each element of the citation Pub. L. No. 94-583 mean?

3. How many titles does the U.S. Code consist of?

4. What are the names of the two annotated versions of the U.S. Code?

5. In addition to the federal statutes, what else do the annotated codes offer the legal researcher?

6. What information is contained in the following federal statute citation? 17 *U.S.C.A.* § 567

7. What are the three tools that let you find a federal statute by its popular name if you don't know its citation?

8. What is a statutory scheme?

9. What is the most common method for keeping state and federal annotated codes up-to-date?

10. What tools help you find recently-enacted federal and state statutes that haven't yet been published in a pocket part?

11. What are the eight rules of statutory interpretation?

12. How does *Words and Phrases* help you interpret statutes?

13. What is the most common way to locate legislative history for a federal statute?

14. What special tool is available to help you understand a state statute that is based on a "uniform law"?

15. What publication contains the federal regulations?

Answers

1. Find a good constitutional law hornbook written for law school students.

2. "Pub. L." stands for public law. "94" stands for the Congress that passed the law (the 94th Congress). 583 is the number that has been assigned to the statute.

3. 50.

4. *United States Code Annotated (U.S.C.A.)* and *United States Code Service, Lawyer's Edition (U.S.C.S.)*.

5. They contain information pertaining to each statute, including:

   • one-sentence summaries of court cases that have interpreted the statute;

   • notes about the statute's history (amendments, etc.);

   • cross-references to other relevant statutes;

   • cross-references to administrative regulations that may be helpful in interpreting the statute;

   • citations to the legislative history of the statute; and

   • research guides (references to relevant materials by the same publisher).

6. The 17 means Title 17. *U.S.C.A.* means *United States Code Annotated*. § means section. 567 is the section number.

7. • The "popular names index" that follows the *United States Code Annotated (U.S.C.A.)*

   • The "popular names table" volume that accompanies the *United States Code Service, Lawyer's Edition (U.S.C.S.)*

   • *Shepard's Acts and Cases by Popular Names*.

8. A group of statutes that are related to an overall subject matter. Sometimes an index will alert you to the existence of a statutory scheme by putting an "et seq." at the end of a single statutory reference. ("Et seq." means "and following.")

9. Pocket parts—paper supplements that fit inside each hardcover volume, usually at the back. Pocket parts are published once a year and contain any statutory changes occurring in the interim. When doing legal research in an annotated code, always remember to check the pocket part.

10. Each federal and state annotated code has a monthly advance legislative service that prints statutes a month or two after they have been passed by Congress or the state legislature. The one for *U.S.C.A.* is called the *U.S.C.A. Quarterly Supplement,* while the one for *U.S.C.S.* is known as the *U.S.C.S. Advance Legislative Service*. The names vary for the state advance legislative services.

11. Rule 1: Read the statute over at least three times. Then read it again.

    Rule 2: Pay close attention to the "ands" and "ors."

    Rule 3: Assume that all words and punctuation in the statute have meaning.

    Rule 4: Interpret a statute so that it is consistent with all other related statutes, if possible.

Review (continued)

Rule 5: Interpret criminal statutes strictly.

Rule 6: Interpret ambiguities in statutes in ways that seem to best further the purpose of the legislation.

Rule 7: Interpret the statute so that it makes sense and does not lead to absurd or improbable results.

Rule 8: Track down all cross-references to other statutes and sections.

12. This publication contains one-sentence interpretations of common words and phrases that have been pulled from cases and organized alphabetically. It allows you to find out whether courts have interpreted or used any particular word or phrase you are interested in, and if so, how.

13. Most statutes in the annotated federal codes *(U.S.C.A.* and *U.S.C.S.)* are followed by a reference to the *U.S. Code Congressional and Administrative News*, which contains federal legislative history.

14. A series of books called the *Uniform Laws Annotated (U.L.A.)*, published by West. It contains all of the uniform laws, the original comments accompanying them, a listing of the states that have adopted them, notations of how states have altered each provision in the course of adopting it, summaries of case opinions that have interpreted each statute, and references to pertinent law review discussions.

15. The *Code of Federal Regulations (C.F.R.)*.

Understanding Case Law

Finding the right court decision (case) is the heart of the legal research method outlined in Chapter 2. No matter how clear a statute or regulation may seem on its face—and few fit that description—you need to find out what the courts have done with it in situations like yours. The best path to that result is first to find one relevant case that, through the cross-reference materials covered in Chapter 10, will lead you to others.

This chapter introduces you to cases—what they are and how they influence later disputes. Chapter 8 explains where you find cases. Chapter 9 tells you how to find them.

What Is a Case?

A case starts in the trial court and may end up being appealed to a higher court—an intermediate appellate court or a supreme court. It is the published opinions of these appellate or supreme courts that make up most of the cases you will find in a law library. The books they are published in are called case reports or reporters.

The Nuts and Bolts of a Case

When you look at the beginning of a case in one of the reporters, you will find certain basic information. Look at the beginning of the *Keywell* case, which we have reproduced below, and follow along as we identify the important information contained on the first page.

The Citation. The editors of the *Federal Reporter* make it impossible for you to forget what case you're reading. At the top of each page, the case name is given and you are told that you should cite the case as, for example, 33 F.3d 159 (2nd Cir. 1994).

The Parties. In a civil case, the parties are known as the plaintiff (the one who filed the lawsuit) and the defendant (the one being sued). In a criminal case, the plaintiff is "the People" of the United States Government (if it's a federal case), or "the People" of one of the states (if it's a state case). The defendant is the person being charged with a crime.

Some reported cases are from the trial level. For example, all of the cases in the *Federal Supplement* ("F. Supp") are from United States District Courts, and, in that case, the parties are identified as "plaintiff" and "defendant." When a reported case is from one of the appellate courts, the original parties are also identified as the appellant (the one who lost below and is now bringing the appeal) and the appellee (the one who won below and is now having to defend that victory).

In the *Keywell* case, Keywell Corporation is identified as the "Plaintiff-Appellant." This label tells you that Keywell initiated the lawsuit at the trial level and was the one to file the present appeal. Weinstein and Boscarino were the defendants at the trial level and are the appellees now.

The Docket Number. When a case is filed in the trial court, it is given a number, called the "docket number," by the clerk of the court. While the case remains in the trial court, it is referred to by that number. If the case goes to the appellate level, it will be given a different number by the clerk of the appellate court. If you wanted to examine the court file in either court, you would have to use that number when making your request at the clerk's office. The docket number is also the number that is attached to an opinion when it is first issued (as a "Slip Opinion"), before it goes into the reporter series and gets its permanent cite.

In the *Keywell* case, the docket number is "No. 1208 Docket Number 93-7994." When this case was first listed in *Shepard's*, the listing would have looked like this: "Dk2 93-7994." The "Dk2" tells you that this is a Slip Opinion from the Second Circuit.

The Court. This is the name of the court that wrote the decision. In the *Keywell* case, the decision was written by the United States Court of Appeals for the Second Circuit, which heard the case. In order to find out which trial court had the case originally, you will have to read the Summary, discussed below.

The Dates. Many opinions include the date that the case was argued and the date the court issued the opinion. If the decision announces a new rule of law, or invalidates a statute, the issue date will be important to know. (But watch out: Opinions do not become "final" until the time for granting a re-hearing has passed. The local rules for each court will specify how long that time period may be.)

The Summary. This is usually a one-paragraph summary of the decision, written by the editors of the reporter series and not part of the decision itself. This text cannot be cited. If the opinion is from a trial court (like one you would read in "F. Supp.," which is the reporter series that contains federal district court cases), it will list the issue and the decision. If the opinion is from an appellate-level court, the summary will describe the trial court's decision and will go on to explain the holding of the appellate court.

The Decision. Many summaries end with a one-line phrase describing the holding of the court. In *Keywell*, we are told that the lower court's decision was "Affirmed in part, and reversed and remanded in part." This means that the decision of the trial court was upheld as to one or more

Parties →

Docket Number →

The Court →

The Dates →

The Citation →

KEYWELL CORP. v. WEINSTEIN

Cite as 33 F.3d 159 (2nd Cir. 1994)   **159**

**KEYWELL CORPORATION,
Plaintiff-Appellant,**

v.

**Daniel C. WEINSTEIN and Anthony
Boscarino, Defendants-Appellees.**

No. 1208, Docket 93-7994.

United States Court of Appeals,
Second Circuit.

Argued March 7, 1994.

Decided Aug. 23, 1994.

Summary →

Purchaser of metal recycling plant brought suit under CERCLA against two shareholders, officers, and directors of selling corporation to recover environmental cleanup costs. The United States District Court for the Western District of New York, William M. Skretny, J., granted summary judgment for defendants, and purchaser appealed. The Court of Appeals, Jacobs, Circuit Judge, held that: (1) genuine issue of material fact on reasonableness of purchaser's reliance on seller's misrepresentations precluded summary judgment on fraud claims, but (2) purchaser was not entitled to recover cleanup costs under CERCLA, since parties clearly allocated risk of CERCLA liability to purchaser under terms of purchase agreement.

Affirmed in part, and reversed and remanded in part.

1. Federal Courts ⚖766

When reviewing district court's grant of summary judgment, Court of Appeals must determine whether genuine issue of material fact exists and whether district court correctly applied law.

2. Federal Civil Procedure ⚖2470.1

Summary judgment is appropriate only if, resolving all ambiguities and drawing all factual inferences in favor of nonmoving party, there is no genuine issue of material fact to be tried. Fed.Rules Civ.Proc.Rule 56(c), 28 U.S.C.A.

3. Federal Civil Procedure ⚖2544

Party seeking summary judgment bears burden of demonstrating absence of any genuine factual dispute. Fed.Rules Civ.Proc. Rule 56(c), 28 U.S.C.A.

4. Federal Civil Procedure ⚖2504

Purchaser raised genuine questions of fact on reasonableness of its reliance on sellers' misrepresentations regarding release of hazardous substances on property, precluding summary judgment for sellers on its claim of fraudulent misrepresentation under New York law, since reasonable jury could conclude that purchaser, having conducted environmental due diligence and received report that was consistent with sellers' representations that there had been no dumping or other release of hazardous waste on property, had no obligation to investigate further, despite recommendation for additional testing in environmental audit.

5. Contracts ⚖2

New York law applied to claim questioning validity of contract, though parties chose Maryland law to govern their contract, where contract was made in New York.

6. Contracts ⚖2

Questions concerning validity of contract should be determined by law of jurisdiction in which it was made.

7. Fraud ⚖3

In New York, plaintiff claiming fraudulent misrepresentation must prove that defendant made material false representation, defendant intended to defraud plaintiff thereby, plaintiff reasonably relied on representation, and plaintiff suffered damage as result of such reliance.

8. Fraud ⚖22(1)

When party is aware of circumstances that indicate certain representations may be false, that party cannot reasonably rely on those representations, but must make additional inquiry to determine their accuracy.

9. Fraud ⚖31

Defrauded party is permitted to affirm contract and seek relief in damages, rather than choose remedy of rescission.

Opinion in *Keywell Corp. v. Weinstein*

160   33 FEDERAL REPORTER, 3d SERIES

10. Health and Environment ⚌25.5(5.5)

Purchaser of metal recycling plant was not entitled to recover costs of environmental cleanup from two officers, directors, and majority shareholders of selling corporation as signatories to purchase agreement, where agreement clearly allocated risk of CERCLA liability, which purchaser assumed when indemnity period expired, as shortened by the signing of release. Comprehensive Environmental Response, Compensation, and Liability Act of 1980, §§ 107(a), 113(f), 42 U.S.C.A. §§ 9607(a), 9613(f).

11. Health and Environment ⚌25.5(5.5)

Private parties may contractually allocate among themselves any loss they may suffer by imposition of CERCLA liability. Comprehensive Environmental Response, Compensation, and Liability Act of 1980, § 107(e)(1), 42 U.S.C.A. § 9607(e)(1).

———

Stuart A. Smith, New York City (Alfred Ferrer III, Piper & Marbury, Joseph G. Finnerty, Jr., Charles P. Scheeler, of counsel) for plaintiff-appellant.

Thomas E. Lippard, Pittsburgh, PA (Craig E. Frischman, Thorp Reed & Armstrong, of counsel) for defendant-appellee Weinstein.

Jeremiah J. McCarthy, Buffalo, NY (Phillips, Lytle, Hitchcock, Blaine & Huber, of counsel) for defendant-appellee Boscarino.

Before: WALKER, JACOBS, Circuit Judges and CARMAN,* Judge.

JACOBS, Circuit Judge:

Keywell Corporation ("Keywell") has incurred costs for environmental cleanup at an industrial facility that it purchased in 1987 from Vac Air Alloys Corporation ("Vac Air"). Defendants–Appellees Daniel C. Weinstein ("Weinstein") and Anthony Boscarino ("Boscarino") were shareholders, officers and directors of Vac Air prior to the purchase and at the time of the transaction, and were signatories to the Purchase Agreement. Keywell has brought suit against Weinstein

———
* Honorable Gregory W. Carman of the United States Court of International Trade, sitting by

and Boscarino, (i) alleging that they induced Keywell to buy the property by making misrepresentations bearing upon the environmental risks at the premises, and (ii) alleging that, as owners and operators of Vac Air, they are strictly liable to Keywell for their equitable share of response costs pursuant to §§ 107(a) and 113(f) of the Comprehensive Environmental Response, Compensation, and Liability Act ("CERCLA"). 42 U.S.C. §§ 9607(a) and 9613(f). Following the parties' submission of cross-motions for summary judgment, the district court dismissed Keywell's claims, finding as a matter of law that Keywell could not have reasonably relied on the allegedly fraudulent misrepresentations, and that Keywell had contractually released its right to sue defendants under CERCLA.

We affirm the dismissal of the CERCLA claims on the ground that the parties allocated the risk of CERCLA liability in their Purchase Agreement, the terms of which establish that such risk now falls on Keywell. However, we reverse the dismissal of the diversity fraud claims and remand for further proceedings. The Decision ←

BACKGROUND

The facts, drawing all justifiable inferences in favor of the non-movant Keywell, are as follows. Weinstein founded Vac Air in 1966 and, until the time Keywell purchased certain Vac Air assets in December 1987, was a principal shareholder, president, chief executive officer, and member of the board of directors of the company. Boscarino joined Vac Air in 1971 as an assistant to the secretary/treasurer, and by 1978 he had become a stockholder, director, and vice-president of the company. Both Weinstein and Boscarino took an active part in conducting the business of Vac Air, which included the operation of a metals recycling plant located in Frewsburg, New York (the "Frewsburg plant").

From the time Vac Air was founded in 1966 until Keywell's acquisition of assets in December 1987, the Frewsburg plant recycled scrap metal—a process that entailed the

designation.

issues, but that they were reversed on other issues and the case was sent back to the trial court for further proceedings as directed by the appellate decision.

How the Opinion Itself Is Organized

Normally, every intermediate appellate or supreme court opinion contains four basic elements:

1. A detailed statement of the facts that are accepted by the court as true. These facts are taken from the lower court's determination of the facts, unless the lower court's determinations were clearly in error. For intermediate appellate courts, the lower court is usually the trial court. For supreme courts, the lower court is usually the intermediate appellate court.

2. A statement of the legal issue or issues presented by the appealing parties for resolution.

3. An answer to the issues presented for resolution—this is called the ruling or holding. In appeals, the court always takes some specific action. If it agrees with the lower court's conclusions and the relief it ordered for one or both of the parties, the lower court decision is "affirmed." If the court disagrees with either or both of these aspects of the lower court's decision, the decision is "reversed."

    Sometimes lower court decisions are affirmed in part and reversed in part. If the intermediate appellate or supreme court agrees substantially with the lower court, but disagrees with some particular point, it may modify or amend the decision. Usually, in the case of a complete or partial reversal, the case is sent back to the lower court to take further action consistent with the intermediate appellate or supreme court's opinion. This is called a remand.

4. A discussion of why the ruling was made—the court's reasoning or rationale.

    The court's reasoning is usually the longest part of the case and the most difficult to understand, for a number of reasons:

    - The legal issues are complex and require a complex chain of reasoning to unravel.
    - The court doesn't understand the legal issues but has to address them anyway because the legal world expects it.
    - The court decides the case contrary to established law and spends a lot of time trying to explain this fact away.
    - The judge doesn't know how to write.

    A major part of law school training is how to analyze this element of court opinions and apply it to other cases. This book can't replace law school, but most researchers get the hang of legal reasoning after reading a few dozen cases. Also, consider reading Statsky and Wernet, *Case Analysis and Fundamentals of Legal Writing* (Thomson Learning, 1994) for a structured introduction to case analysis.

Many court opinions present these four components—facts, issues, decision and reasoning—in this order. Others do not. For instance, one format used by some courts is a summary of the issue and the decision in the first couple of paragraphs, followed by a statement of the facts and the reasoning.

The actual opinion issued in a case called *Deason v. Metropolitan Property & Liability Insurance Co.* is shown below. The four elements described above are labeled.

DEASON v. METRO. PROP. & LIABILITY INS. CO.   Ill.   783
Cite as 474 N.E.2d 783 (Ill.App. 5 Dist. 1985)

130 Ill.App.3d 620
85 Ill.Dec. 823

Mary Kaye **DEASON**, Administratrix of the Estate of David A. Deason, Deceased, and Mary Kaye Deason, Plaintiff-Appellee,

and

Florence Petro, Administrator of the Estate of George Petro, deceased; Sherrill Josephson, Administratrix of the Estate of Mathew Josephson, deceased; and Michael Petro, Counter-Plaintiffs-Appellees,

v.

METROPOLITAN PROPERTY & LIABILITY INSURANCE COMPANY, a Corporation, Defendant-Appellant,

and

Auto-Owners Insurance Company, a Corporation, et al., Defendants.

No. 5–84–0073.

Appellate Court of Illinois, Fifth District.

Jan. 10, 1985.

Action was brought against automobile insurer seeking a judgment declaring that policy issued to driver's parents afforded secondary coverage in connection with an accident which occurred while insureds' son was driving his grandmother's automobile. The Circuit Court, St. Clair County, Richard P. Goldenhersh, J., entered judgment in favor of plaintiffs, and insurer appealed. The Appellate Court, Harrison, J., held that automobile operated by driver was not a "temporary substitute vehicle" under terms of automobile policy issued to parents so as to afford secondary coverage in connection with driver's accident.

Reversed.

1. Declaratory Judgment ⟜168

Case involving question whether coverage existed under terms of automobile insurer's policy was proper subject for declaratory judgment action.

2. Insurance ⟜435.2(4)

Where driver's use of his grandmother's automobile was not to be temporary, but regular and permanent, and the automobile was not intended by driver's parents to be a substitute for either of two automobiles owned by driver's father, under terms of automobile policy issued to parents, the automobile operated by driver was not a "temporary substitute vehicle" so as to afford secondary coverage in connection with driver's accident.

See publication Words and Phrases for other judicial constructions and definitions.

3. Evidence ⟜200

In action brought against automobile insurer seeking a judgment declaring that policy issued to driver's parents afforded secondary coverage in connection with an accident which occurred while insureds' son was driving his grandmother's automobile, trial court correctly noted in its judgment that statements by certain employees of insurer to the effect that they believed driver's parents' policy afforded coverage were merely opinions and were not binding on a court in its consideration of the legal question presented.

Feirich, Schoen, Mager, Green & Associates, Carbondale, for defendant-appellant.

C.E. Heiligenstein, Brad L. Badgley, Belleville, for Mary Kaye Deason.

H. Carl Runge, Jr., Runge & Gumbel, P.C., Collinsville, for Beth Martell, a minor, by her father and next friend, John Martell, John Martell and Patsie Gott, Administratrix of the Estate of Lisa J. Gott, Deceased.

Michael P. Casey, Edward R. Vrdolyak, Ltd., Chicago, for Florence Petro & Sherrill Josephson & Michael Petro.

HARRISON, Justice:

[1] Metropolitan Property & Liability Insurance Company (hereinafter referred to as Metropolitan) appeals from a judgment of the circuit court of St. Clair Coun-

ty declaring that a policy of insurance issued by Metropolitan afforded secondary coverage in connection with a November 30, 1980, accident involving a 1975 Mercury Comet driven by Christopher Warner. The primary issue for our consideration is whether the trial court properly concluded that, under the terms of the policy issued by Metropolitan to Christopher Warner's parents, the Comet operated by Christopher Warner was a "temporary substitute automobile". Because this case involves the question of whether or not coverage exists under the terms of Metropolitan's policy, it is a proper subject for a declaratory judgment action. *Reagor v. Travelers Insurance Co.* (1980), 92 Ill.App.3d 99, 102–03, 47 Ill.Dec. 507, 415 N.E.2d 512.

The policy in question provides coverage to the insured for accidents arising out of the ownership, maintenance or use of an owned or non-owned automobile. The terms "non-owned automobile" and "owned automobile" are defined in the policy as follows:

" *'[N]on-owned automobile'* means an *automobile* which is neither owned by nor furnished nor available for the regular use of either the *named insured* or any *relative*, other than a *temporary substitute automobile*, and includes a *utility trailer* while used with any such *automobile:*

 •   •   •   •   •   •

'[O]wned automobile' means

(a) a *private passenger automobile* or *utility automobile* owned by the *named insured* and described in the Declarations to which the Automobile Liability Coverage of the policy applies and for which a specific premium for such insurance is charged, or

(b) a *private passenger automobile* or *utility automobile* ownership of which is newly acquired by the *named insured*, provided (i) it replaces an *owned automobile* as defined in (a) above, or (ii) METROPOLITAN insures all *automobiles* owned by the *named insured* on the date of such acquisition and the *named in-*

sured notifies METROPOLITAN within thirty (30) days of such acquisition of his election to make this and no other policy issued by METROPOLITAN applicable to such *automobile* and pays any additional premium required therefor, or

(c) a *temporary substitute automobile:*"

The policy defines "temporary substitute automobile" in this manner:

" *'[T]emporary substitute automobile'* means an *automobile* not owned by the *named insured* or any resident of the same household, while temporarily used with the permission of the owner as a substitute for an *owned automobile* when withdrawn from normal use for servicing or repair or because of breakdown, loss or destruction: "

The facts relevant to a determination of whether the 1975 Comet was a temporary substitute automobile are not in significant dispute. Christopher Warner spent the summer of 1980 in Ohio with his grandmother, Vera Fry. Ms. Fry, an Ohio resident, owned the 1975 Comet, which was insured by a company other than Metropolitan. During that summer, arrangements were made whereby Christopher would take the Comet with him when he returned to his parents' Cobden, Illinois home at the end of the summer. It was further agreed that Christopher would return to Ohio at Christmas time and pay Vera Fry $100 after which she would have the title to the Comet transferred to Christopher and one of his parents. Christopher did in fact bring the Comet back to Cobden in August, 1980, and he and his parents used it regularly. On November 30, 1980, before Christopher had paid any money to Vera Fry, and before title to the Comet had been transferred, the accident in question occurred.

On the date of the accident, Andrew Warner, Christopher's father, owned a 1973 Mercury and a 1974 Dodge pickup truck. Both of these vehicles were insured by Metropolitan. Neither was operable at

Opinion in Deason v. Metropolitan *(continued)*

DEASON v. METRO. PROP. & LIABILITY INS. CO.   Ill.   78£
Cite as 474 N.E.2d 783 (Ill.App. 5 Dist. 1985)

the time of the accident; the Mercury had a defective transmission and the Dodge had a twisted drive shaft. Both vehicles were put back into operation shortly after the accident involving the Comet. During his deposition, Andrew Warner testified as follows:

"Q. Did you have any intention if the Comet hadn't been wrecked, did you have any intention to dispose of either of these other two cars just because you got the Comet?

A. Oh, no."

[2] In ruling that Metropolitan's policy afforded secondary coverage in connection with the accident involving the 1975 Comet, the court found that Christopher Warner was "a relative operating a temporary substitute" automobile. Metropolitan contends that this conclusion is incorrect, and we are compelled to agree. Under the terms of the policy, a temporary substitute automobile is defined as one "temporarily used with the permission of the owner as a substitute for an owned automobile when withdrawn from normal use for servicing or repair or because of breakdown, loss, or destruction." Here, the unequivocal deposition testimony of all concerned establishes that Christopher Warner's use of the Comet was not to be temporary, but regular and permanent, as it was the intention of both Vera Fry and Christopher Warner that he would pay $100 for the car at Christmas time, and would not return it to her. Moreover, the Comet was not intended by the Warners to be a substitute for either the Mercury or the Dodge; rather, it was to be kept as a third car, and the fact that the Dodge and Mercury broke down during the Warners' use of the Comet was entirely coincidental. Under these circumstances, the "temporary substitute" provision of the policy issued by Metropolitan did not encompass Christopher Warner's use of the Comet on the date of the accident. (See *Sturgeon v. Automobile Club Inter-Insurance Exchange* (1979), 77 Ill. App.3d 997, 1000, 34 Ill.Dec. 66, 397 N.E.2d 522.) This conclusion is buttressed by the holding of *Nationwide Insurance Compa-*

ny v. Ervin* (1967), 87 Ill.App.2d 432, 436-37, 231 N.E.2d 112, wherein it was recognized that a "temporary substitute" provision of the type under consideration here is to be applied to those situations where an insured automobile is withdrawn from use for a short period, and not where, as here coverage is sought to be extended to an additional automobile for a significant length of time.

[3] *Providence Mutual Casualty Company v. Sturms* (1962), 37 Ill.App.2d 304 185 N.E.2d 366, relied on by appellees, is not on point. *Sturms* addresses the question of whether coverage afforded on a temporary substitute automobile expires immediately upon repair of the insured's regular automobile (37 Ill.App.2d 304, 306 185 N.E.2d 366), and does not discuss the more fundamental issue of when a vehicle is considered to be a temporary substitute in the first place. While appellees also suggest that portions of Metropolitan's claim file show that certain Metropolitan employees believe that the policy in question afforded coverage, the trial court correctly noted in its judgment that these statements are merely opinions, and are not binding on a court in its consideration of the legal question presented. 31A C.J.S Evidence § 272(b) (1964).

For the foregoing reasons, the judgment of the circuit court of St. Clair County is reversed.

Reversed.

JONES, P.J., and KARNS, J., concur.

Opinion in Deason v. Metropolitan *(continued)*

Courts Where Appeals Are Normally Filed

Courts Cases Appealed From	U.S. Supreme Court	U.S. Court of Appeals	State Supreme Court	State Court of Appeal
U.S. Courts of Appeals	X			
U.S. District Courts	If issued by a 3-judge panel OR when the U.S., its agent or employee is a party, and an act of Congress is held unconstitutional on its face (not as applied)	X		
State Supreme Courts	If a federal question is involved	X		
State Courts of Appeal	If a federal question is involved and the State Supreme Court has denied relief OR declined to hear the case		X	
State Trial Courts			If there's no court of appeal OR it is a special case (appeal of death penalty case)	X

Library Exercise: The Nuts and Bolts of a Case

You are reading an employment discrimination case for a meeting of your research team. You will be expected to be familiar with the procedural aspects of the case. The case can be found at 3 F.3d 873. Locate the case and learn about its structural and procedural aspects.

Questions

1. The name of the case is useful because that is how a case is often referred to by people familiar with it. What is the name of your case?

2. The citation of a case is how it is referred to in written materials, as in a memo to the court. What is the citation of your case?

3. Knowing the docket number of a case and the date of the decision will help you get information or documents from the court. Also, if the opinion is very recent, you need this information to get a copy of the slip opinion from the court or from Lexis or Westlaw. What are the docket number and date of decision of your case?

4. Knowing which court wrote the opinion tells you what other decisions this court had to follow when deciding this case. It also tells you which courts are bound by this decision. What court heard *Moham* and wrote this opinion? By what court decisions were the judges bound, and who is bound by this opinion?

5. A trial is a presentation of evidence (witnesses' testimony and physical evidence) as well as lawyers' arguments linking facts and law. Typically, the judge makes decisions about the application of the law, and the jury makes findings of facts (verdicts). In an appeal, there is no presentation of evidence—the only question to be decided is whether the trial court correctly applied the law. Is *Moham* from a trial court or an appellate court?

6. It is important to know what happened in the lower court in order to understand what issues are being appealed and what will happen as a result of the decision.

6a. In what court was the trial held?

6b. Who was the plaintiff and who was the defendant?

6c. Who won in the trial court?

6d. Who appealed to the Fifth Circuit?

7. What does the Summary of the case tell you about the appellate court's decision?

Answers

1. The name of the case is *Moham v. Steego Corp.* In a discussion, people would call it "Moham."

2. *Moham v. Steego Corp.*, 3 F.3d 873 (5th Cir. 1993).

3. The docket number is 92-5165, and the date of the decision is September 27, 1993.

4. The U.S. Court of Appeals for the 5th Circuit heard this case. The three judges on the appellate panel were bound by prior decisions of the Fifth Circuit. This decision will be precedent for appellate and trial courts within the Fifth Circuit.

5. *Moham* is a decision from an appellate court, and therefore it will discuss whether the lower court correctly understood and applied the law.

6a. The trial was held in the United States District Court for the Western District of Louisiana.

6b. Mr. Moham was the plaintiff, and Steego Corporation was the defendant.

6c. The trial judge found for the employee, Mr. Moham.

6d. Steego Corporation, who lost, was the appellant; and Mr. Moham, who won, became the appellee.

7. It seems that everyone got something as a result of this trip to the appellate courthouse. The decision of the lower court was "affirmed in part" (meaning that some of its decision was left intact); it was "reversed and rendered in part" (meaning that a part of the judge's decision was overturned and the correct decision was substituted by the appellate court); and it was "remanded" (meaning that the case was sent back to the trial court to re-do some aspect of it in accordance with the instructions contained in the appellate decision).

How Appellate Courts Decide Cases

Appellate courts comprise anywhere from three to nine justices. For example, the California Supreme Court and the New York Court of Appeals have seven justices, the Vermont Supreme Court has five and the U.S. Supreme Court has nine. In New York (and in Texas for criminal cases) the highest state court is called the Court of Appeals rather than the Supreme Court.

Only the actual decision of the majority (or plurality) of justices and the principles of law that are absolutely necessary to that decision serve as precedent for other courts. Other discussion in the opinion may be helpful in understanding the decision, but is not binding on other courts. The court's decision and the law necessary to arrive at it are called the "holding." The rest of the decision is called "dicta."

A justice on an appellate court who disagrees with the decision of the majority on a case may issue a "dissenting" opinion, which is published along with the majority's opinion. No matter how passionate a dissent happens to be, it has no effect on the particular case. However, it may have a persuasive effect on judges in future court decisions.

A justice who agrees with the majority decision but disagrees with the reasons given for it may issue a "concurring opinion," which is published along with the majority's opinion. A concurring opinion also can have a persuasive influence on future court decisions.

If the main opinion in the case is supported by less than a majority—called a "plurality" opinion—the concurring opinion can in fact operate as a weak type of authority for future cases. For instance, in a 1985 case, the U.S. Supreme Court issued an opinion in which only four justices joined. A fifth justice, Chief Justice Burger, concurred and swung the court's holding to the plurality's view; if Chief Justice Burger had sided with the other four justices, they might have been the majority (or plurality, if he only concurred with and did not join their opinion).

For a fascinating account of how the U.S. Supreme Court decides its cases, read *The Brethren: Inside the Supreme Court,* by Woodward and Armstrong (Simon and Schuster, 1979).

Using Synopses and Headnotes to Read and Understand a Case

In addition to the court opinions, the publishers of case reports also publish a one-paragraph synopsis of the case and some helpful one-sentence summaries of the legal issues discussed in it. The synopsis and "headnotes" come just before the opinion itself. Below are the headnotes from *Deason v. Metropolitan Property & Liability Insurance Co.*

The headnotes are numbered in the order in which the legal issues they summarize appear in the opinion. The part of the opinion covered by each headnote is marked off in the opinion with a number in brackets. See the *Deason* opinion, above, for an example.

Headnotes can be very useful in several ways. They serve as a table of contents to the opinion, so that if you are only interested in one of the many issues raised in a case, you can skim the headnotes, find the relevant issue and then turn to the corresponding bracketed number in the opinion. Headnotes also allow discussions of legal issues in one case to be cross-indexed to similar discussions in other cases by the use of "digests." (See Chapter 10.) Finally, headnotes are very helpful when you are "Shepardizing" a case. (See Chapter 10.)

⚠ **Headnotes Are Prepared by the Publisher and Are Not Part of the Case As Such.** Because the editors who prepare the headnotes are human and fallible, don't rely on the headnotes to accurately state the issue or principle of law as it appears in the opinion. You must read the pertinent section of the opinion for yourself. Never quote a headnote in any argument you submit to a court.

DEASON v. METRO. PROP. & LIABILITY INS. CO.   Ill. 783
Cite as 474 N.E.2d 783 (Ill.App. 5 Dist. 1985)

130 Ill.App.3d 620
85 Ill.Dec. 823

Mary Kaye DEASON, Administratrix of the Estate of David A. Deason, Deceased, and Mary Kaye Deason, Plaintiff-Appellee,

and

Florence Petro, Administrator of the Estate of George Petro, deceased; Sherrill Josephson, Administratrix of the Estate of Mathew Josephson, deceased; and Michael Petro, Counter-Plaintiffs-Appellees,

v.

METROPOLITAN PROPERTY & LIABILITY INSURANCE COMPANY, a Corporation, Defendant-Appellant,

and

Auto-Owners Insurance Company, a Corporation, et al., Defendants.

No. 5-84-0073.

Appellate Court of Illinois, Fifth District.

Jan. 10, 1985.

Action was brought against automobile insurer seeking a judgment declaring that policy issued to driver's parents afforded secondary coverage in connection with an accident which occurred while insureds' son was driving his grandmother's automobile. The Circuit Court, St. Clair County, Richard P. Goldenhersh, J., entered judgment in favor of plaintiffs, and insurer appealed. The Appellate Court, Harrison, J., held that automobile operated by driver was not a "temporary substitute vehicle" under terms of automobile policy issued to parents so as to afford secondary coverage in connection with driver's accident.

Reversed.

headnote

1. **Declaratory Judgment** ⇐168

Case involving question whether coverage existed under terms of automobile insurer's policy was proper subject for declaratory judgment action.

2. **Insurance** ⇐435.2(4)   ← headnote

Where driver's use of his grandmother's automobile was not to be temporary, but regular and permanent, and the automobile was not intended by driver's parents to be a substitute for either of two automobiles owned by driver's father, under terms of automobile policy issued to parents, the automobile operated by driver was not a "temporary substitute vehicle" so as to afford secondary coverage in connection with driver's accident.

> See publication Words and Phrases for other judicial constructions and definitions.

3. **Evidence** ⇐200   ← headnote

In action brought against automobile insurer seeking a judgment declaring that policy issued to driver's parents afforded secondary coverage in connection with an accident which occurred while insureds' son was driving his grandmother's automobile, trial court correctly noted in its judgment that statements by certain employees of insurer to the effect that they believed driver's parents' policy afforded coverage were merely opinions and were not binding on a court in its consideration of the legal question presented.

Headnotes from Deason v. Metropolitan Property & Liability Insurance Co.

How Cases Affect Later Disputes

Past decisions in appellate cases are powerful predictors of what the courts are likely to do in future cases given a similar set of facts. Most judges try hard to be consistent with decisions that either they or a higher court have made. This consistency is very important to a just legal system and is the essence of the common law tradition. (Common law—the decisions of courts over the years—is discussed in Chapter 3.) For this reason, if you can find a previous court decision that rules your way on facts similar to your situation, you have a good shot at persuading a judge to follow that case and decide in your favor.

There are two basic principles to understand when you're reading cases with an eye to using them to persuade a judge to rule your way. One is called "precedent," the other "persuasive authority."

Precedent

In the legal sense, a "precedent" is an earlier case that is relevant to a case to be decided. If there is nothing to distinguish the circumstances of the current case from the already-decided one, the earlier holding is considered binding on the court.

The idea of a precedent comes from a basic principle of the American common law system: *stare decisis* (Latin for "Let the decision stand"). Once a high court decides how the law should be applied to a particular set of facts, this decision controls later decisions by that and other courts. For example, a majority of the present U.S. Supreme Court is thought to dislike the common law rule that illegally seized evidence cannot be used in a criminal prosecution. Yet, because this rule was created in past Supreme Court cases, the present court continues to uphold it (while minimizing the effect of the rule by carving out more and more exceptions).

A case is only a precedent as to its particular decision and the law necessary to arrive at that decision. If, in passing, a judge deals with a legal question that is not absolutely essential to the decision, the reasoning and opinion in respect to this tangential question are not precedent, but non-binding "dicta."

Example: A Court of Appeals rules that the lesser dung beetle is protected under the Endangered Species Act. As part of his reasoning, the judge writing the opinion states that as he reads the statute, even mosquitoes are entitled to protection. Since the court was asked to rule on the lesser dung beetle, the judge's comments on mosquitoes are dicta—language unnecessary to deciding the case before the court—and not binding as to any future dispute on that point.

It is common for courts to avoid overruling earlier decisions by distinguishing the earlier one from the present one on the basis of some insignificant factual difference or small legal issue. It is much easier to get a court to "distinguish" an old case than openly overrule it. Simply put, it is sometimes difficult to tell whether an earlier case has been overruled (and is clearly no longer precedent) or distinguished (and therefore technically still operative as precedent).

On the other hand, prior decisions are sometimes expressly overruled as not being consistent with the times. When the U.S. Supreme Court decided *Brown v. Board of Education* in 1954, it held that separate educational facilities for black and white students were unconstitutional. That overruled a 19th-century case called *Plessy v. Ferguson*, which had held that such "separate but equal" facilities were constitutional.

A case is only precedent as to a particular set of facts and the precise legal issue decided in light of those facts. The more the facts or legal issues vary between two cases, the less the former operates as precedent in respect to the latter. Teaching the art of distinguishing cases on the basis of the facts and issues decided is what most of law school is all about.

In addition to the degree of similarity between an earlier and a later case, the precedential value of the earlier case is affected by which court decided it. Here are some guidelines for determining the effect that one court's decisions have on another's:

- Appellate court cases (including supreme court cases) operate as precedent with respect to future decisions by the same courts.

  Example: In 2020, the Indiana Supreme Court rules that county general relief grants cannot be terminated without first providing the recipient with a hearing. In 2021, a fiscally strapped county cuts everyone off general assistance without hearings. A group of recipients seeks court relief. In 2021, the issue gets to the Indiana Supreme

Court, which orders the recipients reinstated on the ground of its earlier ruling.

- U.S. Supreme Court cases are precedent for all courts in respect to decisions involving the U.S. Constitution or any aspect of federal law.

    Example: In 2020, the U.S. Supreme Court rules that under the First Amendment to the U.S. Constitution, non-lawyers may help the public use self-help law books without being charged with the unauthorized practice of law. In 2021, the Nebraska Bar Association sues a non-lawyer to stop him from telling people how to use a self-help divorce book. He claims a violation of his First Amendment rights and wins on the basis of the U.S. Supreme Court case.

- U.S. Courts of Appeals cases are precedent for U.S. District Courts within their circuits (that is, the states covered by the circuit) and for state courts in this area with respect to issues concerning the U.S. Constitution and any aspect of federal law. (The country is divided into 12 circuits—see list in Chapter 8.)

    Example: In 2005, the U.S. Court of Appeals for the First Circuit rules that the Eighth Amendment to the U.S. Constitution requires that bail in a criminal case be set in an amount that the defendant can reasonably afford to raise. In 2008, Perry is charged in the U.S. District Court for New Hampshire with the crime of assault against a federal officer. Since the U.S. District Court for New Hampshire is within the First Circuit, it must follow the rule for bail laid down by the Court of Appeals for that circuit. However, if Perry were charged with the crime in the U.S. District Court in Vermont—which is in the Second Circuit—the First Circuit case would not be binding.

    If Perry were charged with a crime in a New Hampshire state court, he would still be entitled to the new bail rule, since it is based on the U.S. Constitution and New Hampshire is within the First Circuit.

- U.S. District Court case opinions are never precedent for other courts. (They may be persuasive authority; see "Persuasive Authority," below.)

    Example: A U.S. District Court in Hawaii rules that the Federal Endangered Species Act applies to mosquitoes. A U.S. District Court in Houston is asked to stop a local development because it threatens an endangered mosquito species. The U.S. District Court in Houston is free to follow the Hawaii case or reach a different conclusion.

- State supreme court cases are precedent with respect to all courts within the state.

    Example: The Nevada Supreme Court rules that casinos may not require female employees to wear sexy outfits. This ruling is binding on all Nevada courts that are later faced with this issue.

- State intermediate appellate court cases are precedent with respect to the trial courts in the state. In larger states (for example, California), where the intermediate appellate courts are divided into districts (for instance, the fifth appellate district or the second appellate district), any particular intermediate appellate court's decision is sometimes only regarded as precedent by the trial courts within that district.

    Example: In 2006, the intermediate appellate court for the fifth appellate district in California rules that preparing an uncontested divorce petition for another is not the practice of law. As long as this is the only intermediate appellate court ruling on this issue in the state, it is binding on all California trial courts. In 2007, the intermediate appellate court for the second appellate district rules that preparing an uncontested divorce petition is the practice of law and can be done only by attorneys. The first ruling, from the fifth appellate district, is binding on the trial courts located within that district—for example, those in Fresno. The second ruling is binding on trial courts in the second appellate district—for instance, Los Angeles. Trial courts in other appellate districts may follow either precedent, until their intermediate appellate courts issue their own rulings.

Persuasive Authority

If a case is not precedent (binding on later courts) but contains an excellent analysis of the legal issues and provides guidance for any court that happens to read it, it is "persuasive authority." For example, the landmark California Supreme Court case of *Marvin v. Marvin*, the first major case establishing the principle of "palimony," was considered persuasive authority by many courts in other states when considering the same issue, though the *Marvin* decision was not binding on courts outside California.

As a general rule, the higher the court, the more persuasive its opinion. Every word (even dicta) of a U.S. Supreme Court opinion is considered important in assessing the state of the law. Opinions written by an intermediate appellate court in a small state, however, are not nearly so influential on other courts.

Example: In the case partially set out below, a Colorado court used cases from Hawaii, Texas and Virginia as guidance in arriving at its own decision.

How to Analyze the Effect of an Earlier Case on Your Issue

Reading cases and understanding how they apply to your issue can be vexing. Most law and paralegal schools offer an entire course on case analysis. Obviously this book can't replace that training. The sidebar below offers one possible approach, and a close reading of Statsky's *Case Analysis* will definitely help. But you may have to put in a number of hours of practice before you feel comfortable with the case analysis process.

Steps to Analyzing the Effect of an Earlier Case

Step 1. Identify the precise issues decided in the case—that is, what issues of law the court had to decide in order to make its ruling.

Step 2. Compare the issues in the case to the issues you are interested in and decide whether the case addresses one or more of them. If so, move to Step 3. If not, the case is probably not helpful.

Step 3. Carefully read and understand the facts underlying the case and compare them to the facts of your situation. Does the case's decision on the relevant issues logically stand up when applied to your facts? If so, move to Step 4. If not, go to Step 5.

Step 4. Determine whether the court that decided the case you are reading creates precedent for the trial or appellate courts in your area. If so, the case may serve as precedent. If not, move to Step 5.

Step 5. Carefully read and understand the legal reasoning employed by the court when deciding the relevant issues and decide whether it logically would help another court resolve your issues. If so, the case may be persuasive authority.

Arguing the Law

You can often find two attorneys in the same courtroom relying on the same case to support two diametrically opposed positions. This is, at least in part, because lawyers are adept at hairsplitting. Distinguishing one very similar fact situation from another so that the distinguished case will not be used as precedent or persuasive authority in the case you are arguing is a highly-developed art. If you want to succeed in the legal world, you must be ready to hairsplit with the best of them. For assistance in learning this valuable legal skill, consult Statsky and Wernet, *Case Analysis and Fundamentals of Legal Writing* (West Group, 1995).

must inevitably result in suppressing protected speech." *Id.* at 526, 528, 78 S.Ct. at 1342, 1343.

Presumptions similar or identical to the one at issue here have been invalidated as unconstitutional by various courts. In *State v. Bumanglag*, 63 Hawaii 596, 634 P.2d 80 (1981), for example, the court held that such a presumption [18] impermissibly inhibited free expression: "Its application would tend to limit public access to protected material because booksellers may then restrict what they offer to works they are familiar with and consider 'safe.' The distribution of protected, as well as obscene, matter may be affected by this self-censorship." [19] 634 P.2d at 96.

In *Davis v. State*, 658 S.W.2d 572 (Tex. Crim.App.1983), the court perceived a similar danger to the guarantees of the first amendment, noting that, especially in the case of a large establishment, "[t]he risk of suppressing freedom of expression is not negligible; ... it rises to astronomical proportions." 658 S.W.2d at 579. In addition to observing that the presumption cannot survive due process analysis, *see Leary v. United States*, 395 U.S. 6, 89 S.Ct. 1532, 23 L.Ed.2d 57 (1969), the Texas court concluded that "[f]reedom of expression is too important a right to allow it to be seriously impeded or impaired by a presumption such as the one implicated in this case." 658 S.W.2d at 580. *See also Grove Press, Inc. v. Evans*, 306 F.Supp. 1084 (E.D.Va.1969); *Skinner v. State*, 647 S.W.2d 686 (Tex.App. 1982) (presumption impermissibly shifts burden of proof and eliminates element of

scienter); Model Penal Code § 251.4(2), comment 11 (1980) ("A presumption that one who disseminates or possesses obscene material in the course of his business does so knowingly or recklessly places a severe burden of prior examination and screening on legitimate business. It seems unlikely today that such a presumption would pass constitutional scrutiny."); Note, *The Scienter Requirement in Criminal Obscenity Prosecutions*, 41 N.Y.U.L.Rev. 791, 797–99 (1966) (evidentiary presumptions similar to the one at issue here are invalid after *Smith v. California*).

The Supreme Court has, on one occasion, expressly declined to reach the issue of the constitutionality of such presumptions. *Ginsberg v. New York*, 390 U.S. 629, 632 n. 1, 88 S.Ct. 1274, 1276 n. 1, 20 L.Ed.2d 195 (1968). More recently, however, in a case in which the same issue was raised, the Supreme Court dismissed an appeal for want of a substantial federal question in *People v. Kirkpatrick*, 32 N.Y.2d 17, 343 N.Y.S.2d 70, 295 N.E.2d 753 (1973), *appeal dismissed*, 414 U.S. 948, 94 S.Ct. 283, 38 L.Ed.2d 204 (1973). In *Kirkpatrick*, the state courts upheld the constitutionality of a statutory presumption that the seller of obscene materials knows the contents of that material, and also held that there was sufficient independent evidence of scienter to support the conviction.

[23] This dismissal, in its procedural context, was equivalent to an adjudication of the federal issue on its merits.[20] *Hicks*

---

18. HRS § 712–1214 provided that:
    (1) A person commits the offense of promoting pornography if, knowing its content and character, he:
    (a) Disseminates for monetary consideration any pornographic material....
    The presumption at issue, contained in HRS § 712–1216, provided that:
    (1) The fact that a person engaged in the conduct specified by sections 712–1214 or 712–1215 is prima facie evidence that he engaged in that conduct with knowledge of the character and content of the material disseminated or the performance produced, presented, directed, participated in, exhibited, or to be exhibited....

19. Additionally, the court in *Bumanglag* implied that the challenged presumption violated due process. The court agreed that salespeople generally were less likely than not to know the contents of their entire stock: "We find this difficult to discount, for a conclusion that a person who sold a book also was familiar with its character and content does not comport with what common sense and experience tell us about booksellers, salesclerks and their knowledge of the contents of books." 634 P.2d at 96.

20. We are aware that summary affirmances have sometimes been accorded less than full precedential weight by the Supreme Court. *See Edelman v. Jordan*, 415 U.S. 651, 671, 94 S.Ct. 1347, 1359, 39 L.Ed.2d 662 (1974); *Richardson*

Library Exercise: Anatomy of a U.S. Supreme Court Case

You are reading another employment discrimination case for your research team. This one is a U.S. Supreme Court case and, in addition to understanding the facts and the holding of the case, you will be expected to explain the structural details of the case. The case can be found on page 538 of volume 108 of the *Supreme Court Reporter*.

Questions

1. What is the name of the case?
2. What is the citation? This is how you will refer to the case in written memos to your boss or to a court. (Note that United States Supreme Court decisions are printed in three reporters. Citations to all of them are included in a complete written citation, with the official reporter (U.S.) listed first.)
3. What is the docket number, and what is the date of decision?
4. What happened in the lower courts? Where do you look for a quick answer to this question?
5a. The Supreme Court made a decision that affected the individuals involved (the probation officer and the judge); it also explained or announced a rule of law that others can rely upon and should follow. What happened as far as the individuals were concerned? What does "reversed and remanded" mean?
5b. What legal rule did the Supreme Court decide should be used in the case?
6. If you wanted to read the Court of Appeals' opinion which had been vacated by the grant of *certiori* in this case, where would you find it?
7. How could you find out what happened to the parties in this case after they returned to the trial court?
8. At the end of page 539, there is a syllabus (synopsis of the case). Is this text a part of the opinion, and can it be cited and used as authority?
9. Where does the opinion itself start?
10. Who wrote the headnotes numbered 1 through 6 on page 539?
11. On page 543, about two-thirds of the way down the left column, there is a paragraph with a "[5]" in front of it. What does the "[5]"mean?

Answers

1. The name of the case is *Forrester v. White*.

2. *Forrester v. White*, (1988) 484 U.S. 219, 98 L.Ed.2d 55, 108 S. Ct. 538.
3. The docket number is #86-761, and the decision was issued on January 12, 1988.
4. A quick summary of the decision is found directly after the argument and decision dates. At the trial in the U.S. District Court, the plaintiff, a probation officer, alleged she was demoted and fired by her superior (a judge) because of sexual discrimination. The judge, who was the defendant, claimed that hiring and firing probation officers was a judicial function and that, consequently, he was protected from suit by disgruntled former employees by virtue of his judicial immunity. The jury decided in favor of the plaintiff, but the court granted the defendant's motion for summary judgment on the grounds that he was immune from civil suit. The Court of Appeals affirmed (agreed with) the District Court's decision. Forrester (the plaintiff) then appealed to the U.S. Supreme Court.
5a. "Reversed" means that the Supreme Court disagreed with the Court of Appeals as to what the rule of law should be. "Remanded" means that, having set the appellate court straight, the Supreme Court sent the case back to the appellate court to decide the issues remaining in the appeal in keeping with the Supreme Court's instruction on the law.
5b. The Supreme Court held that a state court judge was not immune from being sued for sexual discrimination when he dismissed a probation officer because this was an administrative, rather than a judicial, function.
6. The original Court of Appeals opinion would be found at 792 F.2d 647. This citation was included in the summary.
7. The end of the summary notes that the "Opinion on remand" will be found at 846 F.2d 29.
8. No, the "Syllabus" was written by an editor who works for the reporter series (West's), and it may not be cited.
9. The portion of the opinion that may be cited as authority begins at the end of page 540.
10. The editors of the reporter read the opinion and assigned headnotes to various sections.
11. This is the part of the opinion that is summarized in headnote 5.

Review

Questions

1. What is a "case" for the purpose of discussing the law?
2. What elements does every intermediate appellate or supreme court opinion contain?
3. What is a dissenting opinion, and what effect does it have?
4. What is a concurring opinion, and what effect does it have?
5. How are headnotes helpful in legal research?
6. What is a precedent?
7. What is persuasive authority?

Answers

1. Cases are the published opinions of appellate or supreme courts.
2. Almost all published cases contain:
   - A detailed statement of the facts that are accepted by the court as true;
   - A statement of the legal issue or issues presented by the appealing parties for resolution;
   - An answer to the issues presented for resolution (called the ruling or holding);
   - A discussion of why the ruling was made—the court's reasoning or rationale.
3. A justice on an appellate court who disagrees with the decision of the majority on a case may issue a dissenting opinion, which is published along with the majority's opinion. No matter how passionate a dissent happens to be, it has no effect on the particular case. However, it may have a persuasive effect on judges in future court decisions.
4. A justice who agrees with the majority decision but disagrees with the reasons given for it may issue a concurring opinion, which is published along with the majority's opinion. A concurring opinion can also have a persuasive influence on future court decisions.
5. - They serve as a table of contents to the opinion.
   - They allow discussions of legal issues in one case to be cross-indexed to similar discussions in other cases by the use of "digests."
   - They are very helpful when you are "Shepardizing" a case.
6. An earlier case that is relevant to a case to be decided. If there is nothing to distinguish the circumstances of the current case from the case that has already been decided, the earlier holding is considered binding on the court. A case is only precedent as to a particular set of facts and the precise legal issue decided in light of those facts.
7. If a case is not precedent (binding on other courts), but contains an excellent analysis of the legal issues and provides guidance for any court that happens to read it, it is "persuasive authority."

How Cases Are Published

Cases are published in volumes called "case reports," "reports," or "reporters." We use the term "reporter" throughout this chapter, except when a particular publication uses a different term. When we refer to a particular publication we also give its citation. We discuss citations in detail in Chapter 9.

Cases are also "published" online and are available over the Internet. Courts publish their own recent cases (access is free) and proprietary entities such as Lexis, Westlaw, Loislaw and Versuslaw publish cases (both recent and archived) that are available to their subscribers for a fee.

If you are in a law library as you read this, locate the volumes of the *Federal Supplement*—the reporter containing published U.S. District Court cases. You will see hundreds of numbered hardcover volumes; more than 20 volumes a year are added to the collection. If you look around, you will see that some sets of volumes reporting the cases of the other court systems are even larger. All told, there are many thousands of books containing court cases—courts have been cranking out opinions for a long, long time.

There are many separate reporters for different courts and for geographical areas; an opinion may be published in more than one. For example, New York Court of Appeals cases are found in a publication titled *New York Appeals* and in a regional reporter called the *Northeastern Reporter*, which contains state court cases from New York, Illinois, Indiana, Massachusetts and Ohio.

California Supreme Court cases are found in three publications:

- *California Reports* (California Supreme Court cases only);
- *California Reporter* (all California Appellate and Supreme Court cases); and
- *Pacific Reporter* (a regional reporter that collects cases from the appellate courts of 15 Western states).

Federal Cases

Federal court cases are published according to the court they are decided by.

U.S. District Court Cases

Only a very small percentage—those deemed to be of widespread legal interest—of U.S. District Court cases are published. This means that occasionally a case can be on the front page of your local paper for weeks and never be reported. There is no automatic connection between sensational facts and legal import. All published U.S. District Court cases are collected in the *Federal Supplement* (F. Supp.) or *Federal Rules Decisions* (F.R.D.).

Bankruptcy Court Cases

Decisions of the U.S. bankruptcy courts are reported in the *Bankruptcy Reporter* (B.R.), published by West.

U.S. Court of Appeals Cases

All published decisions by the U.S. Courts of Appeals are collected in the *Federal Reporter*. This is currently in its third series and is abbreviated as "F.", "F.2d", or "F.3d" (*Federal Reporter, Second Series*).

The U.S. Court of Appeals (the intermediate federal appellate court) is divided into 12 circuits and a special court called the Federal Circuit that hears appeals relating to patents and customs. Below is a table of the states in each circuit.

U.S. Supreme Court Cases

Last, but certainly not least, there are three separate reporters for United States Supreme Court cases. Each of them contains the same cases but different editorial enhancements.

You might wonder why it is necessary to have three reporters for a single court. It's really not; many small law libraries only buy one, or two at the most.

United States Supreme Court Reports (U.S.)

This reporter is the so-called "official" reporter, commissioned by Congress. Other reports that cover these cases are termed unofficial reports. This doesn't mean the opinions collected in the official reporter are more accurate or authoritative than those in the unofficial reporters; for basic legal research purposes there is little difference between the official and unofficial reporters. However, most courts require a citation to the official reporter when referring to a U.S. Supreme Court case in court documents.

Supreme Court Reporter (S. Ct.)

This reporter is part of the West Group series of reporters, which means it is also part of an elaborate cross-reference system known as the "key system" (explained in Chapter 10). If you are using the West research system, it is a good idea to use this reporter.

Supreme Court Reports, Lawyer's Edition (L. Ed.)

This reporter is published by Lexis Publishing and is very handy if you are using that company's research system. This reporter contains not only all of the U.S. Supreme Court cases (as do the other two reports), but also provides considerable editorial comment about the case's impact, including an annotation that relates the case to other cases on the same subject. This reporter is currently in its second series.

Circuits of the U.S. Court of Appeals

1st Circuit

Maine	New Hampshire	Rhode Island
Massachusetts	Puerto Rico	

2nd Circuit

Connecticut	New York	Vermont

3rd Circuit

Delaware	Pennsylvania	Virgin Islands
New Jersey		

4th Circuit

Maryland	South Carolina	West Virginia
North Carolina	Virginia	

5th Circuit

Canal Zone	Mississippi	Texas
Louisiana		

6th Circuit

Kentucky	Ohio	Tennessee
Michigan		

7th Circuit

Illinois	Indiana	Wisconsin

8th Circuit

Arkansas	Missouri	North Dakota
Iowa	Nebraska	South Dakota
Minnesota		

9th Circuit

Alaska	Hawaii	Nevada
Arizona	Idaho	Oregon
California	Montana	Washington
Guam		

10th Circuit

Colorado	New Mexico	Utah
Kansas	Oklahoma	Wyoming

11th Circuit

Alabama	Florida	Georgia

District of Columbia Circuit

Washington, D.C.

Federal Circuit

Patent and Customs Cases

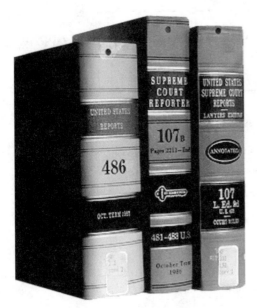

Supreme Court Reports

State Court Cases

Each state arranges for its appellate court cases to be published in official state reporters. In the larger states, there are usually two official reporters: one for the highest court cases and another for the intermediate appellate court cases. If you are interested in using the official reporters for your state while doing your research, ask your law librarian where the official state reporter is shelved.

In addition to these official reporters, the cases of each state—both supreme court and appellate—are published in a series of reporters called "regional reporters," published by the West Group. West has divided the country into seven regions, and the cases produced by the courts of each state in a region are published together. For example, cases from Alabama, Florida, Louisiana and Mississippi are all published in the *Southern Reporter*.

West also publishes state-specific versions of its regional reporters. For this reason, the *Southern Reporter* found in an Alabama library might contain only Alabama cases.

Most academic law libraries carry both the official reporters for their own state and the regional reporters for the entire country. However, when it comes to cases from other states, they probably won't have state-specific reporters. So if you are in New Hampshire and want to look up a New Hampshire case, you will have a choice between the New Hampshire official reports and the *Atlantic Reporter* (the regional reporter for the Northeast). However, if you want to find a Florida case, you will most likely need to use the *Southern Reporter*.

Keeping Case Reporters Up-to-Date

A significant time lag usually exists between the date a case is decided and publication of a new hardcover reporter. To make new cases available during the interim, reporters have weekly update pamphlets called "advance sheets." The chances are great that if a case was decided within several months (or even years for some Supreme Court cases) of when you are doing your research, it will be found in an advance sheet rather than in the latest hardcover volumes.

It is important to remember that all appellate opinions (and some at the trial level) are followed by a period of time during which the parties can request and the court can grant a rehearing before the same court. Also, most decisions are appealable by means of a petition for hearing or a writ of *certiori* to the next higher court. Opinions may appear in the advance sheets during this time period. If either a rehearing or a petition for hearing or *certiori* is granted, the underlying opinion is rendered null and void, and it cannot be cited. For this reason, the advance sheets have subsequent case history tables that you should consult whenever you cite to a case that is still in the advance sheets.

Most law libraries shelve advance sheets next to the hardcover volumes. Sometimes, however, they are kept behind the reference desk to avoid theft.

The National Reporter System

Full Name of Reporter	Abbreviation	State Courts Included
Atlantic Reporter (First and Second Series)	A. and A.2d	Supreme and intermediate appellate courts in D.C., Connecticut, Delaware, Maine, Maryland, New Hampshire, New Jersey, Pennsylvania, Rhode Island and Vermont
Northeastern Reporter (First and Second Series)	N.E. and N.E.2d	Court of Appeals in New York and supreme and intermediate appellate courts in Illinois, Indiana, Massachusetts and Ohio
Northwestern Reporter (First and Second Series)	N.W. and N.W.2d	Supreme and intermediate appellate courts in Iowa, Michigan, Minnesota, Nebraska, North Dakota, South Dakota and Wisconsin
Pacific Reporter (First and Second Series)	P. and P.2d	Supreme and intermediate appellate courts in Alaska, Arizona, California (Sup. Ct. only since 1960), Colorado, Hawaii, Idaho, Kansas, Montana, Nevada, New Mexico, Oklahoma, Oregon, Utah, Washington and Wyoming
Southeastern Reporter (First and Second Series)	S.E. and S.E.2d	Supreme and intermediate appellate courts in Georgia, North Carolina, South Carolina, Virginia and West Virginia
Southern Reporter (First and Second Series)	So. and So.2d	Supreme and intermediate appellate courts in Alabama, Florida, Louisiana and Mississippi
Southwestern Reporter (First and Second Series)	S.W. and S.W.2d	Supreme and intermediate appellate courts in Arkansas, Kentucky, Missouri, Tennessee and Texas
New York Supplement	N.Y.S.	All New York supreme and intermediate appellate courts
California Reporter (First and Second Series)	Cal. Rptr. and Cal. Rptr. 2d	All California supreme and intermediate appellate courts

The Newest Cases

When an opinion is issued by a judge, it has a life of its own before it appears in the weekly advance sheets. Typically, the opinion is signed by the judge(s) and then sent to the clerk's office for distribution to the public. Copies go to the parties, the general press, the local legal newspapers, the case reporter services (for inclusion in the next advance sheet booklet) and *Shepard's*. Some clerk's offices have a basket on the counter with that day's opinions sitting in it.

During the time that the opinion is simply a bundle of stapled pages, it is referred to as a "slip opinion," and it is identified by its docket number—the court number the case received when it was first filed. When it appears in the next week's advance sheets it will get a regular citation;

but before that time, it may be picked up by *Shepard's* if it cites other cases. *Shepard's* will refer to the case by its docket number. If you need to see an opinion that is identified only by its docket number, your best bet is to go to an Internet site or use one of the computerized research services (Lexis or Westlaw).

It is risky to cite a slip opinion. As with opinions in the advance sheets, slip opinions can be wiped off the books if a rehearing is ordered or a higher court decides to take the case. Slip opinions do not become "final" and citable until the time for filing these motions has passed. If you cite a slip opinion, be sure to thereafter track its course through the advance sheets, by checking to see if it appears and whether it shows up in the subsequent case history table.

Researching California Cases

In California, unlike most other states, there is a good reason to use the official reporters—*California Reports* for California Supreme Court cases and *California Appellate Reports* for California Court of Appeal cases. This is because the California Supreme Court frequently "depublishes" published Court of Appeal opinions. Depublished opinions can no longer be relied on as correct statements of California law. When a case is "depublished," its conclusion remains intact as far as the case's parties are concerned, but it is taken out of the official reports and replaced with a notation to that effect. It usually remains in the unofficial reports. By using the unofficial reports, you run a small risk of relying on a case that appears helpful but no longer exists from a legal standpoint.

In California, the advance sheets for the official case reports published by Lexis contain a section at the back that tells you what has happened to cases since they were published in the reports. Cases are sometimes re-heard, taken for hearing by the Supreme Court, or ordered depublished. A table that appears in the advance sheets—called the cumulative Subsequent History Table—informs you when this happens. You may also use *Shepard's Citations for Cases* (discussed in Chapter 10), to find out whether a case has been depublished.

Although the concept of depublication appears Orwellian, its purpose is to allow the Supreme Court to administratively weed out misstatements of the law without having to handle the errant case on appeal. Also, it allows a weak or divided Court to render impotent a decision by a lower court that creates new law or is controversial in nature. Depublication allows the appellate court decision to operate as far as the parties to that case are concerned, but its decision does not become a precedent upon which others can rely.

Law Week and Other Loose-leaf Publications

A weekly loose-leaf publication called *United States Law Week* contains the full text of U.S. Supreme Court decisions, often within a week or two of their release by the Court. *Law Week* also publishes opinions from other courts around the country that its editors deem to be of general interest. If you are looking for a recent U.S. Supreme Court case or other cases of interest decided by other courts, try this service. The weekly pamphlets are collected in a large loose-leaf binder and indexed both by subject matter and case name.

If you are looking for a recent case involving a topic that is covered by one of the loose-leaf services covered in Chapter 5 (such as family law, environmental law, or media law), or you might find the case in one of these publications. For example, the CCH tax service regularly publishes all new court cases of significance in the tax field.

While *Law Week* and the other loose-leaf services are good places to read a recent case, you will definitely want to learn the case reporter citation for the case when it becomes available, so you can use the tools discussed in Chapter 10 to find your way to other relevant cases.

Publishing Cases on the Internet

Cases have been published online for many years—and more recently over the Internet. The two large legal databases—Lexis and Westlaw—charge substantial fees for their use and have pretty much been inaccessible to the common, garden-variety legal researcher. However, many law libraries now subscribe to one or both of these services and make them available to their patrons. So, if you have access to a law library that gives you access to Westlaw or Lexis, the law librarian can get you started on your case research. After a few minutes, you'll have the hang of it.

Two other services that originated as pure Internet services charge considerably less than Lexis and Westlaw, but also offer correspondingly less information. One of these, VersusLaw, is described in more detail in Chapter 9. Recent state and federal appellate cases (typically from the past several years) are often published online for free by the courts that decide them.

Review

Questions

1. What are the books that contain published court opinions called?
2. What series publishes decisions by U.S. District Courts?
3. What series publishes decisions by the U.S. Court of Appeals?
4. What series publishes decisions by the U.S. Supreme Court?
5. What series publishes all state court cases, by region?
6. How are new cases first published?
7. What service does *U.S. Law Week* provide?

Answers

1. Cases are published in volumes called "case reports," "reports," or "reporters."
2. *Federal Supplement.*
3. *Federal Reporter* (three series).
4. *United States Supreme Court Reports, Supreme Court Reporter* and the *Supreme Court Reports, Lawyer's Edition.*
5. The "regional reporters," published by the West Publishing Co.
6. Reporters have weekly update pamphlets called "advance sheets."
7. The full text of U.S. Supreme Court decisions, often within a week or two of their release by the Court.

Finding Cases

Every reported (published) case has a unique citation. As long as you have the citation, you can find any case published in a standard case reporter. This chapter tells you how to interpret these citations and use them to find a case.

Interpreting Case Citations

A case citation consists of five or six items:

- the case name—usually the names of the plaintiff and defendant;
- the name of the reporter(s) where the case is published;
- the volume number(s) of the reporter(s) where the case is published;
- the page number where the case begins;
- the year the case was decided; and
- for federal Court of Appeals cases, a designation of the circuit; for federal District Court cases, the state and judicial district where the court is located; for state cases, an indication of the state if it's not apparent from the name of the reporter.

Let's take a closer look at each of the elements in a case citation.

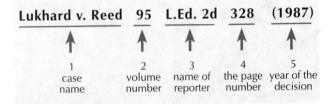

Citation Form

Citations often take slightly different forms. For example, it is not uncommon to see the date immediately following the case name or different abbreviations that designate the reporter. A nationwide system of citations is contained in a book titled *A Uniform System of Citation,* 18th ed. (colloquially called the "Harvard Blue Book"). It has been developed primarily for law school use, but is used in federal courts and most state courts. We follow it here for the most part.

Case Name

The first element of a case citation is the case name. *People v. Fields* is a case name. So is *Lukhard v. Reed*. There are usually two names, one on either side of a "v." that stands for versus. This format reflects the adversarial aspect of our justice system; one name is the plaintiff's, the other the defendant's. Usually, the first name is the plaintiff's and the second name is the defendant's. But not always. The plaintiff in the *People v. Fields* case was "the people" (this tells us it was probably a criminal case), and the defendant was Fields. In *Lukhard v. Reed*, however, the original plaintiff was Reed, and the defendant was Lukhard. But when Lukhard appealed a lower court decision in favor of Reed, his name was put first.

Sometimes, cases only have one name with some Latin attached. For example, *In re Gault* is the name of a juvenile case; the "in re" means "in the matter of." These types of case names normally appear where the proceeding is brought by the state for the individual's best interest, or where the proceeding is not considered to be an adversary proceeding that warrants the "v."

Finally, cases are sometimes referred to by the subject matter of the dispute. For instance, divorce cases commonly carry such names as *Marriage of Sullivan* (last name of the divorcing couple) or *In the Matter of Schmidt*.

Volume Number

A case citation provides the volume number of the reporter in which the case is located. The volumes of each separate reporter are numbered consecutively.

Name of Reporter

Obviously a citation wouldn't be much help without the name of the reporter. That information comes immediately after the volume number. In the *Lukhard* case, the full name of the reporter is *U.S. Supreme Court Reports: Lawyer's Edition*.

Examples of abbreviations for other reporters:

- "A." (*Atlantic Reporter*)
- "P." (*Pacific Reporter*)
- "U.S." (*United States Reports*)
- "F. Supp." (*Federal Supplement*)
- "F." (*Federal Reporter*)

Most reporters have been published in two or more series. For example, the *Lukhard* case is published in the

second series of the L. Ed. reporter (L. Ed. 2d). Cases decided in the nineteenth and early twentieth century were published in the first series (L. Ed). In litigious states like California, the case reporters are up to their fourth series. For instance, a citation for a recent California case is *Arroyo v. State of Calif.*, 34 Cal. App. 4th 755 (1995).

⚠️ Do not worry about memorizing all of these abbreviations. Virtually every legal research tool that you'll be using contains a table of abbreviations for the various case reports. Also, as you do research within your own state, you'll quickly get to know the most commonly-used abbreviations. If you are ever in doubt, law librarians will come to the rescue.

The Page Number

You have undoubtedly already figured out what the next item of a citation is for. It provides the page number the case starts on.

Year of the Decision

Citations also carry the year the case was decided. This information can be helpful because old law tends to be bad law. When you're doing research, you usually want to first check the most recent cases relating to your problem.

Now you know that the citation *Lukhard v. Reed*, 95 L. Ed. 2d. 327 (1987) means that a case called *Lukhard v. Reed* was decided in 1987 and can be found in Volume 95 of *U.S. Supreme Court Reports: Lawyer's Edition*, starting on page 327.

Federal Cases: The Circuit, State or District

Citations to cases decided by the federal Courts of Appeal usually include the circuit of the court deciding the case. A case decided by the Court of Appeals for the 3rd Circuit is cited as 654 F.2d 925 (3rd Cir. 1984). A U.S. District Court citation should indicate the state and judicial district of the case; for example, in *Peter v. Jones*, 509 F. Supp. 825 (E.D. Pa. 1981), the E.D. Pa. means Eastern Judicial District for Pennsylvania.

Parallel Citations

As mentioned in Chapter 8, cases are often found in more than one reporter. For example, U.S. Supreme Court cases can be found in three separate reporters. When you see a U.S. Supreme Court case referred to (that is, "cited"), you will often see three citations following the case name.

Example: *Lukhard v. Reed*
- 481 U.S. 368
  United States Reports
- 95 L. Ed. 2d 328
  Lawyer's Edition, 2d Series
- 107 S. Ct. 1807 (1987)
  Supreme Court Reporter

These three citations are known as *parallel citations* because they parallel each other (that is, refer to the same case).

Citations to Advance Sheets

Advance sheets are numbered and paginated in accord with the rest of the reporter and serve as the reporter until a new hardcover reporter is produced. For example, a 1991 U.S. Supreme Court advance sheet (for *U.S. Supreme Court Reports, Lawyer's Edition*) is labeled Vol. 113 L. Ed. 2d., No. 2. One of the cases reported in this advance sheet is *Columbia v. Omni Outdoor Advertising*, on page 382. The citation for this case (as published in this reporter) is 113 L. Ed. 2d 382 (1991).

When the hardcover book containing the case is published, the volume number for the hardcover is the same as is on the advance sheet, and the case is found on the same page. In short, the citation doesn't change.

Internet Citations

As a general rule, citations to very recent cases from online services such as Lexis or Westlaw will be accepted by a court. Also, cases published by the Lexis, Westlaw and Versuslaw services typically include the hard copy citation, which is always acceptable.

How to Find Cases in the Law Library

Now that you know how to read citations to the publications described in Chapter 8, it's time to focus on finding a citation that will get you to the case you need. There are a number of ways to do this depending on where you are coming from in your research.

- If you have found a relevant statute and want to read cases that interpret the provisions you are interested in, you can probably find an appropriate citation in the case notes following the statute ("Case Notes That Follow Statutes," below), or in the listings for that statute in "*Shepard's Citations for Statutes*" (below).
- If your research involves primarily common law (cases), you might find a helpful citation in a background resource ("Background Resources," below) or in the subject index to a case digest ("The Case Digest Subject Index," below).
- If you know the name of a case that you want to find but not its citation, you can use the table of cases in a case digest ("The Digest Table of Cases," below). If the case is very recent (within the past several months) and not yet listed in the case digest table of cases, you can find it by searching the tables of cases in the advance sheets or recently published hardcover case reporter volumes ("The Case Reporter Table of Cases," below).
- If you have a case citation for one reporter and you need the citation for a second reporter (that is, the parallel citation), you can find it by using *Shepard's Citations for Cases*. (See Chapter 10.)

Below we examine in more detail each of these approaches to finding an appropriate citation to that one good case.

Background Resources

Most of the background materials discussed in Chapter 5 are copiously footnoted with citations to cases that discuss specific points of law covered in the main discussion. For example, consider the page from *California Jurisprudence*, a California legal encyclopedia, shown below.

Although we generally recommend that you proceed directly from background reading to any pertinent statutes —and then to cases—it is also common to go directly to any case that appears to be relevant, or to at least note the citation for later reference. For example, if you want to know what your constitutional rights are in the event you are accused of a zoning violation, the case of *Los Angeles v. Gage* (cited in footnote 42 on the page shown below) appears to bear directly on that point. Before you search for a statute related to this issue, you might first read this case to see what light it sheds on your problem. The case itself may discuss relevant statutes.

Case Notes That Follow Statutes

If you are searching for a case that has interpreted a relevant statute, check the listings after the text of the statute in an "annotated" version of the code. You should be able to find annotated versions of your state's code and of the *United States Code* in the law library.

In the annotated code, one-sentence summaries of court cases that interpret the statute directly follow the notes on the statute's history. These summaries are actually head-notes (see Chapter 7) that have been lifted from the case reporter. Some statutes have been interpreted by the courts so many times that the publisher includes a little index to the case summaries, which are organized by issues raised by the statute. The example below is taken from the *Michigan Compiled Laws Annotated*.

It is often difficult to tell from such a brief summary whether or not a case is in fact relevant to the problem you are researching. Remember that the editor who wrote these blurbs may not have had her second cup of coffee when she wrote the one you're interested in. Fortunately, the summaries also contain a case citation that allows you to look up the case and read it for yourself. It is essential that you read the case itself and not just rely on what it says in the annotation.

Annotations Online. KeyCite at www.keycite.com provides annotations for the U.S. Code and the codes of all 50 states. The cost is $4 per statute searched. See Chapter 10 for more on KeyCite.

§ 210   ZONING AND OTHER LAND CONTROLS

additional time not exceeding a specified number of days as the court may, within the original number of days, allow, but in no event later than a designated number of days after entry of the order, petition the proper reviewing court to review such order by writ of mandate. No such order of vacation is effective, nor may it be recorded in the office any county recorder, until the time within which a petition for writ of mandate may thus be filed has expired.[41]

§ 211. Defenses

Generally speaking, any matter that is germane to a cause of action to enforce a zoning or planning enactment and that presents a legal reason why the plaintiff should not succeed therein may constitute a good defense. It is a good defense, for instance, that the enactment under which complaint is made is unconstitutional or invalid, either in toto or as applied to the defendant's property.[42] In order to plead this defense, however, the defendant must have exhausted the administrative remedies available to him under the enactment.[43] And the partial invalidity of

---

41. *Deering's Gov C § 65908 subd (b).*

42. *Los Angeles v Gage, 127 CA2d 442, 274 P2d 34; People v Gottfurcht (2d Dist) 62 CA3d 634, 133 Cal Rptr 270.*

Regarding validity of zoning enactments generally, see §§ 43 et seq., supra.

Practice References: 8 POF2d p. 53, Unreasonableness of Zoning Restriction §§ 1 et seq.; 13 POF2d p. 373, Vested Right in Continuation of Zoning §§ 1 et seq.; 14 POF2d p. 117, Zoning—Nonconforming Use §§ 1 et seq.

43. *San Mateo v Hardy, 64 CA2d 794, 149 P2d 307.*

A church and a member thereof failed to exhaust their administrative remedies before defending on constitu-

tional grounds against the enforcement of an ordinance requiring a use permit as a prerequisite to operation of church on property in a residential zone, where it did not appear that the member even applied for any such permit, and the church dismissed its appeal from the planning commission's decision to the city council before decision by the council. *Chico v First Ave. Baptist Church, 108 CA2d 297, 238 P2d 587.*

Property owners whose auto wrecking yard was found to be a nonconforming use and was ordered terminated by the county board of supervisors on recommendation of the county planning commission were not denied procedural due process, where a public hearing after 15 days' notice was held by the planning commission at which hearing the property owners were represented by counsel and witnesses were

---

Page From *California Jurisprudence*

Historical and Statutory Notes

Source:
P.A.1931, No. 328, § 451a, added by P.A. 1969, No. 243, § 1, Eff. March 20, 1970.

C.L.1948, § 750.451a.
C.L.1970, § 750.451a.

750.452. House of ill-fame; keeping, maintaining or operating

Sec. 452. KEEPING, ETC., A HOUSE OF ILL-FAME—Any person who shall keep, maintain or operate, or aid and abet in keeping, maintaining or operating a house of ill-fame, bawdy house or any house or place resorted to for the purpose of prostitution or lewdness shall be guilty of a felony, punishable by imprisonment in the state prison for not more than 5 years or by a fine of not more than 2,500 dollars.

Historical and Statutory Notes

Source:
P.A.1931, No. 328, § 452, Eff. Sept. 18.
C.L.1948, § 750.452.
C.L.1970, § 750.452.

Prior Laws:
R.S.1846, c. 158, § 10.
C.L.1857, § 5865.

C.L.1871, § 7700.
How. § 9286.
P.A.1887, No. 34.
C.L.1897, § 11697.
C.L.1915, § 15471.
P.A.1927, No. 37, § 1.
P.A.1927, No. 40, § 1.
C.L.1929, §§ 16826, 16860.

Cross References

Disorderly persons, see § 750.167.
Public nuisances, abatement, see § 600.3801.

Library References

Disorderly House ⚖5.
WESTLAW Topic No. 130.
C.J.S. Disorderly Houses § 5.

Notes of Decisions

mini-index

Conduct or use of house 3
Elements of offense 1
Evidence 6-8
   In general 6
   Reputation 7
   Weight and sufficiency of evidence 8
House, building or place 2
Indictment or information 5
Instructions 10
Jury questions 9
Keeping of house 4
Reputation, evidence 7
Review 12
Sentence and punishment 11
Weight and sufficiency of evidence 8

case summaries

1. Elements of offense

Under this section providing that "Any person who shall keep, maintain or operate, or aid and abet in keeping, maintaining or operating a house of ill-fame, bawdy house or any house

or place resorted to for the purpose of prostitution * * * shall be guilty of a felony, * * *.", it is only where the operation or maintenance of a house of ill fame is charged that the reputation of the premises is an essential element. People v. Mayes (1973) 205 N.W.2d 212, 44 Mich.App. 482.

A person who solicited a female, who was at the time a prostitute, and inmate of a house of ill fame, to become an inmate of another such house, was not guilty of a violation of How. § 9286, which provided for the punishment of any person who solicited a female to enter such house for the purpose of "becoming" a prostitute. People v. Cook (1893) 55 N.W. 980, 96 Mich. 368.

2. House, building or place

Evidence that defendant kept a house to which men resorted for purposes of prostitution, that frequent acts of prostitution were there committed with her, and that the house

362

Finding Recent Cases That Have Interpreted a Statute

Each volume of a case reporter has a "table of statutes" that are mentioned by the cases reported in that volume. The table is usually in the front of the volume. It can be helpful if you know that a statute has been interpreted in some case within a specific period of time.

For example, suppose you hear of a 2008 Illinois court decision that interprets that state's statute governing stock issuances of small corporations. You are familiar with the statute and would like to read the case, but you don't know its name or where to find it. What to do? The most direct approach is to check for the particular statute in the table of statutes in each volume of the *Northeastern Reporter* that contains 2008 Illinois cases. If the statute you are interested in was, in fact, interpreted by a case, the table of statutes will tell you precisely which one and provide its citation. Remember to check the advance sheets for the reporter if you think the case was very recent.

Shepard's Citations for Statutes

There are several different research tools provided by a service known as *Shepard's*. *Shepard's Citations for Statutes* provides a complete listing of each time a particular statute, regulation or constitutional provision has been referred to and perhaps interpreted by a published decision of a federal or state court. In the next chapter, we'll discuss *Shepard's Case Citations*, which tells you every time a particular case has been referred to by a later case. *Shepard's* for both statutes and cases are tools you will definitely want to master.

Here are the basics for using *Shepard's Citations for Statutes*:

- *Shepard's Citations for Statutes* are dark red, thick, hardcover volumes with separate update pamphlets that may be gold, red or white, depending on how recently the hardcover volumes were published.
- A separate *Shepard's* exists for the statutes of each state and for federal statutes.
- *Shepard's* hardcover volumes for the statutes of a state or the federal government cover different time periods. For example, one hardcover volume

may contain all references made by court decisions before 1980, another may contain all references made between 1980 and 1990, and a third may contain all references made between 1990 and 1998.

- To use *Shepard's*, you need the exact number (citation) of the statute. It is very helpful to know the approximate year it was passed.
- Each *Shepard's* volume is organized in the same way as the statutes being referred to are labeled in the codes of each state or the federal government. So if you want to know whether a particular New York criminal statute has been interpreted by a court, you would first locate the place in the New York *Shepard's Citations for Statutes* that covers the New York criminal laws, and then look for the specific statute by number. In other states, where statutes are not grouped by topic but only by sequential number, you would only need to find the statute by its number.
- Once you find the statute you are "Shepardizing" in *Shepard's*, you will see whether or not any court decisions have referred to it. If so, the citations tell you the reporter, the volume and the page where the reference occurred.
- *Shepard's Citations for Statutes* are kept in different places in different libraries. Some libraries have their *Shepard's* in a central location, while others have their *Shepard's* at the end of the statutes for each state and at the end of the federal code. Still other libraries have *Shepard's* at the end of the volumes of cases for each state.

Four Warnings When You're Using Shepard's

1. Make sure you use the *Shepard's* that covers the state in which you are interested.
2. When you look up a statute in *Shepard's*, make sure you use the part that deals with statutes (marked clearly on the front of the volume and the top of the page), and not with the part that deals with cases, regulations or the constitution.
3. Use the *Shepard's* volumes for the appropriate years. A hardcover volume that contains citations from 1980 through 1985 will not do you any good for a statute enacted in 1986. You should use only the volumes that contain citations to cases decided after the statute was passed.
4. Look in all hardbound volumes and paperback supplements that may contain citations.

Sheperdizing Statutes Online. You can use Westlaw to find cases that have referred to a particular statute. Visit Westlaw by Credit Card at http://creditcard.westlaw.com. Click the register button at the top of the screen and provide the requested information, including your credit card number. Then follow these steps:

- Sign in using your login name and password;
- Click the "Check a Citation Using a KeyCite Template" link just below the KeyCite search box;
- For a state statute, select your state from the drop-down menu at the top;
- Scroll down to the publication containing the statute you wish to check, enter the citation, and click "Go"; and
- For a federal statute, scroll down to the bottom of the first "Template" page, enter the United States Code Annotated citation that you wish to research, and click "Go."

Your credit card will be docked $6.25 for each citation request. While this may seem impossibly steep, you can obtain a list of all cases that have referred to the statute in question. You can also use this service to read the cases. However, it will cost $9.00 per case, so a more cost-effective strategy would be to read the cases for free on the internet (for recent cases) or in a law library. You also can subscribe to Versuslaw for $11.95 a month, which will probably give you access to the cases.

Many law libraries provide their patrons with free access to KeyCite; check with your local law library before spending your own money.

You can also use Lexis by Credit Card to *Shepardize* statutes. Enter the following URL in your browser: http://web.lexis.com/xchange/ccsubs/cc_prods.asp.

- Click the "Continue" button.
- Check the citation formats for the statute you wish to *Shepardize*.
- Enter the citation and click "Go."
- If you are using this for the first time, you will be asked to register your credit card. If you have already registered, enter your login ID and password.

Your credit card will be charged $6.00 per search. This is relatively inexpensive for what you get. For example, we *Shepardized* a California statute on the unauthorized practice of law (Business and Professions Code Section 6125) and produced a list of over 100 citations to cases that referred to that statute.

Summing Up
How to *Shepardize* Federal Statutes

✔ Note the year the statute you wish to *Shepardize* was passed.
✔ Find *Shepard's Citations for Statutes*.
✔ Select the volumes covering the years since the statute was passed.
✔ Find the title of the citation as it appears in boldface at the top of the page (for example, Title 251 U.S.C.).
✔ Under the appropriate title number, find the section number of the statute (for example, Title 25 U.S.C. § 863).
✔ Copy the citations listed under the section number. The citations refer to the exact page in the case where the statute is referred to.
✔ Follow this procedure for all volumes and pamphlets up to the most recent.

Summing Up
How to *Shepardize* State Statutes

✔ Note the year the statute you wish to *Shepardize* was passed.
✔ Find the *Shepard's* volume for your state's statutes.
✔ Select the volumes covering the years since the statute was passed.
✔ If your state statutes are organized into codes, find the title of the code in the upper margin in boldface (for example, *Penal Code*). If your state goes by a title system, find the title number at the top of the page. If your state's statutes are consecutively numbered without reference to a code or title, find the place in *Shepard's* where the number appears in boldface.
✔ If you are dealing with a code or title, find the section number of the statute (for example, Title 19, § 863).
✔ Note the citations under the section number. These citations are to the book and pages where the statute is referred to.
✔ Follow this process for all volumes and pamphlets up to the most recent.

FLORIDA STATUTES—FLORIDA STATUTES ANNOTATED

1983 , 827.03

The following are the citator columns as printed, read top-to-bottom, left-to-right.

361So2d406 · 377So2d1158 · 379So2d422 · 383So2d713 · 425So2d189 · 460So2d492 · 40FlS103 · 440F2d339 · 20MiL591 · 25MiL418 · 26MiL318 · 26MiL601 · 66CR681 · 78CR108 · 1A452n · Subsec. 1 · 295So2d690 · 317So2d864 · C354So2d867 · 425So2d188 · Subsec. 2 · 295So2d691 · 317So2d864 · C354So2d867 · 355So2d130 · 425So2d188 · 28MiL375 · Subsec. 3 · C356So2d314 · 377So2d1158 · 383So2d692 · 430US677 · 51LE734 · 97SC1415 · **827.04** · Ad1974C383 · A1975C298 · A1977C429 · 346So2d992 · 361So2d407 · 379So2d408 · 385So2d1054 · 425So2d189 · 453So2d799 · 78CR108 · Subsec. 1 · 420So2d919 · 462So2d833 · Subsec. 2 · C361So2d406 · C376So2d862 · 388So2d563 · 425So2d188 · 33MiL970 · 33MiL1100 · Subsec. 3 · Ad1977C73 · C370So2d1 · C377So2d674 · 378So2d831 · 440So2d631 · 443So2d180 · 32MiL1108 · **827.05** · A1971C136 · A1975C298 · A1977C429 · U346So2d992 · 361So2d407 · 385So2d1054 · 388So2d563 · 425So2d189 · 20MiL591 · 25MiL418 · 32MiL1104 · 33MiL970

827.06 · Ad1974C383 · 517F2d788 · Subsec. 1 · A1975C298 · Subsec. 2 · **827.071** · Ad1983C75 · A1971C136 · 16MiL195 · **827.08** · A1979C298 · A1980C293 · 6FSU694 · **828.02** · 8So2d392 · 63So2d508 · 351So2d864 · 401So2d1112 · 150Fla592 · torture · 310So2d43 · **828.03** · A1975C223 · A1976C102 · 30MiL161 · Subsec. 2 · A1977C174 · **828.05** · A1980C188 · A1984C105 · 28MiL828 · **828.073** · Ad1975C223 · Subsec. 2 · A1976C102 · A1978C12 · A1979C234 · Subsec. 3 · A1976C102 · A1978C12 · Subsec. 4 · A1971C136 · A1979C102 · Subsec. 6 · Subd. b · A1976C102 · **828.08** · A1971C136 · A1971C272 · R1974C383 · Re-en · [1975C298 · **828.12 to** · **828.14** · 63So2d509 · **828.12** · A1970C50 · A1982C116 · 63So2d508 · 210So2d443 · 310So2d43 · C401So2d · [1111 · 451So2d880 · 4FlS2d108 · **828.121** · Ad1971C12 · A1976C59 · A1981C224 · Subsec. 4 · A1982C116

828.13 · A1971C136 · A1981C17 · A1982C116 · Subsec. 1 · Subsec. 2 · 464So2d668 · Subd. a · C464So2d668 · Subd. b · C464So2d668 · **828.14** · Subsec. 1 · A1971C136 · **828.15** · U63So2d508 · **828.16** · A1971C136 · **828.161** · Ad1967C177 · Subsec. 4 · A1971C136 · **828.17** · A1973C334 · **828.23** · Subsec. 1 · A1971C377 · **828.24** · Subsec. 2 · A1977C104 · **828.26** · Subsec. 1 · A1971C136 · Subsec. 2 · A1971C136 · **831.01** · et seq. · 257So2d92 · 298So2d551 · 358So2d889 · 426So2d79 · **831.01** · A1971C136 · A1973C334 · 9So2d712 · 46So2d453 · 74So2d370 · 75So2d195 · 76So2d645 · 107So2d379 · 111So2d460 · 114So2d198 · 117So2d408 · 117So2d737 · 118So2d193 · 118So2d630 · 123So2d464 · 133So2d74 · 192So2d45 · 200So2d829 · 227So2d524 · 243So2d437 · 256So2d223 · 257So2d93 · 267So2d702 · 298So2d551 · 312So2d808 · 330So2d160 · 341So2d539 · 345So2d363 · 351So2d377 · 355So2d818 · 366So2d1208 · 404So2d762 · 428So2d363 · 451So2d993 · 451So2d1048

452So2d957 · 458So2d423 · 462So2d1131 · 151Fla293 · 423US441 · 445US270 · 46LE619 · 63LE388 · 96SC836 · 100SC1137 · 469F2d1345 · 580F2d766 · 631F2d1258 · 219FS263 · 17MJ783 · 10MLQ200 · 22MiL607 · 28MiL897 · **831.02** · A1971C136 · 74So2d370 · 75So2d195 · 114So2d198 · 117So2d408 · 117So2d737 · 118So2d193 · 133So2d74 · 181So2d231 · 192So2d45 · 192So2d293 · 200So2d829 · 214So2d516 · 256So2d223 · 257So2d93 · 266So2d695 · 274So2d18 · 278So2d643 · 290So2d77 · 292So2d72 · 313So2d432 · 317So2d853 · 330So2d160 · 332So2d354 · 339So2d172 · 341So2d539 · 345So2d363 · 355So2d818 · 356So2d347 · 356So2d870 · 357So2d491 · 361So2d826 · 366So2d1208 · 367So2d695 · 368So2d634 · 397So2d410 · 402So2d1288 · 415So2d50 · 415So2d1174 · 426So2d81 · 428So2d363 · 435So2d963 · 438So2d974 · 452So2d957 · 445US270 · 63LE388 · 100SC1137 · 627F2d707 · 219FS262 · 17MJ783 · 22MiL272 · 22MiL606 · 28MiL897

831.03 · A1971C136 · 469F2d1345 · **831.04** · Subsec. 1 · A1971C136 · Subsec. 2 · A1971C136 · **831.05** · A1971C136 · **831.06** · 266So2d695 · 28MiL897 · **831.07** · A1971C136 · 358So2d889 · 630F2d393 · **831.08** · A1971C136 · 345So2d363 · 440So2d507 · 630F2d393 · **831.09** · A1971C136 · 358So2d888 · **831.10** · A1971C136 · 152So2d755 · 18MiL395 · 20MiL272 · **831.11** · A1971C136 · 262So2d457 · 28MiL897 · **831.13** · A1971C136 · 440So2d507 · **831.15** · A1971C136 · 345So2d363 · 440So2d507 · **831.16** · A1971C136 · 440So2d507 · **831.17** · 152So2d755 · 18MiL395 · 20MiL272 · **831.18** · 428So2d734 · **831.20** · A1973C334 · **831.22** · A1971C136 · **831.23** · A1971C136 · 9FLR293 · **831.24** · A1971C136 · **831.25** · A1971C136 · **831.26** · A1971C136 · A1977C104 · **831.27** · A1971C136 · **831.29** · A1969C313 · A1971C136 · A1973C334 · C407So2d231 · 20MiL276

831.30 · Ad1971C331 · A1972C234 · Subsec. 1 · A1973C331 · **831.31** · 442So2d287 · 444So2d64 · C446So2d · [1185 · 463So2d1144 · 469So2d231 · 469So2d957 · Subsec. 2 · Subd. b · 469So2d231 · **832.04** · et seq. · 1975C189 · 257So2d92 · 305So2d188 · 30MiL84 · **832.04** · Subsec. 1 · A1971C136 · 95So2d23 · 113So2d387 · 9FLR293 · → **832.041** · 285So2d428 · 290So2d123 · 20MiL245 · Subsec. 1 · A1971C136 · **832.05** · 1965C1503 · C95So2d20 · 105So2d505 · 113So2d384 · 123So2d753 · 126So2d540 · 145So2d736 · 153So2d850 · 193So2d691 · 193So2d706 · 255So2d264 · 301So2d109 · C305So2d187 · 324So2d191 · 333So2d63 · 339So2d213 · 341So2d216 · 356So2d347 · 368So2d948 · 372So2d489 · 390So2d1199 · 396So2d1108 · 403So2d616 · 404So2d749 · 433So2d1249 · 433So2d1336 · 470So2d88 · 470So2d835 · 452US921 · 69LE426 · 101SC3060 · 444F2d235 · 16BRW212 · 16MiL234 · 22MiL258 · 22MiL606 · 33MiL870 · Subsec. 1 · A1984C297 · C95So2d20 · 433So2d1250

444F2d235 · Subsec. 2 · A1984C297 · 84So2d42 · C95So2d20 · 113So2d383 · 113So2d387 · 115So2d169 · 123So2d335 · 123So2d753 · 128So2d757 · 136So2d633 · 153So2d850 · 161So2d697 · 188So2d861 · 203So2d174 · 235So2d751 · 239So2d857 · 325So2d466 · 326So2d63 · 370So2d800 · 393So2d1188 · 444F2d235 · 16FLR260 · 16MiL234 · 18MiL396 · 26MiL367 · Subd. a · 302So2d577 · 336So2d686 · 341So2d217 · 343So2d58 · 361So2d159 · 372So2d489 · 420So2d880 · 36FlS195 · 444F2d237 · Subd. b · A1971C136 · 113So2d384 · 345So2d397 · 444F2d237 · Subsec. 3 · Ad1979C98 · 455So2d1154 · Subd. a · 444So2d564 · Subsec. 4 · A1984C297 · 113So2d384 · 113So2d387 · 123So2d335 · 123So2d752 · 128So2d757 · 136So2d633 · 148So2d261 · 153So2d849 · 161So2d696 · 184So2d698 · 188So2d861 · 190So2d621 · C196So2d218 · 203So2d174 · 231So2d31 · 235So2d751 · 239So2d857 · 264So2d121 · 305So2d188 · 305So2d459 · 337So2d415 · 345So2d829 · 356So2d346 · 356So2d838 · C358So2d545 · 360So2d486 · 363So2d165

368So2d948 · 393So2d1188 · 404So2d792 · 16MiL234 · 18MiL395 · 20MiL245 · 20MiL275 · 24MiL258 · 24MiL350 · 30MiL670 · Subd. a · 235So2d752 · 255So2d264 · 274So2d18 · 277So2d310 · C358So2d546 · 393So2d1188 · 420So2d880 · 26MiL367 · 28MiL898 · Subd. b · A1971C136 · 113So2d387 · 123So2d335 · 123So2d753 · 128So2d757 · 404So2d792 · Subsec. 5 · 360So2d486 · Subsec. 7 · 84So2d42 · 95So2d20 · 123So2d464 · 153So2d849 · C287So2d134 · 305So2d188 · 335So2d1 · 339So2d213 · 341So2d218 · 30MiL670 · **832.06** · Subsec. 1 · A1969C77 · A1974C348 · A1977C174 · A1979C11 · **832.07** · Ad1975C189 · A1980C301 · 360So2d486 · 368So2d948 · 444So2d564 · 461So2d979 · 30MiL84 · 34MiL524 · 35MiL494 · Subsec. 1 · Subd. a · A1977C174 · A1979C345 · 360So2d487 · 442So2d1019 · 444So2d564 · 461So2d979 · 34MiL524 · **832.11** · 433So2d1344 · **833.04** · 17MJ783 · **836.01** · et seq. · 448So2d528

```
                          444F2d235      368So2d948
                          Subsec. 2      393So2d1188
                          A1984C297      404So2d792
                          84So2d42       16MiL234
                          C95So2d20      18MiL395
                          113So2d383     20MiL245
                          113So2d387     20MiL275
                          115So2d169     24MiL258
                          123So2d335     24MiL350
                          123So2d753     30MiL670
                          128So2d757     Subd. a
                          136So2d633     235So2d752
                          153So2d850     255So2d264
                          161So2d697     274So2d18
                          188So2d861     277So2d310
                          203So2d174     C358So2d546
                          235So2d751     393So2d1188
                          239So2d857     420So2d880
                          325So2d466     26MiL367
                          326So2d63      28MiL898
                          370So2d800     Subd. b
                          393So2d1188    A1971C136
                          444F2d235      113So2d387
                          16FLR260       123So2d335
                          16MiL234       123So2d753
                          18MiL396       128So2d757
                          26MiL367       404So2d792
                          Subd. a        Subsec. 5
                          202So2d577     360So2d486
                          336So2d686     Subsec. 7
                          341So2d217     84So2d42
                          343So2d58      95So2d20
                          361So2d159     123So2d464
                          372So2d489     153So2d849
              832.05      420So2d880     C287So2d134
              1965C1503   36FlS195       305So2d188
              C95So2d20   444F2d237      335So2d1
              105So2d505  Subd. b        339So2d213
              113So2d384  A1971C136      341So2d218
              123So2d753  113So2d384     30MiL670
              126So2d540  345So2d397     832.06
              145So2d736  444F2d237      Subsec. 1
              153So2d850  Subsec. 3      A1969C77
              193So2d691  Ad1979C98      A1974C348
              193So2d706  455So2d1154    A1977C174
          →   255So2d264  Subd. a        A1979C11
              301So2d109  444So2d564     832.07
              C305So2d187 Subsec. 4      Ad1975C189
              324So2d191  A1984C297      A1980C301
              333So2d63   113So2d384     360So2d486
              339So2d213  113So2d387     368So2d948
              341So2d216  123So2d335     444So2d564
              356So2d347  123So2d753     461So2d979
              368So2d948  128So2d757     30MiL84
              372So2d489  136So2d633     34MiL524
              390So2d1199 148So2d261     35MiL494
              396So2d1108 153So2d849     Subsec. 1
              403So2d616  161So2d696     Subd. a
              404So2d749  184So2d698     A1977C174
              433So2d1249 188So2d861     A1979C345
              433So2d1336 190So2d621     360So2d487
              470So2d88   C196So2d218    442So2d1019
              470So2d835  203So2d174     444So2d564
              452US921    231So2d31      461So2d979
              69LE426     235So2d752     34MiL524
              101SC3060   239So2d857     832.11
              444F2d235   264So2d121     433So2d1344
              16BRW212    305So2d188     833.04
              16MiL234    305So2d459     17MJ783
              22MiL258    337So2d415     836.01
              22MiL606    345So2d829     et seq.
              33MiL870    356So2d346     448So2d528
              Subsec. 1   356So2d838
              A1984C297   C358So2d545
              C95So2d20   360So2d486
              433So2d1250 363So2d165
```

Section 832.05

The Case Digest Subject Index

If you haven't found a helpful case through one of the first three methods, you can proceed directly to a case digest. Digests are collections of headnotes from cases that are organized and indexed according to legal issues. Digests are fully discussed in Chapter 10 as a means of finding additional cases once you find a good relevant case to get you to that phase of your research. But the subject index to a digest may also help you discover "that one good case."

For example, if you want to know whether a father who doesn't support his child because he has lost his job can legally be denied visitation rights, you would be dealing with the topics of "child visitation," "child support" and "child custody." You could use the subject indexes (and tables of contents) in a case digest for your state to find a relevant case that deals with your questions.

The Digest Table of Cases

It is common to hear well-known cases referred to by name only. Lawyers might talk about the *Roe v. Wade* abortion case, or a politician might still rant and rave about the harm that the *Miranda* case is doing to the country. Many people have heard of *New York Times v. Sullivan*, the Supreme Court case that extended First Amendment protection to media that report statements by public officials. If you know the name of a case but need its citation to locate and read it, the West Digest system is extremely helpful. Each digest is accompanied by a Table of Cases that lists all the cases referred to in that digest. By using the correct digest and accompanying Table of Cases, you can find the name of any case that was decided long enough ago—usually a year or more—to find its way into the Table of Cases.

The Table of Cases is organized with the plaintiff's name first. If you don't find your case in the Table of Cases, consult the Defendant-Plaintiff table.

When a case starts out in the trial court, the first name is the plaintiff's, and the name after the "v." is the defendant's. However, if an appeal is brought by the defendant, sometimes the defendant's name is put first in the appeal. Since most cases are opinions issued by appellate courts, a case name may in fact consist of the defendant's name in front of the "v." and the plaintiff's name after. This fact gives rise to an extremely important rule of legal research: If you can't find a case under one name, reverse the names and try again. For instance, if you can't find the case you're looking for under *Jones v. Smith*, try *Smith v. Jones*. It works more often than you might think.

Federal Cases

The table of cases that is part of the West *Federal Practice Digest, Fourth Series*, lists every case reported since 1992, alphabetically by case name. The *West Federal Digest, Third Series* lists cases reported between 1975 and 1992. The West *Federal Digest, Second Series*, lists cases reported between 1961 and 1975. For pre-1961 cases, the Table of Cases for the West *Modern Federal Practice Digest* should be consulted. Moore's *Federal Practice Digest* Table of Cases can also be used for earlier federal cases.

Assume, for example, that you are interested in the rights of unwed fathers with respect to decisions affecting their children. You have heard that a U.S. Supreme Court case

called *Caban v. Mohammed* held as unconstitutional a New York law that allows an unwed mother, but not an unwed father, to object to a child's adoption. You want to read this case but don't have a citation for it. You could go to the West *Federal Practice Digest* Table of Cases (start with the *Third Series*) and look it up. In the Table of Cases for the *Second Series* you would find what is shown below.

Now you have the citation and can go to the appropriate report and read the case for yourself. Easy.

While you can use the *Federal Digest* Table of Cases for U.S. Supreme Court cases, as we showed in the example, you could also utilize the Table of Cases for the West *Supreme Court Digest*.

Library Exercise: How to Use *Shepard's Citations:* Statutes

You are researching the federal law governing custody proceedings involving Native American children living in New Mexico. The statutes involved are Title 25 *U.S.C.*, sections 1901 through 1923. You want to find out how these statutes have been interpreted by the U.S. Supreme Court and by the Tenth Circuit Court of Appeals (New Mexico's circuit). You also want to know whether the statutes have been discussed in an *American Law Reports (A.L.R.)* article.

Questions

1. Which particular volumes of which *Shepard's* will tell you every time sections 1911 and 1912 of Title 25 *U.S.C.* were cited in U.S. Supreme Court and Tenth Circuit Court of Appeals cases?

2. Check all hardcover and paperbound supplements. What are the citations for two Tenth Circuit Court of Appeals cases that cited § 1911 and § 1912?

3. What are the citations of three Tenth Circuit U.S. District Court cases that cited subsection b of § 1911?

4. What is the *Lawyer's Edition 2d., U.S. Supreme Court Reports* citation to a Supreme Court case that cited § 1912 as a whole?

5. Are there any *A.L.R.* annotations that cite § 1911(a)? Any that cite 1912? Any that cite 1912(b)?

Answers

1. *Shepard's Citations* has volumes for cases and volumes for statutes. In the Federal Statute Citations volumes, you find Title 25, sections 1911

and 1912. The first volume, which includes Title 25, is Statute Edition, vol. 3, 1996; there are also supplemental volumes that include Title 25 and the paperbound supplements.

2. Cases decided by federal Courts of Appeals are published in the *Federal Reporter*, first, second and third series (F, F.2d, F.3d). The Tenth Circuit Court of Appeals case that cited both Sections 1911 and 1912 is found in 967 F.2d 437 and in 94 F.3d 1394. A case citing section 1912 is 53 F.3d 304. A case citing section 1911 is 53 F.3d 301.

3. Cases decided by U.S. District Courts are published in the *Federal Supplement* (F. Supp). Citations for the cases that cited subsection b of § 1911 are 624 FS 133, 847 FS 874 and 760 FS 1463. There are no new cases as of March 2004.

4. The *Lawyer's Edition 2d, U.S. Supreme Court Reports*, is abbreviated in *Shepard's* as *LE2*. The citation you are looking for is 104 LE2 40.

5. In *Shepard's, American Law Reports* and other secondary sources are listed at the end of all the cases that cited your case. 21 A.L.R. 5th 411n cited subsection a of § 1911 (the "n" means that the cite is found in a note at the bottom of page 411). In the 1996-2001 hardbound Supplement, volume 2, we find that 89 A.L.R. 5th 201n cites § 1912, and in the 2001-2003 hardbound Supplement, volume 1, we find that 92 A.L.R. 5th 385n cites section 1912(b).

82 F P D 2d—61 **CALIFANO**

References are to Digest Topics and Key Numbers

C., Inc. v. Brookside Drug Store, Inc., Bkrtcy.Conn., 3 B.R. 120. See Brookside Drug Store, Inc., Matter of.

→ **Caban v. Mohammed,** U.S.N.Y., 99 S.Ct. 1760, 441 U.S. 380, 60 L.Ed.2d 297.— Adop 2, 7.2(3), 7.4(1); Const Law 70.- 3(1), 70.3(6), 224(1), 224(2).

Caban v. Nelson, D.C.Conn., 475 F.Supp. 865. See Velez v. Nelson.

Caban, U. S. ex rel., v. Rowe, D.C.Ill., 449 F.Supp. 360. See U. S. ex rel. Caban v. Rowe.

Cabezal Supermarket, Inc., Matter of, D.C.N.D., 406 F.Supp. 345.—Bankr 303(6), 441.5, 442, 446(8.1).

Caesars Palace Securities Litigation, D.C.N.Y., 360 F.Supp. 366.—Fed Civ Proc 161, 176.

Cafeteria and Restaurant Workers Union, Local 473, AFL–CIO v. McElroy, U.S.Dist.Col., 81 S.Ct. 1743, 367 U.S. 886, 6 L.Ed.2d 1230.—Const Law 278.- 4(3), 278.6(1).

Cafferty v. Trans World Airlines, Inc., D.C.Mo., 488 F.Supp. 1076.—Fed Cts 1145; Labor 416.4, 968.

Cagle's, Inc. v. N. L. R. B., C.A.5, 588 F.2d 943.—Labor 290, 367, 379, 382.2, 388.1, 394, 574, 577, 705.

& Supply, Inc., 98 Idaho 495, 567 P.2d 1246.

Calderon v. McGee, C.A.Tex., 589 F.2d 909.—Elections 12; Fed Cts 922.

Calderon v. McGee, C.A.Tex., 584 F.2d 66, vac in part and reh 589 F.2d 909.— Schools 53(1).

Caldwell v. Board of Ed. of City of St. Louis, C.A.Mo., 620 F.2d 1277. See Adams v. U. S.

Caldwell v. Califano, D.C.Ala., 455 F.Supp. 1069.—Social S 142.30.

Caldwell v. Camp, C.A.Mo., 594 F.2d 705. —Courts 508(1), 508(2), 508(7); Fed Civ

Table of Cases in *Federal Practice Digest*

Summing Up
How to Find Federal Cases When the Citation Is Unknown

✔ Locate the Table of Cases for West's *Federal Practice Digest 4th* (Fourth Series) for the most recent cases (1992 to the present); *3d* (Third Series) for cases reported from 1975 to the beginning of *4th*; *2d* (Second Series) for cases between 1961 and 1975; and *Modern Federal Practice Digest* for earlier cases.

✔ Find the case name in the hardcover volume or pocket part and note the citation.

✔ If there is more than one entry for the case name, determine from the information provided with each entry (its date and issues decided) which case is the correct one. If cases involve the same topic, note both citations and read both cases.

✔ If you don't find an entry for the case name, reverse the names and look again. If you still don't find it, look in the Defendant-Plaintiff Table of Cases under both names.

Summing Up
How to Find U.S. Supreme Court Cases When the Citation Is Unknown

✔ Locate the Table of Cases for the *U.S. Supreme Court Digest* or *Federal Practice Digest*.

✔ Find the case name in the hardcover volume or pocket part and note the citation.

✔ If there is more than one entry for the case name, determine from the information provided with each entry (its date and issues decided) which case is the correct one. If cases involve the same topic, note both citations and read both cases.

✔ If you don't find an entry for the case name, reverse the names and look again. If you still don't find it, look in the Defendant-Plaintiff Table of Cases under both names.

State Cases

If you're looking for a citation for a state case, use the West state or regional digests. For example, suppose you want to read the landmark Oregon Supreme Court case of *Burnette v. Wahl*, which held that children can't sue their parents for abandonment. To find the citation, locate the West *Regional Digest* that covers Oregon (the *Pacific Digest*) or the *Oregon Digest* and get the volume containing the Table of Cases. When you turn to *Burnette*, you would find the page shown below.

57 P.D.(367 P.2d)—121   **BURR**

References are to Digest Topics and Key Numbers

Burnett v. State Acc. Ins. Fund, Or.App., 563 P.2d 1234, 29 Or.App. 415. See Kelly, Matter of.

Burnett v. Superior Court of Orange County, Cal., 528 P.2d 372, 117 Cal. Rptr. 556.—Courts 26; Crim Law 237, 241; Ind & Inf 15(4), 141; Mand 48, 61.

Burnett v. Tisdell, Okl., 370 P.2d 924.— App & E 717, 854(6), 867(2), 977(3); Cust & U 18; New Tr 6, 163(2).

Burnett v. Western Pac. Ins. Co., Or., 469 P.2d 602, 255 Or. 547.—Decl Judgm 322, 329; Insurance 514.9(2), 514.10(1), 514.12, 616.1, 616.2; Judgm 713(2), 720.

Burnette v. McClearn, Colo., 427 P.2d 331, 162 Colo. 503.—Extrad 34.

→ Burnette v. Wahl, Or., 588 P.2d 1105, 284 Or. 705.—Action 3; Const Law 70.-1(11); Parent & C 11.

Burney v. State, Okl.Cr., 594 P.2d 1226. —Crim Law 683(2), 1137(5), 1153(1), 1202(4), 1202(6); Witn 269(1).

Burnford v. Blanning, Colo., 540 P.2d 337, 189 Colo. 292.—App & E 1008.1(3); Contracts 352(6); Frds St of 119(2), 131(1); Spec Perf 44; Ven & Pur 85.

Burnford v. Blanning, Colo.App., 525 P.2d 494, 33 Colo.App. 444, rev 540 P.2d 337, 189 Colo. 292.—Contracts 252; Frds St of 129(1), 129(3), 129(5); Ven & Pur 85.

Burnham v. Bankers Life & Cas. Co., Utah, 470 P.2d 261, 24 Utah 2d 277, appeal after remand 484 P.2d 155, 26 Utah 2d 9.—Insurance 11.1, 255, 256.1, 365.2, 365.3; Judgm 181(2).

Burnham v. Burnham, Wash.App., 567 P.2d 242, 18 Wash.App. 1.—Lim of Act 145(1), 148(1), 149(1).

Burnham v. Calfee, Or.App., 608 P.2d 606. See Woelke v. Calfee.

Burnham v. Eshleman, Or., 479 P.2d 501, 257 Or. 400.—App & E 1050.4; Autos 243(1); Evid 380; Trial 56, 251(1).

Burnham v. Nehren, Wash.App., 503 P.2d 122, 7 Wash.App. 860.—Autos 160(1), 160(3), 160(4), 206, 216, 217(1), 217(2), 217(5), 245(6), 245(72), 246(58); New Tr 38.

Burnham v. Yellow Checker Cab, Inc., N.M., 391 P.2d 413, 74 N.M. 125.—App & E 928(1); Autos 245(91), 246(58); Neglig 83.1, 83.6; Trial 203(1).

Burningham v. Ott, Utah, 525 P.2d 620. —Judgm 178, 181(2), 185(1), 186; Lim of Act 104½.

Burnison v. Fry, Kan., 428 P.2d 809, 199 Kan. 277.—Judgm 524, 660, 668(1), 720, 739; Parties 29.

Burnkrant v. Saggau, Ariz.App., 470 P.2d 115, 12 Ariz.App. 310.—Admin Law 229; App & E 1, 781(7); Mand 79; Schools 177.

Burns, Application of, Hawaii, 407 P.2d 885, 49 Haw. 20.—Atty & C 76(4); Divorce 165(6), 402(1), 402(7); Hab Corp 90, 99(3); Infants 18; Judgm 399, 817, 818(1); Parent & C 2(18).

Burns v. A. G. C., Or., 400 P.2d 2, 240 Or. 95.—Insurance 146.7(1), 169(1), 178.-3(2).

Burns v. Anchorage Funeral Chapel, Alaska, 495 P.2d 70.—Dead Bodies 9; Ex & Ad 426, 438(1); Lim of Act 124; Parties 52, 60, 76(1), 80(1), 84(1), 96(2); Plead 408.

Burns v. Atchison, T. & S. F. Ry. Co., Okl., 372 P.2d 36.—App & E 207, 230, 261, 499(1), 501(1), 1060.1(1), 1072; R R 350(1); Trial 131(3), 133.6(8).

Burns v. Burns, Okl.App., 585 P.2d 1126. See Burns' Estate, Matter of.

Burns v. Burns, Ariz., 526 P.2d 717, 111 Ariz. 178.—Const Law 70.1(11); Divorce 313.

Burns v. Burns, Ariz.App., 519 P.2d 190, 21 Ariz.App. 337, vac 526 P.2d 717, 111 Ariz. 178.—Com Law 14; Courts 90(6); Divorce 313; Hus & W 205(2).

Burns v. Burns, Colo., 454 P.2d 814, 169 Colo. 79.—Atty & C 81; Contracts 143(3); Divorce 287; Evid 397(6), 450(1), 455; Hus & W 279(2).

Burns v. Burns, Colo., 392 P.2d 662, 155 Colo. 96.—Hus & W 279(6).

Burns v. Burns, Mont., 400 P.2d 642, 145 Mont. 1, 13 A.L.R.3d 1355.—Divorce 55, 164, 238, 240(2), 286(1).

Burns v. Denver Post, Inc., Colo.App., 606 P.2d 1310.—Libel 6(1).

Burns v. Dills, Wash., 413 P.2d 370, 68 Wash.2d 377.—Autos 163(1), 169, 219, 242(3), 243(1), 246(19), 246(22), 246(30); Evid 472(1); New Tr 39(6); Statut 223.2(20).

Burns v. Ferguson, Okl.App., 576 P.2d 784.—Guar 6.

Burns v. Hand, Kan., 375 P.2d 637, 190 Kan. 471.—Hab Corp 113(9).

Burns v. Herberger, Ariz.App., 498 P.2d 536, 17 Ariz.App. 462.—Const Law 60; Tax 28, 42(1), 347, 348(3), 348.1(1), 348.-1(3), 362¼, 485(1), 485(3).

Burns v. Newell, Or.App., 507 P.2d 414, 12 Or.App. 621.—Hab Corp 92(1); Pardon 14.11, 14.15.

Burns v. Norwesco Marine, Inc., Wash. App., 535 P.2d 860, 13 Wash.App. 414. —Atty & C 20, 21; Corp 1.4(1), 1.4(2), 1.4(4), 1.6(3), 1.6(7); Judges 51(2); Pretrial Proc 724.

Burns v. Ottati, Colo.App., 513 P.2d 469. —Autos 227, 246(58); Evid 553(4), 555; Neglig 83.1, 83.6, 83.8, 141(9).

Burns v. Page, Okl.Cr., 446 P.2d 622.— Crim Law 1216(1); Prisons 15(2).

Burns v. Payne, Wash., 373 P.2d 790, 60 Wash.2d 323.—Judgm 106(1); Pretrial Proc 588.

Burns v. Ramsey, Colo.App., 520 P.2d 137.—Insurance 103, 103.1(2).

Burns v. Sheriff, Carson City, Nev., 569 P.2d 407.—Const Law 250.2(1), 263; Crim Law 224; Hab Corp 85.5(2); Homic 139; Ind & Inf 10.2(12).

Burns v. Sheriff, Clark County, Nev., 554 P.2d 257, 92 Nev. 533.—Crim Law 238(3), 404(4); Drugs & N 46; Hab Corp 25.1(2).

Burns v. Slater, Okl., 559 P.2d 428.— Const Law 208(3); Elections 22; States 200.

Burns v. Sommerfeld 96 Idaho 336, 528 P.2d 680. See Andersen v. Burns.

Burns v. Sommerfeld Agency, Idaho, 528 P.2d 680, 96 Idaho 336. See Andersen v. Burns.

Burns v. Southwestern Preferred Properties, Inc., Okl., 580 P.2d 986.—Work Comp 974, 978.

Burns v. State, Kan., 524 P.2d 737, 215 Kan. 497.—Burg 49; Crim Law 273.-1(1), 273.1(2), 274(3), 986, 991(1), 998(14), 998(16), 1158(1); Larc 88.

Burns v. State, Nev., 495 P.2d 602, 88 Nev. 215.—Crim Law 412.1(1), 412.2(3), 706(3), 763(1), 1159.2(5), 1170½(3), 1170½(6), 1202(1), 1202(4); Larc 65.

Burns v. State, Okl.Cr., 595 P.2d 801.— Arrest 63.1, 68; Crim Law 394.1(3), 814(17), 863(2), 1044.1(1); Searches 7(26).

Burns v. State, Okl.Cr., 547 P.2d 978.— Crim Law 1211.

Burns v. State, Wyo., 574 P.2d 422.— Crim Law 986(4), 942(2), 1043(3), 1114(1), 1137(3); Rob 24.3.

Burns v. State, Bureau of Revenue, Income Tax Division, N.M., 439 P.2d 702, 79 N.M. 53, cert den 89 S.Ct. 119, 393 U.S. 841, 21 L.Ed.2d 111.—Tax 28, 31, 959, 959, 966; U S 3.

Burns v. State Dept. of Social and Health Services, Wash.App., 581 P.2d 1069, 20 Wash.App. 585.—Social S 4.5, 11, 194.1, 194.13, 194.19; States 4.13.

Burns v. Superior Court of Pima County, Ariz., 397 P.2d 448, 97 Ariz. 112, 18 A.L.R.3d 1169.—Ex & Ad 130(1), 314(1), 315.6(1); Mand 10, 12, 24, 42.

Burns v. Transcon Lines, N.M.App., 595 P.2d 761, 92 N.M. 791, cert den 598 P.2d 1078, 92 N.M. 675.—Work Comp 89.

Burns v. U & S Motor Co., Inc., Utah, 562 P.2d 233. See Chrysler Credit Corp. v. Burns.

Burns v. U & S Motor Co., Inc., Utah, 527 P.2d 655. See Chrysler Credit Corp. v. Burns.

Burns v. Wheeler, Ariz., 446 P.2d 925, 103 Ariz. 525.—App & E 1002; Autos 157, 197(7), 245(82), 246(10), 246(28); Costs 203; Pretrial Proc 718; Trial 244(4).

Burns v. Yuba Heat Transfer Corp., Okl.App., 615 P.2d 1029.—Work Comp 545, 597, 1418, 1492, 1506, 1989.11(5).

Burns, City of. See City of Burns.

Burns Const. Co. v. Bilbo, Okl., 370 P.2d 913.—Sales 267, 273(1), 441(3).

Burns' Estate, Matter of, Kan., 608 P.2d 942, 277 Kan. 573.—Courts 202(5); Ex & Ad 256(5); Ven & Pur 199.

Burns' Estate, Matter of, Okl.App., 585 P.2d 1126.—Adv Poss 58; Des & Dist 83; Ex & Ad 85(8); Ten in C 3; Trusts 1, 44(1), 62, 86, 88, 89(1), 89(5), 91, 95, 107, 109, 110.

Burns Realty & Trust Co. v. Mack, Colo., 450 P.2d 75. See D. C. Burns Realty & Trust Co. v. Mack.

Burns, State ex rel., v. Blair, Idaho, 417 P.2d 217, 91 Idaho 137. See State ex rel. Burns v. Blair.

Burns, State ex rel., v. City of Livingston, Mont., 395 P.2d 971, 144 Mont. 248. See State ex rel. Burns v. City of Livingston.

Burns, State ex rel., v. Kelly, Idaho, 403 P.2d 566, 89 Idaho 139. See State ex rel. Burns v. Kelly.

Burns, State ex rel., v. Steely, Okl.Cr., 600 P.2d 367. See State ex rel. Burns v. Steely.

Burnside v. Burnside, N.M., 514 P.2d 36, 85 N.M. 517.—Divorce 223, 226, 231, 235, 239.

Burnside v. Landon, Idaho, 487 P.2d 957. See Brown v. Burnside.

Burnside v. Runstetler, Ariz.App., 504 P.2d 1299, 19 Ariz.App. 76.—App & E 846(5); Divorce 165(2), 386(2).

Burnworth v. Burnworth, N.M., 605 P.2d 222, 93 N.M. 714.—Divorce 287.

Burnworth v. Burnworth, Okl.App., 572 P.2d 301.—Divorce 62(1), 160; Judgm 141, 382, 386(3).

Burr v. Burr, Nev., 611 P.2d 623.—Divorce 151, 223, 286(4), 308, 309.4.

Burr v. Capital Reserve Corp., Cal., 458 P.2d 185, 80 Cal.Rptr. 345, 71 C.2d 983. —Brok 8(3); Princ & A 14(1), 24; Usury 12, 16, 18, 42, 102(1), 102(5), 113, 119, 138.

Burr v. Carey, 407 P.2d 779, 2 Ariz.App. 238. See Burr v. Frey.

Burr v. Department of Revenue, Mont., 575 P.2d 45.—Tax 861, 887.

Burr v. Frey, Ariz.App., 407 P.2d 779, 2 Ariz.App. 238.—Hab Corp 113(8).

Burr v. Green Bros. Sheet Metal, Inc., Colo., 409 P.2d 511, 159 Colo. 25.—Autos 205; Neglig 131; Witn 267, 269(2), 276, 282, 405(2), 406.

Burr v. Lane, Wash.App., 517 P.2d 988, 10 Wash.App. 412, 661.—App & E 731(2), 733; Garn 191; Insurance

The Case Reporter Table of Cases

Each case reporter volume has a Table of Cases, usually at the front. This table contains a listing of all cases in that volume of the reporter and their page references. This is a very valuable tool if you are searching for a case that you know only by name and that was decided too recently to be listed in a Digest Table of Cases (generally, within the previous six months to one year).

If the case is more recent than the dates of the cases in the latest hardcover case reporter, use the Table of Cases in the advance sheets. But remember that there is usually a one- to two-month lag between the decision in a case and its publication in an advance sheet. If the case is old enough to be in the hardcover volumes, start with the table of cases in the latest hardcover volume and work backwards.

The Case Reporter Subject Index

Each case reporter volume has a subject index, usually at the back. If the reporter is published by West Group (most are), the index is in fact organized according to the key numbers that have been assigned to the cases contained in the volume. If you know that a case involving a specific topic was decided during a certain time period, but don't know its name, you may be able to find it by looking in the subject index for each volume containing cases for that time period.

For example, suppose you want to read a 1992 Illinois court decision that interprets that state's statute governing stock issuances of small corporations. You could find what you were looking for by using the subject index for the volumes containing cases decided in 1992. Simply look under "corporations," "stock," or "business" until you find what you are looking for, and the index will refer you to the proper case. (See Chapter 4 for help in using a legal index.)

Be prepared to look under more than one topic when trying to find a case through this method. Also be aware that the volume may contain the case you're looking for even though it's not described in the subject index.

Library Exercise: Finding Cases by Popular Name

You are researching famous cases in which several defendants were identified by the public as a group. Your research has yielded two popular case names—the *Chicago Seven* case and the *Scottsboro* case. You have searched the Table of Cases for all digests and have come up empty.

Questions

1a. To find the citations to the *Chicago Seven* case, what index will you use?

1b. What do you find under *Chicago Seven*?

1c. Find the case in 472 F.2d and write out its full citation.

2. How many cases are known as the *Scottsboro* cases? Is there any way to tell whether they are related without going further than *Shepard's*?

Answers

1a. In *Shepard's Acts and Cases by Popular Names: Federal and State*, in the third volume, are federal and state cases cited by popular names. The set is followed by a paperbound supplement.

1b. The *Chicago Seven* case is listed with two citations. The first is 461 F.2d 389; the second one is 472 F.2d 340.

1c. Going to the *Federal Reporter,* 2d series, volume 472, page 340, you find *United States v. Dellinger,* 472 F.2d 340 (1972), cert. den. 93 S. Ct. 1443.

2. *Shepard's Acts and Cases by Popular Names: Federal and State* seems to show five different cases. Although the *Alabama Reporter* (Ala.) citations are different, they are not very far away from each other; in addition, they each have one Supreme Court citation (U.S.) in common with at least one other.

Summing Up
How to Find the Text of a U.S. Supreme Court Case Decided Over One Year Ago

✔ If you have the case citation, find the indicated reporter, volume and page.

✔ If you don't have a citation but know the name of the case, consult the volume containing the Table of Cases for the *United States Supreme Court Digest* (West Group). Check both the hardcover volume and the pocket part.

✔ If you don't know the case name, utilize the Digest's subject index, starting with the pocket part. Then, turn to the hardcover volume. Be prepared to look under more than one subject.

✔ If you can't find a citation to the case in the digest but you know the approximate year the case was decided, use the Table of Cases or subject index in each case reporter volume for Supreme Court cases decided during that period of time.

Summing Up
How to Find a State Supreme Court Case Decided More Than One Year Ago

✔ If you have a citation, find the proper volume and page.

✔ If you have no citation but know the name of the case, find its citation by consulting the Table of Cases to either the West Digest for your state or the West Regional Digest that covers your state (if one exists). Check the pocket part first. If you don't find the case name, go to the hardcover volume.

✔ If you don't know the name of the case, use the subject index to the appropriate digest and try to find a summary of the case in the body of the digest. If you do, the citation will be provided.

✔ If you can't find a citation to the case in the digest but you know the approximate year the case was decided, use the table of cases or subject index in each case reporter volume for cases decided during that period of time.

Summing Up
How to Find the Text of a U.S. Supreme Court Case Decided Within the Past Year

If you have the citation, locate the advance sheets of the appropriate report and turn to the indicated page. If you don't have the citation, there are two quick ways to find your case.

U.S. Law Week. If you know the name of the case, consult the *U.S. Law Week* volume for the current year. This loose-leaf weekly publication contains a table of cases that tells you on which page in *U.S. Law Week* the case appears.

If you don't know the name of the case, use the *U.S. Law Week* topical index. By searching the correct topic, you should find a reference to one or more cases whose description resembles the case you're looking for.

Advance Sheets. If you know the name and approximate date your case was decided, start looking in the appropriate advance sheets (the ones dated a month or more after the decision). Descriptions by name and subject of the cases contained in each volume can be found on either the outside or the inside of the cover.

A quick skim will tell you whether a particular advance sheet contains the case you are interested in. Also, if you know the name of your case, each advance sheet contains a cumulative listing of case names and citations of where they can be found. A new cumulative index starts for each new reporter volume number.

Summing Up
How to Find a State Supreme Court Case Decided Within the Past Year

✔ If you have a citation, find the proper volume and page.

✔ If you have no citation but know the name of the case, locate the advance sheets for a report that publishes the Supreme Court decisions for your state. This will probably be either a regional reporter or the official reporter for your particular state.

✔ If you know the approximate date of the case, start browsing through the advance sheets that were published after the case. Each advance sheet should have a case name index to the cases reported in it.

✔ If you know the subject that the case addressed but not its name, use the subject index that is included in each advance sheet.

How to Find State Cases on the Internet

Most states have made their current or recently-decided cases available online. What do the words "current" and "recently-decided" mean in this context? This will depend on the number of cases being cranked out by the court in question. In California, "current" may mean the past several months, while in Vermont, it may mean the past year or two. In the same vein, "recent" may mean within a year or two in California and three or four years back in Vermont.

The best way to find state sites containing these cases is to use one of the following sites that provide links to primary law sources (including state cases):

- Cornell Legal Information Institute [www.law.cornell.edu]
- FindLaw [www.findlaw.com]

Click through to the pages for your state's judiciary and see what you find. If you already know the address for your state judiciary's site, or another address where it maintains its cases, you can go directly there.

Suppose you are searching for a state case that is neither current nor recent. First, you should try one of the sites listed above to see what cases your state has put on the Internet. If you're unable to access the case you need for free, you'll need to try a site that charges for access to cases. We suggest that you use VersusLaw, a fee-based system for finding state and federal cases—both current and past (archived).

Internet Exercise: Finding a State Case on the Internet

You live in Vermont and are a divorced mother of two small children. In a magazine article you read about a Vermont Supreme Court decision that reinterprets the Vermont child support guidelines in a way that will increase the child support levels for many Vermont families. Since you are barely getting by with the support you currently receive from your ex, you want to read the case to see what it might mean for you. You can't remember exactly when the case was decided, but you think it was within the last few years. You want to find a website that contains Vermont cases free of charge.

Note: Sometimes we learn of cases by their case name ("Jones v. Smith"), while other times we learn of them by subject matter only ("that new case on child support"). In this example, we'll show you how to find the case in both situations.

Your Results May Look Different. This example is intended to give you a concrete understanding of how to find information on the Internet. While the example was accurate when originally prepared, it may not be by the time you read this book. This means you may not get the same results that we did if you try to follow along with your own browser. Also, you should not rely on the example as an accurate statement of the law itself.

1. **Start with the Cornell Legal Information Institute (LII).** You'll be able to access recent Vermont cases through this site, free of charge. If the case is older than you can find here, you can then move to a fee service. The LII website is at www.law.cornell.edu. When you enter that URL into your browser, you get the LII home page. From this page, you can select the best link for your research needs.

2. **The LII offers several ways to find legal resources.** A number of subject-matter headings are listed on the left side of the screen. To discover which research tasks are represented by a particular heading, suspend your mouse pointer over it. If you pass your pointer over "Court Opinions," you will get a sublist consisting of four types of opinions:
   - U.S. Supreme Court
   - Other Federal courts
   - New York Court of Appeals, and
   - Other state courts.

3. **By process of elimination** you would select the last option, since you are looking for a state case that isn't from the New York Court of Appeals. This offers a list of links to each state. To find the Vermont case, you would click the Vermont link.

4. **When you click on Supreme Court** you finally come to the actual site containing the Vermont Supreme Court cases, which is maintained by the Vermont Department of Libraries. At the top of this page are links to current Vermont Supreme Court cases. Below those are links to recent volumes of the Vermont Reports, the official reporter of published Vermont Supreme Court cases. These are identified by the volume number of the reporter. You can access the cases in each reporter either in a list by the order they appear in the reporter or through a key word search.

5. **Unless you know the exact citation of a case,** the best way to find it is by key word search. That's what you'll have to do here. Since you can't remember when the case was decided, you can start with the most recent cases and then move backwards. Click the "Search Current Vermont Supreme Court Opinions" link. This produces a search page.

Internet Exercise: Finding a State Case on the Internet (continued)

6. **It's always best to start** with whatever information you have. Let's say that when you read the magazine article, you wrote down the name "Tetreault v. Coon." This should help narrow it down. In the search box, type in "Tetreault"; it is an unusual name and unlikely to call up unrelated cases. Since this is a search by key word, not by title, the search will produce any recent Vermont opinions with the word Tetreault in the name or the text. So, you'll get any cases with Tetreault in the title, as well as any that cite to the Tetreault case.

   At the time we tried this exercise, no recent Vermont opinions contained the name Tetreault. You'll have to try your search again in an older selection of cases. You'll want to start by searching the most recent Vermont Reports volume and work backwards.

   Next, try searching 167 VT Reports for "Tetreault." With this search, you'll find your case: *Tetreault v. Coon*, 167 Vt. 396; 708 A.2d 571 (1996).

   Here's a tip. When we were updating this page, the Vermont statute search engine was out of order. We turned to Google.com (using the Basic Search feature) and entered "Tetreault" and "child support" (both in quotation marks). The first result was a link to the case of *Tetreault v. Coon*. See Chapter 4 for more about using Google to find legal resources on the Internet.

7. **Often, you don't know or remember** the name of the case you want to read. In that event, the search process will be a little more cumbersome, but not much. How would you find this Vermont case concerning child support guidelines if you didn't know its name?

   In this case, you would go through much the same process as above, but instead of typing "Tetreault" in the search box, you would devise a search term consisting of key terms that you think would appear in your case. Given our facts, the term "child support guidelines" would be a fair place to start.

8. **As with our example of the case name search**, start with the link that allows you to search the most recent Vermont opinions. Then, work backwards through the VT Reports until you find your case. If you don't find anything, you can try varying your search term. Using the search term we chose, we didn't find any cases in the more recent Vermont opinions. We did find success, however, in 167 VT Reports. When we told the search engine to look for cases with those key terms, we got a list of cases to choose from.

9. **Which is the case you were looking for?** In this example, you have two ways to find it. You can open each case and read the introduction, or you can back up one step and refine your search by adding more key words, which ought to yield fewer cases.

10. **If your search query produced too many cases** to comfortably open and scan, you'll want to narrow the search. In this example, if we wanted to refine our search and produce a smaller results list, we might think of another word or two that we would expect to be in the case. For instance, if the article identified the Supreme Court justice who wrote the opinion (in this case, Justice Dooley), we could have added "dooley" to the search. Our results would then include only those child support cases heard by Justice Dooley.

Finding Federal Case Law on the Internet

Here we explain how to use the Internet to find a written opinion for a federal case. As we explained in Chapter 8, there are essentially three types of federal opinions, depending on where (by which court) the lawsuit was litigated:

- U.S. Supreme Court opinions;
- Federal Circuit Court of Appeal opinions; and
- U.S. District Court opinions.

Under the U.S. District Court category, there are several specialty courts, including bankruptcy courts.

Here is a rough description of what you can find for free on the Internet at this time:

- U.S. Supreme Court opinions going back about one hundred years;
- Federal Court of Appeals opinions as far back as 1991, depending on the circuit;
- Recent District Court opinions, depending on the district; and
- Most recent bankruptcy court opinions.

The Supreme Court has its own website [www.supreme courtus.gov]. The circuits, districts, and bankruptcy courts have their own sites as well. Generally, the circuit sites follow the form of www.ca<circuit number>.uscourts.gov, such as www.ca9.uscourts.gov for the Ninth Circuit. District court addresses are more variable. If you don't have your circuit, district, or bankruptcy court's direct address, you can find a link to the site at one of the following sites:

- Cornell Legal Information Institute [www.law.cornell. edu];
- Federal Judiciary [www.uscourts.gov/links.html];
- Washburn University School of Law [www.washlaw.edu/searchlaw.html#];
- Emory Law School [www.law.emory.edu/FEDCTS].

Also, as we explained in Chapter 4, most primary legal resources on the Internet can be found through a basic Google key word search as well as by using one of the dedicated legal information sites mentioned above. For instance, if you are aware of a federal district court case that you want to read, entering the case name or key words describing the case's subject matter in the Google search box will likely give you a direct link to the case. It is posted on the county's website. If you aren't able to find what you need at one of the free sites, you'll have to head to a fee-based option. Again, we recommend VersusLaw as the best site for your money.

Using VersusLaw to Research Federal and State Case Law

VersusLaw, a private online publisher of primary legal resources, offers a collection of state and federal court opinions that range from the most recent to those decided 75 years ago. Just how far back VersusLaw goes depends on the state and court. VersusLaw provides this information in their "Complete Library Directory," which is available from the page displayed after signing in. Below, for example, is a reprint of the VersusLaw chart showing the inclusive dates for its different state collections. Similar charts are available for its federal court, tribal court and statute databases.

VersusLaw State Collections

State	Year	State	Year
Alabama	1955	New Hampshire	1930
Alaska	1960	New Jersey	1930
Arizona	1930	New Mexico	1930
Arkansas	1957	New York	1960
California*	1930	North Carolina	1945
Colorado	1930	North Dakota	1943
Connecticut	1950	Ohio	1950
Delaware	1950	Oklahoma	1954
D.C.	1945	Oregon	1950
Florida	1910	Pennsylvania	1950
Georgia	1940	Rhode Island	1950
Hawaii	1930	South Carolina	1950
Idaho	1964	South Dakota	1965
Illinois	1950	Tennessee	1950
Indiana	1940	Texas**	1950
Iowa	1932	Utah	1950
Kansas	1950	Vermont	1930
Kentucky	1943	Virginia	1930
Louisiana†	1980	Washington	1935
Maine	1940	West Virginia	1970
Maryland	1949	Wisconsin	1945
Massachusetts	1930	Wyoming	1960
Michigan	1930	Guam	1996
Minnesota	1930	Puerto Rico	1998
Mississippi	1954		
Missouri	1960		
Montana	1925		
Nebraska	1965		
Nevada	1950		

* California Court of Appeals coverage begins in 1944.
**Texas library contains all but the 10th and 11th Districts.
† Louisiana 4th App. District not available.

Internet Exercise: Finding a Federal Case on the Internet

You work for a publishing company that produces self-help law books and software. Your company, Nolo, has been in business for 35 years and has never been sued by an unhappy customer nor accused by any governmental agency of publishing inaccurate or misleading materials. Out of the blue, the Supreme Court of Texas, through its Committee on the Unauthorized Practice of Law, has decided to investigate your company for practicing law in the state of Texas without a license.

Are Nolo authors and editors sneaking into Texas, setting up shop and handling cases as if they were members of the State Bar? No, it seems that simply selling Nolo materials may constitute the offense.

Your legal training (even your high school civics class) suggests to you that the mere provision of legal information is a matter of free speech, protected by the First Amendment of the United States Constitution. You decide to do a little legal research to find out if there is case authority to back you up. A lawyer friend tells you that he remembers reading a case a few years ago about free speech and licensing that dealt with a securities newsletter. But he can't remember anything else about the case. Before hopping on the bus to go to your local law library, you fire up the computer and begin your search.

For this project, you decide to begin with the Internet search engine FindLaw.

Your results may look different. This example is intended to give you a concrete understanding of how to find information on the Internet. While the example was accurate when originally prepared, it may not be by the time you read this book. This means you may not get the same results that we did if you try to follow along with your own browser. Also, you should not rely on the example as an accurate statement of the law itself.

1. **The FindLaw website** is at www.findlaw.com. Your first step is to choose a FindLaw category. FindLaw's home page is divided into two categories: 1) For the Public, and 2) For Legal Professionals. For this exercise, we'll use the Legal Professionals links.

Since you're looking for a case that will support your position, you initially may wish to use FindLaw's "U.S. Laws: Cases & Codes" category. But don't click on the bold title just yet—notice that you can also go directly into the subcategory of Federal (under "U.S. Laws: Cases & Codes"). This will take you to a number of federal law sources, including a link to the U.S. Supreme Court: Opinions and Website. Since your issue is a pretty hefty one (whether the government can suppress the publication of legal information on the theory that it constitutes the "practice of law"), chances are the Supreme Court has addressed the issue.

2. **Be bold and go straight for the Supremes** (as the Supreme Court is called in the trade).

   From here, you must decide where to begin your search. The top of the page provides links to Supreme Court cases by year, back to 1999. While you could systematically search these links, you would only cover those years, whereas the case or cases you are looking for may have been decided much earlier.

   • If you have the official citation for a case, you can pull up that case. For instance, if you are reading an article and you are directed to a case at 497 US 497, you can simply enter the numbers in the appropriate boxes and go right to the case by clicking the "Get It" button.

   • If you know the name of one of the parties to the case, you can pull up all cases where that name is in the case title. For instance, if you wanted to find the famous *Miranda v. Arizona* case, you could simply enter Miranda in the query box specified for this search and you would get all cases with the name including the one you are interested in.

   • You can search for a case according to the specific words used in the case—that is, you can search by key word.

   In our example, we don't have the name or year of the case or even the volume it was reported in. So our only practical option is to do a key word search (also called a "Full-Text Search").

Internet Exercise: Finding a Federal Case on the Internet (continued)

3. **Wait before you begin typing.** Notice that there is a little hot link next to the box, again called "options." Click it and you'll get two more links to information screens that explain how to formulate an effective full-text search in the FindLaw database:
   - Boolean and proximity operators, and
   - Wildcards.

   The link to Boolean and proximity operators will tell you how to do a Boolean search, which is a much more precise way of formulating a search than simply typing in key words.

   Use this link to help you design a search that will, hopefully, bring you to any Supreme Court cases that will help you establish that the publication of legal information in a book is protected speech under the First Amendment.

4. **As a general rule, we prefer to start with just a word or two** that is likely to pull up a list of candidate cases, and then start narrowing the search from there. Although it may seem more efficient to craft the best possible search from the beginning, sometimes this will be too narrow to find your case, and you'll have to back up and widen your search. We prefer to go wide first and narrow later.

   So, go back up to the box entitled Full-Text Search and type this search: publish near law near first amendment near securities.

   Why use the "near" boolean operator Instead of "and"? The "near" Boolean operator is in one sense the same as the "and" operator, because both operators will bring you cases that have the search phrases or words in them. For example, a search written "first amendment *and* securities" will bring you cases with both "first amendment" and "securities" in them. And a search written "first amendment *near* securities" will also bring you cases with both "first amendment" and "securities." So why use "near"?

   The "near" operator is more sophisticated. It tells the search engine to look for cases in which the two search terms or phrases are not only *in* the case, but next to or close by each other. You'll want to use "near" when you're looking for a concept or phrase, and can anticipate that certain words are likely to be used in a phrase or sentence.

For instance, suppose your legal question concerns the impact of the First Amendment on securities law. If you search for "first amendment *and* securities," the fact that these two search terms are both in the same opinion doesn't necessarily mean that First Amendment is being used in the securities context. (You might get a case that covers two unrelated issues: The First Amendment and advertising, and the need to register as a securities advisor.) However, if the two search terms are near each other, then they are more likely to relate to each other. By ranking your search results in terms of how near these terms are to each other, you will be more likely to have a relevant case at the top of the list.

5. **Using the near operator,** we get a Results page. Now, you will analyze the results of your research. The seventh case shown on the results page is *Lowe v. SEC,* the case your lawyer friend told you about. How do you know? Since securities were involved, it's likely that the SEC (the Securities and Exchange Commission) was a party to the lawsuit.

6 **FindLaw gives you a more surefire way** of determining which case in the string of hits is the one you want. Under each case, you'll see a "Highlight Hits" link. This feature gives you a quick look at the places in the case where your search terms appear. From the context, you can determine the relevancy of the case to your search. When you click the Highlight Hits link under *Lowe,* you quickly see that the case deals with a securities advice newsletter—just as your lawyer friend told you.

   Key word searching means trial and error.
   Searching for case authority by key word involves a lot of trial and error. Even if you tailor your search wisely by using Boolean operators, you may end up scanning materials that aren't helpful in the least. For instance, the successful search terms we used in this example were not the first terms we used. Quite frankly, it took us several tries before we were able to produce search results that put *Lowe v. SEC* near the top of the hit list.

   Besides learning to live with the inherent looseness of key word searching, you have to realize that different search engines behave differently. In other words, a search will bring different results depending on which

Internet Exercise: Finding a Federal Case on the Internet (continued)

engine goes to work on it. For example, one of our searches in FindLaw placed *Lowe v. SEC* in position 33 (meaning you'd have to scan the hits in 32 cases before getting to it). When we used the identical search in VersusLaw, the search engine on that site put the *Lowe* case at the top of the list. The point is, be patient and systematic and you'll likely find what you're looking for in the end.

7. **Now that you've determined** that *Lowe* is the case your friend was thinking of, it's time to read it and find out if it will help you argue that merely selling books about the law is a protected activity under the First Amendment. When you click on the title of the case, FindLaw brings up the text of the opinion.

 If you follow this exercise online and read the case, you'll find that it's not until Part II, Section A, of the concurring opinion that you strike paydirt. (A concurring opinion is when one or more justices

agree with the result in the case but for different reasons than those stated by the majority of justices.) Your friend was right: The concurring justices clearly distinguish the right of the government to regulate the conduct of lawyers through a licensing scheme from the regulation of legal speech contained in a book—which is impermissible.

8. **What's next?** At this point, you might be tempted to think you've found the answer and stop your research. But think for a moment: It might be interesting to find out whether the Supreme Court, your Circuit Court or state courts have used the Lowe v. SEC concurring opinion.

 So don't turn the computer off just yet. In Chapter 10, we explain how to use the reasonably priced Westlaw KeyCite feature, which you can use to update and expand your research.

Versuslaw is not free, but it is the most reasonably priced of all the online publishers that offer archived cases. Versuslaw costs $11.95 a month. You don't have to subscribe for any period of time, so if you are a one-time researcher, $11.95 will give you a month of solid online research; you can discontinue your subscription if your needs do not extend past the initial month subscription.

You can get a good sense of how Versuslaw works by using its "Guest Research" utility. Just provide some basic personal information and you will be able to browse the search facilities and create a search. However, if your search brings up some links to cases that meet your search criteria, you won't be able to read the cases. Instead you'll be prompted to join up to go further. So, no free lunch here, but surely an opportunity to familiarize yourself with this service.

- Enter your search terms in the search box.
- If you can, specify the dates between which the case was decided.
- Start the search.
- Click on a case link that is produced by your search.

Only when you want to actually examine a case are you asked to either enter your username and password or register.

One of the great features of VersusLaw is its online help. The Research Manual and FAQs (links to both appear on the search page) are written in plain English and provide the best research support we've encountered on the Internet. For that reason, we confidently hand you off to VersusLaw for any additional information you want on how to use that site for your online searching needs.

Using Westlaw to Find Cases by Key Words and Other Search Criteria

If your law library offers free access to Westlaw, you're in luck. After you agree to comply with the conditions of use, you'll be taken to a screen that contains search shortcuts and a box for entering key words.

Using the shortcuts, you can call up or locate all the citations for a case if you have the case information. If you aren't sure of the correct method of citing the case, use the "Publications List" to find the correct abbreviation for the publication containing the case you want to research.

You can also use the shortcuts menu to search for a case by party name. For example, if a case name is *Fisher v. Priceless*, you could enter "Priceless" in the search box and

pull up all cases containing that name. You could also use Fisher in the search, but as a general rule it's more efficient to use one name as long as it is unusual.

Westlaw also lets you search by West Key Number by clicking "Key Search" at the top of the screen. Chapter 10 explains how the key number system works.

Finally, Westlaw provides a key-word search box. Chapter 4 describes this search technique. To use this search box you first must indicate what database you want to search. For instance, if you are searching for federal cases, you'll choose the "Allfeds" database. If you aren't sure which database you want, a drop-down menu provides a list of all databases to which your library subscribes. Sometimes this will be a long list; smaller libraries may only carry a few to keep the subscription cost to a minimum.

Westlaw has an ingenious key-word search tool called "Require/Exclude Terms." By clicking that link you can specify which of your terms must be in the case you are checking. Any term not selected for required inclusion will be used in your search but won't prevent a case from appearing on your results list as long as the case has the required terms.

As its name implies, the "Require/Exclude" search tool lets you designate words that will prevent a case from appearing on the results list. See Chapter 4 for how this 'exclude' tool can be used to narrow your search.

The Westlaw key-word search page also links to a thesaurus that you can use to provide a broader range of words in your search. As explained in Chapter 4, the more relevant terms you put in your search, the more likely it is you'll find what you're looking for.

If you find a good case, you have only to click the KeyCite tab at the top of the screen to citate the case. See Chapter 10 for instructions on using KeyCite.

The Next Step

Suppose you find a good, relevant case or cases—then what? It is at this point that your research efforts can really become productive. Once you have located even one relevant case, you have the key to all other relevant case law. By using two basic tools in the law library—*Shepard's Citations for Cases* and the West Digest system—you can parlay your case into a notebook full of both helpful and harmful precedent. You can go from the narrowest point of the hourglass research model (Chapter 2) to a broad base of helpful material. These tools are discussed in the next chapter. You can also use the Internet to perform this same function, albeit by using different tools.

Review

Note: The following citations and case names are fictitious and are used for instructional purposes only.

Questions

1. In what year was the case *Ocean v. River*, 467 F.2d 208 (5th Cir. 1973), decided?

2. What is the name of the defendant in *Ocean v. River*? The plaintiff?

3. What does "5th Cir." mean in the *Ocean v. River* citation?

4. What does the F.2d stand for in the *Ocean v. River* citation?

5. If the *Ocean v. River* case is in volume 467 of F.2d, what page does it start on?

6. How can a background resource lead you to relevant cases?

7. If you find a relevant statute and are looking for good cases in the Notes of Decisions section following the statute, can you tell for sure from a case note whether a particular case is helpful?

8. How does *Shepard's* help you find cases that have interpreted your statute?

9. In addition to the hardbound volumes of *Shepard's*, how many gold, bright red and white paper supplements should you have to look in to bring your Shepardizing completely up-to-date?

10. Each *Shepard's* citation has several abbreviations in it. How can you find out what they stand for?

11. If you can't find any relevant cases by using background resources, case notes or *Shepard's*, how can the digests help?

12. Suppose you are told that a 1990 California case named *Wind v. Rain* is relevant to your problem. You go to the table of cases in the *California Digest* and look under "Wind" but find nothing. What will you try next?

13. You are in a digest table of cases looking for *Snow v. Sleet*, and find two cases by that name. How can you tell which is the one you are looking for?

Answers

1. 1973.

2. River; Ocean.

3. This case was decided by the federal Court of Appeals for the 5th Circuit.

4. This case is published in the *Federal Reporter*, 2d series.

5. Page 208.

6. Most background materials have many footnotes with citations to cases that discuss specific points of law covered in the main discussion.

7. Not really. The case notes are helpful as a weeding-out process, but all possibly relevant cases should be located and read.

8. *Shepard's Citations for Statutes* gives you citations of all cases that have referred to (cited) your statute for any purpose.

9. One of each color, plus "express" citations in blue.

10. Every *Shepard's* volume, hardbound or paper, has a list of abbreviations in the front.

11. The digests have subject indexes that lead you to the topics and key numbers for your issue.

12. Look under "Rain" in the same table; look under "Wind" in the Defendant-Plaintiff table; look under "Rain" in the Defendant-Plaintiff table.

13. If you know the date of the case, look for that; if that doesn't work, look at the list of topics and key numbers following each entry; look up each case under its topic and key number to see what issues it involves. If you still can't decide, you'll have to read both cases.

Shepard's, Digests and the Internet: Expand and Update Your Research

C hapter 9 discussed how to find a specific case that might help you answer your research question. This chapter introduces the tools that let you jump from one case to other cases that may shed light on your issues. These may be cases that directly affect the continuing validity of the "one good case" you found (for instance, cases that overrule or reverse the case), or cases that add to your understanding of your issues without affecting the validity of the case you've already found.

Using Westlaw or LexisNexis to 'Shepardize' a Case

When we refer to 'Shepardizing' a case, we refer to the process of identifying all published cases that have referred to (cited) an earlier case. In addition, the process helps to garner information about why the earlier case was cited by the later cases. This incredibly valuable service was originally provided by a hardcopy trademarked resource known as *Shepard's Case Citations*. LexisNexis acquired *Shepard's* and now provides this information in hardcopy and digital format. As you can imagine, the process of *Shepardizing* a case is ideal for an Internet researcher. The online LexisNexis service is called *Shepardize!*

The process of collecting case citations is not proprietary to *Shepard's* and any company can organize its own *Shepard's*-like system. That's exactly what Westlaw has done with its KeyCite service. Regardless of the brand name for the rival citators, legal professionals often use the term "Shepardize" to refer to any process of locating related citations.

As more and more law libraries offer Westlaw or LexisNexis to their patrons for free, researchers are weaning themselves from the hardcopy *Shepard's* and using the computer as a citator.

Westlaw and LexisNexis also make their citator services available by credit card, which means your credit card gets docked a specific sum for each use you make of the Westlaw or LexisNexis service. In other words, if you have the budget, you can perform this activity in the comfort of your home or office.

As we point out later, you still may need to use the law library, or an affordable legal database such as Versuslaw, to access the cases that your home or office-based research turns up—due to the fact that you must pay $9.00 or $9.25 per case called up for reading. For example, if your *Shepardizing* produces 20 citations you want to check out, LexisNexis would dock your credit card $180.00. You could save that $180.00 dollars by printing out the list of citations and taking them to the library where you can read the cases for free, or, you could subscribe to Versuslaw for $11.95 a month, do your research, and then cancel your subscription for succeeding months.

Before telling you how to use the Westlaw and LexisNexis systems, we explain how to use the hardcopy tools later in this chapter—so you'll know what to look for when you get on the computer.

Shepard's Citations for Cases

Once you have located a case that speaks to your research issues, *Shepard's* gives you a list of every later case that has referred to it. You can use this list to:

- see if the case was affirmed, modified or reversed by a higher court;
- see if other cases affect the value of the case as precedent or persuasive authority; and
- find other cases that may help your argument or give you better answers to your question.

Shepard's works only when the case you are interested in has actually been referred to in the later case by name. If a later case deals with the same subject but doesn't mention your case, *Shepard's* won't help. One of the happy by-products of the adversary system (happy at least for legal researchers) is that attorneys arguing appeals usually dredge up and present to the court every possibly relevant case. These cases, and others located by the court's own clerks, are typically included in the court's opinion. *Shepard's* is therefore an extremely reliable guide to how any given case has been used by the courts.

Read First, Practice Later. As you read the next several pages, you may feel that the information is so dry and technical that you can't absorb it all at once. Don't try. Just understand the broad outline of how the system works. When you actually need to use *Shepard's*, take this book along. After the first few encounters you will surely get the hang of it.

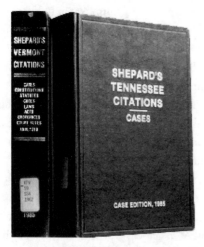

Shepard's Citations for Cases

Shepard's Citations for Cases: **The Basics**

Before learning how to use *Shepard's Citations for Cases*, it helps to know the basics:

- *Shepard's Citations for Cases* are dark red, thick, hardcover volumes with separate update pamphlets that may be gold, bright red or white, depending on how recently the hardcover volumes were published. (If you remember from Chapter 9, *Shepard's Citations for Statutes* look the same.)
- Separate *Shepard's Citations for Cases* are published for each state, for federal court cases and for U.S. Supreme Court cases. Sometimes the *Shepard's Citations for Cases* is in a separate volume; sometimes it is combined in the same volume with *Shepard's Citations for Statutes* for that state.
- The outside of each *Shepard's* volume tells whether it covers statutes, cases or both. For example, the *Shepard's Mississippi Citations* has the following on its outside cover: "Cases, Constitutions, Statutes, Codes, Laws, Etc."

   Minnesota Shepard's, on the other hand, has case citations in one volume and everything else in another.

- *Shepard's Citations for Cases* is organized according to the case reporters that publish cases. Each *Shepard's* volume has a box in the first couple of pages telling you the specific publications covered by that volume. Below is a sample taken from the *Shepard's Citations* for cases contained in the *Northeastern Reporter*.
- To use *Shepard's Citations for Cases*, you need the case citation—the name of the case reporter your case appears in, its volume number and the first page on which the case appears.
- *Shepard's* hardcover volumes for the cases of a particular state's courts, or the federal courts, cover different time periods. For example, one hardcover volume may contain all references made by cases decided before 1980, another may contain all references made by cases decided between 1980 and 1985 and a third may contain all references made by cases decided between 1985 and 1990.
- *Shepard's Citations for Cases* is kept in different places in different libraries. Some libraries have their

---

SHEPARD'S
NORTHEASTERN REPORTER
CITATIONS

**A COMPILATION OF CITATIONS TO
ALL CASES REPORTED IN THE NORTHEASTERN REPORTER**

THE CITATIONS
which include affirmances, reversals and dismissals by higher state courts
and by the United States Supreme Court

APPEAR IN

NORTHEASTERN REPORTER
UNITED STATES SUPREME COURT REPORTS
LAWYERS' EDITION, UNITED STATES SUPREME COURT
 REPORTS
SUPREME COURT REPORTER
FEDERAL CASES
FEDERAL REPORTER
FEDERAL SUPPLEMENT
FEDERAL RULES DECISIONS
ATLANTIC REPORTER
CALIFORNIA REPORTER
NEW YORK SUPPLEMENT
NORTHWESTERN REPORTER
PACIFIC REPORTER
SOUTHEASTERN REPORTER
SOUTHERN REPORTER
SOUTHWESTERN REPORTER
AMERICAN BAR ASSOCIATION JOURNAL

and in annotations of

LAWYERS' EDITION, UNITED STATES SUPREME COURT REPORTS
AMERICAN LAW REPORTS

also in Vols. 1–283 Illinois Appellate Court Reports, Vols. 1–19 Ohio
Appellate Reports and Vols. 1–101 Pennsylvania Superior Court Reports

SECOND EDITION - - - - - - - - - - - - - - VOLUME 2 (1974)

SHEPARD'S CITATIONS, Inc.
COLORADO SPRINGS
COLORADO 80901

Shepard's Citations for Cases **Published
in the *Northeastern Reporter***

Shepard's in a central location, while others have their *Shepard's* at the end of the volumes of cases for each state.

- *Shepard's Citations for Cases* uses its own citation system—which is different than the "Blue Book" system, the one used by this book. Every *Shepard's* volume has a table of abbreviations in case you get confused.

How to Use *Shepard's Citations for Cases*

Step 1. Identify the citation of the case you wish to *Shepardize*. Most cases are published in at least two reporters—the official reporter and a West regional reporter. You may use *Shepard's Citations for Cases* for either. The only parts of the citation you need are the volume, reporter abbreviation and page number—for instance, 112 Cal. Rptr. 456.

Step 2. Find the *Shepard's* volumes that cover the reporter in the citation. If you chose the *Northwestern Reporter* citation, for example, select the *Shepard's* for the *Northwestern Reporter*.

Step 3. If a *Shepard's* volume contains citations for more than one reporter (for example, for both the official reporter and for the West regional reporter), find the part that covers citations for the reporter named in the citation you have selected. For instance, if your citation is for the *Northwestern Reporter*, locate the pages that cover this series rather than the pages that pertain to your state's official reporter.

Step 4. Note the year of the case you are *Shepardizing*. Select the volume or volumes that contain citations for cases decided after the case you are *Shepardizing*. Remember to check the update pamphlets—gold, red and white—if you have started with a hardcover volume. Some researchers prefer to work backwards—checking the pamphlets first and then working back to the earliest relevant hardcover volume. Either way is fine.

Step 5. Find the volume number (in boldface) that corresponds to the volume number in the citation to the case being *Shepardized*. For example, if you are *Shepardizing* a case with the citation "874 F.2d 1035," search for Vol. 874 in bold print at the top of or on the page.

Step 6. Under this volume number, find the page number of the citation for the cited case. To continue the example from Step 5, search for the page number (-1035-) in bold print.

Step 7. Under the bold page number, review the citations given for the citing cases.

Step 8. Use the letters to the left of the citation to decide whether the case is worth reviewing. (See below for a discussion of what these letters mean and when to use them.)

Step 9. Use the numbers to the right of the citation to decide whether the citing case is referring to the cited case for issues you might be interested in. (See below for a discussion of what these numbers mean and how to use them.)

Step 10. After you write down all potentially-useful citations, go on to more recent *Shepard's* volumes and update pamphlets, and repeat these steps.

NORTHEASTERN REPORTER, 2d SERIES

Vol. 231

323FS⁶344
596FS⁶784
650FS437
64A2506s

—70—
(120S26)
(41@p159)
231NE³332
370NE³458
371NE²843
381NE²972
414NE⁴438
453NE⁴664
454NE²1389
488NE927

—71—
(120A68)
(41@p122)
p166NE808
c484NE220
j484NE221
18A2813s

—81—
(120A87)
(41@p163)
432NE⁸212
Cir. 6
577FS⁴1131
Md
513A2d938

—85—
(120A59)
(41@p117)

—91—
(120A83)
(41@p160)
521NE⁴1153
521NE⁶1153
31A3585n

—94—
(120hM127)
(41@p131)

—97—
(87Il2411)
Cert Den
269NE²355
269NE⁶356
273NE¹162
280NE¹²46
283NE¹543
318NE¹²122
326NE⁸468
363NE⁵625
363NE¹²626
369NE¹295
369NE²295
447NE⁴441
458NE⁵1069
f502NE⁶478
18A2633s

—103—
(87Il2181)
Cert Den
323NE²809
323NE⁴809
374NE⁴1140

—107—
(87Il2139)
cc257NE233
317NE¹631
347NE¹70
360NE²¹197
378NE²¹157

—109—
(87Il2182)
Cert Den
262NE¹797
281NE¹388
378NE³606
412NE¹629

—112—
(87Il2432)
241NE¹120
241NE³120
272NE761
274NE³879
287NE¹530
289NE³703
293NE³704
305NE²³417
379NE²66
d412NE⁵632
d412NE⁷632
e427NE⁷130
474NE⁶785
474NE⁷785
481NE¹45
497NE³479
502NE²¹295
510NE²¹183
Ga
221SE482
Iowa
174NW383
N C
198SE56
39A4333n

—115—
(87Il2159)
m243NE225
231NE¹³713
367NE²395

—120—
(20NY417)
(284NYS2d
[441)
j437NE1095
437NE⁴1095
287NYS2d
[467
298NYS2d
[645
300NYS2d
[397
f304NYS2d
[263
318NYS2d
[653
335NYS2d
[749
387NYS2d
[718
e388NYS2d
[472
j452NYS2d
[338
452NYS2d⁴
[338

453NYS2d
[597
513NYS2d72
Cir. 2
d282FS⁴73
j282FS⁴82
f292FS⁴115
439FS⁴975
439FS⁴977
Cir. 4
339FS⁴499
Cir. 6
311FS⁴1191
Calif
90CaR921
94CaR604
484P2d580
Colo
509P2d1272
Iowa
247NW271
Mich
164NW37
N H
400A2d53
Wash
496P2d516
W Va
279SE408
34A2155s
65A31069n

—126—
Case 1
(20NY792)
(284NYS2d
[449)
s282NYS2d
[664
242NE²395
295NYS2d
[163

—126—
Case 2
(20NY793)
(284NYS2d
[449)
s238NE502
s278NYS2d
[770
s291NYS2d12

—127—
Case 1
(20NY793)
(284NYS2d
[450)
s275NYS2d
[960
s282NYS2d
[973

—127—
Case 2
(20NY794)
(284NYS2d
[450)
s272NYS2d
[446
294NYS2d77

—128—
Case 1
(20NY794)
(284NYS2d
[451)
s274NYS2d
[392
s281NYS2d
[974

—128—
Case 2
(20NY795)
(284NYS2d
[451)
s281NYS2d
[985

—128—
Case 3
(20NY796)
(284NYS2d
[452)
s281NYS2d
[864
468NYS2d
[161

—129—
Case 1
(20NY796)
(284NYS2d
[452)
s282NE³201n
[438

—129—
Case 2
(20NY797)
(284NYS2d
[453)
292NYS2d45
j292NYS2d47
307NYS2d
[191
321NYS2d
[842
426NYS2d
[843
432NYS2d
[156

—130—
Case 1
(20NY798)
(284NYS2d
[454)

—130—
Case 2
(20NY798)
(284NYS2d
[458)

—130—
Case 3
(20NY798)
(284NYS2d
[455)
s242NE486
s280NYS2d
[952

—131—
(20NY799)
(284NYS2d
[455)
s232NE652
s234NE840
s261NYS2d
[336
s271NYS2d
[523
s285NYS2d
[621
s287NYS2d
[886
Cir. 2
9BRW824

—132—
Case 1
(20NY801)
(284NYS2d
[456)
s219NE295
s269NYS2d
[368
s272NYS2d
[782
s388US41
s18LE1040
s87SC1873
59LE962n
37A3630n
57A3178n
57A3201n
82A3376n
60ARF710n

—132—
Case 2
(20NY801)
(284NYS2d
[457)
s229NE192
s245NYS2d
[524
s272NYS2d
[353
s282NYS2d
[974
[497
385NYS2d
[681
39A3497n
65A3512n
44A4888n
44A4893n
68ARF957n

—133—
(20NY801)
(284NYS2d
[458)
Cert Den
US cert den
in390US971
s229NE220
s282NYS2d
[538
495NYS2d
[539
33A41132n

—134—
Case 1
(20NY802)
(284NYS2d
[459)
s189NE620
s239NYS2d
[124

—134—
Case 2
(20NY802)
(284NYS2d
[459)

—134—
Case 3
(20NY802)
(284NYS2d
[460)
s205NE879
s257NYS2d
[960
s282NYS2d
[174

—135—
Case 1
(20NY803)
(284NYS2d
[460)
s273NYS2d
[572
s282NYS2d
[639
250NE582
265NE924
288NYS2d
[246
j288NYS2d
[247
303NYS2d
[524
317NYS2d
[629
391NYS2d
[220
392NYS2d28
433NYS2d
[657
434NYS2d
[278
497NYS2d
[530
42A4828n

—135—
Case 2
(20NY804)
(284NYS2d
[461)
s275NYS2d
[674
527NYS2d
[585

—136—
(20NY805)
(284NYS2d
[462)
s274NYS2d
[850
268NE646
j295NYS2d
[970
24A3327n

24A3363n

—138—
(249Ind173)
304NE⁴877
336NE692
339NE97
430NE²787
452NE1006
526NE1229

—140—
(249Ind178)
242NE42
f363NE226
e400NE²¹111

—145—
(249Ind141)
338NE¹262
j403NE811

—147—
(249Ind144)
360NE604
f408NE620
f408NE⁴621
f408NE⁵621
f408NE⁶621
409NE⁶1272
409NE⁶1274
j437NE113
441NE⁵22
471NE⁵731
471NE⁶731
486NE¹662
Mass
j440NE776
Calif
140CaR294
Conn
261A2d296
Tex
547SW624
61A31210n
61A31219n
1A475n

—151—
(249Ind168)
241NE¹368
309NE²845
309NE³847
316NE²689
323NE¹239
e331NE¹780
399NE¹368
Me
318A2d498

—154—
(141InA649)
274NE⁵742
301NE¹243
310NE²279
348NE¹81
Ala
361So2d9
Minn
222NW80
4COA569§3
16A4192n
17A4494n

—157—
(142InA154)
241NE¹77
Nebr
421NW3

—159—
(141InA669)
d252NE²606
d252NE³606
254NE²219
255NE¹829
j275NE¹856
278NE¹336
278NE²336
280NE²865
316NE¹593
316NE²593
339NE¹112
340NE¹813
357NE¹256
387NE²1339
433NE²21

—161—
(141InA655)
233NE²805
256NE³923
322NE⁸103
323NE¹238
f355NE⁷438
f355NE⁸438
393NE⁸810
417NE⁷338
486NE⁸442
9A21044s

—165—
(141InA672)
231NE¹863
j235NE¹99
242NE⁴140
261NE⁶602
308NE²878
Okla
541P2d861
40A342n
40A358n
40A375n

—169—
(141InA662)
f239NE¹173
249NE516
j249NE³517
j251NE³26
j251NE⁴26
251NE¹34
269NE³767
j269NE⁴770
270NE767
e272NE⁴629
e272NE³633
272NE⁴874
f273NE²553
f273NE³553
277NE606
280NE³303
284NE³735
286NE¹698
297NE¹471
307NE¹504
383NE1085

Continued

Cases That Cite *Nationwide Insurance v. Ervin*, 231 N.E.2d 112 (1967)

How *Shepard's* Works: An Example

This example shows how Steps 1 through 7 work. Steps 8 and 9 are covered below. We are searching for cases that have referred to *Nationwide Insurance v. Ervin*, 231 N.E.2d 112 (1967). We call *Ervin* the "cited case," and any case that has referred to it is called a "citing" case.

Step 1. Identify the citation for the *Ervin* case. We will use the West regional reporter citation, 231 N.E.2d 112 (1967).

Step 2. Find the volume that contains citations to cases published by the *Northeastern Reporter*.

Step 3. Use the part of the volume that contains *Northeastern Reporter* citations. The volume that contains citations for *Northeastern Reporter* cases also contains citations for the official case reporter (*Illinois Appellate Reports*).

Step 4. Find the volume for the correct period. We only want to use volumes that have citations for cases decided after 1967, the year *Ervin* was decided. In this example, all volumes of *Shepard's Citations for Cases* that contain *Northeastern Reporter* citations have at least some citations to cases that have been decided after 1967, so we must check them all, including the pamphlets.

Step 5. Find the volume number appearing in the Northeastern Reporter citation for *Ervin*—Vol. 231.

Step 6. Find the page number. The *Ervin* page number appears as -112-.

Step 7. Review the citations. Under the page number (-112-) appear the citations to every case that has referred to the *Ervin* decision.

See the illustration of this example on the following page.

That is basically the way you use *Shepard's* to find cases that have referred to the case you're interested in. But you often want to know a little bit more about the citing case before you take the time to read it. Does it bear directly on the validity of the cited case? Does it help you understand whether the cited case is precedent or persuasive authority? Does it mention the cited case for the same reasons that interest you?

Fortunately, *Shepard's* provides some guidance on each of these points; see below.

Was the Cited Case Directly Affected by the Citing Case in an Appeal?

Once you have a case in which you are interested, you first want to find out whether it has been appealed and, if so, whether the appeal affected the case as a source of law. *Shepard's* uses a code next to its citations that instantly gives you this information.

For example, suppose you read a case called *Jones v. Smith*, which is located at 500 F. Supp. 325. Since the case is published in the *Federal Supplement*, we know it was decided by a U.S. district court. (See Chapter 8.) The district court case may not have had the last word, however; the case quite possibly was appealed to a higher court—typically, a U.S. Circuit Court of Appeals, but in rare instances the U.S. Supreme Court.

Once a case is appealed, the published opinion of the lower or intermediate appellate court may or may not continue to be a valid expression of the law. When a higher appellate court reverses a published decision of a lower court, it usually vacates the lower court's opinion. This means that the opinion is not to be considered as law for any purpose. The underlying case may also be affirmed or modified on appeal. In these situations, the lower court's opinion will usually remain in existence to provide guidance for future courts, but sometimes also may be ordered vacated and replaced with the higher court's opinion.

When a case is directly affected by a higher court on appeal, *Shepard's* places a small letter just before the citation of the case. For instance, if the higher court vacated the cited case's opinion, a "v" will appear next to the citation, as shown below.

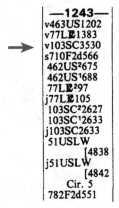

Citation Showing Vacating of Lower Court Opinion

Abbreviations used to indicate information about a case on appeal include those shown below.

Shepard's Abbreviations: Appeal of the Cited Case

a	affirmed	r	reversed
cc	connected case	s	same case
D	dismissed	v	vacated
m	modified		

Abbreviations Showing Action by the Supreme Court

When an unsuccessful attempt has been made to take the cited case before the U.S. Supreme Court, *Shepard's* uses certain notations to tells you exactly what happened.

US cert den. This means that the U.S. Supreme Court refused to issue a writ of certiorari. When this happens, the cited case is considered to be very good law, since the Supreme Court refused to review it.

US cert dis. This means that the petition for cert was dismissed, usually for procedural reasons. It's possible that the case may still be taken by the Supreme Court at a later time.

US reh den. This only appears when the cited case is a U.S. Supreme Court case, and means that the U.S. Supreme Court refused to grant a rehearing in that case.

US reh dis. This means that a request for a rehearing was dismissed.

Do Other Cases Affect the Value of the Case as Precedent or Persuasive Authority?

The law is constantly changing. New facts call for different decisions in order to reach a just result. New social or technological developments (for example, in vitro fertilization, changing attitudes about race, the computer) give rise to entirely new legal theories and cause massive changes in existing legal doctrine. This means that a case you find in your research may or may not represent the way current courts would decide the same issue. Accordingly, each time you find a case that appears relevant, you must find out whether it is still "good law." *Shepard's* helps you do this by using a second set of abbreviations to explain why the citing case referred to the cited case. This set of abbreviations is used only when the citing case is unrelated to the cited case—that is, not reviewing the cited case on appeal. The most commonly-used abbreviations are shown below.

The sample page from *Shepard's Citations for Cases*, below, shows how these abbreviations appear next to the citations.

If you are using *Shephard's* primarily as a means of checking a case for its precedential or persuasive value, you can skim down a list of the citations under the cited case and search for these abbreviations. If none appear, or the ones that do appear indicate that your case is still good law, you might stop there (but see our word of caution below). But if the cited case was questioned, criticized or overruled by the citing case, you would definitely want to read that citing case.

If there is no letter to the left of the citation, it usually means that the cited case was mentioned in passing and wasn't important to the decision in the citing case.

> ⚠ If you have the time, it is better to read any case that pertains to your issue (see below) and not rely on the abbreviations. The *Shepard's* editors sometimes make mistakes and fail to tag a citation with the proper letter.

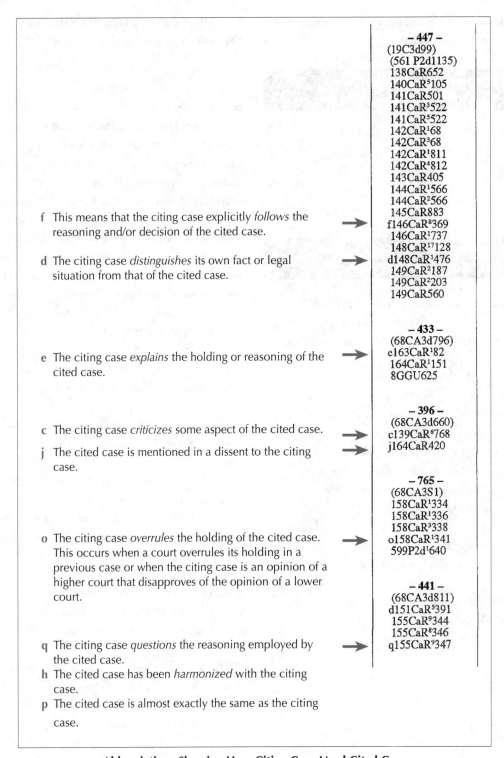

f   This means that the citing case explicitly *follows* the reasoning and/or decision of the cited case.

d   The citing case *distinguishes* its own fact or legal situation from that of the cited case.

e   The citing case *explains* the holding or reasoning of the cited case.

c   The citing case *criticizes* some aspect of the cited case.

j   The cited case is mentioned in a dissent to the citing case.

o   The citing case *overrules* the holding of the cited case. This occurs when a court overrules its holding in a previous case or when the citing case is an opinion of a higher court that disapproves of the opinion of a lower court.

q   The citing case *questions* the reasoning employed by the cited case.

h   The cited case has been *harmonized* with the citing case.

p   The cited case is almost exactly the same as the citing case.

Abbreviations Showing How Citing Case Used Cited Case

Does the Citing Case Discuss the Issue You Are Researching?

Shepard's was designed primarily as an updating tool. However, as we've pointed out, it can be used for much more than updating. Once you've found a case that's relevant, *Shepard's* can be used to find other cases dealing with the same issue. Every citing case is potentially relevant; thus, if you start out with one cited case, you may find any number of useful cases that have referred to it. Then, each of these citing cases can itself be *Shepardized*.

Suppose, for example, *Shepard's* lists five cases that have referred to your initial case. Then you *Shepardize* each of these five cases and find an additional two citing cases for each one. In very little time, you have a list of over ten cases that may be relevant to your situation.

There is a catch to this, however. We have seen that *Shephard's* gives you a list of every case that has referred to the cited case. But most cited cases deal with a number of legal issues, and a citing case will usually only mention the cited case in connection with one (or perhaps several) of those issues.

For example, if a cited case touches on 20 different legal issues, a citing case may refer to it for only three of these. If the issues in which the citing case is interested are the same as the issues in which you are interested, the citing case may be helpful in your research. However, if the citing case refers to the cited case for issues in which you aren't interested, the citing case won't do you any good.

To help you separate the wheat from the chaff and avoid this time trap, *Shepard's* identifies the specific issues in which the citing case was interested in when it referred to the cited case. It does this by:

- identifying the issue from the cited case that is being discussed by the citing case;
- selecting the headnote in the cited case that most closely states the issue being discussed in the citing case; and
- placing that headnote number just to the right of the citation to the citing case.

Example: *Nationwide Insurance v. Ervin*, 231 N.E.2d 112 (1967) is referred to (cited) in *Deason v. Metropolitan Property & Liability Insurance Co.*, 474 N.E.2d 783 (1985).

DEASON v. METRO. PROP. & LIABILITY INS. CO.   Ill. 785
Cite as 474 N.E.2d 783 (Ill.App. 5 Dist. 1985)

the time of the accident; the Mercury had a defective transmission and the Dodge had a twisted drive shaft. Both vehicles were put back into operation shortly after the accident involving the Comet. During his deposition, Andrew Warner testified as follows:

"Q. Did you have any intention if the Comet hadn't been wrecked, did you have any intention to dispose of either of these other two cars just because you got the Comet?

A. Oh, no."

[2] In ruling that Metropolitan's policy afforded secondary coverage in connection with the accident involving the 1975 Comet, the court found that Christopher Warner was "a relative operating a temporary substitute" automobile. Metropolitan contends that this conclusion is incorrect, and we are compelled to agree. Under the terms of the policy, a temporary substitute automobile is defined as one "temporarily used with the permission of the owner as a substitute for an owned automobile when withdrawn from normal use for servicing or repair or because of breakdown, loss, or destruction." Here, the unequivocal deposition testimony of all concerned establishes that Christopher Warner's use of the Comet was not to be temporary, but regular and permanent, as it was the intention of both Vera Fry and Christopher Warner that he would pay $100 for the car at Christmas time, and would not return it to her. Moreover, the Comet was not intended by the Warners to be a substitute for either the Mercury or the Dodge; rather, it was to be kept as a third car, and the fact that the Dodge and Mercury broke down during the Warners' use of the Comet was entirely coincidental. Under these circumstances, the "temporary substitute" provision of the policy issued by Metropolitan did not encompass Christopher Warner's use of the Comet on the date of the accident. (See *Sturgeon v. Automobile Club Inter-Insurance Exchange* (1979), 77 Ill. App.3d 997, 1000, 34 Ill.Dec. 66, 397 N.E.2d 522.) This conclusion is buttressed by the holding of *Nationwide Insurance Compa-*

ny v. Ervin (1967), 87 Ill.App.2d 432, 436–37, 231 N.E.2d 112, wherein it was recognized that a "temporary substitute" provision of the type under consideration here is to be applied to those situations where an insured automobile is withdrawn from use for a short period, and not where, as here, coverage is sought to be extended to an additional automobile for a significant length of time.

[3] *Providence Mutual Casualty Company v. Sturms* (1962), 37 Ill.App.2d 304, 185 N.E.2d 366, relied on by appellees, is not on point. *Sturms* addresses the question of whether coverage afforded on a temporary substitute automobile expires immediately upon repair of the insured's regular automobile (37 Ill.App.2d 304, 306, 185 N.E.2d 366), and does not discuss the more fundamental issue of when a vehicle is considered to be a temporary substitute in the first place. While appellees also suggest that portions of Metropolitan's claim file show that certain Metropolitan employees believe that the policy in question afforded coverage, the trial court correctly noted in its judgment that these statements are merely opinions, and are not binding on a court in its consideration of the legal question presented. 31A C.J.S. *Evidence* § 272(b) (1964).

For the foregoing reasons, the judgment of the circuit court of St. Clair County is reversed.

Reversed.

JONES, P.J., and KARNS, J., concur.

Page From *Deason v. Metropolitan Property & Liability Insurance Co.*

Therefore, in this example, *Ervin* is the cited case and *Deason* is the citing case. If you *Shepardized Ervin*, you would find the citation to the page in *Deason* where the *Deason* court cited *Ervin*, as shown below.

NORTHEASTERN REPORTER, 2d SERIES

Vol.231

323FS⁶344	—107—	453NYS2d	—128—	—131—	—134—	24Æ363n	—157—
596FS⁴784	(87IlÆ139)	[597	Case 1	(20NɎ799)	(20NɎ802)		(142InA154)
650FS437	cc257NɆ233	513NYS2d72	(20NɎ794)	(284NYS2d	(284NYS2d	—138—	241NɆ⁴77
64Æ506s	317NɆ¹631	Cir. 2	(284NYS2d	[455)	[459)	(249Ind173)	Nebr
	347NɆ¹70	d282FS⁴73	[451)	s232NɆ652	s189NɆ620	304NɆ⁴877	421NW3
—70—	360NɆ²1197	j282FS⁴82	s274NYS2d	s234NɆ840	s239NYS2d	336NɆ692	
(12♦S26)	378NɆ¹1157	f292FS⁴115	[392	s261NYS2d	[124	339NɆ97	—159—
(41♦p159)		439FS⁴975	s281NYS2d	[336		430NɆ¹787	(141InA669)
231NɆ²332	—109—	439FS⁴977	[974	s271NYS2d	—134—	452NɆ1006	d252NɆ²606
370NɆ²458	(87IlÆ82)	Cir. 4		[523	Case 2	526NɆ1229	d252NɆ²606
371NɆ³843	Cert Den	339FS⁴499	—128—	s285NYS2d	(20NɎ802)		254NɆ²219
381NɆ²972	262NɆ¹797	Cir. 6	Case 2	[621	(284NYS2d	—140—	255NɆ¹829
414NɆ⁴438	281NɆ¹388	311FS⁴1191	(20NɎ795)	s287NYS2d	[459)	(249Ind178)	j275NɆ¹856
453NɆ⁴664	378NɆ³606	Calif	(284NYS2d	[886		242NɆ42	278NɆ¹336
454NɆ²1389	412NɆ¹629	90CaR921	[451)	Cir. 2	—134—	e400NɆ²1111	278NɆ²336
488NɆ927		94CaR604	s281NYS2d	9BRW824	Case 3		280NɆ²865
	—112—	484P2d580	[985		(20NɎ802)	—145—	316NɆ¹593
—71—	(87IlÆ432)	Colo		—132—	(284NYS2d	(249Ind141)	316NɆ²593
(12♦A68)	241NɆ¹120	509P2d1272	—128—	Case 1	[460)	338NɆ¹262	339NɆ¹112
(41♦p122)	241NɆ³120	Iowa	Case 3	(20NɎ801)	s205NɆ879	j403NɆ811	340NɆ¹813
p166NɆ808	272NɆ761	247NW271	(20NɎ796)	(284NYS2d	s257NYS2d		357NɆ¹256
c484NɆ220	274NɆ³879	Mich	(284NYS2d	[456)	[960	—147—	387NɆ²1339
j484NɆ221	287NɆ¹530	164NW37	[452)	s219NɆ295	s282NYS2d	(249Ind144)	433NɆ²21
18Æ813s	289NɆ²703	N H	s281NYS2d	s269NYS2d	[174	360NɆ604	
	293NɆ³704	400A2d53	[864	[368		f408NɆ620	—161—
—81—	305NɆ²417	Wash	468NYS2d	s272NYS2d	—135—	f408NɆ⁴621	(141InA655)
(12♦A87)	379NɆ²66	496P2d516	[161	[782	Case 1	f408NɆ⁵621	233NɆ²805
c432NɆ⁴212	d412NɆ²632	W Va		s388US41	(20NɎ803)	f408NɆ⁶621	256NɆ²923
Cir. 6	d412NɆ⁷632	279SɆ408	—129—	s18LɆ1040	(284NYS2d	409NɆ⁶1272	322NɆ³103
577FS⁴1131	e427NɆ⁷130	34Æ155s	Case 1	s87SC1873	[460)	409NɆ⁴1274	323NɆ¹238
Md	474NɆ⁶785	65Æ31069n	(20NɎ796)	59LɆ962n	s273NYS2d	j437NɆ113	323NɆ⁸238
513A2d938	474NɆ⁷785		(284NYS2d	37Æ3630n	[572	441NɆ²22	f355NɆ⁷438
	481NɆ⁴45	—126—	[452)	57Æ3178n	s282NYS2d	471NɆ⁵731	f355NɆ⁸438
—85—	497NɆ³479	Case 1	s282NYS2d	57Æ3201n	[639	471NɆ⁶731	393NɆ²810
(12♦A59)	502NɆ²1295	(20NɎ792)	[438	82Æ3376n	250NɆ582	486NɆ¹662	417NɆ²338
(41♦p117)	510NɆ²1183	(284NYS2d		60ÆRF710n	265NɆ924	Mass	486NɆ⁸442
	Ga	[449)	—129—		288NYS2d	j440NɆ776	9Æ1044s
—91—	221SɆ482	s282NYS2d	Case 2	—132—		Calif	
(12♦A83)	Iowa	[664	(20NɎ797)	Case 2	—146—	140CaR294	—165—
(41♦p160)	174NW383	242NɆ395	(284NYS2d	(20NɎ801)	j288NYS2d	Conn	(141InA672)
521NɆ⁴1153	N C	295NYS2d	[453)	(284NYS2d	[247	261A2d296	231NɆ¹863
521NɆ⁶1153	198SɆ56	[163	292NYS2d45	[457)	303NYS2d	Tex	j235NɆ¹99
31Æ3585n	39Æ333n		j292NYS2d47	s229NɆ192	[524	547SW624	242NɆ⁴140
		—126—	307NYS2d	s245NYS2d	317NYS2d	61Æ31210n	261NɆ⁶602
—94—	—115—	Case 2	[191	[353	[629	61Æ31219n	308NɆ878
(12OhM127)	(87IlÆ159)	(20NɎ793)	321NYS2d	s272NYS2d	391NYS2d	1Æ475n	Okla
(41♦p131)	m243NɆ225	(284NYS2d	[842	[974	[220		541P2d861
	231NɆ¹³713	[449)	426NYS2d	s282NYS2d	392NYS2d28	—151—	40Æ342n
—97—	367NɆ²395	s238NɆ502	[843	[497	433NYS2d	(249Ind168)	40Æ358n
(87IlÆ411)		s278NYS2d	432NYS2d	385NYS2d	[657	241NɆ¹368	40Æ375n
Cert Den	—120—	[770	[156	[681	434NYS2d	309NɆ²845	
269NɆ²355	(20NɎ417)	s291NYS2d12		39Æ3497n	[278	309NɆ²847	—169—
269NɆ⁵356	(284NYS2d		—130—	65Æ3512n	497NYS2d	316NɆ²689	(141InA662)
273NɆ¹162	[441)	—127—	Case 1	44Æ4888n	[530	323NɆ¹239	f239NɆ¹¹73
280NɆ¹246	j437NɆ1095	Case 1	(20NɎ798)	44Æ4893n	42Æ4828n	e331NɆ¹780	249NɆ516
283NɆ¹⁵43	437NɆ⁴1095	(20NɎ793)	(284NYS2d	68ÆRF957n		399NɆ¹368	j249NɆ³517
318NɆ¹²122	287NYS2d	(284NYS2d	[454)		—135—	Me	j251NɆ³26
326NɆ⁸468	[467	[450)		—133—	Case 2	318A2d498	j251NɆ⁴26
363NɆ⁵625	298NYS2d	s275NYS2d	—130—	(20NɎ801)	(20NɎ804)		251NɆ¹34
363NɆ¹²626	300NYS2d	[960	Case 2	(284NYS2d	(284NYS2d	—154—	269NɆ²767
369NɆ¹295	[397	s282NYS2d	(20NɎ798)	[458)	[461)	(141InA649)	j269NɆ⁴770
369NɆ²295	f304NYS2d	[973	(284NYS2d	Cert Den	s275NYS2d	274NɆ⁵742	270NɆ767
447NɆ⁴441	[263		[454)	US cert den	[674	301NɆ¹243	e272NɆ⁴629
458NɆ⁵1069	318NYS2d	—127—	s282NYS2d	in390US971	527NYS2d	310NɆ²279	e272NɆ³633
f502NɆ⁴478	335NYS2d	Case 2	[934	s229NɆ220	[585	348NɆ¹81	272NɆ⁴874
18Æ633s	[749	(20NɎ794)		s282NYS2d		Ala	f273NɆ²553
	387NYS2d	(284NYS2d	—130—	[538	—136—	361So2d9	f273NɆ⁸553
—103—	[718	[450)	Case 3	495NYS2d	(20NɎ805)	Minn	277NɆ606
(87IlÆ181)	e388NYS2d	s272NYS2d	(20NɎ798)	[539	(284NYS2d	222NW80	280NɆ²303
Cert Den	[472	[446	(284NYS2d	33Æ41132n	[462)	4COA569§ 3	284NɆ³735
323NɆ²809	j452NYS2d	294NYS2d77	[455)		s274NYS2d	16Æ4192n	286NɆ¹698
323NɆ⁴809	[338		s242NɆ486		[850	17Æ4494n	297NɆ¹471
374NɆ⁴1140	452NYS2d⁴		s280NYS2d		268NɆ646		307NɆ¹504
	[338		[952		j295NYS2d		383NɆ1085
					[970		
					24Æ3327n		*Continued*

Page From *Shepard's*

The little numbers (6 and 7) between the N.E.2d and the page number (785) are the numbers of the headnotes in *Ervin* that, in the opinion of *Shepard's*, best describe the issues which the case is being cited for in *Deason*. These headnotes are shown below.

NATIONWIDE INSURANCE COMPANY v. ERVIN   Ill. 113
Cite as 231 N.E.2d 112

1. Insurance ⬅138(1)

Parties to insurance contract are free to incorporate such provisions into it, if not unlawful, as they see fit and it is then the duty of the court to enforce those provisions.

2. Insurance ⬅146.7(8)

Rule that all ambiguities in policy will be construed most strongly against insurance company, as the party that drafted the policy, only has application where ambiguity in fact exists and court may not distort the contract to create the ambiguity itself.

3. Insurance ⬅146.2

Insurance contract should be construed in accordance with the general contract rule of construction that the agreement should be ascertained as a whole to determine intention of parties and purpose which they sought to accomplish.

4. Insurance ⬅435.2(2)

Enumeration in automobile policy of those few situations where coverage is afforded to the insured with reference to other than named automobile serves to limit areas of risk assumed by insurer.

5. Insurance ⬅435.3(1)

Provision of automobile policy limiting coverage for additional owned automobile to 30 days after acquisition by insured permits owner adequate opportunity to acquire necessary additional insurance and is not intended to cover two automobiles for any protracted period.

6. Insurance ⬅435.2(4)

Provision in automobile policy granting coverage to insured for temporary substitute automobile, not owned by the insured, applies to those situations where the named automobile is in repair shop or withdrawn from use for short period.

7. Insurance ⬅435.3(1)

Where insured had bought second automobile in July 1964 after transmission "went

231 N.E.2d—8

out" of automobile which was named in policy and which remained inoperable in driveway of his home until repair in spring of 1966, and had accident with second automobile on September 26, 1964, the second automobile was not a "replacement" for the named automobile within policy provision extending coverage to replacement automobile.

Barrick, Jackson & Switzer, Rockford, for appellant.

Nordquist & Anderson, Rockford, for appellees.

ABRAHAMSON, Justice.

The Nationwide Insurance Company brings this appeal from a decree of the Circuit Court of the 17th Judicial Circuit, Winnebago County, entered December 29, 1966, that found that an automobile insurance policy issued by it to Douglas Ervin "covered" an accident that had occurred on September 26, 1964, and that a certain automobile operated by Ervin at the time of the accident was a "replacement" as defined in the policy.

On August 16, 1963, Nationwide issued its policy of automobile insurance number 94-441-489 to Ervin for coverage of his 1958 Chevrolet. In July of 1964 the transmission of the Chevrolet, according to Ervin, "went out" and he purchased a 1958 Cadillac. The Chevrolet was retained by Ervin, although inoperable, and left in the driveway of his home.

On September 26, 1964, Ervin was in an automobile accident with the Cadillac that involved a truck owned by the Jones Transfer Company, an Illinois Corporation, and another automobile in which Robert Holmes was a passenger. Holmes subsequently brought suit against Ervin and Jones Transfer for injuries allegedly suffered as a result of that accident. Nationwide was called upon by Ervin to defend him in that suit pursuant to the policy.

Headnotes From *Ervin*

Thus, *Deason* used *Ervin* when it discussed the issues summarized in these two headnotes. If the issues in these two headnotes were the reason you were *Shepardizing Ervin*, you would definitely want to read *Deason*. However, if you were not interested in the issues discussed in headnotes 6 and 7, you might wisely choose not to read *Deason*.

If there is no headnote number next to the citation—that is, the citation doesn't identify the issue for which the cited case is being mentioned—it means that the reference to the cited case appeared, to the *Shepard's* editors, to be general rather than in reference to a specific legal issue. The citing case may or may not be of interest, so you should at least skim it.

Summing Up
How to *Shepardize* State Court Cases

✔ Select one of the parallel citations of the case you wish to *Shepardize*.

✔ Note the year of the case you are *Shepardizing*.

✔ Find the *Shepard's* volumes—and if necessary the parts of these volumes—that cover the reporter in the citation.

✔ Select the volume or volumes that contain citations for cases decided after the case you are *Shepardizing*.

✔ Find the volume number (in boldface) that corresponds to the volume number of the case being *Shepardized*.

✔ Under this volume number, find the page number (in boldface) of the citation for the cited case.

✔ Under this page number, review the citations given for the citing cases.

✔ Use the letters to the left of the citation to decide whether the case has been directly affected by a higher court in an appeal.

✔ Use the numbers to the right of the citation to decide whether the citing case is referring to the cited case for issues in which you might be interested.

✔ After you write down all potentially useful citations, repeat these steps with the more recent *Shepard's* volumes and update pamphlets.

Summing Up
How to *Shepardize* U.S. Supreme Court Cases

✔ Select one of the three parallel citations for the case you wish to *Shepardize*.

✔ Note the year of the case.

✔ Find the *Shepard's* labeled *United States Case Citations*.

✔ Select the volume or volumes that contain citations for cases decided after the date of the case you are *Shepardizing*.

✔ Select the part of the *Shepard's* volume that pertains to the citation you are using. For instance, if your citation is for the *U.S. Supreme Court Reporter* (S. Ct.), locate the pages that cover this report rather than the pages that pertain to the *United States Reports* (U.S.) or the *Supreme Court Reports, Lawyer's Edition* (L. Ed.).

✔ Find the boldface volume number that corresponds to the volume number of the case being *Shepardized*.

✔ Under this volume number, find the page number of the cited case.

✔ Under the page number, review the citations of the citing cases.

✔ Use the letters to the left of each citation to decide whether the case has been directly affected by a higher court in an appeal.

✔ Use the numbers to the right of the citation to decide whether the citing case is referring to the cited case for issues in which you might be interested.

✔ After you write down all potentially useful citations, repeat these steps with the more recent *Shepard's* volumes and update pamphlets.

Library Exercise: Using *Shepard's Citations*: Cases

Now it's time to use the library to apply what you've just learned. This exercise asks you to use *Shepard's Citations for Cases* to find references to a relevant case that you have discovered in the course of your research. Additional research exercises that include these and other skills are in Chapter 11.

Questions

1. You are researching flag burning cases and have found *Street v. New York*, 394 U.S. 576 (1969).
   a. Only the *Supreme Court Reporter* (West) is available in your law library. Use *Shepard's* to find the case's citation in the *Supreme Court Reporter*.
   b. *Shepardize* the *Supreme Court Reporter* citation.
      1. Find the citation to the Fourth Circuit case that followed *Street* on the matter treated in headnote 16.
      2. Find a Ninth Circuit case that distinguished itself from *Street* on the matter covered by headnote 2.
      3. Find the references to two *American Law Reports* annotations that cite *Street*. *Not*
2. You are researching the effect of bankruptcy on child support and alimony in New Mexico. You find a helpful case: *Yeates v. Yeates (In re Yeates)*, 807 F.2d 874 (10th Cir. 1986). You want to use this case to find a case that deals specifically with New Mexico law.
   a. *Shepardize Yeates* and find a New Mexico case that has cited *Yeates*.
   b. Find an *American Law Reports* annotation that cites *Yeates*.
3. You are researching the issue of whether a judge may rule that a defendant was not guilty by reason of insanity, even though the jury convicted him. You have a citation to *Douglas v. United States*, 239 F.2d 52 (1956), which holds that a judge may do this in an appropriate case, but must do so with caution because of the deference usually given to the jury's resolution of factual issues. This statement could be very helpful to you.
   a. Find the case. Which headnote includes the statement in which you are interested?
   b. *Shepardize Douglas*.

1. What does the (99 ADC 232) following the case citation mean?
2. Are there any citations listed for cases that followed *Douglas* on the issue dealt with in headnote 3?
3. Are there any cites for cases that distinguished themselves from *Douglas* on the matter dealt with in headnote 3?
4. Are there any citations for cases in which a dissenting opinion cited *Douglas* in support of the statement contained in headnote 3?

Answers

1. a. Go to *Shepard's United States Citations*. The parallel citation is given only the first time the case is listed in *Shepard's*, so go to the earliest volume that includes 394 U.S. (Volume 1.6 of Case Edition 1994). When you look under *United States Reports*, volume 394, page 576, the citations in parentheses right after the citation to your case are the parallel citations (citations to the same case published in other reporters). The citation you are looking for is 89 S. Ct. 1354.
   b. Go to *Shepard's United States Citations*; you want to start with the earliest volume that includes 89 S. Ct. (Volume 3.5, Case Edition 1994), and then continue forward to all other volumes and paper supplements that include 89 S. Ct.
      1. The citation you are looking for is 317 F.Supp. 141 (the reference to *Street* is on page 141; the case starts on some page before that). You know that this case followed *Street* because of the "f" in the margin to the left of the citation; you know it followed on the matter treated in *Street's* headnote 16 because of the tiny "16" up and to the right of the FS. (FS is the abbreviation used by *Shepard's* for the *Federal Supplement*.)
      2. 462 F.2d 102. You know that this case distinguished itself from *Street* because of the "d" in the left margin. You know it distinguished itself regarding the matter treated in *Street's* headnote 2 because of the tiny "2" above and to the right of the F.2d (*Shepard's* abbreviation for *Federal Reporter,* 2d series).

Library Exercise: Using *Shepard's Citations:* Cases (continued)

3. 9 A.L.R.3d 462s (the "s" means the citation of *Street* is in the pocket part). 41 A.L.R.3d 505n (the "n" means the citation to *Street* is in a footnote on page 505). Note: The list of citations is long. We are interested in the last two citations in the hardbound volume.

2. a. Go to *Shepard's Federal Citations*, starting with the first volume that includes 807 F.2d (volume 13, 1995) and then proceeding forward to all later volumes and supplements that include 807 F.2d. Looking under all listings for *Federal Reporter*, 2d series, volume 807, page 874, you find, under a subheading "NM", meaning New Mexico, the following citations: 784 P.2d 425 and 109 NM 238.

   b. 74 A.L.R. 2d 758s (the "s" means the citation to *Yeates* was in the pocket part to the annotation).

3. a. Headnote 3 contains that statement.

   b. Go to *Shepard's Federal Citations*, starting with the first volume that includes 239 F.2d (volume 6, 1995) and then proceeding forward to all later volumes and supplements that include 239 F.2d.

      1. The citation in parentheses means that *Douglas* is also reported in volume 99 of *Appeal Cases, District of Columbia Reports*, on page 232. This is called a parallel citation. Abbreviations are listed in the front of every volume of *Shepard's Citations*.

      2. 251 F.2d 879. You know that this case followed *Douglas* because of the "f" in the margin to the left of the citation; you know it followed on the matter treated in *Douglas'* headnote 3 because of the tiny "3" up and to the right of the F.2d (*Shepard's* abbreviation for *Federal Reporter*, 2d series).

      3. 213 F. Supp. 454. You know that this case distinguished itself from *Douglas* because of the "d" in the left margin. You know it distinguished itself regarding the matter treated in *Douglas'* headnote 3 because of the tiny "3" above and to the right of the FS (*Shepard's* abbreviation for *Federal Supplement*).

      4. 251 F.2d 881; 284 F.2d 254; 325 F.2d 622. You know that *Douglas* was cited in the dissenting opinions of these cases because of the "j" in the margin to the left of each citation. You know that the dissents cited *Douglas* for the matter contained in *Douglas'* headnote 3 because of the tiny "3" up and to the right of the F.2d (*Shepard's* abbreviation for *Federal Reporter*, 2d series).

Library Exercise: Using *A.L.R.*, Case Headnotes and *Shepard's*

Your employer has taken on several paid "trainees" for the summer. They are paralegal students. While the regular assistant office administrator is away or busy, they will do work that is regularly done in the office: filing, preparing billings, running to various courts to file documents, and going to law offices around town to pick up or deliver papers.

Your boss thinks that he can pay these "trainees" below the minimum wage required for employees by the Fair Labor Standards Act. He thinks that they are not "employees" because they are in training, will learn how a law office works and will gain "resume value." He has been told that *50 A.L.R. Fed.* has an article on this topic and that an important case in your Circuit (the 4th) is *Wirtz v. Wardlaw*. (The use of *A.L.R.* (American Law Reports) and *A.L.R. Fed.* are discussed in Chapter 5.)

Questions

1. Where in the library do you find the *A.L.R. Fed.* article?

2. How do you find the case?

3. Scan those sections and find *Wirtz*. Where is the case first mentioned, and does this use of the case suggest that it is relevant to your question?

4. Find the case.

5. Look through the headnotes. This case treats several issues other than the specific one with which you are concerned. Which headnote is about the point made in the *A.L.R.* article?

6. *Shepardize* the case: Using the Federal *Shepard's*, find all the volumes that cover *Federal Reporter 2d*, including volume 339. (You will consult the main set, bound supplements and paper supplements.) What cases cited *Wirtz* for the issue covered by that headnote?

7. What does the "e" mean in "e473 FS 469"?

Answers

1. The article will be in *A.L.R. Federal*, in volume 50. In the front of the volume is an alphabetical list of articles in that volume arranged by subject. Under "Employees," you soon see, "When is an individual in training an 'employee' for purposes § 3(e)(1) of the Fair Labor Standards Act (29 U.S.C.S. § 203(e)(1)), 50 A.L.R. Fed 632?"

2. Turn to page 632. There isn't a list of cases, but there is a Table of Courts and Circuits. Cases from the Fourth Circuit are cited in §§ 2, 3, 5, 6 [a,b] and 7. On page 638 is *Wirtz v. Wardlaw*.

3. The case is first mentioned on page 635. The text describes the test for determining whether trainees are employees (are their efforts integral to the employer's business?), and cites *Wirtz* as framing this question by asking whether the trainees' efforts actually helped the business of the employer (if they were truly mere trainees, they probably just got in the way!).

4. The citation is to 339 F.2d 785. It is found in volume 339 of *Federal Reporter*, 2nd series, on page 785.

5. Headnote 3 concerns the designation of trainees as employees.

6. 406 FS 1307, e473 FS 469 and 992 F.2d 1026. Each of these cites includes a small elevated "3" directly following the "FS" or the "F.2d," which indicates that these cases deal with the issue described in headnote 3.

7. It means that the case at 473 *Federal Supplement* cites *Wirtz* on page 469 and explains *Wirtz* regarding the issue covered by headnote 3.

Shepardize! Online

If you've found a helpful case on the Internet, you might be tempted to call it a day. Frustrations with Boolean operators and endlessly-reworked key word searches have earned you some time off. But don't switch off the computer just yet. As you know from reading *"Shepard's Citations for Cases,"* above, you can't march out the door of the library without confirming that the case you've found in the Reporter is the latest, most direct legal opinion on the subject you're researching; and you shouldn't leave the web without being assured of the same thing. We'll show you how to do it.

Looking for an Updated Case

You can use the Internet to find cases that have used a helpful case. If you're lucky, you'll get a recent case that adds legal ammunition to the point you need to argue. Or, if you're unlucky, you'll find that your helpful case has been overruled or not followed by later courts. But even here, you'll be saved the embarrassment of using a case that is no longer good law.

Using Westlaw's KeyCite

Westlaw also offers a citator tool with functions similar to *Shepardize!*, called KeyCite. As with the LexisNexis *Shepardize!* tool, you can access KeyCite with a credit card at http://creditcard.westlaw.com/ as well as using it for free in the law library if Westlaw is available.

To use KeyCite with a credit card, click the "register" link, provide the requested information, and follow the online instructions. Each time you wish to cite a case, you'll be warned that your credit card will be charged $6.25 and you'll be asked to approve the purchase. If you are citing many cases, the cost will mount in a hurry. However, if you only need to cite several cases, which is usually the case, the cost will be little more than what it would take to get to the law library to use its free resources.

Once you reach the Westlaw homepage after registering your credit card, you either may use the "Check this citation in KeyCite text box" or the "Check a Citation Using a KeyCite Template" link. We recommend the template approach for beginners, as it provides helpful structure in correctly entering the citation you wish to cite. Importantly, KeyCite comes with help at every juncture. Take a little time to read it. Also, check out the sidebar, "A Law Librarian's Tips.")

A Law Librarian's Tips

Here are some tips for using KeyCite in the law library—prepared for her patrons by Bonnie Perkins, law librarian at the Lake County Law Library in Northern California

On the screen that comes up when you log into Westlaw, you'll find the words KeyCite printed in the left hand column. Under "KeyCite," you find a blank spot for typing in your search request. Type in your case citation (for example 202 F.3rd 839, a federal case, or 108 Cal.App.3rd 339, a California state court case.) Do not surround the citation with quotation marks.

The case whose citation you typed in the search box will appear at the top of the page of a list of cases. Below your case, you'll see more cases chronologically listed. By definition, all of these cases were decided after the case you are citing.

If the case you are citing originally appeared in a West publication, you will probably only be interested in topics covered in one or two headnotes. Each case on the list produced by KeyCite is followed by the numbers of the headnotes (in bold) that your original case is being cited for. For example, if you are looking for a case discussing the issue raised in headnote 5 of the original case, and all the case produced by KeyCite involve other headnotes, you needn't pull up any of the cases on the list—since they aren't relevant.

If you see a red flag on a case you wish to examine, be careful. A red flag means that particular case is no longer good law, due to it being overruled by a higher court or ordered depublished. If you see a yellow flag on a case you wish to examine, be careful. This reasoning of the case has been called into question by another court.

To use *Shepardize!*, you must register and provide the website with a credit card number. Once you are registered, you can use your username and password to access this site. Enter the following URL in your browser: http://web.lexis.com/xchange/ccsubs/cc_prods.asp.

To start the registration process, enter any citation in the citation box and click "Go." You'll then be asked to log in

or register, which means provide a little information about yourself and a credit card number. Once your registration is approved, you'll be prompted to sign in, using your new user name and password. After this step, you'll go through several order screens for each citation that you *Shepardize*.

![!] **Spend Your Money Wisely.** The fee for each *Shepardize!* search is currently $6.00. This is unrelated to how much time you spend doing your search or using the site's help feature. If you find a relevant case and want to use the *Shepardize!* document retrieval feature to view it, you'll be charged an additional $9.

While the headnote and other *Shepardize!* features are very powerful, beware the mounting costs. For example, to order your results according to the keynote (which we do below), you will be charged an additional $6.00. The good news is that *Shepardize!* warns you whenever you are about to incur a new charge. And when you sign off, you will be told the number of transactions you engaged in (multiply this number by $6.00 to get your total charge that will come off your credit card).

If you limit yourself to the *Shepardize!* results and resist pulling up documents, you shouldn't be hit too hard. If the cases you find are recent, you may be able to find them on the Internet for free (see Chapter 9). And if they are older cases, you can use a flat-fee service like VersusLaw to find them. Keep in mind, you can get a whole month of basic VersusLaw searching for a few dollars more than the price of one document retrieved through *Shepardize!*.

Once your *Shepardize!* request goes through, you'll see a list of cases that refer to the case cited. Spend a little time exploring your options—referred to as "restrictions." You can restrict the search results according to jurisdiction, date, and headnotes, but this involves a small learning curve. For instance, in order to see what footnote the citing case is referring to the cited case for, you'll need to click the "Custom Form" button at the top of the search results page, click the "Headnotes" link on the custom form page, and then check the "Headnote" check boxes. Finally, click "Show Restrictions." The citations will now indicate the relevant headnotes of the cited case.

The West Digest System

When researching case law, you're looking for cases with facts that are as close to your facts as possible. The closer the facts, the more authority a case will provide for your position. Obviously, the more cases you examine that have taken up the same legal issue, the better the chance of finding a case with facts like yours.

In Chapter 9, we saw how digests can help you find a good case to open up your research. They can also provide invaluable assistance in finding similar cases.

Digests Defined

Digests are collections of headnotes—the one-sentence summaries of how a particular case decided specific legal issues—that are taken from cases as reported in case reporters and grouped together by topic. For example, in *Nationwide Insurance Co. v. Ervin*, 231 N.E.2d 112 (1967), one of the issues is classified under "Insurance." The court's holding on that issue is summarized in Headnote 5, shown below, and has been assigned a topic key number, 435.3(1).

That headnote has also been published in West's *Northeastern Digest*, with headnotes from other cases that have been assigned the same key topic and key number. (See "The West Key System," below.) The *Ervin* headnote, as it appears in West's *Northeastern Digest*, is shown below and in context on page 205. West has stopped publishing a digest for this region, and for the Southern and Southwestern regions as well. Consequently, some states are not included in regional digests. They can be found in the *General Digest*, and some of them have their own digests.

> **Ill.App. 1967.** Provision of automobile policy limiting coverage for additional owned automobile to 30 days after acquisition by insured permits owner adequate opportunity to acquire necessary additional insurance and is not intended to cover two automobiles for any protracted period.—Nationwide Ins. Co. v. Ervin, 231 N.E.2d 112, 87 Ill.App.2d 432.

Digest Entry

The West Key System

Let's take a closer look at the West Digest system. The most important point to understand about this system is that West Group reports virtually all published cases that emerge from the state and federal courts. This means that West has been able to create a uniform and comprehensive classification scheme for all legal issues raised in these cases. This classification system is called the West Key Number system.

The West Digest key number system has 414 key topics and many numbered subtopics. Any given headnote from one case anywhere in the U.S. is grouped with the head-notes from all other cases that deal with that same issue. For example, a particular issue dealing with insurance on replacement automobiles can be assigned a subtopic number and grouped with headnotes from other state and federal court cases that carry the same topic and subtopic number.

This means that all the researcher needs to crack the digest system is one headnote labeled by key topic and number. That key topic and number can then be used to find all other headnotes with the same key topic and number that appear in cases in the geographic area the digest covers. The topic label and subtopic number together constitute the "key" to finding other cases in the digest that have discussed the same or similar issue.

There are a number of different West Digests. There is an overall digest that groups all headnote entries from all parts of the country and from all courts. This is made up of two sub-digests—the *Decennials* and the *General Digest*. West has divided this huge digest into smaller ones:

- The *U.S. Supreme Court Digest* covers only U.S. Supreme Court cases;
- The *Federal Practice Digest* covers all federal courts (including the U.S. Supreme Court) ;
- State digests (for example, the *Illinois Digest* covers only the cases from that state); and
- Regional digests (the states have been grouped into four regions: *Atlantic, Pacific, Northwestern* and *Southeastern*).

Each of these digests is discussed below. As you can see, some digests overlap. For instance, both the *U.S. Supreme Court Digest* and the *Federal Practice Digest* cover U.S. Supreme Court cases. And both the *Pacific Regional Digest* and the *California Digest* cover California cases. All of the entries in these digests are duplicated in the *Decennial* and *General Digests*. Because all West Digests use exactly the same classification system (the key number system), an entry in the *California Digest* (for example) will be found in the *Pacific Digest* under the same key topic and subtopic number.

In the event of an overlap, which digest should you start with? Generally, it pays to start with the specific and move to the more general only if the specific doesn't satisfy your research needs. For example, if you are looking for a California case on a specific point, start with the *California Digest*. Then, if you are not satisfied with what you find, you can consult the *Pacific Digest* for cases decided by the courts of the other states in that region. You won't find any additional California cases under your key topic and number, since they would have been contained in the *California Digest*. And the cases in the *California Digest* will show up in the *Pacific Digest*. If, after using the *Pacific Digest*, you're still not satisfied, then go to the *Decennial* or *General Digest*.

Always remember to check the pocket part of any digest you use to get the most recent cases.

Most law libraries do not subscribe to the entire West Digest system. However, most medium to large libraries have the West Digest for that state, the West Digest for the region the state is located in, the West *Federal Practice Digest* and the *Decennials*.

State and Federal Digests Published by West

NATIONWIDE INSURANCE COMPANY v. ERVIN   Ill. 113
Cite as 231 N.E.2d 112

1. Insurance ☞138(1)

Parties to insurance contract are free to incorporate such provisions into it, if not unlawful, as they see fit and it is then the duty of the court to enforce those provisions.

2. Insurance ☞146.7(8)

Rule that all ambiguities in policy will be construed most strongly against insurance company, as the party that drafted the policy, only has application where ambiguity in fact exists and court may not distort the contract to create the ambiguity itself.

3. Insurance ☞146.2

Insurance contract should be construed in accordance with the general contract rule of construction that the agreement should be ascertained as a whole to determine intention of parties and purpose which they sought to accomplish.

4. Insurance ☞435.2(2)

Enumeration in automobile policy of those few situations where coverage is afforded to the insured with reference to other than named automobile serves to limit areas of risk assumed by insurer.

5. Insurance ☞435.3(1)

Provision of automobile policy limiting coverage for additional owned automobile to 30 days after acquisition by insured permits owner adequate opportunity to acquire necessary additional insurance and is not intended to cover two automobiles for any protracted period.

6. Insurance ☞435.2(4)

Provision in automobile policy granting coverage to insured for temporary substitute automobile, not owned by the insured, applies to those situations where the named automobile is in repair shop or withdrawn from use for short period.

7. Insurance ☞435.3(1)

Where insured had bought second automobile in July 1964 after transmission "went

231 N.E.2d—8

out" of automobile which was named in policy and which remained inoperable in driveway of his home until repair in spring of 1966, and had accident with second automobile on September 26, 1964, the second automobile was not a "replacement" for the named automobile within policy provision extending coverage to replacement automobile.

———◆———

Barrick, Jackson & Switzer, Rockford, for appellant.

Nordquist & Anderson, Rockford, for appellees.

ABRAHAMSON, Justice.

The Nationwide Insurance Company brings this appeal from a decree of the Circuit Court of the 17th Judicial Circuit, Winnebago County, entered December 29, 1966, that found that an automobile insurance policy issued by it to Douglas Ervin "covered" an accident that had occurred on September 26, 1964, and that a certain automobile operated by Ervin at the time of the accident was a "replacement" as defined in the policy.

On August 16, 1963, Nationwide issued its policy of automobile insurance number 94–441–489 to Ervin for coverage of his 1958 Chevrolet. In July of 1964 the transmission of the Chevrolet, according to Ervin, "went out" and he purchased a 1958 Cadillac. The Chevrolet was retained by Ervin, although inoperable, and left in the driveway of his home.

On September 26, 1964, Ervin was in an automobile accident with the Cadillac that involved a truck owned by the Jones Transfer Company, an Illinois Corporation, and another automobile in which Robert Holmes was a passenger. Holmes subsequently brought suit against Ervin and Jones Transfer for injuries allegedly suffered as a result of that accident. Nationwide was called upon by Ervin to defend him in that suit pursuant to the policy.

18 N E D—53

INSURANCE ⬤=435.3(1)

Always Consult Cumulative Bound Supplement

Ill.App. 1970. Where automobile liability insurer's policy, by truckmen's endorsement, classified automobiles as (1) automobile owned by named assured, (2) automobile hired on behalf of named assured, with two exceptions, and (3) nonowned automobile defined as "any other automobile", two exceptions to "hired automobile" category fell into classification of "any other automobile" and any automobile falling within either exception was "non-owned automobile."—Kern v. Michigan Mut. Liability Co., 263 N.E.2d 134, 129 Ill.App.2d 423.

Ohio App. 1969. Purpose of provision in automobile liability policy obligating insurer to pay damages arising out of use of nonowned automobile, defined as automobile not owned by or furnished for regular use of either named insured or any relative, was to protect insurer from situation where insured would pay for but one policy and be covered while regularly driving other automobiles owned by members of his family.—Napier v. Banks, 250 N.E.2d 417, 19 Ohio App.2d 152.

Where recently divorced woman stored her furniture and moved temporarily into upstairs room in her parents' home, she and her parents were not members of "same household" within her automobile liability policy, defining covered nonowned automobiles as those not owned by or furnished for regular use of either named insured or any relative, which was defined as relative of insured who is resident of same household, and policy covered accident occurring while woman was driving parents' automobile.—Id.

Ohio App. 1970. Where automobile was delivered to purchaser by dealer with ten-day license cards, she was in possession with dealer's permission and was not, before delivery of certificate of title, owner of automobile within terms of automobile policy held by her father. R.C. § 4505.04.—Oberdier v. Kennedy Ford, Inc., 261 N.E.2d 348.

Ohio Com.Pl. 1967. Where dealer delivered possession of automobile to buyer on October 21 but certificate of title was not issued to buyer until November 4, dealer's policy which excluded from coverage any person other than named insured with respect to automobile possession of which had been transferred to another by named insured pursuant to agreement of sale did not provide coverage to accident which occurred on October 31.—Grange Mut. Cas. Co. v. Clifford, 230 N.E.2d 686, 13 Ohio Misc. 12.

Ohio Com.Pl. 1968. Where divorced daughter was employed in city some 27 to 30 miles away from her parents' home, daughter moved to residence of her parents as a "tentative place to stay," and daughter was driving her father's automobile and had an accident which resulted in a judgment against daughter, and all of the judgment but $10,000 was satisfied by father's insurer, daughter was not a "resident of the same household" of her parents within meaning of daughter's automobile liability policy which excluded coverage of nonowned automobile if insured was a resident of the same household of a relative.—Napier v. Banks, 248 N.E.2d 472, 19 Ohio Misc. 36, affirmed 250 N.E.2d 417, 19 Ohio App.2d 152.

Ohio Com.Pl. 1970. Under automobile liability policy clause defining "non-owned automobile" as an automobile not owned by or furnished for regular use of either named insured or any relative, named insured was not covered while operating automobile titled in the name of his brother who resided in the same household.—Roskin v. Aetna Ins. Co., 263 N. E.2d 923, 25 Ohio Misc. 95.

⬤=**435.2(6). Hired automobiles.**
Ohio App. 1966. Greasing "fifth wheel" (a coupling between tractor and trailer), was not necessary to working condition of tractor and was not part of maintenance which lessor-driver of tractor had agreed to perform but was necessary to use of tractor in combination with lessee's trailer, and collision occurring while lessor-driver was en route to obtain grease to apply to "fifth wheel" of tractor occurred while tractor was being used exclusively in business of lessee for purposes of lessor-driver's liability policy, which was inapplicable while vehicle was being used in lessee's business, and lessee's liability policy, which applied to hired vehicles and persons using them with permission of lessee exclusively in business of lessee.—Hartford Acc. & Indem. Co. v. Allstate Ins. Co., 215 N.E.2d 416, 5 Ohio App.2d 287.

⬤=**435.2(7). Operator's or nonowner's policy.**
Ill.App. 1971. Automobile "operator's policy" insures person or operator while he is in act of operating nonowned vehicles. S.H.A. ch. 95½, §§ 7–315(a), 7–317.—Kenilworth Ins. Co. v. Chamberlain, 269 N.E.2d 317.

Automobile operator's policy did not cover insured while he was driving automobile which he owned, in view of statute providing for both "owner's policy" and "operator's policy," despite contention that purpose of Financial Responsibility Law and public policy required construction in favor of insured, and despite fact that Secretary of State accepted certification of insurance under operator's policy as proof of financial responsibility. S.H.A. ch. 95½, §§ 7–315, 7–317.—Id.

⬤=**435.3(1). In general.**
Ill.App. 1964. Purpose of "automatic insurance clause" or "newly acquired automobile clause" in automobile liability policy is to provide insurance coverage where owned automobile is not described in policy, and once specific insurance is purchased, and automobile becomes described in policy, automobile is no longer "newly acquired automobile" but is then "described automobile," and terms and provisions under "automatic insurance clause" or "newly acquired automobile clause" are no longer applicable.—Cook v. Suburban Cas. Co., 203 N.E. 2d 748, 54 Ill.App.2d 190.

Ill.App. 1967. Provision of automobile policy limiting coverage for additional owned automobile to 30 days after acquisition by insured permits owner adequate opportunity to acquire necessary additional insurance and is not intended to cover two automobiles for any protracted period.—Nationwide Ins. Co. v. Ervin. 231 N.E.2d 112, 87 Ill.App.2d 432. ⟵

Where insured had bought second automobile in July 1964, after transmission "went out" of automobile which was named in policy and which remained inoperable in driveway of his home until repair in spring of 1966, and had accident with second automobile on September 26, 1964, the second automobile was not a "replacement" for the named automobile within policy provision extending coverage to replacement automobile.—Id.

Ill.App. 1968. Automobile which was reacquired by insured after it had been given to insured's son was "newly acquired automobile" within liability policy.—Country Mut. Ins. Co. v. Murray, 239 N.E.2d 498, 97 Ill.App.2d 61.

In order for automobile to be "newly acquired automobile" within provisions of policy its acquisition must occur during policy period. —Id.

"Newly acquired automobile" within terms of policy is not limited to vehicle which had never been previously owned.—Id.

Ohio Com.Pl. 1965. Where insured's nephew purchased automobile when he was living with insured who did not secure coverage on nephew's automobile, and nephew after moving to an apartment permitted his automobile to be driven by insured's wife who permitted

State Digests

West publishes individual digests for every state (and Washington, D.C.) except Nevada, Utah and Delaware, but many other states' digests are being phased out over time. If you are looking for decisions of the courts of your state, it is usually most efficient to start with the West Digest for that state. On the other hand, if you live in a small state and are accustomed to using the law produced by courts in adjoining states, you might want to start with the regional digest.

Regional Digests

West publishes digests for four regions of the country: Atlantic, Northwestern, Pacific and Southeastern. The regions are the same as those used in the regional reporter system (Chapter 8). Accordingly, if the cases decided by your state's courts are reported in the *Pacific Reporter*, start with the *Pacific Digest*. If they are reported in the *Southeast Reporter,* use the *Southeastern Digest*. If your case has been reported in the *Atlantic Reporter* but you want to locate similar cases from California, you can use either the *California Digest* or the *Pacific Digest*.

Federal Court Digests

If you want summaries of federal court decisions, go to the federal case digests in the West system. West publishes the *Federal Practice Digest* in four series:

- The *Modern Federal Practice Digest* (for cases decided before 1961);
- The *Federal Practice Digest Second Series* (for cases decided between 1961 and 1975);
- The *Federal Practice Digest Third Series* (for cases decided between 1975 and 1992); and
- The *Federal Practice Digest Fourth Series* (for cases decided since 1992).

West also publishes the *Supreme Court Digest* (for all cases decided by the U.S. Supreme Court).

The *Federal Practice Digest* (all four series) contains headnotes from cases reported in:

- the *Supreme Court Reporter* (S. Ct.);
- the *Federal Reporter* (which publishes U.S. Court of Appeal cases); and
- the *Federal Supplement* (which publishes U.S. District court cases).

The *Supreme Court Digest* also contains headnotes from the U.S. Supreme Court cases reported in the *Supreme Court Reporter* (S. Ct.). So the *Supreme Court Digest* and the *Federal Practice Digest* overlap with respect to U.S. Supreme Court cases.

Decennial and *General Digests*

The *Decennial* and *General Digests* contain all the headnotes from all courts and all parts of the country. Most of the time it is more useful to use a state or regional digest for state cases, and a *Federal Practice Digest* or *Supreme Court Digest* for federal cases, than it is to use the *Decennial* or *General Digests*. After all, you rarely need to know what courts across the whole country have said about a particular issue. But there may be times when you want to do an extremely thorough research job. In that event, you will find the *Decennial* or *General Digests* a great help.

Initially, *Decennial Digests* were published in editions covering ten years' worth of cases. As of 1976, the *Decennials* are cumulated every five years and issued in two parts. For example, the *Ninth Decennial Digest* Part 1 covers 1976 to 1981, and Part 2 covers cases from 1981 to 1986.

Between publication of each new *Decennial* series, headnotes are collected in a publication called the *General Digest*. About ten of these are published each year, so about fifty will be on the bookshelves before a new *Decennial* emerges. For example, Part 1 of the *Tenth Decennial* will be on the shelves in 1992, covering the period between 1986 and 1991. The *Eleventh Decennial*, however, will not be published until 2001. Until the *Eleventh Decennial* emerges, the *General Digests* must be used for cases decided after 1991. Once the *Eleventh Decennial* is published, the *General Digests* start anew and the *Decennials* can be used for all cases decided before 1991.

A Shortcut When Using the *General Digest*

Each volume of the *General Digest* includes all West key topics and numbers. This means that if you are chasing down the key topic and number of a particular headnote, a relevant case summary might appear in any and all volumes. To make your search more efficient, each tenth volume of the *General Digest* contains a Table of Key Numbers that tells you which volumes in the preceding ten volumes have entries under your key topic and subtopic number.

Library Exercise: Using Digests

This exercise revisits the factual issue discussed in the last Library Exercise, but if you haven't done that one, don't worry.

Your employer has taken on several "trainees" for the summer. They are paralegal students and will do work that is regularly done in the office, such as filing, preparing billings, running to various courts to file documents and going to law offices around town to pick up or deliver papers.

Your boss thinks that "trainees" can be paid below the minimum wage required by the Fair Labor Standards Act because, unlike regular employees, they are in training, will learn how a law office works and will gain "resume value." He has been told that an important but old case in your Circuit (the 4th) is *Wirtz v. Wardlaw*, 339 F.2d 785.

Questions

1. Find *Wirtz* and skim the headnotes following the synopsis. Which headnote appears to deal with minimum wage and employees-in-training, and what is its key number?

2. Which Digest would you use to find other federal cases and, in particular, other 4th Circuit cases on this issue?

3. Because you need current law on this issue, go to the latest edition of that digest. What is it?

4. The volumes' contents are arranged alphabetically, with each book's contents listed on the spine. Find the volume and its paperback supplement which cover Labor Relations 1178. Which volume is it?

5. In both the main text and the supplement (pocket part), examine the cases listed under Labor Relations 1178. Are there any 4th Circuit Court of Appeal cases about whether a trainee is entitled to protection under the Fair Labor Standard Act? Where did they arise?

6. Are there other cases listed that, although not from the appellate level of the 4th Circuit, might be useful?

Answers

1. Headnote 3, Key number "Labor Relations 1178" deals with employees in training and minimum wage requirements.

2. *Federal Practice Digest.*

3. The 4th.

4. Volume 71.

5. Yes; *McLaughlin v. Ensley,* 877 F.2d 1207 (4th Cir. N.C. 1989) is an appellate-level case. The information in parentheses tells you that a three-judge panel of the Fourth Circuit Court of Appeals heard a case being appealed from a district court in North Carolina.

6. Yes; a district court sitting in the Western District of North Carolina considered the issue in *McLaughlin v. McGee Bros. Co., Inc.,* 681 F. Supp. 1117 (W.D. N.C. 1988). Although other district courts within the 4th Circuit are not bound by a mere district court holding, some judges might find it persuasive nonetheless. Also, *Reich v. Parker Fire Protection Dist.,* 992 F.2d 1023, rehearing denied (10th Cir. Colo. 1993).

Finding Cases in Your State That Are Similar to Out-of-State Cases

During your research, you may come across a case that was decided just the way you think it should have been. It would be very helpful to your own situation—except that it was decided by another state's court. With the West Digest system, you can take a case that has been assigned a West topic and key number (any case in a regional reporter or other reporter published by West) and discover whether or not a similar case has been decided in your state.

For example, suppose you are a resident of Kansas and want to find out how to dissolve a partnership you formed with a friend. You read an article in the legal encyclopedia *Am. Jur. 2d* (see Chapter 5) about partnerships and come across a helpful statement to the effect that all you have to do is give notice of your intent to dissolve your partnership. The statement is footnoted with an Illinois Court of Appeals case, *Ljo v. Cooper,* 331 N.E.2d 206 (Ill. App. 1975).

Since you are in Kansas, you naturally wonder if this Illinois rule is the law in your state. Fortunately, the West *Regional Digest* system can be used to locate any Kansas

case law on this very point. (Because most states have adopted the Uniform Partnership Act, you should also check the Kansas version of that Act on this particular point if you are really interested.) Here's how you do this:

1. Read the citation: 331 N.E.2d 206 (Ill. App. 1975).
2. Locate the *Ljo* case in Volume 331 of the *Northeast Reporter, Second Series* at page 206.
3. Locate the headnote that most closely matches the statement you found in *Am. Jur. 2d*.
4. Note the key topic and number. In this case, the key topic is "Partnerships" and the key number is 259 1/2.
5. Locate the regional digest for Kansas, the *Pacific Reporter*. The regions are listed on a map in the front of each regional reporter.
6. In the *Pacific Digest*, look under Partnerships, key number 259 1/2. There you would find headnotes that resemble the one taken from *Ljo v. Cooper*. Note the one from *Craig v. Hamilton*, 518 P.2d 539 (1974), a Kansas case right on point.
7. Check the pocket part.

Alternatively, you could use the *Decennials* and *General Digest* to more inefficiently accomplish the same result.

Don't Rely on Digest Summaries to Tell You the Law. The case summaries in digests are written by the editors of the case reports and do not constitute the actual opinion of the court. While digests are good for finding cases that deal with a similar issue, you must read a case itself before you rely on its holding.

Research Tip. If you are using the West Key system to research the case law from scratch, remember that issues are classified by editors. Thus, two identical cases may be classified differently by two different editors. The result is that the digest doesn't refer to both cases under the same topic and key number. Always look under several key numbers.

Summing Up
How to Find Similar Cases in
Different States

✔ Find the case in your state as it is reported by West Group. Usually, this will be in the regional reporter.

✔ Locate the headnotes that most accurately summarize the issues with which you are concerned, and note the key topic and key number.

✔ Find the West digest that covers cases decided by the courts in which you're interested. If you want to find all similar cases regardless of the state, find the West *Decennial* and *General Digests*.

✔ In the digests you are using, locate the topic heading and key number of the relevant headnotes and skim over the case summaries.

✔ Find and read any cases that look relevant to your question.

✔ Remember to consult the pocket part to the digest if it has one. For the *Decennials,* use the volumes of the *General Digest* to obtain the most up-to-date case summaries.

Library Exercise: Using the *American Digest* System

Now it's time to use the library to apply what you've just learned. This exercise asks you to use the *American Digest* (West) to find cases that treat the same issue treated by a relevant case you've found in the course of your research. Additional research exercises that include these and other skills are in Chapter 11.

Problem

Sylvia Jones lived and died in West Virginia. She left an unwitnessed will that was written, signed and dated by her in her own handwriting. The form on which it was written had "Last Will and Testament" printed at the top and the words "by my hand and seal," "signature" and "date" printed at the bottom.

You are researching the validity of the will. You learn from a background resource that an unwitnessed will that is written, signed and dated entirely in the handwriting of the decedent—called a holographic will—is valid in West Virginia, but that an unwitnessed will on a form containing preprinted words may not be. As authority for this statement, the background resource cites an Arizona case, *Matter of Estate of Johnson*, 630 P.2d 1039 (Ariz. App. 1981). You need a West Virginia case that speaks to this same issue.

Your first step is to find the *Johnson* case and identify one or more of the headnotes that discuss the issue of printed material on handwritten wills, in order to find a helpful key topic and number. All the headnotes for *Johnson* are assigned the key topic and number "Wills 132."

Questions

1. Using the *American (Decennial* and *General) Digest* system, find a 1982 West Virginia case that says: "Under the 'surplusage theory,' non-handwritten material in a holographic will may be stricken with the remainder of the instrument being admitted to probate if the remaining provision makes sense standing alone." What is the citation for this case?

2. Continuing in the *Decennial* and *General Digests*, find a 1987 West Virginia case that says "Holographic wills are valid if they are wholly in the handwriting of the testator, if they are signed, and if they evidence testamentary intent."

3. Use the *Tenth Decennial, Part 2, Eleventh Decennial Digest*, Part 1 and the *General Digest* for years after the *Eleventh*, Part 1 to find other more recent West Virginia cases.

4. What can you now conclude?

Answers

1. The *Ninth Decennial* Part 2 contains cases dated 1981 to 1986. In the volume containing the topic Wills, under key number 132, you find *In re Teubert's Estate*, 298 S.E.2d 456 (1982).

2. The *Tenth Decennial,* Part I, covers cases from 1986 to 1991. Look under Wills 132 to find *Siefert v. Sanders*, 358 S.E.2d. 775 (1987).

   If your law library does not have the *Tenth Decennial,* use the *General Digest.* Each volume contains all the topics, from A to Z. To save the time it would take to look in every volume under Wills 132, go to every tenth volume (Volumes 10, 20, 30, etc.) and look for the Table of Key Numbers in the center of the volume—after the case notes arranged by topic and before the table of cases. Find your topic and key number (Wills 132) in the Table and it will tell you which volumes contain case notes under that key number.

3. When we wrote this exercise in March 2004, there were, after the *Tenth Decennial*, Part 1, *Tenth Decennia*, Part 2, *Eleventh Decennial*, Part 1 and the *General Digest* Ninth series (1996–2001 complete) and the *Tenth* series (2001–2002 up to volume 14). For Question 2, we already checked the *Tenth Decennial*, Part 1, so to find more recent cases, we go to the *Tenth Decennial*, Part 2, the *Eleventh Decennial*, Part 1 and any *General Digest* volumes we need to search for the years after *Eleventh Decennial*, Part 1. In the *Tenth Decennial* Part 2, under Wills 132, there are no West Virginia cases. In the *Eleventh Decennial*, Part 1, we find a very helpful case, *Charleston National Bank v. Thru the Bible Radio Network* 507 S.E. 2d 703 (W. Va. 1998), which held that despite a handwritten portion, a holographic will may be valid if it evidences testamentary intent; this is a case definitely worth reading and updating.

Library Exercise: Using the *American Digest* System (continued)

Because the *Eleventh Decennial,* Part 1 goes to 2001, we check the *General Digests* for 2001 and after. *General Digest* Ninth series volume 60 (2001), Table of Key Numbers, sent us to Volume 52 that had no West Virginia cases under Wills 132. *General Digest,* Tenth series volume 10, Table of Key Numbers, referred us to Volumes 4 and 5; no West Virginia cases. Volumes 11-14 of the *General Digest* tenth series cited no cases under Wills 132.

4. It appears that *Charleston National Bank v. Thru the Bible Radio Network* is the latest word on holographic wills in West Virginia, and that under its holding, Sylvia Jones' will may well be valid. *Sheparizing* would be the next step.

Review

Questions

1. When you look up your case in *Shepard's,* what information can you find about your case?
2. What information about your case do you need in order to *Shepardize* it?
3. If the case you are *Shepardizing* is in the *Pacific Reporter,* Volume 50, what volumes of the *Pacific Shepard's* do you need to look in?
4. How do you know from *Shepard's* whether the opinion in your case has been made invalid (vacated) by a higher court?
5. What does an "f" preceding the citation of the citing case mean?
6. What does an "e" mean?
7. What does a "q" mean?
8. What are digests?
9. What digest contains headnotes from all state and federal cases in the United States of America from 1976 to 1981?
10. In what digests could you look to find headnotes for cases from California that are reported in *California Reporter* and in *Pacific Reporter*?
11. If you found a California case that deals with your issue, but you are in Texas and need Texas cases on that topic, what digest would you use?
12. If you are using a state digest, where do you look to find the most up-to-date case summaries?

Answers

1. • Whether the case was affirmed, modified or reversed by a higher court.
   • Whether other cases affect the value of the case as precedent or persuasive authority.
   • Other cases that may help your argument or give you better answers to your question.
2. To use *Shepard's Citations for Cases,* you need the case citation—the name of the case reporter your case appears in, its volume number and the first page on which the case appears.
3. All volumes that include 50 *Pacific Reporter:* hardbound volumes and update pamphlets.
4. A "v" will appear in the margin to the left of the citing case citation (the citing case is the one that vacated your case's opinion).
5. The citing case explicitly *follows* the reasoning and/or decision of the cited case.
6. The citing case *explains* the holding or reasoning of the cited case.
7. The citing case *questions* the reasoning employed by the cited case.
8. Collections of the headnotes from cases, arranged according to the specific legal issues.
9. The *Ninth Decennial Digest, Part 1.*
10. *California Digest, Pacific Digest* and *Decennial* and *General Digest.*
11. The *Texas Digest.*
12. The pocket part.

CHAPTER 1

How to Write a Legal Memorandum

Do the words "legal memorandum" conjure up images of dusty desks, bleary eyes and massive leather-bound tomes at least two inches thick? If so, your first step is to relax and forget all such notions. A legal memorandum can be a couple of paragraphs long, written in good English and (trust us on this one) fun to prepare. Whether you are doing research for yourself or for a lawyer, the main purpose of a legal memo is to force you to put the results of your search in writing.

Why Prepare a Legal Memorandum?

Why is this important? There are three basic reasons. The first is that you won't really know whether your research is done until you try to write it up. You have undoubtedly had the experience of thinking you understood something until the moment when you had to put pen to paper. The same is true of legal research. You may think you have answered the question you started out with, but you can't be sure until it plays in black and white. Although you may believe that the formal structure for the memorandum suggested here is unnecessary for this purpose, we think that it serves as a checklist for your research. Later, as you become more proficient, you may wish to adopt a more informal way of checking your results.

The second important function of a legal memorandum is to provide you with an accessible record of the fruits of your research after time has erased the memories from your mind. It is unfortunately common for people to put in a day or two of research in the law library on a particular issue, neglect to take an extra hour or two to write it up, and later have to spend another day in the library because they are unable to use their notes to reconstruct what they found.

The third important function of a legal memorandum is to communicate the results of your research to someone else. This will be necessary if you are a paralegal doing research for a supervising lawyer, or if you are researching your own case and wish to inform the judge and opposing party of what you've found.

Now that you're convinced of the importance of preparing a legal memorandum, let's take a look at how to do it. For a much more intensive, yet well-written, presentation of how to analyze case law and prepare a memorandum, see Statsky and Wernet, *Case Analysis and Fundamentals of Legal Writing* (West Group 1995).

How to Prepare a Legal Memorandum

In this section, we tell you how to prepare a legal memorandum. Obviously this is a skill that requires lots of practice. As a follow-up, we suggest that you do at least one of the research hypotheticals later in this chapter (if the necessary materials are available in your law library) and prepare a memorandum based on your work. Then compare your memorandum with the one accompanying each hypothetical. If you are able to do all of the exercises, your writing skills will get even better.

Overview

In Chapter 7, we stated that judicial opinions almost always have four primary elements:
- a statement of the facts;
- a statement of the issue or issues;
- a decision or holding on the issue or issues; and
- a discussion of the reasoning underlying the holding.

We also pointed out that these elements don't necessarily appear in any particular order. Like case opinions, legal memoranda should include a statement of the facts, a statement of the issue or issues, a conclusion about what the law is (equivalent to the holding) and a brief discussion of why you reached your conclusion. Also, like judicial opinions, it is not necessary to put these items in any particular order (unless your boss tells you differently, of course). It is also a good idea to assign a topic heading to your memo.

Distinguishing Internal From External Memoranda

In this discussion, we are talking about internal memoranda —i.e., memoranda intended solely for your own use or the use of your employer. However, legal memoranda are also prepared for external purposes. Commonly called "briefs" or "memoranda of points and authorities," these documents are ordinarily submitted to the court in the course of a lawsuit to advance a particular position with the utmost vigor (or so the client hopes). The brief submitted for the other side of the case will do the same with respect to that side. A brief presents all the law that is helpful to one's side and attempts to distinguish and downplay any law that is harmful.

There is a great difference of opinion among lawyers as to how much you have to acknowledge and deal with cases and authorities that are against you. If the contrary authority is obscure and hard to find, or its bearing on your situation marginal at best, you might decide to gamble and not mention it, hoping that the other side, the judge and the judge's clerk, will either not find it or will consider it inapplicable. On the other hand, if there is authority that is squarely against you, your failure to mention it will undermine your credibility.

Legal memoranda in the sense we are talking about, on the other hand, are not intended to be arguments advancing a particular position. Rather, they are intended to accurately summarize the fruits of the legal research regardless of whether they help or harm one's position. Both sides need to be presented, whether the memorandum is for your own use or is to be turned over to a supervisor. Of course, when you get to court (if you do), you or the attorney you are assisting will want to emphasize the arguments and legal authority that best advance your position.

Internal Consistency

The main idea is to structure your legal memorandum so that it is internally consistent. For example, you have to include enough relevant facts in the memo for your statement of the issue to make sense. If your issue is whether a new owner of an apartment house can evict a tenant for having pets even though the prior landlord allowed them, your statement of facts would have to include such items as:

- the kind(s) of pet(s) in question;
- the date ownership was transferred;
- information about any rental agreement or lease that was executed by the tenant, and so on.

In a similar way, your discussion of the reasoning that you use to arrive at your conclusion has to include cases or statutes that are relevant to the facts that you've listed in the memo. If your law sources and facts don't match up on some level, your reasoning is faulty.

This internal consistency requirement sometimes means that you have to go back and add or subtract a fact or two, or slightly restate the legal issue to square with your conclusion or reasoning. It's very much like fine-tuning a television set or car—all of the operating elements have to be adjusted relative to each other.

Additional Points for Paralegals

Especially if you are a paralegal and are asked to prepare a legal memorandum for your supervising attorney, three additional points may be useful. First, it is usually a good idea to list the resources that you've checked, even if some or many of them didn't pan out. This is because attorneys like to feel secure, and the more thorough your legal research, the more secure they will feel. For example, in any given research project you might check *A.L.R., Am. Jur.,* a local digest or two and some treatises in addition to a local encyclopedia. Even though you only strike pay dirt through the local encyclopedia, the attorney will feel better knowing that you've also checked out the other resources.

Second, keep your sentences short and avoid jargon when possible. It is all too easy to get wrapped up in a research project and produce mile-long, convoluted sentences. Don't.

Third, all statements about what the law is should be supported by some primary legal authority, such as statutes, regulations, cases or ordinances. Other legal materials generally comprise somebody else's opinion about what the law is. It's okay and even desirable to include references to these secondary or background sources, but they cannot replace primary authority.

Research Hypotheticals and Memoranda

In this section we provide you with three self-teaching research problems. Each research problem is set in a particular state: Texas, California and West Virginia. The problems emphasize the use of resources that are available in most states, and most of you should be able to complete at least one of the problems, regardless of the state in which you're doing your research.

In each research problem, we present you with a legal hypothetical, then lead you through the entire research task with a series of questions that directs you to a variety of resources. Answers are provided for each question in case you get stuck. At the conclusion of the research you are asked to write a memorandum of law. A sample memorandum is attached to each research problem.

The method we have followed is good for beginning researchers, as it covers all the bases in a methodical way. As you become more experienced, you will develop both your own well-organized, inclusive method and your favorite background resources.

At the beginning of each research problem, we provide an "estimated time" for completion. This is applicable to anyone who has read this book and completed the library exercises scattered through the text. We recommend doing each problem at one sitting. If you start it one day but don't finish it, you're likely to lose your train of thought and have to go over everything again.

Research Problem: Government Tort Liability Hypothetical (Texas)

Estimated time: 4 hours

The research for this problem will require the following skills:

- brainstorming legal terms for using an index (Chapter 4);
- finding a case from its citation (Chapter 9);
- using the case reporters (Chapter 8);
- using *Shepard's Case Citations* (Chapter 10);
- reading a case, including use of headnotes (Chapter 7);
- using West's Digests (Chapter 10); and
- writing a memorandum of law.

You will also have to know what common law is (Chapter 3). If you don't know what a writ of error is, look it up in a legal dictionary.

The following sources will be needed:

- *Texas Annotated Statutes* (Vernon's);
- *Southwestern Reporter*;
- *Shepard's Southwestern Citations*; and
- *Texas Digest* or *Southwestern Digest* or *American (Decennial* and *General)* digests.

Rachel Pie v. State of Texas

On August 5, 1989, at 2:30 in the afternoon, Robert Roberts, a medical examiner employed by the State of Texas, was driving from Yellow Rose Hospital to Red Ribbon Hospital for his work. He was driving along Elm Street, the main road between the two towns. The road has one lane in each direction, divided by a solid yellow line, and a wide shoulder that is frequently used by bicyclists and occasionally by pedestrians. The street is lined with gas stations and fast food restaurants.

Robert decided to turn in to a Hamburger Queen on his left. He put on his left directional signal and slowed to a stop, waited until there was a long clear stretch of the road with no oncoming cars, then accelerated to cross the oncoming lane and enter the Hamburger Queen lot.

At the same time, Sophie Pie and her daughter Rachel were riding their bicycles along Elm Street on their way from Red Ribbon, where they lived, to Yellow Rose, where they worked in a small factory on the 3-11 shift.

Robert hit Sophie broadside, hurling her and her bicycle through the air in front of Rachel's and many other witnesses' horrified eyes. Rachel threw down her bicycle and, sobbing, "No, no, no," ran over to where Sophie lay in the Hamburger Queen driveway, her body twisted and very bloody. Rachel knelt down at Sophie's side, stroking her mother's forehead and crying. When the police and paramedics arrived, Rachel rode in the ambulance with Sophie. Sophie was unconscious and moaning and Rachel was sobbing, repeating Sophie's name.

"I never saw her," said Robert. "It was as if she materialized out of thin air."

Sophie was in the hospital many weeks and underwent surgery for her head injuries. Despite her doctors' best efforts, she died after suffering considerably. Rachel has suffered from recurrent nightmares in which she relives the moment of impact and the sight of her mother's crumpled body on the pavement.

Everyone agrees that:

- Robert was legally responsible (liable) for Sophie's injuries.
- Had she survived the accident, Sophie's claim against Robert would have been worth approximately $250,000.
- Sophie's claim against Robert can be asserted by her estate as a "survivor's claim." (A survivor's claim is based on the pain and suffering of the deceased up to the point of death, and it is collected by the heirs. A "wrongful death" claim is compensation for being deprived of the companionship and services of the deceased; it is typically brought by the family.)
- As Robert's employer, the State of Texas is also liable to Sophie for her injuries, because Robert was on the job when he hit Sophie.
- Texas law limits the State's liability to $250,000 per accident per victim, and a total of $500,000 per accident.
- Rachel suffered emotional injury as a "bystander" under Texas tort (personal injury) law. (A "bystander" is a person who has witnessed the injury of a close relative and as a result suffers physically and emotionally.)
- Rachel's damages are worth $65,000.
- Robert's negligence caused this injury to Rachel.

- Texas law allows Rachel to recover (get money damages) for this injury from Robert, and from Texas as Robert's employer.
- Robert has no assets or insurance out of which to pay Rachel's claim, and so Rachel's only chance of recovery is from the State of Texas.

The State of Texas, however, contends that its total liability for the accident is limited to $250,000—which it agrees to pay as a "survivor's claim" to Sophie's estate. This contention is based on these arguments by the State:

- The claims of a bystander-victim (Rachel) are derived from (arise out of) the primary victim's (Sophie's) claim.
- Derivative claims should not be treated as separate claims under the Texas Tort Claims Act—the law that governs personal injury claims against the state.
- The State of Texas is therefore not liable to pay Rachel's claim.

Remember, Robert has no assets or insurance to pay Rachel's claim, so Rachel's only opportunity for getting money for her injury is to challenge the State's derivative claim argument. If Rachel sues, the case will be brought in the Travis County Court, which is within the Austin Appellate District. Can she win?

Approach Statement: This case is basically a personal injury (tort) matter. The only issue that needs to be researched is whether a person who sues as a "bystander" is entitled to a separate recovery under the Texas Tort Claims Act. There are several ways to approach this question.

The most thorough approach is to first find a background resource that discusses the Texas Tort Claims Act. This will give you a feeling for how the Act has been applied in the past to bystander cases. Once you have an overview of this issue, the next step is to find the Texas Tort Claims Act, read it and then read one or more cases that interpret the statute in a factual context similar to yours. Finally, as in researching all types of legal issues, you are not finished until you have *Shepardized* the cases and statutes and checked the digests.

For the purpose of this exercise, assume that initial research in background resources has informed you that: (1) the state is immune from suit (governments cannot be held liable by a court) unless the government waives that immunity and allows itself to be sued; (2) the way a government allows itself to be sued is to pass a law called a "government claims act"; and (3) that Texas has a specific law allowing personal injury claims to be filed against the government, called the Texas Tort Claims Act.

The background resources also say that the Texas Tort Claims Act describes in detail the situations in which all levels of government, from municipalities to the State, can be held liable in tort cases. And the Act specifies maximum amounts that the different levels of government can be required to pay in damages. Nothing is said about bystander cases.

Questions

1. Now that you know what a tort claims act is, that Texas has one, and a little about it, it's time to look at the Tort Claims Act itself. What do you look under in the index to Texas Statutes, and what do you find?

2. How do you find out what CP&R means if you don't already know?

3. Which paragraph numbers are included within the statutory scheme known as the Texas Tort Claims Act?

4. Which section is most likely to be relevant to the issue being researched?

5. According to §§ 101.023(a) and (b), how much is the State liable for if one accident injures two people, as in Rachel's case?

6. Are there any amendments to § 101.023(a) in the pocket part?

7. Check the case summaries in the Notes of Decisions. In the Table of Contents at the beginning of the Notes of Decisions, which entry most likely refers to the issue being researched?

8. Do the cases in the Notes of Decisions say anything about the history of § 101.023?

9. Which of these cases is relevant to Rachel's case? Why?

10. Identify the volume number, West Reporter and page number for the relevant case. Find the case.

The following questions are based on reading the *City of Austin v. Davis* case and thinking about it in relation to the case of Rachel Pie.

11. Who is the "Davis" in *City of Austin v. Davis*?

12. What is the name of the legal doctrine under which Mr. Davis made his claim?

13. Did the court find that Mr. Davis had bystander injuries?

14. So far, is *Davis* similar to Rachel's case?

15. Did the City of Austin claim that Mr. Davis's bystander injuries were derivative of his son's wrongful death action? What would be the result if the court found them to be derivative?

16. Is this the same claim that the State of Texas is making about Rachel's case?

17. What did the *Davis* court decide about the issue of "derivative injury"?

18. If the claim was not derivative, did the court say that Mr. Davis was therefore a "person injured" for purposes of the Tort Claims Act limitation of liability?

19. According to the *Davis* court, what is the importance of deciding that Mr. Davis was "suing for injuries he personally suffered" (693 S.W.2d at 34), and not for damages to which a person is entitled just because he is related to a person who is injured or killed?

20. Is *Davis*, then, a good case for you to rely on as authority?

21. Why or why not?

22. Now that you have an authoritative case, *City of Austin v. Davis*, which says what you want it to, how can you make sure that there are no other cases with similar facts and contrary holdings, and that the case is up-to-date and has not been overturned or otherwise affected by subsequent cases? In other words, how do you determine that it is still "good law"?

23. When you *Shepardize Davis* in *Shepard's Southwestern Citations*, the first entry under the citation is "RNRE"; what does this mean?

24. What is the citation for the case that has cited *Davis* on page 595?

25. Is the case that cited *Davis* on page 595 a bystander case?

26. Is it about limits of liability?

27. Why was *Davis* cited in this case?

28. Does this case affect Rachel's case in any way?

Note: In your notes, write down the citation and your conclusions as to why it is not relevant; that way, if it comes up again, you won't have to look it up again.

29. Locate the case that is cited in *Shepard's* as "872 S.W.2d 766." Note that the case has two entries in *Shepard's*: one with a "c" preceding the cite, and the other with a "j." Locate the case and determine its cite. What do those prefixes mean?

30. What does your legal radar tell you about the need to read *Harris*? Consider the fact that the *Davis* case is cited and disapproved in the majority opinion, and cited in the dissenting opinion.

31. Read *Harris*. How does it affect Rachel's case?

32. Another case you find by *Shepardizing* Davis is *Edinburgh Hospital Authority v. Trevino*, 904 S.W.2d 831 (1985). Read the opinion.
   a. What court issued the opinion? Is this court within the Austin appellate district, where Rachel's case will be heard? If not, will it be followed in Rachel's case?
   b. What is the factual context of *Trevino*?
   c. What is the court's holding?
   d. Does the *Trevino* holding affect your case?

33. Remember, no competent researcher is finished until she's updated her research.
   a. What do you find when you *Shepardize* the Appellate level decision in *Trevino*?
   b. What court issued the opinion?
   c. Does this new case affect your results?

Note: We will save you the time and trouble; the other citations of *Davis* listed in *Shepard's* are no more relevant to Rachel's case than those discussed above. Of course, a complete research job would mean looking at every case that cited *Davis* to make sure of not missing any case that might affect your situation.

34. Where would you go next to make sure that there are no other cases that could affect Rachel's case or the authority of *Davis*?

35. How do you choose under what topic and key number to look when you use a West Digest?

36. What is the appropriate digest to use to make sure that there are no other cases with similar facts and issues that have contrary holdings?

37. Can you find in the digests reference to any case that might affect the authority of *Davis* on the issue of limitation of liability?

Answers

1. Under "Tort Claims Act," the index says, "Generally, CP&R 101.001 et seq."

2. Consult the list of code sections at the front of the index volume. The abbreviation means Civil Practice and Remedies Code.

3. §§ 101.001-101.109.

4. § 101.023. There is a table of contents to chapter 101. Scanning it, we see 101.001 Definitions, 101.021 Governmental liability and 101.023 Limitation on liability. Because our issue is not about liability (the State agrees it is liable), but only about the limits on liability, go first to § 101.023. You can go back to the definitions section if necessary. Don't forget to check the pocket part. Here, the pocket part tells you to look at the soft paperback volume for updates.

5. Subsection (a) provides that the state government's liability is limited to $250,000 for "each person" and $500,000 for each single occurrence for bodily injury. This would seem to mean that if Rachel and Sophie are each considered a "person injured," then the state's limit for the two of them would be $500,000, not $250,000, as the State claims. Subsection (b) applies to local governments and is therefore not relevant to our case.

6. No. § 101.023 in the pocket part says, "See main volume for (a) to (c)." This means that no change has been made to (a), (b) or (c). Subsection (d) deals with volunteer fire departments, so we can ignore it.

7. Persons.

8. Each case description refers to Vernon's Ann. Civ. St. art. 6252-19 and says that that statute has been repealed and is now "this chapter" (the statute we are reading).

9. *City of Austin v. Davis.* The most important reason is that it is the only one of the three cases in the notes that is about limitation of liability in a bystander case (your issue). Secondly, it is from the same appellate jurisdiction in which Rachel would litigate her case (Travis County). Also, it is a recent case.

10. *City of Austin v. Davis* is in Volume 693 of the *Southwestern Reporter*, Second Series at page 31. The "ref. n.r.e." means "Application for writ of error refused, no reversible error."

11. The father of a boy who died as a result of the negligence of a City of Austin hospital, and who suffered emotional and physical injuries as a result of coming upon his son's body.

12. The Bystander Doctrine.

13. Yes.

14. Yes; and the State of Texas agrees that Rachel has injuries as a bystander.

15. Yes, the City tried to argue that the father's suit was "derivative," which would mean that he would be bound by the recovery limitation imposed on the main, wrongful death, suit of the child's family. In other words, if the father's claim were viewed as "derivative," he and any other wrongful death beneficiaries would have to share in the amount recoverable by "each person."

16. Yes.

17. The *Davis* court decided that the father's injuries were personally suffered by him as a bystander and were not derivative of his son's claim against the City.

18. Yes. In the discussion, the court referred to a $100,000 per person limitation, because that was the limit at that time for municipal (city) governments. The principle is the same for our case; just the numbers are different.

19. The importance of the distinction, the *Davis* court explains, is that if the person's injuries are derivative, then the damages for the other person (Sophie, in our case) and the plaintiff (Rachel, in our case) are lumped together and the total damages are subject to the "each person" limitation. If the plaintiff is found to be a bystander, and is found to have personally suffered the injuries, then he or she has his or her own cause of action (legal claim) and is a separate "person injured" for purposes of the limitation.

20. Yes.

21. The facts and issues are similar to Rachel's case, and the holding favors your client. Also, the court is the appeals court, which has jurisdiction over the Travis County District Court in which Rachel would file her claim.

22. *Shepardize* and use West's Digests.

23. By looking in the front of the *Shepard's* volume, you find that RNRE means "Application for Writ of Error refused, no reversible error." This means that *Davis* has been upheld upon review by the higher court.

24. 731 S.W.2d 590. (The case starts on page 590; *Davis* is cited on page 595.)

25. Yes.

26. No.

27. Yes, about bystander issues.

28. No. Our issue is limits of liability; this case is not about that.

29. The case begins on page 759 of Volume 872 of S.W.2d. It is called *Harris County Hospital District v. Estrada* (Tex App.-Houston [1st Dist.] 1993). The "c" means that *Davis* was criticized on page 766, and the "j" means that it was cited in the dissenting opinion on page 770.

30. *Harris* ought definitely to be read, because its interesting use of *Davis* suggests that there may be some new wrinkles on the "derivative" vs. "separate person" analysis of bystander claim status in Texas.

31. The court in *Davis* was concerned solely with whether a bystander's claim was independent or derivative. Once it decided that the claim was independent, it implicitly acknowledged that the father was a "person injured" because it allowed his claim. The claim of the wrongful death beneficiaries was allowed as well.

In *Harris*, however, the court was not concerned with revisiting the issue of whether the bystander claim is derivative. Instead, the court focused on the phrase "each person," and decided that the phrase referred only to the first person physically injured by the state (namely, the deceased). The court decided that the state's liability for "each person injured" referred only to that person, and that all claims would have to share in that single award. Whether a claim was derivative or independent was therefore beside the point.

If *Harris* is applied to Rachel's case, she will not collect as an independent "person injured," despite the fact that her bystander claim is independent and non-derivative, because the only "person injured" will be Sophie. Only one $250,000 award will be available to satisfy both Rachel's and the survivor's claim. Rachel will hope that since *Harris* is from an appellate district (Houston) other than her own (Austin, the home of the *Davis* opinion), her trial court will not follow *Davis*.

32. a. *Trevino* is an opinion of the Thirteenth Appellate District Court of Appeals in Corpus Christi, Texas. Rachel's case will be heard in the Third Appellate District. Because *Trevino* is from a different District, if it is relevant it will be considered persuasive, but not binding.

b. *Trevino* is a medical malpractice case in which the parents of a fetus sued the hospital for the negligent death of the fetus. In addition to other claims, each parent made a bystander claim for emotional inju-

ries suffered as the result of the death of the stillborn child.

c. *Trevino* holds that the parents have causes of action as bystanders for damages, which are separate from each other and separate from their direct claims.

d. Yes; the *Trevino* opinion cites *Davis* in support of the principle that mental anguish is considered to be bodily injury under the Tort Claims Act. It also cites *Davis* in support of the principle that a bystander's claim for mental anguish is not derivative of the claim of the primary person injured, but is the plaintiff bystander's own separate claim.

33. a. The first *Trevino* opinion from the Corpus Christi Court of Appeals was overturned by an opinion found at 941 S.W. 2d 76.

b. This is an opinion of the Supreme Court of Texas. Since the opinion is from the state's highest court, if it is relevant it will definitely have to be followed by the trial court in Rachel's case.

c. There are two main parts of the Supreme Court's opinion. The first part deals with whether the hospital owed a duty of care towards the unborn child (if they did not, then there is no primary claim that a bystander can use as the source of her derivative claim). The Court decided that the hospital owed no duty to an unborn child and, consequently, could not be sued on a derivative theory claimed by the mother. This issue is not present in Rachel's case, since it is undisputed that Robert owed a duty of care towards pedestrians and bicyclists (who include Sophie).

Secondly, the Court considered whether Texas should allow bystander claims in a hospital setting, where the bystander is typically not present in the operating or emergency room where the claimed injury occurs. While other states have relaxed the traditional requirement that a bystander literally witness the injury to his or her loved one, Texas has not. The experience of getting the bad news from the doctors or nurses is not enough, in Texas, to establish bystander status.

The Supreme Court's decision is not relevant to Rachel's situation because we are not dealing with medical malpractice and it is undisputed that Rachel actually saw the accident and its aftermath.

34. The digests.

35. If you have an authoritative case like *Davis*, you look at the topic and key number of the headnotes of that case that are most relevant to your research issues. These are headnotes 7 and 8, for which the topics and key numbers are Action Key number 38(3) and Hospitals Key number 7. You would also want to pursue *Harris*, whose Headnote 17 (Counties Key number 141) deals with the issue of several independent claimants having to share a single liability award.

36. Start with the latest edition of *Texas Digest* or *Southwestern Digest*.

    If you are not in Texas or one of the other states included in the *Southwestern Reporter* region, and your library does not have the *Southwestern Digest*, you will have to use the latest *Decennial Digest* and then all the volumes of the *General Digest* that update the *Decennial* and are cumulated every five years.

37. No. Under Hospitals, Key number 7, "Liability of proprietors, officers and employees," the Texas cases revolve around a hospital's liability under the Texas Tort Claims Act. This was an issue in *Davis* with which we are not concerned.

    Under Action Key number 38(3) and Counties Key number 141, there are no relevant cases. Given the *Harris* departure from the older rule in *Davis*, however, it would not be surprising to find other appellate districts in Texas beginning to state their own views on the matter.

Legal Memorandum

Okay, you're done with your research. The very final step is to write up what you found in the form of a legal memorandum, using the guidelines set out above. Then compare your result with the sample memorandum we've prepared for this research (set out below).

Memo From: Terry Paralegal
To: Ruth Lawyer
Topic: Limitation of Liability Under the Texas Tort Claims Act for
            Rachel Pie

Facts:

In August 1989, Robert Roberts, a state employee, negligently struck
with his car and gravely injured Sophie Pie, who was riding a bicycle. Rachel Pie, Sophie's daughter, was riding another bicycle right behind Sophie
and witnessed the accident and Sophie's injuries. Sophie died from her injuries. Every night, Rachel has nightmares in which she relives the accident.

All the parties, including the State, agree that Sophie's damages ex-
ceed $250,000 and that Rachel's damages are $65,000. Sophie's damages are
being asserted as a survivor's claim by her estate. Roberts has no assets
or insurance, and the parties agree that under the Tort Claims Act, the
State of Texas is liable for damages caused by Roberts.

The State accepts liability as Robert's employer as provided by the
Tort Claims Act and agrees that Rachel has damages as a bystander under
Texas tort law. But it insists that Rachel's bystander damages are derivative of Sophie's, so both Sophie's and Rachel's damages are limited to a
total of $250,000.

Issue:

If a person is injured in an accident, and another person who witnesses
the accident is considered a "bystander" under Texas law, is she a "separate person" injured under the limits of liability provisions of the Tort
Claims Act § 101.023, as interpreted by the courts within this [Austin] Appellate District?

Conclusion:

Yes. Because she is a "bystander," Rachel's injuries are considered to
be personally suffered by her, not derivative from Sophie's injuries. However, a recent case from the Court of Appeals in Houston suggests that, in
spite of the fact that Rachel has an independent claim, she may be limited
in her recovery if the state's liability limitation is read to extend to
the limit for each person physically injured by the state.

Reasoning:

At common law, the State is immune from liability. When Texas waives
that immunity in certain situations and within certain limits, it is only
liable insofar as it has specifically waived the immunity.

The Texas Tort Claims Act (Vernon's Ann. Texas Stat. CP&R §§ 101.001
et seq.), makes the state liable for property damage, personal injury and
death negligently caused by an employee of the state while driving a motor
vehicle in the scope of his employment if the employee would be held liable
under Texas law. § 101.023 limits that liability to $250,000 for each per-

son and $500,000 for each single occurrence for bodily injury or death.

According to Texas case law pursuant to the Texas Tort Claims Act, when a bystander suffers injuries as a result of witnessing the injuries suffered by a close relative, the bystander suffers those injuries personally and is therefore a separate "person injured" for purposes of limits of liability.

In City of Austin v. Davis, 693 S.W.2d 31 (Tex. App. Dist.--Austin 1985), the father of a boy whose death was due to the negligence of a city hospital was found to be a bystander. In Davis, the City claimed that the father's injuries were derivative from the son's claim for the purposes of limitation of liability under the Tort Claims Act. The Davis court held that the bystander injuries sustained by the father were suffered personally by him and were not derivative of the wrongful death of his son. Therefore, the court held, the father was a "person injured" for the purposes of the Tort Claims Act limitation of liability, and he was thus entitled to recover up to the per-person limitation for his own injuries.

The issue in Davis is the same as Rachel's: If the bystander's injuries are considered to be derivative of those of the person whose injury they witnessed, then the per-person liability limit applies to the total of both persons' injuries. Also the relevant facts of Davis are the same as in Rachel's case: Mr. Davis witnessed the death of his son. Rachel witnessed the accident that gravely injured her mother. Both Mr. Davis and Rachel suffered physically and emotionally. The Davis opinion comes out of the Appellate Court for this District, so its holding is authoritative. Just as Mr. Davis was found to have suffered his injuries personally, the Court would decide that Rachel is a separate person injured and is thus entitled to recover up to $250,000 for her injuries. Because the parties have agreed that Rachel's injuries amount to $65,000, she will be entitled to collect that full amount from the state, unaffected by the limitation on Sophie's damages.

A worrisome note, however, has been stuck by the Court of Appeals sitting in Houston. In Harris County Hospital District v. Estrada (Tex App.-- Houston [1st Dist.] 1993), the majority expressly declined to follow Davis and limited the recovery of two independent, non-derivative types of claims to the single statutory amount specified in the Texas Tort Claim Act. In Harris, the court acknowledged that the bystander claim was non-derivative, but it did not end its inquiry there. Focusing on the "each person injured" language of the statute, the court narrowed that term to refer to the first person physically hurt by the state's negligence. By restricting the definition of the "person injured," the court forced all claimants (regardless of their derivative or non-derivative status) to share in that one recovery limit. If the state raises Harris, our best response will be to note that it is not controlling in our District and that its premise (to deny that the other independent claimants are not also "persons injured") is unwise.

Research Problem:
Burglary Hypothetical (California)

Estimated Time: 4 hours

The research for this problem will require the following skills:

- finding and reading annotated statutes (Chapter 6);
- using a legal encyclopedia (Chapter 5);
- reading a case, including use of headnotes (Chapter 7);
- using the digests (Chapter 10);
- using *Shepard's Case Citations* (Chapter 10); and
- writing a memorandum of law.

You will also need to know what common law is (Chapter 3).

The following sources will be needed:

- California Annotated Code (West's or Deering's);
- *American Jurisprudence (Am. Jur.)*;
- *California Reporter* or *California Appellate Decisions, 3d*;
- *Shepard's California Citations*; and
- *California Digest* or *Pacific Digest* or *American (Decennial* and *General) Digest*.

Charlene owns a house in San Francisco, CA. She lived there until her employer sent her to Los Angeles in January 1989, on a special two-year project at the Los Angeles office. The company provided Charlene with a small furnished apartment in Los Angeles.

Charlene rented out the house in San Francisco, but in June of 1990 the tenant moved out; Charlene decided to keep the house empty until her return, scheduled for January 1991. Charlene hired Sally to maintain the premises, and every week Sally went to the house to clean, change the pattern of the random automatic lighting, and otherwise make the house look lived-in.

In October 1990, Alix broke into the house at night to steal whatever she could find and was caught red-handed by the police.

Alix has been charged with first-degree burglary, but insists that it should be only second degree because first-degree burglary only applies to inhabited premises, and, Alix says, Charlene wasn't living there. You are a paralegal working for the prosecutor's office and have been assigned to research the matter.

Approach Statement: Criminal law is almost completely a creature of statute. For a person to be convicted of a criminal act, she or he must have *intended* to do the illegal thing and to have had "notice" that it was illegal. (A person is considered to have notice if the law has been published, as in an annotated code.) So, when researching a criminal law issue, the first thing to do is to find and read the appropriate statutes in an annotated code. Second, consult background resources to fill out your understanding of the area of law you are researching. The third step is to find one or more cases that interpret the statute in a factual context as similar to yours as possible. Finally, as in researching all types of legal issues, you are not finished until you have *Shepardized* the cases and statutes and checked the digests.

Questions

1. What index should you use to locate the appropriate state statute governing your research issue?
2. Under what topics should you look for our problem?
3. Where does the index send you?
4. Find Penal Code § 459 and read it. What does § 459 teach you?
5. The first element of the crime of burglary, as defined in § 459, is that the accused must *enter* the house or apartment. In our case, has this element been satisfied?
6. What is the next element of the crime of burglary, as defined in § 459?
7. Has this element been satisfied in our case?
8. How would you find out if Alix's intended crime was of the type required by the statute—grand or petit larceny or a felony?
9. Does § 459 say anything about the issue of "inhabited"? Remember, Alix claims that the burglary is only second degree because Charlene wasn't living there.
10. Now read Penal Code § 460. What is the title of the section?
11. According to § 460, what is the relationship between the question of whether the house is inhabited and the degree of burglary?

Note: So now we know, from § 460, that if Alix is to be found guilty of first-degree burglary, Charlene's house must have been "inhabited." We also know, from § 459, that inhabited means "currently used for dwelling purposes, whether occupied or not." What we don't know is whether Charlene's house would be considered "currently being used

for dwelling purposes" when no one is using the premises to sleep in.

This is the time to go to a background resource to find out how the courts in California have dealt with cases like ours, where the owner of the house is away for a short or long time, and the issue or question is whether the house was occupied when the person accused of burglary did the foul deed.

Unless you are familiar with criminal law, the law of burglary and the issue of "inhabited," we suggest that you wait to look at the Notes of Decisions following the statute until after you have gained some familiarity with the subject from a background resource.

12. Of the general national background resources, we recommend trying *American Jurisprudence 2d (Am. Jur. 2d)*, because it gives explanations of the law in language that is not too technical, and also because it will refer you to helpful annotations in the *American Law Reports (A.L.R.)*—because both resources are published by Bancroft-Whitney/Lawyers Coop.

a. What word do you look under in the General Index to *Am. Jur. 2d* to find out how a temporarily unoccupied dwelling house affects a burglary conviction?

b. What helpful entries are there?

c. In the volume that includes burglary, § 1 is a basic common law definition of burglary. Is this definition similar to the definition in the California statute?

d. Which section deals with our issue, a temporarily unoccupied dwelling?

e. What does that section say about the owner being temporarily absent?

f. What does it say about the importance of the length of time the owner is absent?

Now, this is helpful information for us, and gives us a good sense of what factors are important in our case. There is an *A.L.R.* annotation cited, but it is from the first series, which is quite old, and no California case is cited to support the statements made in the text.

g. What is the next step before leaving *Am. Jur. 2d*?

h. Where do you look in the pocket part, and what do you find there?

i. From the description in the *Am. Jur.* notes, what does the case seem to hold?

j. Could this case be important to Charlene's case against Alix?

You will want to write down the citation to *People v. Marquez* and to the *A.L.R.* article, so that you will be able to find them later without going back to *Am. Jur. 2d*.

The same *A.L.R.* annotation could have been found by looking in the *A.L.R.* index under "burglary." It is a helpful annotation because it is an entire article all about the issue of whether a dwelling is "inhabited" in a burglary case if the owner is temporarily absent. If you went to *A.L.R.* first, you would find a discussion of *People v. Marquez* in the pocket part.

Now we need to go back to the annotated code to see how courts in California have dealt with a situation like ours, where the owner or tenant had been away for a while at the time of the burglary.

13. Go to the annotated code and look at the notes of decisions following § 460 to find any cases with facts and issues similar to ours. There are many cases listed. How do you find the ones about this issue?

14. Looking through the Notes of Decisions (remember to also look in the pocket part), you find several cases in which the owner or renter was absent for a night or other short period. Do you find any cases that indicate in the notes that the owner was gone for a long time, as in Charlene's situation?

15. Find *People v. Marquez*. Read it, using the headnotes to help you. From reading the case, answer the following questions:

a. In the case of Charlene and Alix, Charlene had been absent from the house for almost two years. In *Marquez*, had the owner been absent for a similarly lengthy period of time?

b. Charlene was actually living in another place; was that true in *Marquez* as well?

c. Was it important to the court in *Marquez* that the owner had not indicated any intent to not return and that the home was being maintained for her by others?

16. If the court in *Marquez* were deciding the case of Alix and Charlene, do you think it would conclude that Charlene's house was "currently used for dwelling purposes" and therefore "inhabited" at the time Alix broke in?

Note: The answer to Question 16 means that *Marquez* can be used as authority for the position that Alix is guilty of first-degree burglary, as was the defendant in *Marquez*.

17. Now you have an authoritative case that says what you want it to say. How can you make sure that there are not other cases with similar facts and contrary holdings, and that the case is up-to-date and has not been overturned or otherwise affected by subsequent cases?

18. *Shepardize Marquez* under both the *California Reporter* citation and the *California Appellate Decisions, 3d* citation.
    a. How can you determine whether there are cases that cite *Marquez* about the issue of "inhabited"?
    b. Are there cases that might have cited *Marquez* about the issue of "inhabited"?

19. What is the name of the case that cited *Marquez* at 198 *California Reporter* 607?

20. Why did the *O'Bryan* court cite *Marquez*? Is this a case about the issue of "inhabited"?

21. What is the name of the case that cites *Marquez* at 259 *California Reporter*, pages 130 and 131?

22. Is it about the issue of "inhabited"?

23. Is it about whether a house is "inhabited" if the owner is absent?

24. Now go to the digests to find other relevant cases and to make sure that other cases do not affect your determination of the law in our case.
    a. How do you go from the case to the digests?
    b. What is the appropriate digest to use to make sure that there are no other cases with similar facts and issues that have contrary holdings?
    c. Find the case in which, because the renters had moved out and did not intend to return, the burglary of their apartment (despite their *right* to return, and the presence of some of their belongings) could not be classified as first degree. Do you find any other cases that might affect our case or the authority of *Marquez*?

Answers

1. The index to the annotated collection of California statutes. In California this is *West's Annotated Code* or *Deering's Annotated Code.* California also has *LARMAC,* a separately-published index to statutes.

2. Since you know that Alix has been charged with burglary, look under "burglary." You also know that the issue is about some difference between first and second degree. "Burglary" is an Index entry, "degrees" is a subheading.

3. Under "Burglary" and the subheading "degrees," West refers you to Pen (the abbreviation for Penal Code) 460. Deerings refers you to Penal 459.

4. § 459 is a general description of the crime of burglary. That is, it sets out what factors or elements the State must prove in order for a person to be found guilty of the crime.

5. Yes. In our case there is no question that Alix *entered* (she broke a window and climbed in).

6. Intent. The person must enter with the intent or purpose to commit grand or petty larceny or a felony. Actually, this is two elements: (1) the entry must be made with the intention to commit a crime and (2) the intended crime must be grand or petit larceny or a felony.

7. Yes. Alix entered with the intent to "steal whatever she could find." The term "steal" is vernacular for larceny.

8. By looking up the definitions of grand and petit larceny in the statutes in the annotated code; you would start by looking up larceny in the index. To save you the trouble of actually looking this up, we'll tell you that Alix's intention was to commit either grand larceny or petit larceny (which would depend on the value of the property Alix intended to steal).

9. Yes. It says, "In this chapter, 'inhabited' means currently being used for dwelling purposes, whether occupied or not."

10. *West*: "Degrees; construction of section."
    Deering's: "Degrees."

11. "Every burglary of an inhabited dwelling house ... is burglary of the first degree." In subsection (b), we are told that all other kinds of burglary are of the second degree.

12. a. Look in the index volume under "burglary."
    b. "Burglary."
    "Dwelling house, generally Burgl §§ 1-4."
    "Occupancy, generally Burgl sections 4, 27."
    c. Yes, except that the *Am. Jur. 2d* definition includes "in the night time," an element not included in California's statute.
    d. § 4.
    e. We are told that the owner must have left with the intention of returning if the house is to be considered "inhabited."

f. The length of time the house is unoccupied seems to be of little importance. "The intention to return is determined mainly from the condition in which the house was left."

g. Time to look in the pocket part!

h. Under Burglary § 4 in the pocket part, you find a new *A.L.R.* annotation, 20 *A.L.R.* 4th 349, and a California case, *People v. Marquez*, which seems to have facts similar to our case. The other California cases are less relevant.

i. The case seems to say that the house was "inhabited," and the defendant is therefore guilty of first-degree burglary.

j. Yes, if it deals with the issue of "inhabited" in a context of relevant facts similar to ours.

13. At the beginning of the Notes of Decisions following § 460 is a table of contents to the notes. If you are using *West's Annotated California Code*, you'll find:

"Inhabited dwelling or building 4-8

Temporary absence 5."

The numbers represent the Note sections. When you refer to the pocket part at the back of the bound volume, you will know to go directly to those section numbers in the pocket part's Notes of Decisions. (The *Deering* set has a similar arrangement. "Inhabited dwelling 1-3 in relation to first-degree burglary." Inhabited dwelling 2 is for an element of burglary with which you are less concerned.)

14. There is only one case note that indicates that the owner was absent for a long time, and even had "moved to a boarding home …" *People v. Marquez* (again!), 192 Cal. Rptr. 193, 143 Cal. App. 3d 797 (1983). In West § 460 note 4, the case appears in the main volume. In *Deering* § 460 note 13, the case appears in the pocket part.

15. a. Yes. In *Marquez*, the owner had been absent for several years.

b. Yes; the owner was living in some kind of care facility.

c. Yes. The *Marquez* court said that the important thing in terms of deciding whether premises are inhabited when the owner is absent is whether the owner intends to return. The fact that the home was maintained for her supported the conclusion that she intended to return.

16. Yes. The important (relevant) facts are very similar, and the court was deciding the same issue raised by Alix: whether the house was inhabited for the purpose of determining whether the burglary was of the first or second degree pursuant to Penal Code § 460.

17. *Shepardize* the case and use the appropriate West's case digests.

18. a. *Shepard's California Citations* shows that a number of cases have cited *Marquez*, but most of them for points of law dealt with by the *Marquez* court with which we are not concerned. If you look at the headnotes for the *Marquez* opinion, you will see that our issue is dealt with in headnotes 2, 3 and 4, and there are several cases that *Shepard's* says cited *Marquez* for issues dealt with in other headnotes.

b. Yes: There are three citations that either cited one of the three headnotes with which we are concerned or that cited to the case as a whole (no specific headnote). We have to look at these to make sure there is no problem. *Shepard's* also tells us that an *A.L.R.* annotation cited *Marquez* in the pocket part (20 A.L.R. 4th 349s). You will want to make a note of the *A.L.R.* article in case you need more information or more cases.

19. *People v. O'Bryan*.

20. No. *O'Bryan* cited *Marquez* about an issue regarding burglary (was the place a residence), but NOT about the issue of "inhabited."

In your research notes, mark this case as not relevant.

21. *People v. Hines*.

22. Yes it is.

23. No. It's about whether a guest house that was broken into was a part of the "inhabited dwelling house." Therefore, it is not a matter of concern to us, because it would not affect the authority of *Marquez*. Make your notes specific on this point.

24. a. By using the key topic and number assigned to the headnotes relevant to your issue.

b. Taking the key topic and number from the relevant headnotes of *Marquez*, Burglary Key number 10, go to the latest edition of the *California Digest*.

c. In *California Digest 2d* under Burglary Key number 10, we see that the section is titled "degrees," and after looking at the notes for a few cases, we see that this section contains cases about many issues other than "inhabited." Just keep plugging, and you'll pick out cases about "inhabited" in this section. And don't forget the pocket part.

One of the cases you will find is *People v. Cardona*. You may recall that this was one of the cases noted in the Notes of Decisions following

Penal Code § 460, and we told you not to bother looking these up as they were about very short-term absences. This is also true of *People v. Lewis* and *People v. Stewart*. Eventually, you will find *Marquez* again, but no other relevant cases. So, after all the looking, you can conclude there is nothing here that would affect our case or the authority of *Marquez*.

Legal Memorandum

Okay, you're done with your research. Now the very final step is to write up what you found in the form of a legal memorandum. After giving it a good try, using the general approach outlined above, compare your result with the following memo.

Memo from: Terry Paralegal

To: Ruth Lawyer

Topic: Whether Charlene's house was inhabited at the time Alix entered for the purpose of larceny, so as to make Alix guilty of first-degree burglary.

Facts:

In October 1990, Alix broke into a house in San Francisco, owned by Charlene, with the intent to steal. At the time, Charlene was not occupying the house as she had been sent to Los Angeles by her employer for a temporary assignment; she planned to return in January 1991. In her absence the house was maintained by Sally, whom Charlene had hired for that purpose. Alix was seen entering the premises and was arrested there by the police.

Issue:

For purposes of deciding whether a person is guilty of first-degree burglary under Penal Code § 459, was the house "inhabited" under the following circumstances?

- No one was actually living in the house when it was broken into.
- The owner/resident was absent from the house for an extended period but intended to return.
- The house was maintained for the owner/resident in her absence.

Conclusion:

The issue of whether a house is inhabited if the owner/resident is absent from the premises depends on the intent of the owner/resident to return. The length of the absence is relevant only insofar as a factor in determining the intent. Charlene showed intent to return, so her house was "inhabited," and Alix is guilty of first-degree burglary.

<u>Reasoning:</u>

California Penal Code defines burglary as the entering of a building for certain criminal purposes (Pen. Code sec. 459). It then goes on to set up a distinction between first- and second-degree burglary (Pen. Code sec. 460). First degree is when the building entered is an "inhabited dwelling house." In our case, there is no doubt that the act of Alix was burglary and that the building entered was a dwelling house. Regarding the issue of whether the house was inhabited, case law indicates that only the owner's intent is determinative. In <u>People v. Marquez</u>, 192 Cal. Rptr. 193, 143 Cal. App. 3d 797 (1983), the elderly owner had moved to a care facility for several years and friends and relatives maintained the house, expecting her to return. The <u>Marquez</u> court held that the length of absence from a person's home is relevant only insofar as it may bear on the determination of whether she intends to return, that the residence was inhabited and the defendant was guilty of first-degree burglary.

In our case, Charlene was gone for a long time (almost two years), but she left for a temporary job with a specific two-year duration and a specific return date of January 1991, and employed Sally to create the appearance that the house was occupied. There were no indications that Charlene did not intend to return.

Therefore, based on the holding in <u>People v. Marquez</u>, the court should find that Charlene's house was "inhabited" and that Alix is guilty of burglary in the first degree.

Research Problem: Alimony Hypothetical (West Virginia)

Estimated Time: 2½ hours

The research for this problem will require the following skills:

- using background resources (Chapter 5);
- finding a case from its citation (Chapter 9);
- using the case reporters (Chapter 8);
- Using *Shepard's Case Citations* (Chapter 10);
- using West's Digests (Chapter 10);
- reading a case, including use of headnotes (Chapter 7); and
- writing a memorandum of law (Chapter 11).

The sources required to fully research this problem are:

- *American Law Reports (A.L.R.)*;
- *Southeastern Reporter;*
- a law dictionary;
- *Shepard's Southeastern Citations*; and
- *Virginia and West Virginia Digest* or *Southeastern Digest* or the *Decennial/General* digest.

Joan and Michael Hamish were married in 1952. Joan filed for divorce in early 1981 in the circuit court near their home in West Virginia. Their three children were grown and independent. Michael (55 years old in 1982) was a successful surgeon; Joan (50 years old in 1982) had been a teacher before the children were born and in 1980 had gone back to school for a Ph.D. in psychology with the plan to become a psychotherapist. At the time of the divorce she was working part time in a clinic as part of her school program and earning $6,000 per year.

They made the following agreement, which was approved by the court in a decree dated June 1, 1982.

1. Joan was to keep the family home, and the car she used, in her name.
2. Michael was to keep the family boat, and the car he used, in his name.
3. All other property and debts were to be divided equally.
4. Michael was to pay Joan alimony as follows: $3,000 per month for 5 years (60 months) starting June 1, 1982; then $2,000 per month for 3 years (36 months); then $1,000 per month for 10 years (120 months). The purpose of the payments is to support Joan while she finishes her degree and becomes self-supporting through her psychotherapy practice, but she may use the funds for any purpose. In any event, the payments will cease on May 1, 2000.

On October 1, 1990, Michael died of a heart attack. His estate was worth over $2 million, but his will made no provision for Joan. The executor was his best friend, Jose Nuñez, M.D. Michael had made the October alimony payment, which at that time was down to $1,000, and Joan was well on the way to being self-supporting, although she was relying on the $1,000 monthly payment for ten more years.

Joan called Jose after the funeral and asked him when she might expect the next payment. Jose talked to his lawyer and then told Joan, "Alimony payments terminate when the paying spouse dies. Too bad, Joan, but I can't do anything about it." Joan wants to know whether Jose is right.

Approach Statement: Family law (divorce, child support, alimony, adoption, etc.) is a mixture of common law and statutes, with many cases interpreting the statutes, and then more statutes putting the cases into effect (called "codifying the cases").

For this type of research problem, start with a background resource that will help you gain an overview of the issues. Then study the cases and statutes that are mentioned by the resource as bearing on your research question. Finally, *Shepardize* the cases and statutes on which you plan to rely and check the digests.

General national background resources include *A.L.R., Am. Jur., C.J.S.* and law review articles. We suggest starting with *A.L.R.* to learn about alimony in West Virginia and the issue of termination of alimony payments on the death of the payor (paying spouse). We recommend trying *A.L.R.* first if you can find a recent annotation about your issue, because it gathers all the cases on a single issue into an easy-to-use, well-organized form and discusses cases from all states.

Questions

1. Does *A.L.R.* have an annotation (article) about your issue? Under what topic do you look in the index?
2. Go to the annotation. Does the *A.L.R. 9th* article discuss West Virginia cases? If so, in which sections?
3. The "Summary and Comment" at the beginning of the article first discusses whether unpaid and overdue alimony payments may be recovered from the estate of a deceased payor spouse. Is this an issue in our case?
4. What does the summary tell us about what happens to regular periodic alimony payments upon the death of the obligor (paying spouse)?

5. Now it is time to look at the sections that contain West Virginia cases. What West Virginia case is cited in § 2[b]?

6. Make a note of the name and citation of the case and the section you found it in for easy reference later. What does this case seem to say about our problem?

7. What West Virginia case is discussed (not just cited, but discussed) in § 4[a]?

8. What does this case, as summarized in *A.L.R.*, tell us about our question?

9. Do the discussions in §§ 5[a] and 6[a] concern the issue in our case?

10. What is the West Virginia case cited in § 29[a]?

11. Is this case also discussed in § 29[b]?

12. Does § 29[a] refer to the case for the same reason that 29[b] does?

13. § 29 is titled "Alimony in Gross." In order to understand what is meant by this in West Virginia, you will need to read *Weller*. Where do you find the *Weller* case?

14. Read the *Weller* case. What situation does the court define as "alimony in gross"?

15. Was the alimony "in gross" in the *Weller* case? What facts were relevant to that determination?

16. Following the rule of *Weller* for determining whether alimony is "in gross," is the alimony in our case "in gross"?

17. Concerning our issue of whether the payments to Joan are payable to her by Michael's estate, what does the *Weller* court say is the importance of the alimony being "in gross"?

18. What does "vested" mean? The *Weller* court doesn't define it, so where would be the best place to look?

19. What does the *Weller* court say is the relationship between the alimony being vested and it being "in gross"?

20. Applying the reasoning of the *Weller* court, will Joan's alimony payments survive Michael's death and be payable to her by Michael's estate?

21. In *Weller*, did the court say when Mrs. Weller was to receive the money?

22. Are there difference between the facts of *Weller* and our case?

23. If so, are these differences relevant? That is, would these differences affect the reasoning and conclusion of the *Weller* court if it were examining our case?

24. Which statutes does the court discuss that might be relevant to your issue?

25. What is the rule of § 48-2-15(f)?

26. Does 48-2-15(f) affect Joan's case? Why?

27. According to *Weller*, what is the court supposed to do in cases where 48-2-15(f) does not apply?

28. Now that you have an authoritative case that says what you want it to, and have determined that the alimony statute does not affect your case, what do you have to do to make sure that there are no other cases with similar facts and contrary holdings, and that the case is up-to-date and has not been overturned or otherwise affected by subsequent cases (in other words, how do you make sure that *Weller* is still "good law")?

29. Shepardize *Weller*. Are there any cases that have cited *Weller*?

30. a. The first citation, 385 S.E.2d 389, has a "j" in front of it in *Shepard's*. What does the "j" mean?

    b. Read the citing case. Does it affect the holding of *Weller* as it relates to Joan's situation?

31. a. The second citing case is shown in *Shepard's* as citing Weller twice. The first one has a "d" in front of it, one has a small "1" after the S.E.2d and the other has a small "2" after the S.E.2d. What do these notations mean?

    b. Could *Weller* headnotes 1 or 2 be relevant to our case?

    c. Read the case, especially the part on page 479. Does the case in any way change the effect of *Weller* on our case?

32. The third citing case also cites to *Weller's* headnote 1. Find the case and read it. Does it change the effect of *Weller* on our case?

33. Well, that's it for *Shepard's*. Now, what is the appropriate digest to use to make sure that there are no other cases with similar facts and issues that have contrary holdings to *Weller*?

34. Under what do you look in that digest?

35. Did you find anything that disturbs the authority of *Weller*? 374 S.E. 2d 712.

36. How would you calculate the amount owed by Michael's estate to Joan?

Answers

1. If you look in the *A.L.R. Index* under the heading "ALIMONY" and the subheading "Death" (don't forget the pocket part in the back of the Index volume you are using), you will find a reference to "obligor spouse's death as affecting alimony," 79 *A.L.R.4th* 10. You're in

luck; this seems to be exactly what you're looking for. There is also a reference to "husband's death as affecting alimony 39 *A.L.R.2d* 1406," but this is a much older article (*A.L.R.2d*), so go first to the newer article; if that one doesn't address your issue, go to the older one.

2. The Table of Jurisdictions represented at the beginning of the annotation shows that there are West Virginia cases in §§ 2[b], 4[a], 5[a], 6[a], 29[a] and 29[b].

3. No. Michael wasn't in arrears at the time of his death—that is, he didn't owe any back support; his payments were up-to-date.

4. The summary tells us that the rule of most courts is that an award for regular periodic alimony payments (as in our case) ends on the death of the obligor (payor, paying) spouse, but that the courts of varying jurisdictions hold widely diverging views on this issue.

5. *Re Estate of Hereford*, 162 W. Va. 477, 250 S.E.2d 45 (1978).

6. Because *Hereford* is cited in footnote 7, read the text preceding the "7." From the text, *Hereford* seems to concern issues about the daily ability of the obligee spouse (the receiver of alimony) to support her/himself and the sufficient size of the obligor's estate to pay the alimony claim. This might be helpful if we don't find anything better.

7. *In Re Estate of Weller*, 374 S.E.2d 712 (W. Va. 1988), on page 30 of the article.

8. This section is about whether a court may order that periodic alimony continue after the death of the obligor spouse. The West Virginia court seems to say that a court may order the obligation to be paid out of the obligor's estate.

9. No. The issue treated in § 5[a] is whether parties getting divorced may provide in their agreement that the payments will survive the death of the payor spouse. This is not our issue; the parties in our case did not so provide, and now it is too late. The issue discussed in § 6[a] concerns whether, if the divorce decree says the payments are to continue until the death of the payee spouse, this shows an intent that they would continue after the death of the payor spouse. This is not our issue; in our case there was no such provision.

10. *In Re Estate of Weller*, 374 S.E.2d 712 (1988).

11. Yes.

12. No. § 29[a] says that the cases referred to in that section stand for the proposition that alimony may survive the death of the obligor spouse, whereas § 29[b] says just the opposite.

13. The citation is 374 S.E.2d 712. This case is in volume 374 of the *Southeastern Reporter 2nd* series, starting on page 712.

14. On page 716, the *Weller* court says an alimony award will be characterized as alimony in gross when the total amount of the alimony payments and the date the payments will cease can be determined from the divorce decree.

15. Yes. In *Weller*, the amount of each payment was designated in the decree, and the exact number of payments could be determined from the decree. Therefore, by simple arithmetic, the total amount of money that the payor spouse was to pay the payee spouse could have been calculated on the date of the divorce decree.

16. Yes. On the date of the Hamish's divorce decree, it would have been possible to determine the total amount Michael was to pay Joan, because the exact number of payments and the amount of each payment are stated in the decree.

17. The *Weller* court says that if alimony is "in gross," it is vested as of the date of the divorce decree.

18. The best place to look it up is in a law dictionary, another type of background resource. Two widely-used law dictionaries are *Black's Law Dictionary* and Oran's *Dictionary of Legal Terms*, where you will find that "vested" means the vested thing is absolutely yours and will come to you without your having to do anything except, perhaps, wait.

19. On pages 715-716, the *Weller* court says, "Mrs. Weller had a vested right to receive a total sum of $9,000 … and her award may therefore be properly characterized as 'alimony in gross ….'" Therefore, the obligation of the payor spouse survived his death and was payable to the payee spouse by the payor's estate.

20. Yes. Once it is determined that the alimony is "in gross," it follows that it is also "vested." Alimony that is vested survives the death of the payor spouse, and must be paid to the payee spouse out of the payor's estate.

21. The *Weller* court states on page 716, in the last paragraph of the case, "… Mrs. Weller is entitled to the $6,600.00 she stood to receive from Dr. Weller had he lived, such amount now being payable from Dr. Weller's estate."

22. There are differences in facts between the *Weller* case and ours: the length of time payments were to be made, the amount of the individual payments and the total amount to be paid.

23. No. The court never attaches any significance to the number of payments or their amount, except to calculate the amount owed.

24. West Virginia Code § 48-2-15(f) and § 48-2-36.

25. The code section states that a divorce agreement or decree must state whether or not alimony is to survive the death of the payor party.

26. No. The *Weller* court held that § 48-2-6 provides that § 48-2-15 (enacted in 1984) does not have retroactive effect on alimony payments. Joan and Michael's decree was dated June 1, 1982, so it would not be affected by § 48-2-15(f).

27. The court writes that: "We believe the better result will be reached in this case by examining the plain language of the divorce decree …"

28. Use digests and *Shepardize*.

29. In *Shepard's Southeastern Citations*, under 374 *Southeastern Reporter, 2d Series*, page 12, we learn that there are three cases in the *Southeastern Reporter* that cited *Weller*. There are also other citations, but these only show that *Weller* was cited in 79 *A.L.R.4th* (the *A.L.R.* article we found it in)!

30. a. By looking in the front of the volume you will find a list of abbreviations. The "j" means that Weller was cited in that case in a dissenting opinion.

    b. No. This case is about a completely different issue. The dissenting judge cited *Weller* in support of the statement that the Court's decisions in recent years, including *Weller*, have been requiring fair and just treatment for married women.

31. a. The "d" means that the case on page 749 in volume 424 of S.E.2d distinguished the facts of that case from *Weller*. The little "1" means that the issue for which it cited *Weller* was described in *Weller* in headnote 1. The little "2" means that the court also cited *Weller* for the issue described in *Weller's* headnote 2.

    b. Maybe. Headnote 1 says the court has the power to say that alimony will survive the death of the payor. Headnote 2 states the general rule that alimony ends when a spouse dies unless the decree specifically states that it is binding on the payor's estate.

    c. No. The case offers no legal principles that would change the rule of *Weller* about alimony in gross surviving the death of the payor spouse.

32. No. The court cites *Weller* and makes a finding consistent with *Weller* and other similar cases. It has no effect on *Weller* or our case.

33. Go to the latest edition of the *Virginia and West Virginia Digest*, or the *Southeastern Digest* or, if your library has neither of these, then the *American (Decennial* and *General) Digest*. Don't forget the pocket parts and don't forget you are looking for West Virginia cases only.

34. Taking the key number from the relevant headnotes of *Weller*, you look under Divorce keys 241 and 247.

35. Not as of March 2004.

36. The amount due is calculated as follows:

Payments to be made:

$3,000 per month for 60 months	$180,000
$2,000 per month for 36 months	$ 72,000
$1,000 per month for 120 months	$120,000
TOTAL	$372,000

Michael paid:

at $3,000 per month 6/1/82-5/1/87	$180,000
at $2,000 per month 6/1/87-5/1/90	$ 72,000
at $1,000 per month 6/1/90-10/1/90	$ 5,000
TOTAL	$257,000

$372,000–257,000 = $115,000

Legal Memorandum

Okay, you're done with your research. The very final step is to write up what you found in the form of a legal memorandum, using the guidelines set out above. Then compare your result with the sample memo we've prepared for this research (set out below).

fam

Memo from: Terry Paralegal

To: Ruth Lawyer

Topic: The liability of Michael Hamish's estate for alimony payments to
               Joan Hamish

Facts:

Joan and Michael Hamish were divorced in 1982. Among other terms,
the divorce decree, dated June 1, 1982, provided that Michael was to pay
Joan alimony starting June 1, 1982 and ending May 1, 2000. The amounts of
the payments were specific: $3000 per month for 60 months; then $2000 per
month for 36 months; then $1000 per month for 120 months. On October 1,
1990, Michael died; he had made the October 1 payment. Joan is planning to
file a claim against Michael's estate for the remaining payments, a total
of $115,000. Michael's executor resists Joan's demand on the basis that
alimony payments terminate upon the death of the payor spouse.

Issue:

Do alimony payments that are for specified amounts and for a specified
number of payments terminate upon the death of the payor spouse before all
payments have been made?

Conclusion:

Because the total amount of the alimony payments could have been calculated on the date of the divorce decree, they vested as of that date.
Therefore the balance of payments due to Joan as of the date of Michael's
death are owed to Joan by Michael's estate.

Reasoning:

West Virginia Code § 48-2-15(f) provides that in all divorce decrees containing alimony payments, there must be a statement as to whether the payments survive the death of the payor spouse. The Hamish's decree contained
no such provision. However, in our case as well as in Re Estate of Weller,
374 S.E.2d 712 (W.Va. 1988), the statute is not applicable because as the
Weller court stated, § 48-2-36 provides that the statute, enacted in 1984,
is not applied retroactively to prior divorce decrees.

Re Estate of Weller is a case similar to ours in that in Weller, as in our
case, the alimony payments were for specified amounts and a specified number
of payments, and the payor spouse died before all payments were made. In
Weller, the Supreme Court stated that whether alimony payments survive the
death of the payor spouse, where the statute is not applicable, depends on
whether the payments are in "in gross" and therefore vested as of the date
of the divorce decree. The court said that, although in general alimony
payments terminate upon the death of the payor spouse, if the total amount
of the payments could be determined as of the date of the decree, then the

alimony was in gross; this was possible in both our case and <u>Weller</u>. If the alimony is in gross and therefore vested as of the date of the decree, the Court said, and the payor spouse dies before all the payments are made, the estate of the deceased payor has to pay now to the surviving spouse, the amount she stood to receive had the paying spouse lived.

Therefore, based on the holding in <u>Weller</u>, a West Virginia court should award to Joan the sum of $115,000, payable to her now by Michael's estate.

Online Research Project, March 2007

A client of your firm lives in Colorado, has cancer and is undergoing chemotherapy. Her doctor tells her that she must eat to keep up her strength, but one of the side effects of her treatment is severe nausea. Her doctor has suggested she try marijuana, which the doctor has read relieves the nausea and stimulates appetite. She consults your firm as to the legalities and how she should proceed.

Legal Question: May a resident of Colorado, suffering severe nausea resulting from cancer treatments, who has a "prescription" from her physician to smoke or ingest marijuana to ameliorate said severe nausea, legally purchase or grow marijuana for her own use?

Conclusion: The law regarding the medical use of marijuana is in a state of change, with a number of state statutes and constitutional amendments allowing medical marijuana use and the federal government banning medical uses of marijuana under its general prohibition of marijuana growth and use. In Colorado, a constitutional amendment, administered by the Colorado Department of Public Health and the Environment (CDPHE), allows individual use of marijuana for medical purposes and issuance of "Registry Cards" to qualifying persons that allow small amounts to be grown or purchased and protects such registrants from Colorado prosecution. The state cannot protect these people from federal prosecution, but both state and federal officials in Colorado are now saying they will not prosecute users of small quantities of medical marijuana.

Research Procedure and Findings

We began our research by entering "medical marijuana law Colorado" in the Google search box.

We used the term 'medical marijuana' because it is in common use; we were prepared to try medical uses of marijuana, but that proved unnecessary. We used "law" because we wanted to find the law and not all other material on medical marijuana, and "Colorado" to narrow the search to our jurisdiction.

It is apparent from looking at the first few hits that these are the websites of advocacy groups. This means that we must evaluate the information we get from them in this way: they may slant the facts to make their points. To be certain our information is correct, we must read the documents to which they refer and rely on official sources as much as possible. We want to know what the law is and what we can depend on, not what advocates want it to be.

On March 24, 2007, these were the hits we got; on another day, they will be different but similar.

The first, stopthedrugwar.org, presents us with an article dated June 2001; although pretty old, it does have a link to an official source, the CDPHE, the Colorado Department of Health and the Environment. The article, written shortly after the law was implemented on June 1, 2001, is informative and seems to be a good introduction to the medical marijuana law in Colorado. Getting past the rhetoric, we can conclude that both state and federal officials in Colorado do not plan to prosecute those who register. There is information at the end that "registered patients can legally possess up to two ounces ..." This appears to be accurate, but we hope to see the actual amendment, the document from which the information presumably comes. The unnamed author then refers us to a website to see the medical marijuana rules.

Clicking on the link to CDPHE, we find that there is something wrong with the link. If we go to the address (URL) box at the top of our screen and shorten the address to delete everything after the us, (leaving www.cdphe. state.co.us) we arrive at the CDPHE site. There is a search box at top right and if we enter medical marijuana law, and click on the first item in the resulting list, we come to the Medical Marijuana Registry Program Update (as of February 28, 2007.) Here we have an official report, which tells the facts and nothing but the facts! Befitting the Department of Health, there are many statistics and simple statements of problems that have come up.

We learn several pertinent facts: our client must apply for a registration card and pay a $110 fee; applicants have been turned down who had various problems not deemed remediable by use of marijuana, but "Table II - Conditions" includes severe nausea as one of the conditions for which cards have been issued. We also learn that there have been two marijuana-related convictions of patients on the registry.

The last paragraph before the tables states "Questions have arisen surrounding interpretations of statutory language..."

Now we must find the statute (constitutional amendment) and see that language for ourselves. We would also like to know more detail about those convictions. We could try to get more information about them by contacting CDPHE: you can email questions to cdphe. information@state.co.us.

Let's go back to our Google search.

The second hit, sensiblecolorado.org, is more up to date and has a good link to CDPHE, but offers not much more to us except the information that it was Constitutional Amendment 20 that was passed to allow medical marijuana use in Colorado in 2000.

Back to our Google search.

We are now looking for the text of Amendment 20. After several futile attempts, we strike pay dirt at medicalmarijuanaprocon.org. There we find a description of the Colorado law and a link at the top of the Colorado box which takes us to the actual Amendment.

Click Colorado, then click Ballot Amendment 20 and *Voila!*

Let's examine the Amendment for relevant matters. *2008* The first page is taken up with Part (1) definitions, from debilitating illness to written documentation. We see that debilitating illness includes both cancer and severe nausea. Part (2) concerns what affirmative defenses a person who has a registry card would have if arrested for "violation of the state's criminal laws related to the patient's medical use of marijuana." Part (2) also addresses the rights and protections of physicians and primary care givers. Part (3) concerns the registry requirements and confidentiality. Parts (4) and (5) describe limitations on the rights of medical marijuana patients. These sections are critical to our client's protection. The no use in plain view or open to the public and the limit of six plants, three in flower and three not, or two ounces of usable marijuana, should merit close attention. In addition, several of the advocacy websites have noted that there is no way under the Amendment for a patient to legally buy the plants or the "usable marijuana."

Now that we have seen the text of Amendment 20, we need to update our information. We do have the CDPHE report from 2007, with all the statistics about Coloradoans use of the program, but are there any other statutes or cases that could affect a medical marijuana user?

Back to the Google search results.

Hit #11, stopthedrugwar.org, has a "newspaper article" from their publication "Drug War Chronicle," describing the arrest of Mr. and Mrs. Masters, who were registered medical marijuana users and were, they allege, growing marijuana for other registered users in addition to themselves. Again getting past the rhetoric, it seems their situation points out a grey area in the law: although the registry registers only patients, not caregivers, it allows registrants on their applications to name primary care-

givers who are defined in section (1)(f) of the Amendment and, in (2)(a)(III), are given the affirmative defense that a patient would have in defense of a charge of possession.

What if one person is designated as a primary care-giver by several registrants and carries out those responsibilities required of a primary care-giver for all of them—may that person be in possession of amounts allowed to all those naming him? And what about the "plain view" prohibition?

It is looking more like our advice to our client would be: grow a few plants in your basement just for your own use and keep it quiet. Where will she get the plants? And how will she learn to grow, dry, and do whatever processing is necessary? Remember, she is an ill and debilitated person.

Back to our Google search: Hit 18 is the website of the Rocky Mountain News, a Colorado daily newspaper, an article dated June 6, 2005 about the U.5 Supreme Court case, handed down shortly before. In a 6-3 decision the Court held that although states were free to have medical marijuana laws, those laws were trumped by federal law, which outlaws marijuana use with rare exceptions.

However, the reporter quoted several federal and state officials in Colorado who said "they have bigger criminals to catch and no resources forgoing after users of small quantities. ' The United States Attorney's office in Colorado continues to focus on large-scale drug distribution organizations.' ... 'The police have much better things to do with their time and so do prosecutors.' ... 'But people who claim they are growing marijuana for medical use when they are actually growing and selling big commercial pot crops are another matter.'"

So, what can we now conclude? It is difficult to advise a client when state law says one thing, federal law, recently reiterated by the U.S. Supreme Court case *Gonzales v. Raich*, says another, but federal and state officials in Colorado say they are not interested in prosecuting small users of medical marijuana. And the *Masters* case will continue to unfold; it doesn't look as if it will affect a single medical marijuana user, but it should be watched. Our conclusion has to be that at this time we can only advise our client that she is unlikely to be arrested in Colorado for growing and using the product of three mature plants and three immature plants, in a way not open to public view.

Work still to do: follow up Colorado Amendment 20 and *Gonzales v. Raich*, to see if any cases have cited them. See Chapter 10 on how to use the ~~Westlaw KeyCite~~ or LexisNexis *Sherpardize* tools to update cases and statutes online.

Google

Web   Images   Video   News   Maps   **more »**

medical marijuana law Colorado

Search

Advanced Search
Preferences

Web   Results **1 - 10** of about **1,150,000** for **medical marijuana law Colorado**. (**0.11** seconds)

Colorado Medical Marijuana Law Now in Effect: Governor
and ...
Colorado Medical Marijuana Law Now in Effect: Governor and
Attorney General Urge Feds to Bust Patients, Feds Say No Thanks
6/8/01 ...
stopthedrugwar.org/chronicle/189/**colorado**.shtml - 22k -
Cached - Similar pages

Sensible **Colorado** :: **Colorado's Medical Marijuana Law**
Colorado law allows qualified patients to have access to **marijuana** for **medical**
purposes. In 2000, **Colorado** voters approved Amendment 20 which allows ...
sensible**colorado**.org/mm/**law**.php - 5k - Cached - Similar pages

ASA : Becoming a Patient in **Colorado**
The **Colorado Medical Marijuana Law** specifically states that patients are not
permitted ... **Colorado medical marijuana law** also does not address the issue of ...
www.safeaccessnow.org/article.php?id=1998 - 37k - Cached - Similar pages

    ASA : **Colorado's Medical Marijuana Laws**
    Medical cannabis (**medical marijuana**) **laws** in **Colorado**.
    www.safeaccessnow.org/section.php?id=190 - 13k - Cached - Similar pages

Colorado - NORML
Sign-up for the free NORML e-zine with specific **Colorado** updates ... to recognize the
medical use of **marijuana**. The **law** took effect on June 1, 2001. ...
www.norml.org/index.cfm?Group_ID=4526&wtm_view=**medical** - 34k -
Cached - Similar pages

    Active State **Medical Marijuana** Programs - NORML
    CONTACT INFORMATION: Application information for the **Colorado medical**
    marijuana ... Other amendments to Oregon's **medical marijuana law** redefine
    "mature ...
    www.norml.org/index.cfm?Group_ID=3391 - 60k - Cached - Similar pages
    [More results from www.norml.org]

AlterNet: DrugReporter: **Colorado Medical Marijuana Law** Now in Effect
"The **law** says we will keep the names confidential, and it's our plan to do that." ...
Colorado's medical marijuana rules can be read at online. ...
www.alternet.org/drugreporter/11034/ - 27k - Cached - Similar pages

American Civil Liberties Union : California's **Medical Marijuana ...**
California's **Medical Marijuana Laws** Get Nod from Court (11/16/2006) ... including
Colorado, Hawaii and Oregon, which permit **medical** use of **marijuana**. ...
www.aclu.org/drugpolicy/med**marijuana**/27446prs20061116.html - 26k -
Cached - Similar pages

State by State **Medical Marijuana Laws** - **Medical Marijuana** ProCon.org
I. Eleven states have enacted **laws** that legalized **medical marijuana**. Alaska - 1999;
California - 1996; **Colorado** - 2000; Hawaii - 2000 **...**
www.**medicalmarijuana**procon.org/pop/StatePrograms.htm - 34k -
Cached - Similar pages

Ken Gorman, **Colorado Medical Marijuana** Advocate, Shot and Killed **...**
Last weekend, CBS4's Rick Sallinger did an investigation on **Colorado's medical
marijuana law** that centered on Gorman. Gorman had recently been giving **...**
www.cannabisculture.com/articles/4902.html - 24k - Cached - Similar pages

Result Page: 1 2 3 4 5 6 7 8 9 10   **Next**

medical marijuana law Colorado   (Search)

Search within results | Language Tools | Search Tips | Dissatisfied? Help us improve

Google Home - Advertising Programs - Business Solutions - About Google

©2007 Google

medical marijuana law Colorado - Google Search   http://www.google.com/search?client=firefox-a&rls=org.mozilla%3A...

Sign in

Google

Web   Images   Video   News   Maps   **more »**

| medical marijuana law Colorado | Search   Advanced Search
                                                  Preferences

Web   Results **11 - 20** of about **1,150,000** for <u>medical</u> <u>marijuana</u> <u>law</u> <u>Colorado</u>. **(0.08** seconds)

<u>Medical Marijuana: **Colorado** Case Will Test State's **Law** |
Stop the ...</u>
A Fort Collins couple will be the first in **Colorado** to seek to use the
state's **medical marijuana law** as a defense to **marijuana**
cultivation and distribution ...
stopthedrugwar.org/chronicle/468/
colorado_**medical**_**marijuana**_case_will_test_state_**law** - 34k -
<u>Cached</u> - <u>Similar pages</u>

<u>MPP: **Colorado** - Home</u>
Colorado's medical marijuana law has also been getting a lot of press recently.
John and Lisa Masters, **medical marijuana** patients and the parents of two ...
co.mpp.org/ - 24k - <u>Cached</u> - <u>Similar pages</u>

   <u>MPP: **Colorado** - Frontpage News Listing</u>
   DENVER — A recent CBS4 Investigation into **Colorado's medical marijuana law**
   gained national attention in the New York Times as the newspaper examined how the
   ...
   co.mpp.org/.../apps/nl/content2.asp?content_
   id=%7B202F31B5-14FB-45B0-B779-3B31D1FF02D8%7D&notoc=1 - 15k -
   <u>Cached</u> - <u>Similar pages</u>
   [<u>More results from co.mpp.org</u>]

<u>Medical Marijuana in **Colorado**</u>
The **law** does not clearly state where **marijuana** plants may be grown or if two ...
Does not add to 100% as some patients report using **medical marijuana for ...
www.cdphe.state.co.us/hs/**Medicalmarijuana**/**marijuana**update.html - 28k -
<u>Cached</u> - <u>Similar pages</u>

<u>Sensible **Colorado** :: **Medical Marijuana**</u>
As part of this Campaign, Sensible **Colorado** is tracking pending **medical** ... About
Colorado's Medical Marijuana Law · Frequently Asked Questions about ...
www.sensible**colorado**.org/mm/ - 8k - <u>Cached</u> - <u>Similar pages</u>

<u>High Court to Weigh **Medical Marijuana Laws**</u>
The appeals court said states were free to adopt **medical marijuana laws** as long ...
The other states with such **laws** are Alaska, Arizona, **Colorado**, Hawaii, ...
www.commondreams.org/headlines04/1125-04.htm - 16k - <u>Cached</u> - <u>Similar pages</u>

<u>**Marijuana** Policy Project - Gonzales v. Raich: The impact of the ...</u>
Colorado Attorney General John Suthers. "The Attorney General's Office ... State
medical marijuana laws have continued to provide near total relief for ...
www.mpp.org/site/c.glKZLeMQIsG/b.2038565/k.CD83/
Gonzales_v_Raich_The_impact_of_the_US_Supreme_Courts_deci... - 20k -
<u>Cached</u> - <u>Similar pages</u>

Colorado Law :: News - Discussion on Recent **Medical Marijuana** Case
Discussion on Recent **Medical Marijuana** Case. October 30, 2005 **...** the current
Colorado Solicitor General and CU **Law** Professor, Allison Eid made comments on **...**
lawweb.**colorado**.edu/news/showArticle.jsp?id=141 - 20k - Cached - Similar pages

Rocky Mountain News: Local
"You can't hide behind the **medical marijuana** certificate to grow lots of **marijuana**
and sell it," Dorschner said. **Colorado's law** allows people with certain **...**
www.rockymountainnews.com/drmn/local/article/0,1299,DRMN_15_3836147,00.html -
32k - Cached - Similar pages

Medical Marijuana / California Prop 215
Colorado will vote on the issue again in November, 2000. A broader **medical**
marijuana law is also included in Alaska's Prop 5, which is on the November **...**
www.chrisconrad.com/expert.witness/Prop215.html - 14k - Cached - Similar pages

Google

Result Page: **Previous** 1 **2** 3 4 5 6 7 8 9 10 11   **Next**

| medical marijuana law Colorado | Search |

Search within results | Language Tools | Search Tips

Google Home - Advertising Programs - Business Solutions - About Google

©2007 Google

The Legal Research Method: Examples

In Chapter 2, we showed you an overall method for undertaking a legal research project. And, in each of the following chapters, we explained an important part of that method. Now it is time to pull it all together in an example.

Time Warp: The example set out below was originally crafted in 1982 and revised in 1997. Ten years later, as you will see, some of the dates of the source materials have long passed. For that reason, you would have trouble following this example in the law library. However, if you just read through the example and pretend it's 1997, you should have no trouble understanding it, and will be able to pick up on the basics for conducting legal research in a law library.

The Facts

Assume the following facts: Laura has enrolled her child Amy in a day care center in California. (Although the law in your state may be different, the method of research will be the same.) Laura came to pick up Amy at the end of the day, but arrived a little early so that she could watch Amy play and could interact with the staff and other parents (a practice that was encouraged by the day care center). Laura stood nearby and chatted with some of the parents as she watched Amy conclude her teeter-totter game.

Amy's joyful play came to a horrific end as, in front of her mother's eyes, she flew off the teeter-totter when the wooden seat detached from the bar. Laura took her immediately to the hospital, where an X-ray disclosed a cranial hemorrhage. Amy was operated upon immediately to relieve the pressure on her brain.

The surgery was a success and the prognosis for Amy was favorable. Laura, however, has suffered extreme anxiety in the form of recurrent nightmares, difficulty in concentrating and fits of uncontrollable crying. She has been unable to forget the awful sight of her daughter flying through the air and landing with a thud on the hard cement of the play yard. Laura's psychological distress has reached the point where she cannot work and has trouble functioning on a daily basis.

Laura has been told by several friends that she ought to see a lawyer. She found out that the wooden play structure that fell apart had been a source of concern to the day care center for some time (they knew that the wood was rotting and had attempted to fix the bolts on the teeter-totter seat). Laura knows that Amy's parents can sue the day care center for Amy's physical injuries, but Laura is less sure whether she herself can recover money damages for her own emotional torment.

Before she sees a lawyer, Laura wants to do a little legal research for herself. As a mother who witnessed her daughter's accident, can she sue for the emotional distress that scene produced? How should she proceed?

Classify the Problem

Following the suggestions made in Chapter 4, Laura must:
- determine whether state or federal law is involved;
- determine whether the matter is civil or criminal; and
- determine whether her research will involve procedural or substantive questions.

Since it's apparent that Laura's dispute with the day center involves a personal injury (Laura's emotional distress), and since most personal injury ("tort") cases are controlled by state law (see Chapter 4), Laura would tentatively start with a state law classification. While the day care center might receive some federal money, the receipt of federal funds by an independent or community entity would probably not transform Laura's dispute from a state to a federal question unless her dispute had something to do with the funds themselves.

The next step is to determine that the matter is civil rather than criminal. Criminal matters always directly involve the government and a violation of the criminal law. Although there are times when an act violates both the criminal law and a civil duty owed to another person (failure to pay child support is an example, battery is another), this is not such a case. In any event, if the center had committed any criminal act, the charges would be brought by the government upon Laura's complaint, not by Laura herself.

Now that Laura has tentatively classified the problem as one involving state civil law, she needs to determine whether the question is substantive or procedural. In essence, Laura's question is whether she can recover damages for her torment. This type of question is really at the heart of substantive law—that is, determining whether someone has done something wrong. But if she decides that the day care center has legally goofed, she would then also become interested in state civil procedural law—that is, how Laura's case gets into court and stays there until she recovers.

So Laura's next task is to determine under which civil substantive law category her problem falls. By skimming the list of substantive civil law topics in Chapter 4, she quickly narrows the issue down to "torts." Why? Because Laura suffered an injury—emotional suffering—that was arguably caused by the day care center's failure to properly maintain their equipment. Whether Laura can recover money for her suffering under the law of torts remains to be determined.

Select a Background Resource

Now that she has narrowed the issue—a state, civil, substantive tort—Laura needs to select an appropriate legal background resource to supply an overview of the part of tort law that is relevant to her problem. Basically, Laura wants to find out whether the day care center has wronged her in some way—as opposed to Amy—and if so, whether her injury qualifies for damages. Finally, she wants to know what she must show to prove her case. For example, is her testimony enough, or does she need doctors' reports?

Because Laura is in California, a good place to start is with the encyclopedia known as *California Jurisprudence* (*Cal. Jur.*), which we discussed earlier in Chapter 5. In California (and the other states that have state-specific encyclopedias published by one of the major law publishers), this type of publication would be found in any medium to large law library, such as the average county library. It is important to note that *Cal. Jur.* is published in three series. The third series, *Cal. Jur. 3d,* is the most up-to-date and the one you want to use.

Many California researchers start instead with the set called *Summary of California Law.* This series, originally by California legal scholar Bernard Witkin, will give you a quick fix on a legal issue. The other Witkin sets are *California Criminal Law, California Procedure* and *California Evidence.*

Use the Legal Index

Now that Laura has selected a background resource for her project, she needs to deal with the index. This involves writing down as many words and phrases as she can think of that relate to her specific fact situation. (See Chapter 4.) Some of these might be:

- emotional distress
- emotional upset
- emotional suffering
- mental suffering
- negligence
- carelessness
- injury
- child
- parent and child
- anxiety
- damages
- shock
- fright
- sleeplessness
- nightmares

Her next step is to look in the general index of *Cal. Jur. 3d*. While a number of the words and phrases that we listed above would ultimately lead her to the proper discussion, the phrase that will strike pay dirt the fastest is "emotional distress." As you can see from the index entry set out below, this phrase refers you to another entry titled "Pain, Suffering, and Mental Disturbance."

CAL JUR 3d GENERAL INDEX

Consulting that heading in the same index, Laura finds a great number of entries. The first one that appears relevant is "intentional infliction of emotional distress," shown below:

CAL JUR 3d GENERAL INDEX

PAIN, SUFFERING, AND MENTAL DISTURBANCE—Cont'd

Evidence—Cont'd
- judicial notice of physical harm resulting from mental suffering, Evid § 49
- opinion testimony concerning pain, admissibility of, Evid §§ 533, 536

Family and relatives

 generally, Asslt, etc. § 103; Fam Law §§ 552, 554
- child, inflicting pain on, Asslt, Crim L § 2008
- disfigurement of other member of family, recovery for having to see, Damg § 76
- fear of safety of, Damg § 73
- witnessing injury to relative, right to recover for, Negi § 76

Feelings, recovery of damages for injury to, Damg §§ 27, 34

Forcible entry or detainer, damages for mental anguish, Eject § 96

Fraud and deceit, recovery of damages for mental anguish, Fraud § 94

Fright and Shock (this index)

Future pain and suffering, Damg §§ 37, 60, 73, 74

General damages, Damg § 21

Healing Arts and Institutions (this index)

High blood pressure caused by, Damg § 75

Homicide victim, necessity of showing suffering, Crim L § 1633

Impact on person, necessity of showing, Damg § 75

Insurance Contracts and Coverage (this index)

→ Intentional infliction of emotional distress

 generally, Asslt, etc., §§ 98-104
- abuse of process, Asslt, etc. § 19
- abusive language, emotional distress caused by, Asslt, etc. § 103
- apartment, manager's abuse of tenant causing emotional distress, Asslt, etc. § 103
- awareness, susceptibility to emotional distress, Asslt, etc. § 102
- damages

 generally, Damg § 73
- - physical injury, recovery of damages without, Asslt, etc. §§ 98, 101, 102
- debt collection, creditor's outrageous method causing emotional distress, Asslt, etc. § 103; Com & Cr A § 7
- defamation, defense of privilege for infliction of emotional distress, Asslt, etc. § 104
- defenses, infliction of emotional distress, Asslt, etc. §§ 100, 104
- definition, Asslt, etc. § 98

PAIN, SUFFERING, AND MENTAL DISTURBANCE—Cont'd

Intentional infliction of emotional distress —Cont'd
- **Embarrassment, Humiliation, and Disgrace** (this index)
- employer's conduct causing emotional distress, Asslt, etc. § 103
- false imprisonment, recovery for damages for infliction of emotional distress, Asslt, etc. §§ 88, 90
- forcible entry or detainer, Eject § 96
- fraud and deceit, Fraud § 94
- insulting language, infliction of emotional distress, Asslt, etc. § 103
- intent to inflict emotional distress, Asslt, etc. § 100
- jury question, outrageous or unreasonable conduct, Asslt, etc. § 101
- knowledge as affecting susceptibility to emotional distress, Asslt, etc. § 102
- landlord's abuse of tenant causing emotional distress, Asslt, etc. § 103
- language, inflicting emotional distress, Asslt, etc. § 103
- libel and slander, Asslt, etc. § 104
- malicious prosecution, recovery for mental suffering caused by, Asslt, etc. § 342
- master and servant, conduct causing emotional distress, Asslt, etc. § 103
- moral abuse sufficient to establish emotional distress, Asslt, etc. § 103
- Negro, abusive treatment of, Asslt, etc. § 103
- official proceedings, privilege covering statements causing emotional distress in course of Asslt, etc., § 104
- outrageous conduct, recovery for, Asslt, etc. §§ 101-103
- physical injury
- - damages recoverable for, Asslt, etc. §§ 98, 101, 102
- - glandular imbalance as, Asslt, etc. § 102
- - intent as element of recovery for, Asslt, etc. § 100
- - judicial notice, Evid § 49
- - miscarriage, Asslt, etc. § 102
- - nervous system, conduct causing shock to, Asslt, etc. § 102
- - outrageous or unreasonable conduct as justifying recovery without, Asslt, etc. §§ 101, 102
- - suicide as, Asslt, etc. § 102
- privacy, invasion of privacy distinguished from pain, suffering, and mental disturbance, Asslt, etc. §§ 99, 107, 124
- privilege, defense, Asslt, etc. §§ 100, 104

161

Cal. Jur. 3d **General Index**

While Laura might get confused at this point (it is here that a law school education would probably pay off a little) and start reading some of these discussions, she would soon decide that her case probably does not qualify for "intentional" infliction of emotional distress. While the day care center may have been impermissibly careless, they in no way "intended" to cause Laura the anxiety or to hurt Amy.

In fact, by again consulting the list of civil law topics in Chapter 4 (see the entry for torts), Laura determines that the day care center may have been negligent—that is, more careless than a hypothetical "reasonable person" would have been under the circumstances. Once having determined that the emotional distress resulted from negligence rather than from an intentional act, Laura logically follows up on the subentry "Negligence," shown below.

The Difference Between Negligence and Intentional Torts

The difference between negligence and intentional torts is not always as clear-cut as this example might suggest. Generally, any action or inaction can be intentional as well as negligent, and cases such as Laura's are usually prosecuted on the basis of both approaches. For the purpose of this chapter, however, let's stick with negligence.

CAL JUR 3d GENERAL INDEX

PAIN, SUFFERING, AND MENTAL DISTURBANCE—Cont'd

Intentional infliction of emotional distress —Cont'd

- proximate cause, outrageous conduct as, Asslt, etc. § 100
- racial insults, Asslt, etc. § 103
- relationship between parties as affecting recovery of damages, Asslt, etc. § 103; Negl § 76
- severe emotional distress, compensable without physical injury, Asslt, etc. §§ 98, 101, 102
- sole reaction, recovery for emotional suffering as, Asslt, etc. § 102
- susceptibility, generally, Asslt, etc. §§ 102, 103
- unprivileged conduct, Asslt, etc. § 100
- unreasonable conduct, recovery without consequent injury, Asslt, etc. § 101
- witnesses, official proceeding as privileged, Asslt, etc. § 104
- words, generally, Asslt, etc. § 103

Libel and slander, recovery of damages for emotional distress, Asslt, etc. § 104

Malicious prosecution, recovery for mental suffering, Asslt, etc. § 342

Negligence

generally, Negl §§ 74-76
- pleading, Negl § 154
- witnessing injury to third person, Negl §§ 7, 76

Nervous disturbance caused by mental suffering, Asslt, etc. § 102; Damg § 75

Nuisances (this index)

Per diem allowance for pain and suffering, Damg § 60

Physical injury

generally, Damg § 75
- intentional infliction of emotional distress, supra

Physician, opinion of causing pain and suffering, Damg § 73

Privacy, invasion of privacy distinguished from pain, suffering, and mental disturbance, Asslt, etc. §§ 99, 107, 124

Property, recovery for mental anguish for damages to, Damg § 67

Question of fact, mental suffering as, Asslt, etc. § 101; Damg §§ 73, 149

Remoteness of damages, Damg §§ 73, 77

Search and seizure, recovery for mental suffering resulting from wrongful, Crim L § 379

Speculativeness of damages, Damg § 73

Telegrams, mental distress as element of damages in actions involving, Tel & Tel § 40

PAIN, SUFFERING, AND MENTAL DISTURBANCE—Cont'd

Third party, injury to, Damg §§ 73, 76

Trespass, mental suffering flowing from, Damg § 73

Work Injury Compensation (this index)

Wrongful death. Death and Death Actions (this index)

Zone of danger, necessity of person being in, Damg § 76

PAINT AND PAINTING

Licensing of painting contractors, Bldg Contr § 22

Scrapings of paint admissible as evidence, Crim L § 2531

PAINTINGS

Exemption of paintings and portraits from liens, Hotel, etc. § 43

PAJAMAS

Regulation of sale of pajamas with potential inflammability hazards, Consumer L § 60

PALMISTRY

Fortunetelling (this index)

PALMPRINTS

Accused's identification by palmprints, Crim L § 955

PAMPHLETS

Circulars, Brochures, and Pamphlets (this index)

PANDERING

Prostitution and Related Offenses (this index)

PANTOMIME

Witness using pantomime in describing motions, Evid § 596

PAPER AND PAPER PRODUCTS

Counterfeiting, circulation of paper used as money in absence of authority as crime, Crim L § 2818

PAPERS

Books and Papers (this index)

Newspapers and Press Associations (this index)

Service of papers. Process and Service of Process and Papers (this index)

Transmission of Messages or Papers (this index)

PAR

Par and Non-Par Values (this index)

162   **Fig. 12-3**

Cal. Jur. 3d **General Index**

Because "negligence, generally" is a subentry to "pain, suffering, and mental disturbance," Laura might well find a discussion of her topic under the indicated sections (§§ 7 and 74-76).

If Laura had decided to use "negligence" as her first search term instead of "emotional distress," she would have gotten to the same place. Consider the index entry under "Negligence," shown below.

CAL JUR 3d GENERAL INDEX

NEGLIGENCE—Cont'd

Emergency—Cont'd
- awareness of danger, duty, Negl §§ 28, 29, 30, 32
- exemption from liability, Negl § 5
- good Samaritan laws, Negl § 5
- last clear chance doctrine, effect of sudden emergency, Negl § 134
- normal response by third person faced with, effect on causation, Negl §§ 64, 65
- standard of care. Negl § 32
- vehicles. Emergency Vehicles (this index)
- violation of statute, etc., effect of emergency justifying, Negl §§ 32, 104

→ Emotional distress. Pain, Suffering, and Mental Disturbance (this index)

Employer and Employee (this index)

Endorser of product, liability to purchaser, Negl § 11

Engine
- applicability of res ipsa loquitur to engine water cap breaking, Negl § 191
- fire engine making test run, applicability of res ipsa loquitur doctrine to, Negl § 146

Engineers. Architects, Engineers, and Surveyors (this index)

Entrustment, generally, Negl §§ 13, 15

Equity, loss of legal remedy through negligence as availability of equitable relief, Equity § 10

Escalators. Elevators and Escalators (this index)

Estoppel and Waiver (this index)

Evidence and witnesses
- admissibility
    generally, Negl §§ 159, 199-204
- - circumstantial evidence, Negl § 199
- - custom or usage as bearing on issue of negligence, Negl § 24
- - expert testimony, Negl § 204
- - firearms, ordinance prohibiting use and possession of, Negl § 109
- - prior accidents, Negl §§ 200, 201
- - statutory, etc., violation, Negl § 109
- - subsequent accidents or injuries, Negl § 202
- - subsequent repairs or precautions, Negl § 203
- - violation of statute, etc., Negl § 109
- circumstantial evidence, supra
- contributory negligence, Negl § 162
- cross-examination to show prior injuries of plaintiff, Negl § 200
- discovered peril, defendant's knowledge of, Negl § 132

NEGLIGENCE—Cont'd

Evidence and witnesses—Cont'd
- expert and opinion evidence, infra
- habit or custom of care as evidence of due care, Evid § 207
- instructions to jury related to issues arising from, Negl § 207
- insurance coverage, exclusion of evidence as to, Evid § 200
- pleading and proof, variance between, Negl §§ 155, 159
- preponderance of evidence. Presumptions and burden of proof, infra
- presumptions and burden of proof, infra
- prior injury, knowledge of, Negl § 200
- proximate or legal cause, Negl §§ 49, 162
- Res Ipsa Loquitur (this index)
- statute, etc., violation of. Violation of statute, ordinance, safety order, or company rule, infra
- subsequent accidents as, Elect § 22; Negl §§ 58, 202
- third person, witnessing injury to, Negl §§ 7, 76, 81
- variance between pleading and proof, Negl §§ 155, 159
- violation of statute, ordinance, safety order, or company rule, infra

Examinations. Inspections and inspectors, infra

Exculpatory clauses in leases, validity of, Negl § 4

Executors and Administrators (this index)

Exemplary damages. Punitive Damages (this index)

Exemptions
- agreements granting, Negl § 4
- civil defense, Negl § 5
- Good Samaritan laws, Negl § 5
- public policy, exceptions to statutory basis of liability supported by, Negl § 3
- statutory exemptions, generally, Negl § 5

Exhibitions. Amusements and Exhibitions (this index)

Experiments and Tests (this index)

Expert and opinion evidence
    generally, Negl §§ 169, 204
- negligence as fact for jury, Evid § 483

Explosions and Explosives (this index)

Factors and Commission Merchants (this index)

Fact questions. Questions of Law and Fact (this index)

Falls and Falling Objects (this index)

Family and Relatives (this index)

Fan in theater falling, applicability of res ipsa loquitur to, Negl § 191

15

Cal. Jur. 3d General Index

Get an Overview of Your Research Topic

The three pages shown below contain the actual discussion in *Cal. Jur. 3d* on negligent infliction of emotional distress. It indicates that a person can recover damages for emotional or mental distress by the negligent acts of another so long as some type of physical injury is associated with the distress. A shock to the nervous system can constitute such a physical injury, according to the discussion in § 75. Read the sections for yourself.

---

§ 74   NEGLIGENCE

2. EMOTIONAL DISTRESS (§§ 74–76]

§ 74. In general

In an action based on negligence, at least where there is a physical impact, the plaintiff may recover for mental anguish or suffering, in addition to any damages he may recover for physical injuries.[27] And damages are recoverable for mental distress caused by tortious infliction of damage to property, unaccompanied by physical injuries.[28] In a personal injury action, however, emotional distress, unaccompanied by a physical impact is not a compensable injury[29] unless such emotional distress results in a physical injury or illness.[30]

in tort actions, generally, see DAMAGES §§ 58 et seq.

27. *Sloane v Southern C. R. Co., 111 C 668, 44 P 320; Merrill v Los Angeles G. & E. Co., 158 C 499, 111 P 534; Easton v United Trade School Contracting Co., 173 C 199, 159 P 597; Deevy v Tassi, 21 C2d 109, 130 P2d 389; Capelouto v Kaiser Foundation Hospitals, 7 C3d 889, 103 Cal Rptr 856, 500 P2d 880.*

Mental suffering is regarded as an aggravation of damage if it ensues naturally from the defendant's wrongful act. *Sloane v Southern C. R. Co., 111 C 668, 44 P 320.*

28. *Crisci v Security Ins. Co., 66 C2d 425, 58 Cal Rptr 13, 426 P2d 173; Windeler v Scheers Jewelers, 8 CA3d 844, 88 Cal Rptr 39.*

A title company insuring real property against liens and encumbrances of record, negligently failing to discover or disclose a recorded lien or encumbrance or failing to exclude a known recorded lien or encumbrance from coverage, and which, on being notified of the existence of the recorded lien or encumbrance, unjustifiably refuses to take legal action to clear the title or eliminate the cloud, is liable to the purchaser in compensatory damages

for any emotional distress that results. It was entirely foreseeable that plaintiffs would suffer mental anguish and distress when apprised of defendant's negligence since they relied on the preliminary report. *Jarchow v Transamerica Title Ins. Co., 48 CA3d 917, 122 Cal Rptr 470 (ovrld Quezada v Hart, 67 CA3d 754, 136 Cal Rptr 815 noting that the Jarchow Case involved a willful refusal to take action to clear title, and stating that to the extent that the court in Jarchow purported to allow recovery for emotional suffering in cases involving negligence without bad faith and without physical injury, the extension of prior California law was unwarranted).*

Annotations: Recovery for mental shock or distress in connection with injury to or interference with tangible property, 28 ALR2d 1070; Recovery for mental anguish or emotional distress, absent independent physical injury, consequent upon breach of contract in connection with sale of real property, 61 ALR3d 922.

Law Review: 49 CLR 758 (recovery of damages for mental suffering arising from breach of contract).

29. *Sloane v Southern C. R. Co.,*

250   46 Cal Jur 3d

Cal. Jur. 3d, **Negligent Infliction of Emotional Distress**

NEGLIGENCE

§ 75. Physical injury without impact

Since California is a "no impact" jurisdiction, it is not necessary in order for plaintiff to recover damages for physical injuries resulting from emotional distress to show that he also suffered a contemporaneous physical impact on his person.[31] Thus, a plaintiff who, as a result of the defendant's negligence, has suffered an emotional trauma resulting in a nervous disturbance or disorder may recover damages. Such shocks to the nervous system are classified as physical injuries.[32]

111 C 668, 44 P 320; *Easton v United Trade School Contracting Co.*, 173 C 199, 159 P 597.

In parents' action based on hospital's negligence in delivering wrong baby, there was no error in instructing the jury that mental suffering alone would not support an action for damages, and that if the only injury suffered was mental suffering, plaintiffs could not recover. *Espinosa v Beverly Hospital*, 114 CA2d 232, 249 P2d 843.

There can be no recovery for emotional distress unaccompanied by physical harm arising from acts solely negligent in nature. *Gautier v General Tel. Co.*, 234 CA2d 302, 44 Cal Rptr 404.

Annotation: Right to recover for mental pain and anguish alone, apart from other damages, 23 ALR 361, 44 ALR 438, 56 ALR 657.

Form: Instruction to jury that damages are not recoverable for mental suffering caused by negligence without simultaneous physical impact or injury, 12 Am Jur Pl & Pr Forms (Rev), Fright, Shock, and Mental Disturbance, Form 5.

30. As to recovery for physical injury resulting from emotional trauma but unaccompanied by physical impact, see §§ 75, 76, *infra*.

As to the measure and elements of compensatory damages for mental anguish and suffering, generally, see DAMAGES §§ 73 et seq.

31. *Dillon v Legg*, 68 C2d 728, 69 Cal Rptr 72, 441 P2d 912, 29 ALR3d 1316; *Cook v Maier*, 33 CA2d 581, 92 P2d 434; *Vanoni v Western Airlines*, 247 CA2d 793, 56 Cal Rptr 115.

32. *Lindley v Knowlton*, 179 C 298, 176 P 440; *Di Mare v Cresci*, 58 C2d 292, 23 Cal Rptr 772, 373 P2d 860.

In an action against the driver of a vehicle which collided with and killed plaintiff's wife, plaintiff's gastric condition constituted sufficient physical injury if it could be fairly said that it was caused by the husband's shock occasioned by his perception of the collision. *Krouse v Graham*, 19 C3d 59, 137 Cal Rptr 863, 562 P2d 1022.

Where plaintiff was shocked at finding a brush which he thought was a spider in his bottle and believed he had swallowed a part of it, the experience caused him such an emotional paroxysm as to result in compensable physical suffering and worry. *Medeiros v Coca-Cola Bottling Co.*, 57 CA2d 707, 135 P2d 676.

Shock to the nerves and nervous system sufficed as an allegation of physical manifestation. *Vanoni v Western Airlines*, 247 CA2d 793, 56 Cal Rptr 115.

Cal. Jur. 3d, Negligent Infliction of Emotional Distress (continued)

§ 76   NEGLIGENCE

§ 76.   —Witnessing injury to third person

A person may recover damages for physical injuries resulting from emotional trauma upon witnessing the tortious infliction of death or injury on a third party even though the person suffering such damages was not in the zone of danger arising out of the tortious conduct. Recovery in such a situation depends on whether harm to the plaintiff was reasonably foreseeable.[33] In determining whether a defendant should reasonably foresee the injury, the court will take into account such factors as the following: (1) whether plaintiff was located near the scene of the accident as contrasted with one who was a distance from it; (2) whether the shock resulted from a direct emotional impact upon plaintiff from the sensory and contemporaneous observance of the accident, as contrasted with learning of the accident from others after its occurrence; and (3) whether plaintiff and the victim were closely related, as contrasted with an absence of any relationship or the presence of only a distant relationship.[34]

Annotations: Recovery for physical consequences of fright resulting in a physical injury, 11 ALR 1119, 40 ALR 983, 76 ALR 681, 98 ALR 402; Right to recover for emotional disturbance or its physical consequences, in absence of impact or other actionable wrong, 64 ALR2d 100.

Law Review: 24 CLR 229 (recovery of damages for nervous shock without impact).

Forms: Complaint for damages for physical injuries resulting from shock and fright, 12 Am Jur Pl & Pr Forms (Rev), Fright, Shock, and Mental Disturbance, Form 1; Instruction to jury as to damages recoverable for bodily pain and suffering resulting from fright, 12 Am Jur Pl & Pr Forms (Rev), Fright, Shock, and Mental Disturbance, Form 6.

Practice Reference: Liability for injury without impact, 15 Cal Practice, Model Personal Injury Action § 250:12.

33. *Dillon v Legg, 68 C2d 728, 69 Cal Rptr 72, 441 P2d 912, 29 ALR3d 1316* (ovrlg to the extent inconsistent herewith *Amaya v Home Ice, Fuel & Supply Co., 59 C2d 295, 29 Cal Rptr 33, 379 P2d 513*).

34. Obviously, a defendant is more likely to foresee that a mother who observes an accident affecting her child will suffer harm than to foretell that a stranger witness will do so. Similarly, the degree of foreseeability of the third person's injury is far greater in the case of his contemporaneous observation of the accident than that in which he subsequently learns of it. The defendant is more likely to foresee that shock to the nearby, witnessing mother will cause physical harm than to anticipate that someone distant from the accident will suffer more than a temporary emotional reaction. *Dillon v Legg, 68 C2d 728, 69 Cal Rptr 72, 441 P2d 912, 29 ALR3d 1316.*

Cal. Jur. 3d, Negligent Infliction of Emotional Distress (continued)

Laura would then turn to the pocket part to see whether these articles had been updated in any significant way. Assume for a moment that she doesn't find anything.

If she stopped here, she would have to conclude, according to § 75 of the *Cal. Jur. 3d* article on negligence, that California law prohibits her from collecting anything from the day care center for the distress that she suffered. Why? Because according to this discussion, recovery for personal injuries resulting from negligence requires at least some physical manifestation of the injury, and Laura did not experience any physical symptom or injury.

Remember, however, that background resources provide a start for good legal research, but never a finish. Laura now needs to check out the primary law on which the article is based. If a statute exists, this is the first place to go. But there is no California statute covering this subject (and none is mentioned in the articles), and, after some rummaging in the California codes, Laura would come to this conclusion. Next Laura should review the cases on which the article is based. Turning back to § 74, Laura notes that the article refers to several cases in footnote 29.

The lead case is *Sloane v. Southern C.R. Co.*, but further along *Espinosa v. Beverly Hospital* and *Gautier v. General Tel. Co.* are also cited as authority for the proposition that you can't recover for negligently inflicted emotional distress without a physical injury. The full footnote is shown below.

---

29. *Sloane v Southern C. R. Co.,*

111 C 668, 44 P 320; Easton v United Trade School Contracting Co., 173 C 199, 159 P 597.

In parents' action based on hospital's negligence in delivering wrong baby, there was no error in instructing the jury that mental suffering alone would not support an action for damages, and that if the only injury suffered was mental suffering, plaintiffs could not recover. *Espinosa v Beverly Hospital, 114 CA2d 232, 249 P2d 843.*

There can be no recovery for emotional distress unaccompanied by physical harm arising from acts solely negligent in nature. *Gautier v General Tel. Co., 234 CA2d 302, 44 Cal Rptr 404.*

Annotation: Right to recover for mental pain and anguish alone, apart from other damages, 23 ALR 361, 44 ALR 438, 56 ALR 657.

Form: Instruction to jury that damages are not recoverable for mental suffering caused by negligence without simultaneous physical impact or injury, 12 Am Jur Pl & Pr Forms (Rev), Fright, Shock, and Mental Disturbance, Form 5.

Footnote From *Cal. Jur. 3d* Entry

If Laura read these cases, she would learn that they state the law pretty much as the article describes; that is, a person can't recover for emotional distress caused by negligence unless there is a related physical injury. But these cases are quite old. The *Sloane* case, in fact, was decided in the nineteenth century.

Even though the encyclopedia didn't indicate that any changes have occurred—remember, we assumed that for the purposes of this example—Laura can't necessarily rely on that fact. The publishers of background resources like encyclopedias may not be aware of important new cases until a year or two (or even longer) after they are decided. While every attempt is made by the publishers to keep these resources up-to-date, important changes often slip through their fingers.

Therefore, until Laura has determined that the *Sloane* case (and the other cases) are still "good law," her research is not complete. Her next step is accordingly to use *Shepard's* case citations to find out whether these cases are still good law.

Use *Shepard's Citations for Cases*

To begin, Laura would locate the *Sloane* case in *Shepard's*. Looking back to footnote 29, the *Sloane* case is followed by two citations. These are parallel citations (explained in Chapter 9), which means that the *Sloane* case can be found in two different sets of case reports.

Often there are separate *Shepard's* for each separate case report set. In this situation, for example, there is a *Shepard's* for the *Pacific Reporter* (the "P" in 44 P. 320) and a *Shepard's* for cases located in the *California Reports* (the "C" in 111 C. 668) and California cases cited in the *Pacific Reporter*. (*Shepard's* uses its own system of abbreviations for reporters instead of following the Harvard bluebook form. If you refer to cases in court documents, you should use the bluebook's system.)

If Laura finds herself getting hazy at this point, she should turn back to Chapter 10, and review the material there. *Shepard's* is among the most difficult aspects of legal research to learn, but she should take time and regroup before going on.

Let's assume that her law library has both the *Pacific Reporter* and *California Reporter* (obviously, other reports would be relevant if researching this question in another state). We'll use the *Pacific Reporter* citation to *Shepardize Sloane*. Laura would therefore want to locate the volumes of *Shepard's* that are keyed to the *Pacific Reporter*. These will be shelved either in a central location along with all the other *Shepard's*, or immediately after the most current volumes of the *Pacific Reporter*.

Upon locating these volumes, she'll find several hardcover volumes and paperbound updates, reflecting the fact that *Shepard's* is updated in paperback every few months. Remember, you have not *Shepardized* a case until you have checked it through *all* the *Shepard's* volumes that cover the period from the day the case was decided to the most recent monthly update. The most recent update available when this example was prepared was February 1997. By the time you read this, new update pamphlets will be available and you can practice by doing some further updating for yourself.

When we did this research, there were twelve bound *Shepard's* on the shelf. These are Volume 1, Parts 1, 2, 3, 4 and 5, and Volume 2, Parts 1, 2, 3, 4, 5, 6 and 7. These cover all cases through 1994. These are followed by a hardbound volume called "Supplement 1994-1996," and then by a red paperback labeled "CUMULATIVE SUPPLEMENT January 1997," which contains citations to cases decided between the issuance of the hardbound series and January 1997. Last is a white paperback called "ADVANCE SHEET EDITION," dated February, 1997.

To look up the *Pacific Reporter* cite for the *Sloane* case, Laura starts with the book that includes the number 44 (the volume number of the *Pacific Reporter* where *Sloane* is reported), which happens to be Volume 1, Part 1. After pulling this volume, she locates the page in *Shepard's* where this number first appears and flips through to where a -320- appears (the page number where the *Sloane* case starts in the *Pacific Reporter*). There she will find a list of citations to cases that have cited *Sloane* for one reason or another. If she reviewed each of these cases, she would find that most resulted in no change in the law. The cases that do represent a change are outlined below.

Vol. 44 PACIFIC REPORTER

101P[2]926
116P754
e124P[2]541
d137P[2]282
236P[1]331
272P[2]1098
4P2d[1]140
34P2d508
51P2d[1]901
51P2d[2]901
59P2d1003
73P2d[1]626
73P2d[2]626
94P2d[1]1061
101P2d[2]1111
116P2d[2]493
128P2d[2]195
128P2d[1]197
144P2d[2]823
j144P2d[1]836
e144P2d842
144P2d[1]843
144P2d[2]843
j207P2d[2]12
98CaR[2]584
Utah
280P[1]737
Ga
49SE315
Iowa
154NW342
154NW354
Minn
108NW481
W Va
96SE943
Wis
107NW463
150ÆR644n
150ÆR645n
150ÆR657n

– 309 –
(111Cal588)
s53P410
128P[4]750
4P2d[4]980
39P2d[1]880
214P2d[4]410
214P2d[1]411
44CaR[3]615
Idaho
241P[4]1016
5ÆR1226n
3Æ2 1316n
3Æ2 1363n

– 312 –
(111Cal648)
50P[3]680
55P[1]990
57P[4]1069
92P[2]499
95P[4]380
117P[3]791
165P[3]563
193P[3]166
214P[3]239
235P[1]660
d242P505
e257P[2]559
260P[4]910
d262P[4]448
263P[4]311
f265P[3]897
d295P[3]906

j8P2d[4]122
94P2d[3]622
262P2d[3]635
276P2d[4]46
d276P2d[3]848
288P2d[3]636
461P2d[3]365
500P2d[3]615
17CaR[3]116
19CaR[4]464
82CaR[3]165
103CaR[3]703
109CaR[3]740
122CaR[3]10
Ariz
136P[3]282
Mont
f77P[2]54
Nev
145P[2]926
Wash
118P[3]922
Mich
81NW925
134NW688
Nebr
212NW611
So C
67SE317
SD
97NW387
234NW624
4Æ3 680n

– 314 –
(111Cal616)
j45P995
54P[5]590
55P[5]1060
57P[6]572
57P[3]771
57P[3]781
75P[6]103
99P[6]201
114P[8]833
115P[8]316
143P[1]1080
147P[3]471
240P518
253P[8]741
286P[6]478
d15P2d540
145P2d[1]595
145P2d[2]596
152P2d[1]245
213P2d[3]115
j245P2d[6]305
287P2d[5]200
j524P2d[8]848
570P2d[8]1052
595P2d[8]95
74CaR[8]23
j115CaR[5]376
141CaR[8]700
f142CaR[3]709
144CaR[8]235
d147CaR[8]221
j147CaR[8]223
147CaR[5]680
153CaR[8]710
155CaR[8]661
157CaR[8]297
157CaR[8]353
175CaR[8]710
d180CaR715
j180CaR717

223CaR[8]739
f229CaR[8]282
Cir. 9
116F[8]486
Idaho
156P105
216P[8]734
Nev
212P2d716
NM
191P[4]454
Wyo
d92P2d[8]556
Ala
100So671
La
129So731
5So2d361
Mo
113SW1065
Nebr
94NW530
ND
149NW357
95Æ2 354n

– 318 –
(112Cal4)
s34P712
52P[2]827
72P351
73P182
73P829
74P701
92P[1]501
d96P[1]910 →
116P[1]307
124P[2]1001
151P[1]393
169P[2]1001
196P[1]906
217P[1]89
261P520
58P2d[1]190
79P2d198
e289P2d[1]578
298P2d[2]687
58CaR73
Idaho
85P[1]491
90P[1]341
165P2d[1]298
Mont
74P76
Utah
55P[2]382
f84P[2]892
88P[1]671
156ÆR1197n

– 319 –
(111Cal639)
s49P577
cc77P1113
54P532
d57P599
62P58
67P787
67P1056
d70P[1]665
j73P465
74P770
77P660
91P[1]590
100P[1]1083
104P474

151P153
157P15
167P198
171P[1]419
184P25
191P1023
195P[1]273
233P333
240P295
260P350
265P855
60P2d478
75P2d598
Cir. 9
d114F[1]993
260F[1]510
142FS[1]110
206FS[1]442
Idaho
211P536
Mont
124P[1]516
Nev
66P953
Utah
125P[1]869
202P[1]818
Iowa
96NW1082
Va
139SE311
Wis
72NW393
55ÆR1388n

– 320 –
(111Cal668)
p70P118
50P[9]29
53P[1]645
55P[9]327
58P[9]317
61P[6]943
62P[6]307
d63P[2]681
65P479
65P1089
f70P[2]626
83P[1]271
89P[2]851
91P[2]523
92P[1]86
94P[1]854
105P[1]739
108P[1]329
e131P[9]325
137P[5]1087
155P[1]840
159P[1]599
174P[8]308
f176P[3]441
d193P[1]132
d228P738
255P289
261P[6]764
280P[2]166
280P[2]396
13P2d[1]774
67P2d[2]688
77P2d[2]836
92P2d[2]436
107P2d[2]616
130P2d[2]396
f198P2d[2]699
210P2d[2]255
217P2d[1]117

249P2d[2]845
258P2d[2]58
265P2d[2]551
f266P2d[2]819
270P2d[2]945
292P2d[7]83
d319P2d[3]81
353P2d[2]300
373P2d[2]865
d379P2d[2]515
j379P2d[2]531
f441P2d[2]917
f610P2d[1]1334
j610P2d1338
e616P2d[9]817
e616P2d[2]820
5CaR[2]692
17CaR[1]272
17CaR[2]272
17CaR[2]572
23CaR[1]135
23CaR[2]777
d29CaR[2]35
j29CaR[2]51
35CaR[7]330
44CaR[2]407
56CaR117
f69CaR[2]77
88CaR[2]43
136CaR[2]277
f164CaR[1]843
j164CaR847
e167CaR[9]835
e167CaR[2]838
j206CaR6
208CaR[1]533
208CaR[6]533
212CaR856
Cir. 1
396FS1184
Cir. 5
159F[2]7
Cir. 6
237F[3]60
Cir. 8
240F2d[6]756
572FS1204
Cir. 9
100F[3]750
119F404
Cir. 10
244FS[9]315
Idaho
111P[3]1085
Mont
28P2d[2]866
Nev
173P1159
Okla
89P2d[2]778
518P2d[3]59
549P2d[2]396
Ore
51P2d[2]667
Ala
73So208
Ark
45SW352
Fla
42So712
Ga
47SE207
Ind
105NE398

Iowa
73NW1058
80NW678
94NW924
98NW282
126NW781
Md
73At692
98At241
408A2d732
Minn
115NW401
Nebr
203NW648
NY
126NE650
62NYS893
NC
42SE985
69SE635
Ohio
95NE886
193NE749
RI
66At208
So C
29SE909
103SE271
Tenn
194SW902
Tex
54SW945
W Va
95SE800
Wis
123NW626
11ÆR1135n
23ÆR365n
36ÆR1025n
36ÆR1031n
122ÆR1493n
18Æ2 223n
72Æ2 585n

– 325 –
(111Cal662)
d132P[3]775
159P[2]184
288P[2]794
Colo
88P847
Utah
56P2d[1]7
NY
94NE198

– 327 –
Case 1
(5CaU303)
(111Cal xvi)
44P1067

– 327 –
Case 2
(111Cal646)
s27P1094
s28P579
155P625
176P[2]183
f244P[1]331
268P[1]630
61CaR[1]589

– 328 –
(5CaU304)
(111Cal xvii)

cc41P1012
cc53P46

– 330 –
(112Cal42)
49P[1]184
50P[1]399
55P404
59P310
Cir. 9
96F741
96F[2]742

– 331 –
(112Cal91)
61P[1]375
81P129
84P[1]1009
86P[1]985
87P[1]417
88P509
99P[1]397
106P268
152P[1]914
191P[1]969
203P[1]111
238P[1]1104
253P[1]354
284P[1]1049
286P[1]499
f287P[1]152
f287P[1]515
10P2d[1]184
56P2d[1]251
110P2d[1]997
114P2d[1]44
j140P2d[1]391
154P2d[1]380
181P2d75
186P2d[1]680
241P2d[1]1056
302P2d[1]114
136CaR[1]740
Nev
140P2d[1]571

– 332 –
(112Cal14)
s71P171
h51P[1]1080
59P692
92P[1]322
112P300
112P474
e141P[1]927
165P[1]527
182P[1]58
253P782
f264P[1]245
136P2d[1]829
276P2d88
Cir. 9
1FS13
Ariz
318P2d680
Idaho
72P963
Okla
252P[1]849
Iowa
123NW192
59ÆR94n

– 333 –
(112Cal53)
49P[2]201

51P[2]717
61P[2]796
74P[1]852
113P[1]171
136P[1]59
208P329
293P[2]123
d23P2d[2]809
130P2d[2]236
47CaR[2]415
Cir. 9
75FS[1]14
Kan
57P[1]123
154P[2]1023
Utah
50P[1]630
Md
43At813
Mich
153NW721
NJ
59At153
NY
100NE725
NC
138SE432
ND
156NW207
Tex
65SW513
105SW341
11SW565
Wis
26NW150
114ÆR300n
114ÆR314n

– 336 –
(115Cal143)
r46P922
d60P[1]848
78P[1]955
26P2d680
d169P2d[2]448
5ÆR1541n
39Æ2 298n

– 339 –
(112Cal1)
s57P84
152P[1]313
192P[3]537
216P[1]404
282P[2]25
122P2d[1]62
311P2d[2]7
324P2d[1]931
d65CaR[2]779
116CaR592
Cir. 10
69F2d[1]903
Ariz
235P[1]147
Idaho
71P[1]129

– 340 –
Case 1
(112Cal38)
s44P227
cc41P465
300P[1]839
Idaho
f101P[1]598

590

Shepard's Citations for Cases: Citations for 44 P. 320

Laura can tell at once by the number of citations that the *Sloane* case received some judicial attention. Taking a closer look, she learns all of the following:

- A case reported in 610 P.2d cited the *Sloane* case on page 1334 and followed it (the "f" just in front of the citation) in regard to the legal issue summarized in headnote "1" of the *Sloane* case (the "1" just following the "2d" tells you this).
- In the same citing case, *Sloane* was cited in a dissent (the "j" in front of the cite tells you this).
- Another case reported in 616 P.2d cited the *Sloane* case on page 817 and explained (the "e" in front of the cite tells you this) the issue summarized in headnote 9 of the Sloane case (the "9" right after the "2d" tells you this).
- This same case also cited *Sloane* on page 820 and explained headnote 2 of the *Sloane* case.
- A case reported in 136 *California Reporter* (this is what the "CaR" means) cited *Sloane* for the issue summarized in headnote 2 of the *Sloane* case (the "2" directly following the "CaR" tells us this).

- The *Sloane* case is cited by a U.S. District Court case reported in 396 F. Supp. 1184.

The case reported in 616 P.2d and 167 Cal. Rptr. is *Molien v. Kaiser Hospital*, 167 Cal. Rptr. 831, 616 P.2d 813 (1980). This case changed the law on the subject of the negligent infliction of emotional distress. While *Shepard's* indicated that the *Molien* case merely explained *Sloane* (this is what the "e" means), a reading of the case would quickly tell you that the *Sloane* holding on the need for physical injury was actually overruled, and that Laura may now possibly recover damages solely for her non-physical emotional distress.

The excerpts shown below, taken from the *Molien* case as it was published in 167 *California Reporter*, illustrate first how the court deals with the *Sloane* case and then, by its holding, how it changed the law.

As early as 1896, this court recognized that mental suffering "constitutes an aggravation of damages when it naturally ensues from the act complained of." (*Sloane v. Southern Cal. Ry. Co.* (1896) 111 Cal. 668, 680, 44 P. 320, 322.) But such suffering alone, we said, would not afford a right of action. (*Ibid.*) We pondered the question whether a nervous disorder suffered by the plaintiff after she was wrongfully put off a train was a physical or a mental injury: "The interdependence of the mind and body is in many respects so close that it is impossible to distinguish their respective influence upon each other. It must be conceded that a nervous shock or paroxysm, or a disturbance of the nervous system, is distinct from mental anguish, and falls within the physiological, rather than the psychological, branch of the human organism. It is a matter of general knowledge that an attack of sudden fright, or an exposure to imminent peril, has produced in individuals a complete change in their nervous system, and rendered one who was physically strong and vigorous weak and timid. Such a result must be regarded as an injury to the body rather than to the mind, even though the mind be at the same time injuriously affected." (*Ibid.*)

The foundation was thus laid, nearly a century ago, for two beliefs that have since been frequently reiterated: first, recovery for emotional distress must be relegated to the status of parasitic damages; and second, mental disturbances can be distinctly classified as either psychological or physical injury. That medical science and particularly the field of mental health have made much progress in the 20th century is ˌmani- ˌ925 fest; yet, despite some noteworthy exceptions, the principles underlying the decision in *Sloane* still pervade the law of negligence.

The present state of the law is articulated in BAJI No. 12.80 (6th ed. 1977): "There can be no recovery of damages for emotional distress unaccompanied by physical injury where such emotional distress arises only from negligent conduct. [¶] However, if a plaintiff has suffered a shock to the nervous system or other physical harm which was proximately caused by negligent conduct of a defendant, then such plaintiff is entitled to recover damages from such a defendant for any resulting physical harm and emotional distress."

The BAJI language appears to be derived mainly from the opinions in *Vanoni v. Western Airlines* (1967) 247 Cal.App.2d 793, 795–797, 56 Cal.Rptr. 115, and *Espinosa v. Beverly Hospital* (1952) 114 Cal.App.2d 232, 234, 249 P.2d 843, both of which relied on *Sloane*. The principle has been reiterated elsewhere, but in each instance is traceable either directly or indirectly to *Sloane*. (See, e. g., *Fuentes v. Perez* (1977) 66 Cal.App.3d 163, 168, 136 Cal.Rptr. 275; *Leasman v. Beech Aircraft Corp.* (1975) 48 Cal.App.3d 376, 381, 121 Cal.Rptr. 768; *Gautier v. General Telephone Co.* (1965) 234 Cal.App.2d 302, 307, 44 Cal.Rptr. 404.) It therefore appears the rule has been immutable since its early origin, with virtually no regard for the factual contexts in which claims arose, or the alleged causes of emotional distress, or the prevailing state of medical knowledge.

Plaintiff urges that we recognize the concept of negligent infliction of emotional distress as an independent tort. In this inquiry we first seek to identify the rationale for the *Sloane* rule. None appears in the opinion, possibly because the court classified the plaintiff's condition, "nervous paroxysm," as a physical injury, and hence had no need to justify a denial of recovery for psychological injury alone. Neither did the *Espinosa* court provide any justification for its rejection of the plaintiff's attempt to "subvert the ancient rule that mental suffering alone will not support an action for damages based upon negligence." (114 Cal. App.2d at p. 234, 249 P.2d at p. 844.) Therefore, we must look elsewhere.

• • • • • • • • • • • • • •

[6, 7] For all these reasons we hold that a cause of action may be stated for the negligent infliction of serious emotional distress. Applying these principles to the case before us, we conclude that the complaint states such a cause of action. The negligent examination of Mrs. Molien and the conduct flowing therefrom are objectively verifiable actions by the defendants that foreseeably elicited serious emotional responses in the plaintiff and hence serve as a measure of the validity of plaintiff's claim ˌfor emotional distress. As yet another cor- ˌ931 roborating factor, we note the universally accepted gravity of a false imputation of syphilis: by statute it constitutes slander per se. (Civ.Code, § 46, subd. 2; *Schessler v. Keck* (1954) 125 Cal.App.2d 827, 271 P.2d 588.)

It follows that the trial court erred in sustaining the demurrer to the cause of action for emotional distress.

Excerpt From *Molien v. Kaiser Hospital*

Check the Pocket Parts

Obviously it's important that your research cover the most recent developments in the law. As we've mentioned, this means checking the pocket parts to whatever resource you are dealing with. In our example, the *Cal. Jur. 3d* pocket part must be checked for recent cases dealing with emotional distress. Earlier we asked you to assume that the pocket part showed no change. However, the pocket part shown below actually shows a considerable change in the law.

As you can see, there are several references to law review articles on negligent infliction of emotional distress, and consulting any of these would yield an in-depth discussion of the *Molien* case. However, if Laura simply skimmed over the case annotations (mostly contained on subsequent pages not reproduced here), she would find no description of the important change that *Molien* made to the law. This means that the *Cal. Jur. 3d* editors failed to expressly account for the case that changed the rules set out in the hardcover discussion, a serious error. The lesson to be drawn from this is clear: Don't rely on the annotations or updates in encyclopedias to bring you up-to-date. Instead, consult the primary law sources (and update them with *Shepard's*) as we are doing in this example. Moreover, the Shepard's "e" notation preceding the *Molien* cite was quite misleading. Sometimes a court's attempt to say in a later case what the earlier decision "really meant" goes so far as to change the earlier holding in a fundamental way.

---

§ 74. [Emotional distress] In general

Practice aids:

California's new tort of negligent infliction of serious emotional distress. (1981) 18 Cal West LR 101.

California expands liability for negligently inflicted emotional distress. (1981) 33 Hast LJ 291.

Negligent infliction of emotional distress. (1982) 33 Hast LJ 583.

Negligent infliction of emotional distress: reconciling the bystander and direct victim causes of action. (1983) 18 USF LR 145.

Negligent infliction of mental distress (1981) 8 Western LR 139.

The Dillon dilemma: A closer look at the close relationship [bystander recovery for negligent infliction of emotional distress]. (1984) 11 Western LR 271.

Bystander recovery for negligently

46 Cal Jur 3d Supp

---

§ 74 ***Cal. Jur. 3d*** *Pocket Part Entry*

NEGLIGENCE

§ 74

inflicted mental distress. 35 Am Jur Proof of Facts 2d 1.

Recoverability of compensatory damages for mental anguish or emotional distress for tortiously causing another's birth. 74 ALR4th 798.

Case authorities:

In a personal injury action arising from an automobile accident that resulted in plaintiff's injury and his unmarried cohabitant's death, the trial court did not err in sustaining defendants' demurrer to plaintiff's second cause of action for negligent infliction of emotional distress without leave to amend, which cause of action was based on plaintiff's witnessing of his cohabitant's fatal injury. The state has a strong interest in the marriage relationship, and granting unmarried cohabitants the same rights as married persons would inhibit that interest. Allowing such a cause of action would impose on courts the burden of inquiring into relationships to determine whether the emotional attachments of family exist. Further, the number of persons to whom a negligent defendant owes a duty of care must be limited. (Disapproving, insofar as they hold to the contrary, *Ledger* v. *Tippitt* (1985) 164 Cal.App.3d 625 [210 Cal.Rptr. 814], and *Mobaldi* v. *Regents of University of California* (1976) 55 Cal.App.3d 573 [127 Cal.Rptr. 720].) *Elden v Sheldon (1988) 46 Cal 3d 267, 250 Cal Rptr 254, 758 P2d 582, mod (1988) 46 Cal 3d 1003a.*

In an action in which a person seeks to recover from a tortfeasor for emotional shock based on the infliction of injury to or death of another, recovery for such emotional shock may not be had if the shock is caused by hearing of the incident of injury or death from others after occurrence of the incident. However, the fact that a person did not have a visual perception of the incident does not necessarily preclude such recovery. Mental reconstruction of the incident may provide a basis for recovery if such reconstruction occurs

46 Cal Jur 3d Supp

substantially contemporaneously with the incident. *Nazaroff v Superior Court of Santa Cruz County (1978, 1st Dist) 80 CA3d 553, 145 Cal Rptr 657.*

In an action in which the mother of an infant, who died from the effects of near drowning in defendants' swimming pool, sought recovery for physical injuries resulting from her emotional distress at witnessing the infant being pulled from the pool and in participating in attempts to revive the infant, the mother, though she had not witnessed the infant's falling into the pool, was not precluded as a matter of law from recovering for her alleged emotional distress. The mother was alerted to the pool area by a shout, which might have permitted her to reconstruct the scene, and her knowledge of what had occurred was derived from her own senses, rather than from another's recital of an uncontemporaneous event. Furthermore, drowning, or near drowning, though initiated by immersion, is not an instantaneous occurrence. *Nazaroff v Superior Court of Santa Cruz County (1978, 1st Dist) 80 CA3d 553, 145 Cal Rptr 657.*

In a situation in which a child is injured in a swimming pool, or other "attractive nuisance," and in which the child's parent seeks to recover for his or her emotional distress based on the child's injury, an apparent paradox exists in allowing such recovery, because if the parent was present at the time of the child's injury, he or she should have avoided the accident, and if the parent was not present, his or her lack of sensory and contemporaneous observance of the injury would defeat the right to recovery. However, in a rare case, the parent may sense the incident sufficiently contemporaneously with its occurrence, but too late to prevent injury to the child, and recovery for emotional distress would not be barred. *Nazaroff v Superior Court of Santa Cruz County (1978, 1st Dist) 80 CA3d 553, 145 Cal Rptr 657.*

In an action by a husband and wife against a doctor arising out of the

29

Use *Shepard's* and Digests to Find On-Point Cases

The next step is to find cases with fact situations as close as possible to yours. You can use *Shepard's Citations for Cases* and *West Digests* to find cases dealing with the legal issue you are concerned with.

Shepard's Citations for Cases

Although the *Molien* case answered a threshold question in Laura's favor (that is, she need not prove physical injury to recover), the facts of that case were not very similar to Laura's. In *Molien*, a hospital was found liable to a husband for falsely diagnosing his wife as having syphilis. In this case, however, Laura wants to recover for distress caused by the day care center's failure to properly maintain play equipment. In other words, Laura is trying to recover for distress caused by the failure to act rather than by an affirmative act. Rather than stopping her research at this point, therefore, Laura should continue to search for a case that presents facts a bit closer to her situation.

Let's first *Shepardize* the *Molien* case, using its *California Citations*. First check the volume for cases decided in 1985. As it turns out, there is no useful case. But, if Laura perseveres and turns to the supplement dated 1985-1990, she'll find the entry shown below under 167 Cal. Rptr. 831 (the *Molien* case).

The case that is referred to by the citation of "208 CaR" (which explains and follows the *Molien* case) turns out to involve emotional distress suffered by a mother as a result of the failure of her doctor to diagnose Down syndrome in an amniocentesis (a process allowing certain disabilities to be diagnosed in a fetus). In this case, the court indicates that for negligent infliction of emotional distress purposes, there is no difference between the affirmative act of misdiagnosis and the failure to diagnose. Although these facts are still not the same as Laura's, they are at least closer than those in *Molien*.

To be safe, Laura also checks the *Shepard's* California Edition's 1992-1995 bound Supplement, Part 2, and the gold and red paperback updates—but in this case, there is nothing useful.

Vol. 167 — CALIFORNIA REPORTER

234CaR²90
238CaR235
238CaR¹238

−292−
210CaR¹924
d217CaR¹275
224CaR²54
227CaR²826
242CaR¹722
261CaR²609

−296−
210CaR¹839
219CaR⁶110
226CaR721
226CaR¹722
242CaR729
247CaR640
258CaR58
e258CaR⁷286
d260CaR94
c641FS¹737

−303−
d225CaR¹574
j225CaR579

−309−
190CaR864
221CaR⁶49
238CaR³638
f263CaR868

−320−
209CaR¹153
211CaR²926
229CaR²237
232CaR¹538
234CaR²588

−326−
207CaR²436
220CaR⁴317
e221CaR⁵302

−343−
192CaR715
229CaR⁵81
241CaR866
242CaR⁶660

−348−
224CaR¹794
224CaR⁶795
j224CaR798

−351−
238CaR⁴14
238CaR¹16

−353−
215CaR453
230CaR190
245CaR⁸749
249CaR843
263CaR¹578
f263CaR²579
639FS484

−363−
259CaR¹568

−366−
207CaR⁹787
208CaR⁴378

219CaR⁹149
227CaR⁹353
250CaR410
f250CaR¹925
f250CaR⁴926
255CaR³520

−376−
208CaR696
f208CaR⁴697

−392−
209CaR¹⁶127
d216CaR
  [¹⁷242
221CaR⁴232
225CaR125
225CaR652
226CaR381
227CaR¹495
230CaR¹¹288
255CaR²⁷255
257CaR²⁵206
  EL§18.01

−402−
d215CaR775
215CaR⁹75
234CaR⁹825
236CaR¹⁸785
239CaR²219
244CaR¹⁸347
244CaR¹⁸351
f245CaR¹⁵296
246CaR402
251CaR⁹240
252CaR¹⁵797
258CaR631
470US278
84L£263
105SC²1094
53USLW
  [4182

−425−
d215CaR⁶905
216CaR⁵30
240CaR910

−429−
238CaR¹¹456

−436−
q233CaR399

−440−
216CaR¹043
216CaR⁸44
216CaR⁵45
227CaR¹⁰498
230CaR³632
236CaR⁶349
CLH§22.04

−447−
221CaR¹473
228CaR¹177

−461−
209CaR¹658
210CaR647
210CaR³648

−463−
j180CaR411
214CaR³585

214CaR⁴585
217CaR³171
235CaR329
854F2d⁵1262

−481−
s463US1234

−502−
232CaR¹539
259CaR¹840

−510−
213CaR175
219CaR¹208
243CaR³423
244CaR¹81

−516−
214CaR772
222CaR³454

−527−
219CaR¹233
222CaR¹258

−538−
e214CaR²239
e214CaR³239
e214CaR
  [¹¹239
214CaR464
753F2d1467
60BRW¹²782

−545−
229CaR²273

−549−
207CaR⁶249
240CaR¹754
240CaR³754
262CaR⁵336

−552−
224CaR⁵156
241CaR³500

−557−
211CaR¹²147
212CaR246
218CaR¹⁶437
241CaR¹¹562

−571−
207CaR³249
244CaR784
244CaR¹784
244CaR805
j244CaR809
258CaR80
258CaR86
f820F2d¹1092

−573−
211CaR²⁰648
215CaR462
216CaR143
216CaR¹⁷145
j216CaR155
217CaR⁹222
218CaR⁴834
219CaR⁴864
221CaR72
221CaR¹¹176
224CaR853

226CaR²⁰897
226CaR¹¹898
235CaR¹¹198
244CaR³888
d244CaR⁴889
d251CaR³648
255CaR²⁰693
258CaR²⁰406
12WSR409
12WSR675

−584−
212CaR561
230CaR⁷882
235CaR¹372
d235CaR373
248CaR⁹120
253CaR⁷505
253CaR⁹505
254CaR84

−595−
224CaR733
259CaR⁴786
263CaR687
596FS⁴606

−603−
211CaR169
211CaR²170
211CaR³170
236CaR²200
237CaR251

−610−
220CaR⁴623
237CaR⁴859
253CaR¹⁸800
253CaR¹⁹800
253CaR²⁰800

−629−
207CaR239
207CaR686

−636−
210CaR325
210CaR¹⁸549
212CaR210
224CaR¹⁸731
q224CaR
  [¹⁹731
226CaR²⁶183
c227CaR
  [³⁷285
f231CaR²⁷845
f231CaR²⁹845
q234CaR
  [¹⁸562
234CaR²⁸918
c236CaR
  [²⁷409
237CaR²⁹115
247CaR³⁰454
45BRW³⁴913

−666−
f184CaR³627

−671−
209CaR⁴364

−700−
212CaR⁹333
212CaR¹⁰695
216CaR⁸536

226CaR741
230CaR760
233CaR⁶702
235CaR⁷622
235CaR⁸623
239CaR³420

−707−
e207CaR²787

−714−
216CaR³215
221CaR652
230CaR²646

−735−
211CaR⁸301
222CaR⁵481
222CaR⁴482
257CaR798
262CaR⁴910

−741−
217CaR¹648
217CaR²649

−747−
209CaR774
209CaR¹778
d250CaR¹726
SRI§7.21

−749−
221CaR¹361
221CaR⁵361

−760−
209CaR¹807
238CaR¹728
256CaR¹510
c51BRW¹837

−762−
207CaR276
819F2d²889

−768−
215CaR²222
215CaR²645
j215CaR879
218CaR498
219CaR²287
226CaR¹397
232CaR¹219

−772−
j207CaR500
j209CaR105
228CaR³658
228CaR⁸449
24SAC907

−778−
224CaR289

−796−
227CaR¹97
227CaR¹105

−801−
d243CaR³250

−811−
227CaR¹808
26SAC87
26SAC100

−813−
208CaR²622
f208CaR¹802
221CaR²385
226CaR²731
233CaR²594
236CaR222

−816−
225CaR⁵708
225CaR¹709
234CaR⁴73

−820−
f210CaR231
210CaR⁶231
210CaR²233
210CaR⁵340
f210CaR²495
212CaR²561
217CaR825
220CaR²589
229CaR³703
229CaR²706
231CaR²153
235CaR⁶322
235CaR⁸878
248CaR²259
253CaR¹506
253CaR⁶506
253CaR²842
254CaR²84

−831−
d208CaR²27
208CaR892
e208CaR⁴896
f208CaR²903
f208CaR⁷903
j209CaR153
209CaR⁵197
210CaR419
210CaR⁶588
d210CaR⁷754
210CaR¹817
211CaR¹473
212CaR⁵855
212CaR⁶856
212CaR⁸857
216CaR⁴588
216CaR²669
216CaR²674
j216CaR680
218CaR728
e221CaR²378
e221CaR⁴378
e221CaR⁸378
222CaR⁴447
d222CaR⁷448
d222CaR⁸449
223CaR³226
225CaR¹518
228CaR778
e228CaR⁷892
d229CaR²199
d229CaR³199
229CaR769
230CaR¹903
d231CaR²100
d231CaR³100
231CaR185
d231CaR²186
231CaR441
e231CaR⁷441
f231CaR460
232CaR³531

234CaR⁴480
234CaR⁷609
235CaR⁷846
f236CaR94
236CaR⁸469
d236CaR⁷470
236CaR922
j237CaR879
239CaR⁸744
239CaR⁴746
239CaR⁷768
240CaR328
f242CaR²856
243CaR810
245CaR108
245CaR289
f246CaR⁴535
246CaR²539
246CaR⁶544
246CaR⁵545
j246CaR549
d250CaR²192
d250CaR³192
d250CaR⁷192
251CaR⁴70
251CaR770
d252CaR³634
d252CaR⁴634
254CaR⁸484
254CaR632
d254CaR⁷843
j256CaR776
257CaR100
f257CaR²101
f257CaR⁷101
d257CaR108
257CaR⁷867
j257CaR895
258CaR793
259CaR³581
259CaR⁴581
261CaR773
262CaR¹343
262CaR¹845
262CaR⁴898
f797F2d⁴737
803F2d1499
804F2d⁵587
f847F2d⁶603
861F2d⁷443
f861F2d⁴444
j861F2d445
876F2d⁶731
885F2d⁶511
885F2d⁷511
638FS1176
665FS986
697FS⁶372
704FS⁶1004
8CoLR81
DTFV
  §1.28
MMPC§4.04

−844−
190CaR¹⁴485
208CaR¹⁵254
j209CaR345
209CaR¹⁵888
209CaR¹⁶889
210CaR³528
210CaR¹⁴688
212CaR³205
d212CaR
  [¹¹205
212CaR⁴798

212CaR⁵798
212CaR⁶798
212CaR⁷798
f214CaR¹⁰560
j214CaR614
214CaR¹⁴614
215CaR825
216CaR¹⁶266
223CaR¹⁴501
226CaR¹⁵398
228CaR¹⁰90
q228CaR⁸91
229CaR³443
q230CaR⁸480
q230CaR
  [¹⁰480
233CaR¹¹71
233CaR¹699
j233CaR107
233CaR⁴730
233CaR⁸731
233CaR¹⁰731
237CaR32
237CaR⁴160
237CaR⁶160
237CaR226
240CaR¹⁴524
240CaR¹¹134
245CaR⁹245
245CaR¹⁰245
248CaR³555
248CaR607
248CaR¹⁴607
248CaR¹⁵607
j248CaR619
248CaR⁷826
249CaR¹⁶605
d250CaR³673
d250CaR⁴673
d250CaR⁵673
d250CaR⁶673
d250CaR⁷673
252CaR532
254CaR²322
254CaR³322
254CaR⁶600
255CaR¹¹642
c255CaR
  [¹⁰874
261CaR¹⁰602
q261CaR603
q261CaR
  [¹⁶604
262CaR¹⁴834
675FS³716

−854−
207CaR⁷497
209CaR⁹102
209CaR119
212CaR¹⁰867
212CaR¹²867
214CaR366
229CaR²¹148
229CaR¹¹710
229CaR³795
229CaR⁴798
237CaR²⁰173
243CaR671
246CaR²⁰305
246CaR¹¹309
246CaR¹⁵309
251CaR²¹290
252CaR58
f252CaR¹959
Continued

Page From *Shepard's Citations for Cases*

West Digests

Laura's next task is to go on from these cases to find other decisions discussing the same or similar issues. Digests can help Laura determine whether she has a case.

The *Molien* case, as reported in the *California Reporter,* has headnotes that have been prepared in accordance with the West key number system. As discussed in Chapter 10, the key number system takes precise legal issues and classifies them with a topic heading and a sub-category number. The headnote from *Molien* shown below covers the precise legal issue with which Laura started her post-*Molien* research.

---

6. Damages ☞ **49.10**

   Cause of action may be stated for negligent infliction of serious emotional distress.

Headnote From *Molien v. Kaiser Hospital*

The West Key number system has labeled this issue "Damages" and has assigned a sub-category number of 49.10. If you look in any digest prepared by West Publishing Co. (which includes almost all digests) under Damages 49.10, you will find summaries of judicial holdings on the same issue. For example, the page shown below is taken from West's *California Digest.*

First, scan those headnotes and note which court made the decision and when. For example, "D.C. Cal." indicates that the case was decided by the Federal District Court in California, "Cal." refers to the California Supreme Court, and "Cal. App." means that a California Court of Appeal rendered the decision. As discussed in Chapter 9, the higher the court, the more important the decision with regard to the principles of precedent and persuasive authority. (Remember, however, that "D.C. Cal." refers to a federal case, which will not be binding on a state court unless the issue you are researching involves a federal question.) Equally important, though, is the date of the decision. The more current the decision, the more likely it is that the case is still "good law."

In addition to the *California Digest,* Laura might also wish to investigate the West *Regional Digests,* the *Decennials* and the *General Digest,* all of which contain, under the heading Damages 49.10, summaries of cases that have discussed the relationship between negligence and emotional distress.

Note: Although cases from other states might not be of much help in your state, small states often look to the judicial decisions of neighboring states. For example, Vermont and Maine often give serious consideration to the decisions of Massachusetts and New York courts, and California Supreme Court cases have traditionally been given weight throughout the West. Also, if you have found the *Molien* case but live in Arkansas, you would want to find out whether a similar case has been decided in your state. You could do this by locating the regional digest containing Arkansas cases and looking under Damages 49.10.

Summary

Because we've covered a lot of ground, it might be helpful to summarize what we've done. We have:

- Classified the problem;
- Determined the possible words and phrases to look up in a legal index;
- Selected a background resource (*Cal. Jur. 3d* in this case);
- Located the article or discussion that most closely covers our topic;
- Read the cases cited by the article as authority for its statements;
- Used *Shepard's Citations for California Cases* to find out whether the cases cited by the article still represent the state of the law;
- Read cases cited in *Shepard's* that seemed appropriate and found the *Molien* case;
- *Shepardized Molien* to find a case closer to our facts; and
- Used the *West Digest* system to locate similar cases.

18 Cal D 2d—17

Law Rev. 1981. Limiting liability for the negligent infliction of emotional distress: the "bystander recovery".—54 So.Cal.L.R. 847.

⚙=49.10. Nature of action or wrongful act, in general.

U.S.Cal. 1987. Railway Labor Act did not require that narrow "emotional injury" exception be carved out of the Federal Employers' Liability Act, absent any basis for assuming that allowing FELA actions for emotional injury would wreak havoc with the general scheme of RLA arbitration and absent intolerable conflict between the two statutes. Federal Employers' Liability Act, § 1 et seq., 45 U.S.C.A. § 51 et seq.; Railway Labor Act, § 1 et seq., as amended, 45 U.S.C.A. § 151 et seq.—Atchison, Topeka and Santa Fe Ry. Co. v. Buell, 107 S.Ct. 1410, 480 U.S. 557, 94 L.Ed.2d 563, on remand 818 F.2d 868.

C.A.9 (Cal.) 1989. LMRA preempted employee's claims of negligent and intentional infliction of emotional distress; actions serving as basis of those claims required analysis of collective bargaining agreement. Labor Management Relations Act, 1947, § 301, 29 U.S.C.A. § 185.—Jackson v. Southern California Gas Co., 881 F.2d 638.

C.A.9 (Cal.) 1987. Discharged employee's allegations in complaint, in support of claim of intentional infliction of emotional distress, that she was held in a work area against her will by threat of physical force and asked to commit lewd sexual acts alleged a nonpreempted state claim.—Survival Systems of Whittaker Corp. v. U.S. Dist. Court for Southern Dist. of California, 825 F.2d 1416, certiorari denied 108 S.Ct. 774, 484 U.S. 1042, 98 L.Ed.2d 861.

C.A.9 (Cal.) 1986. Employee could not recover damages for emotional distress suffered upon his termination; distress employee suffered was neither substantial nor enduring, as it must be to recover damages for emotional distress under California law.—Gilchrist v. Jim Slemons Imports, Inc., 803 F.2d 1488.

C.A.9 (Cal.) 1986. Although plaintiffs may not recover emotional distress damages under Title VII claim, Title VII does not supplant independent state remedies; thus, where emotional distress arises in conjunction with Title VII claim, damages may be awarded for harm that is distinct from employment discrimination injury. Civil Rights Act of 1964, § 701 et seq., 42 U.S.C.A. § 2000e et seq.—Miller v. Fairchild Industries, Inc., 797 F.2d 727, appeal after remand 876 F.2d 718, opinion amended and superseded 885 F.2d 498, amended in part on denial of rehearing, appeal after remand 885 F.2d 498, certiorari denied 110 S.Ct. 1524, 108 L.Ed.2d 764.

C.A.9 (Cal.) 1985. Damages for emotional distress accompanying physical injuries are recoverable in traditional Federal Employers' Liability Act [45 U.S.C.A. §§ 51–60] actions. Federal Employers' Liability Act, §§ 1–10, as amended, 45 U.S.C.A. §§ 51–60.—Buell v. Atchison, Topeka and Santa Fe Ry. Co., 771 F.2d 1320, certiorari granted 106 S.Ct. 1946, 476 U.S. 1103, 90 L.Ed.2d 356, affirmed in part, vacated in part 107 S.Ct. 1410, 480 U.S. 557, 94 L.Ed.2d 563, on remand 818 F.2d 868.

C.A.Cal. 1983. Damages for mental or emotional distress accompanied by some physical manifestation are recoverable under the Employee Retirement Income Security Act section governing breach of fiduciary's duties. Employee Retirement Income Security Act of 1974, § 409(a), 29 U.S.C.A. § 1109(a).—Russell v. Massachusetts Mut. Life Ins. Co., 722 F.2d 482, certiorari granted 105 S.Ct. 81, 469 U.S. 816, 83 L.Ed.2d 29, reversed 105 S.Ct. 3085, 473 U.S. 134, 87 L.Ed.2d 96, on remand 778 F.2d 542, vacated 778 F.2d 542.

C.A.Cal. 1982. Claims that employer violated implied covenant of good faith and fair dealing, as applied to situation where former employee alleges no more than long service and existence of personnel policies or oral representations showing implied promise by employer not to act arbitrarily in dealing with its employees, sound in both contract and tort and may give rise to emotional distress damages and punitive damages.—Cancellier v. Federated Dept. Stores, 672 F.2d 1312, certiorari denied 103 S.Ct. 131, 459 U.S. 859, 74 L.Ed.2d 113.

N.D.Cal. 1989. Principal and superintendent who listened patiently to concerns of student's parents about lack of diploma because he had not timely handed in paperwork for independent study in physical education behaved in reasonable manner when they refused to force teacher to change her "no mark" grade or to allow student to participate in graduation ceremony, and they could not be held liable for negligent infliction of emotional distress.—Swany v. San Ramon Valley Unified School Dist., 720 F.Supp. 764.

School official did not behave unreasonably, and could not be held liable for negligent infliction of emotional distress on student who was not permitted to participate in graduation ceremonies, by failing to develop solution to problem of student's failure to timely turn in materials for independent study in physical education prior to the time the graduation ceremonies were held.—Id.

N.D.Cal. 1988. Under California law, federal district judge's former secretary's allegation that she was assigned excessive work with Federal Judges Association failed to state claim against judge and association for negligent infliction of emotional distress; severe emotional distress was not reasonably foreseeable as result of such conduct.—Garcia v. Williams, 704 F.Supp. 984.

N.D.Cal. 1986. Whether recovery for negligent infliction of emotional distress will be allowed in any particular case depends on whether plaintiff's emotional distress was foreseeable result of defendant's conduct.—Safeco Ins. Co. of America v. Simmons, 642 F.Supp. 305.

D.C.Cal. 1985. Swine flu inoculation did not proximately contribute to or cause plaintiff's extended psychological problem of anxiety reaction, in absence of evidence of allergic reaction within 30 minutes of inoculation and in view of plaintiff's psychological vulnerability to anxiety reactions and panic attacks.—Wolfe v. U.S., 604 F.Supp. 726.

D.C.Cal. 1983. Paragraphs of complaint seeking recovery for emotional distress suffered as direct and proximate result of negligent care and treatment given child by defendants, interpreted to mean that parents sought recovery for physical or mental injuries sustained in course of caring for child and responding to his needs, stated a claim upon which relief could be granted.—Cortez v. County of Los Angeles, 96 F.R.D. 427.

Cal. 1988. Threats of divine retribution made by members of church were protected religious speech and could not form basis of a claim of intentional infliction of emotional distress by former members of church. U.S.C.A. Const.Amend. 1; West's Ann.Cal. Const. Art. 1, § 4.—Molko v. Holy Spirit Ass'n for The Unification of World Christianity, 762 P.2d 46, 252 Cal.Rptr. 122, 46 C.3d 1092, rehearing denied and modified, certiorari denied 109 S.Ct. 2110, 104 L.Ed.2d 670.

Cal. 1986. Store's "merchant's privilege" did not preclude customer's recovery for negligent infliction of emotional distress where store reported to police erroneous and unsupported suspicion that customer was tendering counterfeit bill.—Pool v. City of Oakland, 728 P.2d 1163, 232 Cal. Rptr. 528, 42 C.3d 1051.

Cal.App. 1 Dist. 1990. Award of emotional distress damages to employee terminated by school district would be sustained, although decision had held that tort remedies were not available for

Appendix

Glossary

ab initio
Latin for "from the beginning." This term is used by lawyers intent on getting their money's worth from a liberal arts education by uttering such statements as, "The judge was against me ab initio."

abatement
A reduction. After a death, abatement occurs if the deceased person didn't leave enough property to fulfill all the bequests made in the will and meet other expenses. Gifts left in the will are cut back in order to pay taxes, satisfy debts or take care of other gifts that are given priority under law or by the will itself.

abstract of title
A short history of a piece of land that lists any transfers in ownership, as well as any liabilities attached to it, such as mortgages.

abstract of trust
A condensed version of a living trust document that leaves out details of what is in the trust and the identity of the beneficiaries. You can show an abstract of trust to a financial organization or other institution to prove that you have established a valid living trust, without revealing specifics that you want to keep private. In some states, this document is called a "certification of trust."

accessory
Someone who intentionally helps another person commit a felony by giving advice before the crime or helping to conceal the evidence or the perpetrator. An accessory is usually not physically present during the crime. For example, hiding a robber who is being sought by the police might make you an "accessory after the fact" to a robbery. Compare accomplice.

accomplice
Someone who helps another person (known as the principal) commit a crime. Unlike an accessory, an accomplice is usually present when the crime is committed. An accomplice is guilty of the same offense and usually receives the same sentence as the principal. For instance, the driver of the getaway car for a burglary is an accomplice and will be guilty of the burglary even though he may not have entered the building.

accord and satisfaction
An agreement to settle a contract dispute by accepting less than what is due. This procedure is often used by creditors who want to cut their losses by collecting as much money as they can from debtors who cannot pay the full amount.

acquittal
A decision by a judge or jury that a defendant in a criminal case is not guilty of a crime. An acquittal is not a finding of innocence; it is simply a conclusion that the prosecution has not proved its case beyond a reasonable doubt.

act of God
An extraordinary and unexpected natural event, such as a hurricane, tornado, earthquake or even the sudden death of a person. An act of God may be a defense against liability for injuries or damages. Under the law of contracts, an act of God often serves as a valid excuse if one of the parties to the contract is unable to fulfill his or her duties—for instance, completing a construction project on time.

action

Another term for a lawsuit. For example, a plaintiff might say, "I began this negligence action last fall after the defendant, Ms. Adams, struck me while I was crossing the street at Elm and Main."

actus reus

Latin for a "guilty act." The actus reus is the act which, in combination with a certain mental state, such as intent or recklessness, constitutes a crime. For example, the crime of theft requires physically taking something (the actus reus) coupled with the intent to permanently deprive the owner of the object (the mental state, or mens rea).

ademption

The failure of a bequest of property in a will. The gift fails (is "adeemed") because the person who made the will no longer owns the property when he or she dies. Often this happens because the property has been sold, destroyed or given away to someone other than the beneficiary named in the will. A bequest may also be adeemed when the will maker, while still living, gives the property to the intended beneficiary (called "ademption by satisfaction"). When a bequest is adeemed, the beneficiary named in the will is out of luck; he or she doesn't get cash or a different item of property to replace the one that was described in the will. For example, Mark writes in his will, "I leave to Rob the family vehicle," but then trades in his car for a jet ski. When Mark dies, Rob will receive nothing. Frustrated beneficiaries may challenge an ademption in court, especially if the property was not clearly identified in the first place.

admissible evidence

The evidence that a trial judge or jury may consider because the rules of evidence deem it reliable. See *evidence, inadmissible evidence.*

admission

(1) An out-of-court statement by your adversary that you offer into evidence as an exception to the hearsay rule. (2) One side's statement that certain facts are true in response to a request from the other side during discovery.

adverse possession

A means by which one can legally take another's property without paying for it. The requirements for adversely possessing property vary between states, but usually include continuous and open use for a period of five or more years and payment of taxes on the property in question.

age of majority

Adulthood in the eyes of the law. After reaching the age of majority, a person is permitted to vote, make a valid will, enter into binding contracts, enlist in the armed forces and purchase alcohol. Also, parents may stop making child support payments when a child reaches the age of majority. In most states the age of majority is 18, but this varies depending on the activity. For example, people are allowed to vote when they reach the age of 18, but in some states can't purchase alcohol until they're 21.

agent

A person authorized to act for and under the direction of another person when dealing with third parties. The person who appoints an agent is called the principal. An agent can enter into binding agreements on the principal's behalf and may even create liability for the principal if the agent causes harm while carrying out his or her duties. See also *attorney-in-fact.*

aggravate

To make more serious or severe.

aggravating circumstances

Circumstances that increase the seriousness or outrageousness of a given crime, and that in turn increase the wrongdoer's penalty or punishment. For example, the crime of aggravated assault is a physical attack made worse because it is committed with a dangerous weapon, results in severe bodily injury, or is made in conjunction with another serious crime. Aggravated assault is usually considered a felony, punishable by a prison sentence.

alternate beneficiary

A person, organization or institution that receives property through a will, trust or insurance policy when the first-named beneficiary is unable or refuses to take the property. For example, in his will, Jake leaves his collection of sheet music to his daughter, Mia, and names the local symphony as alternate beneficiary. When Jake dies, Mia decides that the symphony can make better use of the sheet music than she can, so she refuses (disclaims) the gift, and the

manuscripts pass directly to the symphony. In insurance law, the alternate beneficiary, usually the person who receives the insurance proceeds because the initial or primary beneficiary has died, is called the secondary or contingent beneficiary.

alternative dispute resolution (ADR)

A catchall term that describes a number of methods used to resolve disputes out of court, including negotiation, conciliation, mediation and the many types of arbitration. The common denominator of all ADR methods is that they are faster, less formal, cheaper and often less adversarial than a court trial. In recent years the term "alternative dispute resolution" has begun to lose favor in some circles and ADR has come to mean "appropriate dispute resolution." The point of this semantic change is to emphasize that ADR methods stand on their own as effective ways to resolve disputes and should not be seen simply as alternatives to a court action.

amicus curiae

Latin for "friend of the court." This term describes a person or organization that is not a party to a lawsuit as a plaintiff or a defendant but that has a strong interest in the case and wants to file its opinion with the court, usually in the form of a written brief. For example, the ACLU often submits materials to support a person who claims a violation of civil rights even though that person is represented by a lawyer.

ancillary probate

A probate proceeding conducted in a different state from the one in which the deceased person resided at the time of death. Ancillary probate proceedings are usually necessary if the deceased person owned real estate in another state.

annuity

A purchased policy that pays a fixed amount of benefits each year—although most annuities actually pay monthly— for the life of the person who is entitled to those benefits. In a simple life annuity, when the person receiving the annuity dies, the benefits stop; there is no final lump sum payment and no provision to pay benefits to a spouse or other survivor. A continuous annuity pays monthly installments for the life of the retired worker, and provides a smaller continuing annuity for the worker's spouse or other survivor after the worker's death. A joint and survivor annuity pays monthly benefits as long as the retired worker is alive, and then continues to pay the worker's spouse for life.

annulment

A court procedure that dissolves a marriage and treats it as if it never happened. Annulments are rare since the advent of no-fault divorce, but may be obtained in most states for one of the following reasons: misrepresentation, concealment (for example, of an addiction or criminal record), misunderstanding, and refusal to consummate the marriage.

answer

A defendant's written response to a plaintiff's initial court filing (called a complaint or petition). An answer normally denies some or all facts asserted by the complaint, and sometimes seeks to turn the tables on the plaintiff by making allegations or charges against the plaintiff (called counterclaims). Normally, a defendant has 30 days in which to file an answer after being served with the plaintiff's complaint. In some courts, an answer is simply called a "response."

appeal

A written request to a higher court to modify or reverse the judgment of a trial court or intermediate-level appellate court. Normally, an appellate court accepts as true all the facts that the trial judge or jury found to be true, and decides only whether the judge made mistakes in understanding and applying the law. If the appellate court decides that a mistake was made that changed the outcome, it will direct the lower court to conduct a new trial, but often the mistakes are deemed "harmless" and the judgment is left alone. Some mistakes—such as a miscalculation of money damages—are corrected by the appellate court without sending the case back to the trial court. An appeal begins when the loser at trial—or in an intermediate-level appellate court—files a notice of appeal, which must be done within strict time limits (often 30 days from the date of judgment). The loser (called the appellant) and the winner (called the appellee) submit written arguments (called briefs) and often make oral arguments explaining why the lower court's decision should be upheld or overturned.

appellant

A party to a lawsuit who appeals a losing decision to a higher court in an effort to have it modified or reversed.

appellate court

A higher court that reviews the decision of a lower court when a losing party files for an appeal.

appellee

A party to a lawsuit who wins in the trial court—or sometimes on a first appeal—only to have the other party (called the appellant) file for an appeal. An appellee files a written brief and often makes an oral argument before the appellate court, asking that the lower court's judgment be upheld. In some courts, an appellee is called a respondent.

arbitration

A noncourt procedure for resolving disputes using one or more neutral third parties—called the arbitrator or arbitration panel. Arbitration uses rules of evidence and procedure that are less formal than those followed in trial courts, which usually leads to a faster and less expensive resolution. There are many types of arbitration in common use: Binding arbitration is similar to a court proceeding in that the arbitrator has the power to impose a decision, although this is sometimes limited by agreement—for example, in "hi-lo arbitration," the parties may agree in advance to a maximum and minimum award. In nonbinding arbitration, the arbitrator can recommend but not impose a decision. Many contracts—including those imposed on customers by many financial and healthcare organizations—require mandatory arbitration in the event of a dispute. This may be reasonable when the arbitrator really is neutral, but is justifiably criticized when the large company that writes the contract is able to influence the choice of arbitrator.

arraignment

A court appearance in which the defendant is formally charged with a crime and asked to respond by pleading guilty, not guilty or *nolo contendere*. Other matters often handled at an arraignment are setting the bail and arranging for the appointment of an attorney at public expense if the defendant is unable to afford one.

arrearages

Overdue alimony or child support payments. In recent years, state laws have made it almost impossible to get rid of arrearages; they can't be discharged in bankruptcy, and courts usually will not cancel them retroactively. A spouse or parent who falls on tough times and is unable to make payments should request a temporary modification of the payments before the arrearages build up.

arrest

A situation in which the police detain a person in a manner that, to any reasonable person, makes it clear she is not free to leave. A person can be "under arrest" even though the police have not announced it; handcuffs or physical restraint are not necessary to constitute an arrest. Questioning an arrested person about her involvement in or knowledge of a crime must be preceded by the Miranda warnings if the police intend to use the answers against the person in a criminal case. If the arrested person chooses to remain silent, the questioning must stop.

arrest warrant

A document issued by a judge or magistrate that authorizes the police to arrest someone. Warrants are issued when law enforcement personnel present evidence to the judge or magistrate that convinces her that it is reasonably likely that a crime has taken place and that the person to be named in the warrant is criminally responsible for that crime.

articles of incorporation

A document filed with state authorities (usually the Secretary of State or Corporations Commissioner, depending on the state) to form a corporation. As required by the general incorporation law of the state, the articles normally include the purpose of the corporation, its principal place of business, the names of its initial controlling directors, and the amounts and types of stock it is authorized to issue.

assault

A crime that occurs when one person tries to physically harm another in a way that makes the person under attack feel immediately threatened. Actual physical contact is not necessary; threatening gestures that would alarm any reasonable person can constitute an assault. Compare *battery*.

assignee

A person to whom a property right is transferred. For example, an assignee may take over a lease from a tenant who wants to permanently move out before the lease expires. The assignee takes control of the property and assumes all the legal rights and responsibilities of the tenant, including payment of rent. However, the original tenant remains legally responsible if the assignee fails to pay the rent.

assignment

A transfer of property rights from one person to another, called the assignee.

attestation

The act of watching someone sign a legal document, such as a will or power of attorney, and then signing your own name as a witness. When you witness a document in this way, you are attesting—that is, stating and confirming—that the person you watched sign the document in fact did so. Attesting to a document does not mean that you are vouching for its accuracy or truthfulness. You are only acknowledging that you watched it being signed by the person whose name is on the signature line.

attorney fees

The payment made to a lawyer for legal services. These fees may take several forms:

- hourly;
- per job or service—for example, $350 to draft a will;
- contingency (the lawyer collects a percentage of any money she wins for her client and nothing if there is no recovery); or
- retainer (usually a down payment as part of an hourly or per-job fee agreement).

Attorney fees must usually be paid by the client who hires a lawyer, though occasionally a law or contract will require the losing party of a lawsuit to pay the winner's court costs and attorney fees. For example, a contract might contain a provision that says the loser of any lawsuit between the parties to the contract will pay the winner's attorney fees. Many laws designed to protect consumers also provide for attorney fees—for example, most state laws that require landlords to provide habitable housing also specify that a tenant who sues and wins using that law may collect attorney fees. And in family law cases—divorce, custody and child support—judges often have the power to order the more affluent spouse to pay the other spouse's attorney fees, even when there is no clear victor.

Attorney General

Head of the United States Department of Justice and chief law officer of the Federal government. The attorney general represents the United States in legal matters, oversees federal prosecutors, and provides legal advice to the president and to heads of executive governmental departments. Each state also has an attorney general, responsible for advising the governor and state agencies and departments about legal issues, and for overseeing state prosecuting attorneys.

attorney work product privilege

A rule that protects materials prepared by a lawyer in preparation for trial from being seen and used by the adversary during discovery or trial.

attorney-client privilege

A rule that keeps any communication between an attorney and her client confidential and bars it from being used as evidence in a trial, or even being seen by the opposing party during discovery.

attorney-in-fact

A person named in a written power of attorney document to act on behalf of the person who signs the document, called the principal. The attorney-in-fact has only the powers and responsibilities that are granted in the specific power of attorney document. An attorney-in-fact is an agent of the principal.

attractive nuisance

Something on a piece of property that attracts children but also endangers their safety. For example, unfenced swimming pools, open pits, farm equipment and abandoned refrigerators have all qualified as attractive nuisances.

authenticate

To offer testimony that tells the judge what an item of evidence is and establishes its connection to the case.

avowal

A direct statement or declaration. Also, a statement made by a witness after the judge has ruled that his or her testimony is not admissible at trial. This statement "preserves" the testimony so that it may be considered by the court if the trial's outcome is an appeal.

bail

The money paid to the court, usually at arraignment or shortly thereafter, to ensure that an arrested person who is released from jail will show up at all required court appearances. The amount of bail is determined by the local bail schedule, which is based on the seriousness of the offense. The judge can increase the bail if the prosecutor convinces him that the defendant is likely to flee (for example, if he has failed to show up for court in the past), or he can decrease it if the defense attorney shows that the defendant is unlikely to run (for example, he has strong ties to the community by way of a steady job and a family).

bailiff

A court official usually classified as a peace officer (sometimes as a deputy sheriff, or marshal) and usually wearing a uniform. A bailiff's main job is to maintain order in the courtroom. In addition, bailiffs often help court proceedings go smoothly by shepherding witnesses in and out of the courtroom and handing evidence to witnesses as they testify. In criminal cases, the bailiff may have temporary charge of any defendant who is in custody during court proceedings.

bailor

Someone who delivers an item of personal property to another person for a specific purpose. For example, a person who leaves a broken VCR with a repairperson in order to get it fixed would be a bailor.

bankruptcy

A legal proceeding that relieves you of the responsibility of paying your debts or provides you with protection while attempting to repay your debts. There are two types of bankruptcy: liquidation, in which your debts are wiped out (discharged), and reorganization, in which you provide the court with a plan for how you intend to repay your debts. For both consumers and businesses, liquidation bankruptcy is called Chapter 7. For consumers, reorganization bankruptcy is called Chapter 13. Reorganization bankruptcy for consumers with an extraordinary amount of debt and for businesses is called Chapter 11. Reorganization bankruptcy for family farmers is called Chapter 12.

bankruptcy trustee

A person appointed by the court to oversee the case of a person or business that has filed for bankruptcy. In a consumer Chapter 7 case, the trustee's role is to gather, liquidate and distribute proportionally the debtor's non-exempt property to her creditors. In a Chapter 13 case, the trustee's role is to receive the debtor's monthly payments and distribute them proportionally to her creditors.

battery

A crime consisting of physical contact that is intended to harm someone. Unintentional harmful contact is not battery, no matter how careless the behavior or how severe the injury. A fistfight is a common battery; being hit by a wild pitch in a baseball game is not.

bench

The seat (usually a comfy chair rather than a bench) where a judge sits in the courtroom during a trial or hearing. Sometimes the word "bench" is used in place of the word "judge"—for example, someone might say she wants a bench trial, meaning a trial by a judge without a jury.

bench trial

A trial before a judge with no jury. The term derives from the fact that the stand on which the judge sits is called the bench.

beneficiary

A person or organization legally entitled to receive benefits through a legal device, such as a will, trust or life insurance policy.

bequeath

A legal term sometimes used in wills that means "leave"—for example, "I bequeath my garden tools to my brother-in-law, Buster Jenkins."

bequest

The legal term for personal property (anything but real estate) left in a will.

best evidence rule

A rule of evidence that demands that the original of any document, photograph or recording be used as evidence at trial, rather than a copy. A copy will be allowed into evidence only if the original is unavailable.

beyond a reasonable doubt

The burden of proof that the prosecution must carry in a criminal trial to obtain a guilty verdict. Reasonable doubt is sometimes explained as being convinced "to a moral certainty." The jury must be convinced that the defendant committed each element of the crime before returning a guilty verdict.

bifurcate

To separate the issues in a case so that one issue or set of issues can be tried and resolved before the others. For example, death penalty cases are always bifurcated: The court first hears the evidence of guilt and reaches a verdict, and then hears evidence about and decides which punishment to impose (death or life in prison without parole). Bifurcated trials are also common in product-liability class action lawsuits in which many people claim that they were injured by the same defective product: The issue of liability is tried first, followed by the question of damages. Bifurcation is authorized by Rule 42(b) of the Federal Rules of Civil Procedure.

binding precedent

The decisions of higher courts that set the legal standards for similar cases in lower courts within the same jurisdiction.

blue law

A statute that forbids or regulates an activity, such as the sale of liquor on Sundays.

blue sky laws

The laws that aim to protect people from investing in sham companies that consist of nothing but "blue sky." Blue sky laws require that companies seeking to sell stock to the public submit information to and obtain the approval of a state or federal official who oversees corporate activity.

bond

(1) A written agreement purchased from a bonding company that guarantees a person will properly carry out a specific act, such as managing funds, showing up in court, providing good title to a piece of real estate or completing a construction project. If the person who purchased the bond fails at his or her task, the bonding company will pay the aggrieved party an amount up to the value of the bond. (2) An interest-bearing document issued by a government or company as evidence of a debt. A bond provides predetermined payments at a set date to the bondholder. Bonds may be "registered" bonds, which provide payment to the bondholder whose name is recorded with the issuer and appears on the bond certificate, or "bearer" bonds, which provide payments to whomever holds the bond in-hand.

breach

A failure or violation of a legal obligation.

breach of contract

A legal claim that one party failed to perform as required under a valid agreement with the other party. For example you might say, "The roofer breached our contract by using substandard supplies when he repaired my roof."

brief

A document used to submit a legal contention or argument to a court. A brief typically sets out the facts of the case and a party's argument as to why she should prevail. These arguments must be supported by legal authority and precedent, such as statutes, regulations and previous court decisions. Although it is usually possible to submit a brief to a trial court (called a trial brief), briefs are most commonly used as a central part of the appeal process (an appellate brief). But don't be fooled by the name—briefs are usually anything but brief, as pointed out by writer Franz Kafka, who defined a lawyer as "a person who writes a 10,000 word decision and calls it a brief."

burden of proof

A party's job of convincing the decision-maker in a trial that the party's version of the facts is true. In a civil trial, it means that the plaintiff must convince the judge or jury "by a preponderance of the evidence" that the plaintiff's version is true—that is, over 50% of the believable evidence is in the plaintiff's favor. In a criminal case, because a person's

liberty is at stake, the government has a harder job, and must convince the judge or jury beyond a reasonable doubt that the defendant is guilty.

burglary

The crime of breaking into and entering a building with the intention to commit a felony. Modern burglary statutes often dispense with the "breaking and entering" requirement and operate whenever a person enters a building with the intent to commit any type of felony. For instance, someone would be guilty of burglary if he entered a house through an unlocked door in order to commit a murder.

business records exception

An exception to the hearsay rule that allows a business document to be admitted into evidence if a proper foundation is laid to show it is reliable.

bylaws

The rules that govern the internal affairs or actions of a corporation. Normally bylaws are adopted by the shareholders of a profit-making business or the board of directors of a nonprofit corporation. Bylaws generally include procedures for holding meetings and electing the board of directors and officers. The bylaws also set out the duties and powers of a corporation's officers.

capital case

A prosecution for murder in which the jury is asked to decide if the defendant is guilty and, if he is, whether he should be put to death. When a prosecutor brings a capital case (also called a death penalty case), she must charge one or more "special circumstances" that the jury must find to be true in order to sentence the defendant to death. Each state (and the federal government) has its own list of special circumstances, but common ones include multiple murders, use of a bomb or a finding that the murder was especially heinous, atrocious or cruel.

capital punishment

The decision by a jury, in the second phase of a capital case, that the convicted defendant should be put to death.

caption

A heading on all pleadings submitted to the court. It states basic information such as the parties' names, court and case number.

case

A term that most often refers to a lawsuit—for example, "I filed my small claims case." "Case" also refers to a written decision by a judge—or for an appellate case, a panel of judges. For example, the U.S. Supreme Court's decision legalizing abortion is commonly referred to as the *Roe v. Wade* case. Finally, the term also describes the evidence a party submits in support of her position—for example, "I have made my case," or, "'My case-in-chief' has been completed."

cause of action

A specific legal claim—such as for negligence, breach of contract, or medical malpractice—for which a plaintiff seeks compensation. Each cause of action is divided into discrete elements, all of which must be proved to present a winning case.

certified copy

A copy of a document issued by a court or government agency that is guaranteed to be a true and exact copy of the original. Many agencies and institutions require certified copies of legal documents before permitting certain transactions. For example, a certified copy of a death certificate is required before a bank will release the funds in a deceased person's payable-on-death account to the person who has inherited them.

challenge for cause

A party's request that the judge dismiss a potential juror from serving on a trial jury by providing a valid legal reason why he shouldn't serve. Potential bias is a common reason potential jurors are challenged for cause—for example, the potential juror is a relative of a party or one of the lawyers, or admits to a prejudice against one party's race or religion. Judges can also dismiss a potential juror for cause. There is no limit on the number of successful challenges for cause. Compare *peremptory challenges*.

chambers

A fancy word for a judge's office. Trial court judges often schedule pretrial settlement conferences and other informal meetings in chambers.

Chapter 7 bankruptcy

The most familiar type of bankruptcy, in which many or all of your debts are wiped out completely in exchange for giving up your nonexempt property. Chapter 7 bankruptcy takes three to six months, costs $130 in filing fees and $45 in administrative fees, and commonly requires only one trip to the courthouse.

Chapter 13 bankruptcy

The reorganization bankruptcy for consumers, in which you partially or fully repay your debts. In Chapter 13 bankruptcy, you keep your property and use your income to pay all or a portion of the debts over three to five years. The minimum amount you must pay is roughly equal to the value of your nonexempt property. In addition, you must pledge your disposable net income—after subtracting reasonable expenses—for the period during which you are making payments. At the end of the three-to five-year period, the balance of what you owe on most debts is erased.

charge

A formal accusation of criminal activity. The prosecuting attorney decides on the charges, after reviewing police reports, witness statements and any other evidence of wrongdoing. Formal charges are announced at an arrested person's arraignment.

circuit court

The name used for the principal trial court in many states. In the federal system, appellate courts are organized into 13 circuits. Eleven of these cover different geographical areas of the country—for example, the United States Court of Appeal for the Ninth Circuit covers Alaska, Arizona, California, Hawaii, Idaho, Montana, Nevada, Oregon and Washington. The remaining circuits are the District of Columbia Circuit and the Federal Circuit, (which hears patent, customs and other specialized cases, based on subject matter). The term derives from an age before mechanized transit, when judges and lawyers rode "the circuit" of their territory to hold court in various places.

circumstantial evidence

Evidence that proves a fact by means of an inference. For example, from the evidence that a person was seen running away from the scene of a crime, a judge or jury may infer that the person committed the crime.

civil case

A noncriminal lawsuit, usually involving private property rights. For example, lawsuits involving breach of contract, probate, divorce, negligence and copyright violations are just a few of the many hundreds of varieties of civil lawsuits.

civil procedure

The rules used to handle a civil case from the time the initial complaint is filed through pretrial discovery, the trial itself and any subsequent appeal. Each state adopts its own rules of civil procedure (often set out in a separate Code of Civil Procedure), but many are influenced by or modeled on the Federal Rules of Civil Procedure.

class action

A lawsuit in which the interests of a large number of unnamed people with similar legal claims join together in a group (the class) and are represented by named plaintiffs who have been similarly affected by the wrongdoing alleged in the lawsuit. Common class actions involve cases in which a product has injured many people, or in which a group of people has suffered discrimination at the hands of an organization.

clear and present danger

Speech that poses a "clear and present danger" to the public or government will not be protected under the First Amendment's guarantee of free speech. The classic example is that shouting "Fire!" in a crowded theatre is not protected speech.

close corporation

A corporation owned and operated by a few individuals, often members of the same family, rather than by public shareholders. State laws permit close corporations to function more informally than regular corporations. For example, shareholders can make decisions without holding meetings of the board of directors, and can fill vacancies on the board without a vote of the shareholders.

closing argument

At trial, a speech made by each party after all the evidence has been presented. The purpose is to review the testimony and evidence presented during the trial as part of a forceful explanation of why your side should win. Especially in trials before a judge without a jury, it is common for both parties to waive their closing argument on the theory that the judge has almost surely already arrived at her decision.

codicil

A supplement or addition to a will. Codicils must be signed and witnessed in the same manner as the underlying will. A codicil may explain, modify, add to, subtract from, qualify, alter or revoke existing provisions in a will. Because a codicil changes a will, it must be signed in front of witnesses, just like a will.

collateral

Property that guarantees payment of a secured debt.

collateral estoppel

See *estoppel*.

common law marriage

In some states, a type of marriage in which couples can become legally married by living together for a long period of time, representing themselves as a married couple and intending to be married. Contrary to popular belief, the couple must intend to be married and act as though they are for a common law marriage to take effect—merely living together for a long time won't do it.

community property

A method for defining the ownership of property acquired and the responsibility for debts incurred during marriage. Generally, in states that follow community property principles, all earnings during marriage and all property acquired with those earnings are considered community property. Likewise, all debts incurred during marriage are community property debts. Upon divorce, community property and community debts are generally divided equally between the spouses. At the death of one spouse, his half of the community property will go to the surviving spouse unless he leaves a will that directs otherwise. Community property laws exist in Arizona, California, Idaho, Nevada, New Mexico, Texas, Washington and

Wisconsin. Compare *equitable distribution* and *separate property*.

community property with right of survivorship

A way for married couples to hold title to property, available in Arizona, California, Nevada, Texas and Wisconsin. It allows one spouse's half-interest in community property to pass to the surviving spouse without probate.

comparable rectitude

A doctrine that grants the spouse least at fault a divorce when both spouses have shown grounds for divorce. It is a response to an old common-law rule that prevented a divorce when both spouses were at fault.

competent evidence

Legally admissible evidence. Competent evidence tends to prove the matter in dispute. In a murder trial, for example, competent evidence might include the murder weapon with the defendant's fingerprints on it.

complaint

Papers filed with a court clerk by the plaintiff to initiate a lawsuit by setting out facts and legal claims (usually called causes of action). In some states and in some types of legal actions, such as divorce, complaints are called petitions and the person filing is called the petitioner. To complete the initial stage of a lawsuit, the plaintiff's complaint must be served on the defendant, who then has the opportunity to respond by filing an answer. In practice, few lawyers prepare complaints from scratch. Instead they use—and sometimes modify—pre-drafted complaints widely available in form books.

confidential communication

Information exchanged between two people who (1) have a relationship in which private communications are protected by law, and (2) intend that the information be kept in confidence. The law recognizes certain parties whose communications will be considered confidential and protected, including spouses, doctor and patient, attorney and client, and priest and confessor. Communications between these individuals cannot be disclosed in court unless the protected party waives that protection. The intention that the communication be confidential is critical.

For example, if an attorney and his client are discussing a matter in the presence of an unnecessary third party—for example, in an elevator with other people present—the discussion will not be considered confidential and may be admitted at trial. Also known as privileged communication.

conformed copy

An exact copy of a document filed with a court. To conform a copy, the court clerk will stamp the document with the filing date and add any handwritten notations to the document that exist on the original, including dates and the judge's signature. A conformed copy may or may not be certified.

consanguinity

An old-fashioned term referring to the relationship of "blood relatives"—people who have a common ancestor. Consanguinity exists, for example, between brothers and sisters but not between husbands and wives.

conservator

Someone appointed by a judge to oversee the affairs of an incapacitated person. A conservator who manages financial affairs is often called a "conservator of the estate." One who takes care of personal matters, such as health care and living arrangements, is known as a "conservator of the person." Sometimes, one conservator is appointed to handle all these tasks. Depending on where you live, a conservator may also be called a guardian, committee or curator.

consideration

The basis of a contract. Consideration is a benefit or right for which the parties to a contract must bargain; the contract is founded on an exchange of one form of consideration for another. Consideration may be a promise to perform a certain act—for example, a promise to fix a leaky roof—or a promise not to do something, such as build a second story on a house that will block the neighbor's view. Whatever its particulars, consideration must be something of value to the people who are making the contract.

constructive eviction

A provision for housing that is so substandard that, for all intents and purposes, a landlord has evicted the tenant. For example, the landlord may refuse to provide light, heat, water or other essential services, destroy part of the premises or refuse to clean up an environmental health hazard, such as lead paint dust. Because the premises are unlivable, the tenant has the right to move out and stop paying rent without incurring legal liability for breaking the lease. Usually, the tenant must first bring the problem to the landlord's attention and allow a reasonable amount of time for the landlord to make repairs.

contempt of court

Behavior in or out of court that violates a court order, or otherwise disrupts or shows disregard for the court. Refusing to answer a proper question, to file court papers on time or to follow local court rules can expose witnesses, lawyers and litigants to contempt findings. Contempt of court is punishable by fine or imprisonment.

contest

[as in to contest a will]

To oppose, dispute or challenge through formal or legal procedures. For example, the defendant in a lawsuit almost always contests the case made by the plaintiff. Or, a disgruntled relative may formally contest the provisions of a will.

contingency

A provision in a contract stating that some or all of the terms of the contract will be altered or voided by the occurrence of a specific event. For example, a contingency in a contract for the purchase of a house might state that if the buyer does not approve the inspection report of the physical condition of the property, the buyer does not have to complete the purchase.

contingency fee

A method of paying a lawyer for legal representation by which, instead of an hourly or per job fee, the lawyer receives a percentage of the money her client obtains after settling or winning the case. Often contingency fee agreements—which are most commonly used in personal injury cases—award the successful lawyer between 20% and 50% of the amount recovered. Lawyers representing defendants charged with crimes may not charge contingency fees. In most states, contingency fee agreements must be in writing.

contingent beneficiary

1) An alternate beneficiary named in a will, trust or other document. 2) Any person entitled to property under a will if one or more prior conditions are satisfied. For example, if Fred is entitled to take property under a will only if he's married at the time of the will maker's death, Fred is a contingent beneficiary. Similarly, if Ellen is named to receive a house only in the event her mother, who has been named to live in the house, moves out of it, Ellen is a contingent beneficiary.

continuance

The postponement of a hearing, trial or other scheduled court proceeding, at the request of one or both parties, or by the judge without consulting the parties. Unhappiness with long trial court delays has resulted in the adoption by most states of "fast track" rules that sharply limit the ability of judges to grant continuances.

contract

A legally binding agreement involving two or more people or businesses (called parties) that sets forth what the parties will or will not do. Most contracts that can be carried out within one year can be either oral or written. Major exceptions include contracts involving the ownership of real estate and commercial contracts for goods worth $500 or more, which must be in writing to be enforceable. (See *statute of frauds.*) A contract is formed when competent parties—usually adults of sound mind, or business entities—mutually agree to provide each other some benefit (called consideration), such as a promise to pay money in exchange for a promise to deliver specified goods or services or the actual delivery of those goods and services. A contract normally requires one party to make a reasonably detailed offer to do something—including, typically, the price, time for performance and other essential terms and conditions—and the other to accept without significant change. For example, if I offer to sell you ten roses for $5 to be delivered next Thursday and you say "It's a deal," we've made a valid contract. On the other hand, if one party fails to offer something of benefit to the other, there is no contract. For example, if Maria promises to fix Josh's car, there is no contract unless Josh promises something in return for Maria's services.

conviction

A finding by a judge or jury that the defendant is guilty of a crime.

copyright

A legal device that provides the owner the right to control how a creative work is used. A copyright is comprised of a number of exclusive rights, including the right to make copies, authorize others to make copies, make derivative works, sell and market the work and perform the work. Any one of these rights can be sold separately through transfers of copyright ownership.

corporation

A legal structure authorized by state law that allows a business to organize as a separate legal entity from its owners. A nonprofit is often referred to as an "artificial legal person," meaning that, like an individual, it can enter into contracts, sue and be sued and do the many other things necessary to carry on a business. One advantage of incorporating is that a corporation's owners (shareholders) are legally shielded from personal liability for the corporation's liabilities and debts (unpaid taxes are often an exception). In theory, a corporation can be organized either for profit-making or nonprofit purposes. Most profit-making corporations are known as C corporations and are taxed separately from their owners, but those organized under subchapter S of the Internal Revenue Code are pass-through tax entities, meaning that all profits are federally taxed on the personal income tax returns of their owners.

corpus delecti

Latin for the "body of the crime." Used to describe physical evidence, such as the corpse of a murder victim or the charred frame of a torched building.

cosigner

A person who signs his or her name to a loan agreement, lease or credit application. If the primary debtor does not pay, the cosigner is fully responsible for the loan or debt. Many people use cosigners to qualify for a loan or credit card. Landlords may require a cosigner when renting to a student or someone with a poor credit history.

counterclaim

A defendant's court papers that seek to reverse the thrust of the lawsuit by claiming that it was the plaintiff—not the defendant—who committed legal wrongs, and that as a result it is the defendant who is entitled to money damages or other relief. Usually filed as part of the defendant's answer—which also denies plaintiff's claims—a counterclaim is commonly, but not always, based on the same events that form the basis of the plaintiff's complaint. For example, a defendant in an auto accident lawsuit might file a counterclaim alleging that it was really the plaintiff who caused the accident. In some states, the counterclaim has been replaced by a similar legal pleading called a cross-complaint. In other states and in federal court, where counterclaims are still used, a defendant must file any counterclaim that stems from the same events covered by the plaintiff's complaint or forever lose the right to do so. In still other states where counterclaims are used, they are not mandatory, meaning a defendant is free to raise a claim that it was really the plaintiff who was at fault either in a counterclaim or later as part of a separate lawsuit.

counteroffer

The rejection of an offer to buy or sell that simultaneously makes a different offer, changing the terms in some way. For example, if a buyer offers $5,000 for a used car, and the seller replies that he wants $5,500, the seller has rejected the buyer's offer of $5,000 and made a counteroffer to sell at $5,500. The legal significance of a counteroffer is that it completely voids the original offer, so that if the seller decided to sell for $5,000 the next day, the buyer would be under no legal obligation to pay that amount for the car.

court calendar

A list of the cases and hearings that will be held by a court on a particular day, week or month. Because the length of time it will take to conduct a particular hearing or trial is at best a guess and many courts have a number of judges, accurately scheduling cases is difficult, with the result that court calendars are often revised and cases are often heard later than initially planned. A court calendar is sometimes called a docket, trial schedule or trial list.

court costs

The fees charged for the use of a court, including the initial filing fee, fees for serving the summons, complaint and other court papers, fees to pay a court reporter to transcribe deposition and in-court testimony and, if a jury is involved, to pay the daily stipend of jurors. Often costs to photocopy court papers and exhibits are also included. Court costs must be paid by both parties as the case progresses, but ultimately, the losing party will be responsible for both parties' costs.

covenant

A restriction on the use of real estate that governs its use, such as a requirement that the property will be used only for residential purposes. Covenants are found in deeds or in documents that bind everyone who owns land in a particular development. See *covenants, conditions and restrictions.*

covenants, conditions and restrictions (CC&Rs)

The restrictions governing the use of real estate, usually enforced by a homeowners' association and passed on to the new owners of property. For example, CC&Rs may tell you how big your house can be, how you must landscape your yard or whether you can have pets. If property is subject to CC&Rs, buyers must be notified before the sale takes place.

creditor

A person or entity (such as a bank) to whom a debt is owed.

crime

A type of behavior that has been defined by the state as deserving of punishment, which usually includes imprisonment. Crimes and their punishments are defined by Congress and state legislatures.

criminal case

A lawsuit brought by a prosecutor employed by the federal, state or local government that charges a person with the commission of a crime.

criminal insanity

A mental defect or disease that makes it impossible for a person to understand the wrongfulness of his acts or, even if he understands them, to distinguish right from wrong. Defendants who are criminally insane cannot be convicted of a crime, since criminal conduct involves the conscious intent to do wrong—a choice that the criminally insane cannot meaningfully make.

criminal law

Laws written by Congress and state legislators that make certain behavior illegal and punishable by fines and/or imprisonment. By contrast, civil laws are not punishable by imprisonment. In order for a defendant to be found guilty of a criminal law, the prosecution must show that the defendant intended to act as he did; in civil law, you may sometimes be responsible for your actions even though you did not intend the consequences. For example, civil law makes you financially responsible for a car accident you unintentionally caused.

cross-complaint

Sometimes called a cross-claim, legal paperwork that a defendant files to initiate her own lawsuit against the original plaintiff, a co-defendant or someone who is not yet a party to the lawsuit. A cross-complaint must concern the same events that gave rise to the original lawsuit. For example, a defendant accused of causing an injury when she failed to stop at a red light might cross-complain against the mechanic who recently repaired her car, claiming that his negligence resulted in the brakes failing and, hence, that the accident was his fault. In some states where the defendant wishes to make a legal claim against the original plaintiff and no third party is claimed to be involved, a counterclaim, and not a cross-complaint, should be used.

cross-examination

At trial, the opportunity to question any witness, including your opponent, who testifies against you on direct examination. The opportunity to cross-examine usually occurs as soon as a witness completes her direct testimony—often the opposing lawyer or party, or sometimes the judge, signals that it is time to begin cross-examination by saying, "Your witness." Typically, there are two important reasons to engage in cross-examination: to attempt to get the witness to say something helpful to your side, or to cast doubt on (impeach) the witness by getting her to admit something that reduces her credibility—for example, that her eyesight is so poor that she may not have seen an event clearly.

custodial interference

The taking of a child from his or her parent with the intent to interfere with that parent's physical custody of the child. This is a crime in most states, even if the taker also has custody rights.

custodian

A term used by the Uniform Transfers to Minors Act for the person named to manage property left to a child under the terms of that Act. The custodian will manage the property if the gift-giver dies before the child has reached the age specified by state law—usually 21. When the child reaches the specified age, he will receive the property and the custodian will have no further role in its management.

custody (of a child)

The legal authority to make decisions affecting a child's interests (legal custody) and the responsibility of taking care of the child (physical custody). When parents separate or divorce, one of the hardest decisions they have to make is which parent will have custody. The most common arrangement is for one parent to have custody (both physical and legal) while the other parent has a right of visitation. But it is not uncommon for the parents to share legal custody, even though one parent has physical custody. The most uncommon arrangement is for the parents to share both legal and physical custody.

damages

In a lawsuit, money awarded to one party based on injury or loss caused by the other. There are many different types or categories of damages that occasionally overlap, including:

1. compensatory damages

   Damages that cover actual injury or economic loss. Compensatory damages are intended to put the injured party in the position he was in prior to the injury. Compensatory damages typically include medical expenses, lost wages and the repair or replacement of property (also called "actual damages").

2. general damages

   Damages intended to cover injuries for which an exact dollar amount cannot be calculated. General damages are usually composed of pain and suffering, but can also include compensation for a shortened life expectancy, loss of the companionship of a loved one and, in defamation cases (libel and slander), loss of reputation.

3. nominal damages

   A term used when a judge or jury finds in favor of one party to a lawsuit—often because a law requires them to do so—but concludes that no real harm was done and therefore awards a very small amount of money. For example, if one neighbor sues another for libel based on untrue things the second neighbor said about the first,

a jury might conclude that although libel technically occurred, no serious damage was done to the first neighbor's reputation and consequentially award nominal damages of $1.

4. punitive damages

Sometimes called exemplary damages, awarded over and above special and general damages to punish a losing party's willful or malicious misconduct.

5. special damages

Damages that cover the winning party's out-of-pocket costs. For example, in a vehicle accident, special damages typically include medical expenses, car repair costs, rental car fees and lost wages. Often called "specials."

6. Statutory damages

Damages required by statutory law. For example, in many states if a landlord doesn't return a tenant's security deposit in a timely fashion or give a reason why it is being withheld, the state statutes give the judge authority to order the landlord to pay damages of double or triple the amount of the deposit.

7. treble damages

(Lawyerspeak for triple damages.) To penalize lawbreakers, some statutes occasionally give judges the power to award the winning party in a civil lawsuit the amount it lost as a result of the other party's illegal conduct, plus damages of three times that amount.

debenture

A type of bond (an interest-bearing document that serves as evidence of a debt) that does not require security in the form of a mortgage or lien on a specific piece of property. Repayment of a debenture is guaranteed only by the general credit of the issuer. For example, a corporation may issue a secured bond that gives the bondholder a lien on the corporation's factory. But if it issues a debenture, the loan is not secured by any property at all. When a corporation issues debentures, the holders are considered creditors of the corporation and are entitled to payment before shareholders if the business folds.

debtor

A person or entity (such as a bank) who owes money.

decedent

A person who has died, also called "deceased."

decision

The outcome of a proceeding before a judge, arbitrator, government agency or other legal tribunal. "Decision" is a general term often used interchangeably with the terms "judgment" or "opinion." To be precise, however, a judgment is the written form of the court's decision in the clerk's minutes or notes, and an opinion is a written document setting out the reasons for reaching the decision.

declaration under penalty of perjury

A signed statement, sworn to be true by the signer, that will make the signer guilty of the crime of perjury if the statement is shown to be materially false—that is, the lie is relevant and significant to the case.

declaratory judgment

A court decision in a civil case that tells the parties what their rights and responsibilities are, without awarding damages or ordering them to do anything. Unlike most court cases, where the plaintiff asks for damages or other court orders, the plaintiff in a declaratory judgment case simply wants the court to resolve an uncertainty so that it can avoid serious legal trouble in the future. Courts are usually reluctant to hear declaratory judgment cases, preferring to wait until there has been a measurable loss. But especially in cases involving important constitutional rights, courts will step in to clarify the legal landscape. For example, many cities regulate the right to assemble by requiring permits to hold a parade. A disappointed applicant who thinks the decision-making process is unconstitutional might hold his parade anyway and challenge the ordinance after he's cited; or he might ask a court beforehand to rule on the constitutionality of the law. By going to court, the applicant may avoid a messy confrontation with the city—and perhaps a citation, as well.

dedimus potestatum

An outdated legal procedure that permitted a party to take and record the testimony of a witness before trial, but only when that testimony might otherwise be lost. For example, a party to a lawsuit might use the procedure to obtain the testimony of a witness who was terminally ill and might not be able to testify at the trial. Nowadays, the Federal Rules of Civil Procedure routinely permit the taking of testimony before trial if that testimony might otherwise be lost.

deed

A document that transfers ownership of real estate.

defamation

A false statement that injures someone's reputation and exposes him to public contempt, hatred, ridicule or condemnation. If the false statement is published in print or through broadcast media, such as radio or TV, it is called libel. If it is only spoken, it is called slander. Libel is considered more serious than slander because the communication is permanently recorded in print or because it was broadcast to a large number of people. Defamation is a tort (a civil wrong) that entitles the injured party to compensation if he can prove that the statement damaged his reputation.

For example, if a worker can show that she lost her job because a co-worker started a false rumor that she came to work drunk, she might be able to recover monetary damages. In certain extreme cases, such as a false accusation that a person committed a crime or has a feared disease, the plaintiff need not prove that she was damaged because the law presumes that damage was done. These cases are called "libel per se" or "slander per se." Public officials or figures who want to prove defamation must meet a higher standard than the standard for private citizens; they must prove that the person who issued the false statements knew they were false or recklessly disregarded a substantial likelihood that they were false.

default

A failure to perform a legal duty. For example, a default on a mortgage or car loan happens when you fail to make the loan payments on time, fail to maintain adequate insurance or violate some other provision of the agreement. Default on a student loan occurs when you fail to repay a loan according to the terms you agreed to when you signed the promissory note, and the holder of your loan concludes that you do not intend to repay.

default judgment

At trial, a decision awarded to the plaintiff when a defendant fails to contest the case. To appeal a default judgment, a defendant must first file a motion in the court that issued it to have the default vacated (set aside).

defeasance

A clause in a deed, lease, will or other legal document that completely or partially negates the document if a certain condition occurs or fails to occur. Defeasance also means the act of rendering something null and void. For example, a will may provide that a gift of property is defeasable— that is, it will be void—if the beneficiary fails to marry before the willmaker's death.

defendant

The person against whom a lawsuit is filed. In certain states, and in certain types of lawsuits, the defendant is called the respondent. Compare *plaintiff*, *petitioner*.

demurrer

A request made to a court, asking it to dismiss a lawsuit on the grounds that no legal claim is asserted. For example, you might file a demurrer if your neighbor sued you for parking on the street in front of her house. Your parking habits may annoy your neighbor, but the curb is public property and parking there doesn't cause any harm recognized by the law. After a demurrer is filed, the judge holds a hearing at which both sides can make their arguments about the matter. The judge may dismiss all or part of the lawsuit, or may allow the party who filed the lawsuit to amend its complaint. In some states and in federal court, the term demurrer has been replaced by "motion to dismiss for failure to state a claim" (called a "12(b)(6) motion" in federal court) or similar term.

deponent

Someone whose deposition is being taken.

deposition

An important tool used in pretrial discovery where one party questions the other party or a witness who is in the case. Often conducted in an attorney's office, a deposition requires that all questions be answered under oath and be recorded by a court reporter, who creates a deposition transcript. Increasingly, depositions are being videotaped. Any deponent may be represented by an attorney. At trial, deposition testimony can be used to cast doubt on (impeach) a witness's contradictory testimony or to refresh the memory of a suddenly forgetful witness. If a deposed witness is unavailable when the trial takes place—for example, if he or she has died—the deposition may be read to the jury in place of live testimony.

devise

An old legal term that is generally used to refer to real estate left to someone under the terms of a will, or to the act of leaving such real estate. In some states, "devise" now applies to any kind of property left by will, making it identical to the term bequest. Compare *legacy*.

dictum

A remark, statement or observation of a judge that is not a necessary part of the legal reasoning needed to reach the decision in a case. Although dictum may be cited in a legal argument, it is not binding as legal precedent, meaning that other courts are not required to accept it. For example, if a defendant ran a stop sign and caused a collision, the judge's comments about the mechanical reliability of the particular make of the defendant's car would not be necessary to reach a decision in the case, and would be considered dictum. In future cases, lower court judges are free to ignore the comments when reaching their decisions. Dictum is an abbreviation of the Latin phrase "obiter dictum," which means a remark by the way, or an aside.

direct examination

At trial, the initial questioning of a party or witness by the side that called her to testify. The major purpose of direct examination is to explain your version of events to the judge or jury and to undercut your adversary's version. Good direct examination seeks to prove all facts necessary to satisfy the plaintiff's legal claims or causes of action—for example, that the defendant breached a valid contract and, as a result, the plaintiff suffered a loss.

directed verdict

A ruling by a judge, typically made after the plaintiff has presented all of her evidence but before the defendant puts on his case, that awards judgment to the defendant. A directed verdict is usually made because the judge concludes the plaintiff has failed to offer the minimum amount of evidence to prove her case even if there were no opposition. In other words, the judge is saying that, as a matter of law, no reasonable jury could decide in the plaintiff's favor. In a criminal case, a directed verdict is a judgment of acquittal for the defendant.

discharge (of debts)

A bankruptcy court's erasure of the debts of a person or business that has filed for bankruptcy.

discharge (of probate administrator)

A court order releasing the administrator or executor from any further duties connected with the probate of an estate. This typically occurs when the duties have been completed but may happen sooner if the executor or administrator wishes to withdraw or is dismissed.

dischargeable debts

Debts that can be erased by going through bankruptcy. Most debts incurred prior to declaring bankruptcy are dischargeable, including back rent, credit card bills and medical bills. Compare *nondischargeable debts*.

disclaim

(1) To refuse or give away a claim or a right to something. For example, if your aunt leaves you a white elephant in her will and you don't want it, you can refuse the gift by disclaiming your ownership rights. (2) To deny responsibility for a claim or act. For example, a merchant that sells goods secondhand may disclaim responsibility for a product's defects by selling it "as is."

disclaimer

(1) A refusal or renunciation of a claim or right. (2) A refusal or denial of responsibility for a claim or an act. (3) The written clause or document that sets out the disclaimer. See also *disclaim*.

disclosure

The making known of a fact that had previously been hidden; a revelation. For example, in many states you must disclose major physical defects in a house you are selling, such as a leaky roof or potential flooding problem.

discovery

A formal investigation—governed by court rules—that is conducted before trial. Discovery allows one party to question other parties, and sometimes witnesses. It also allows one party to force the others to produce requested documents or other physical evidence. The most common types of discovery are interrogatories, consisting of written

questions the other party must answer under penalty of perjury, and depositions, which involve an in-person session at which one party to a lawsuit has the opportunity to ask oral questions of the other party or her witnesses under oath while a written transcript is made by a court reporter. Other types of pretrial discovery consist of written requests to produce documents and requests for admissions, by which one party asks the other to admit or deny key facts in the case. One major purpose of discovery is to assess the strength or weakness of an opponent's case, with the idea of opening settlement talks. Another is to gather information to use at trial. Discovery is also present in criminal cases, in which by law the prosecutor must turn over to the defense any witness statements and any evidence that might tend to exonerate the defendant. Depending on the rules of the court, the defendant may also be obliged to share evidence with the prosecutor.

disinherit

To deliberately prevent someone from inheriting something. This is usually done by a provision in a will stating that someone who would ordinarily inherit property—a close family member, for example—should not receive it. In most states, you cannot completely disinherit your spouse; a surviving spouse has the right to claim a portion (usually one-third to one-half) of the deceased spouse's estate. With a few exceptions, however, you can expressly disinherit children.

dissolution

A term used instead of divorce in some states.

distributee

Anyone who receives something. Usually, the term refers to someone who inherits a deceased person's property. If the deceased person dies without a will (called intestate), state law determines what each distributee will receive. Also called a beneficiary.

District Attorney (D.A.)

A lawyer who is elected to represent a state government in criminal cases in a designated county or judicial district. A D.A.'s duties typically include reviewing police arrest reports, deciding whether to bring criminal charges against arrested people, and prosecuting criminal cases in court. The D.A. may also supervise other attorneys, called deputy district attorneys or assistant district attorneys. in some states a district attorney may be called a prosecuting attorney, county attorney or state's attorney. in the federal system, the equivalent to the D.A. is a United States attorney. The country has many U.S. attorneys, each appointed by the president, who supervise regional offices staffed with prosecutors called assistant United States attorneys.

district court

In federal court and in some states the name of the main trial court. Thus, if you file suit in federal court, your case will normally be heard in federal district court. States may also group their appellate courts into districts—for example, the First District Court of Appeal.

diversity jurisdiction

The power of the federal courts to decide cases between two citizens of different states, provided the amount the plaintiff seeks in damages exceeds $75,000.

docket

See *court calendar*.

doing business as (DBA)

A situation in which a business owner operates a company under a name different from his or her real name. When starting a new business that is named in this way, the owner must file a "fictitious name statement" or similar document with the appropriate county or state agency—for example, the county clerk or secretary of state's office. Putting this document on file enables consumers to discover the names of the business owners, which will be important if a consumer needs to sue the business. It also allows the business owner to conduct transactions in the business' name, such as opening bank accounts and obtaining a taxpayer identification number; and to bring lawsuits under the business' name for business-related debts. Filing a fictitious name statement does not in itself confer trademark protection for the name.

dominant tenement

Property that carries a right to use a portion of a neighboring property. For example, property that benefits from a beach access trail across another property is the dominant tenement.

dower and curtesy

A surviving spouse's right to receive a set portion of the deceased spouse's estate—usually one-third to one-half. Dower (not to be confused with a "dowry") refers to the portion to which a surviving wife is entitled, while curtesy refers to what a man may claim. Until recently, these amounts differed in a number of states. However, because discrimination on the basis of sex is now illegal in most cases, most states have abolished dower and curtesy and generally provide the same benefits regardless of sex—and this amount is often known simply as the statutory share. Under certain circumstances, a living spouse may not be able to sell or convey property that is subject to the other spouse's dower and curtesy or statutory share rights.

durable power of attorney

A power of attorney that remains in effect if the principal becomes incapacitated. If a power of attorney is not specifically made durable, it automatically expires if the principal becomes incapacitated. See *durable power of attorney for finances*, *durable power of attorney for health care*.

durable power of attorney for finances

A legal document that gives someone authority to manage your financial affairs if you become incapacitated. The person you name to represent you may be called an attorney-in-fact, health care proxy, agent or patient advocate, depending on where you live

durable power of attorney for health care

A legal document that you can use to give someone permission to make medical decisions for you if you are unable to make those decisions yourself. The person you name to represent you is called an attorney-in-fact.

dynamite charge

An judge's admonition to a deadlocked jury to go back to the jury room and try harder to reach a verdict. The judge might remind the jurors to respectfully consider the opinions of others and will often assure them that if the case has to be tried again, another jury won't necessarily do a better job than they're doing. Because of its coercive nature, some states prohibit the use of a dynamite charge as a violation of their state constitution, but the practice passed Federal constitutional muster in the case of *Allen v. Gainer*. The instruction is also known as a dynamite instruction, shotgun instruction, *Allen* charge or third-degree instruction.

easement

A right to use another person's real estate for a specific purpose. The most common type of easement is the right to travel over another person's land, known as a right of way. In addition, property owners commonly grant easements for the placement of utility poles, utility trenches, water lines or sewer lines. The owner of property that is subject to an easement is said to be "burdened" with the easement, because he or she is not allowed to interfere with its use. For example, if the deed to John's property permits Sue to travel across John's main road to reach her own home, John cannot do anything to block the road. On the other hand, Sue cannot do anything that exceeds the scope of her easement, such as widening the roadway.

easement by prescription

A right to use property, acquired by a long tradition of open and obvious use. For example, if hikers have been using a trail through your backyard for ten years and you've never complained, they probably have an easement by prescription through your yard to the trail.

effluxion of time

The normal expiration of a lease due to the passage of time, rather than due to a specific event that might cause the lease to end, such as destruction of the building.

emancipation

The act of freeing someone from restraint or bondage. For example, on January 1, 1863, slaves in the Confederate states were declared free by an executive order of President Lincoln, known as the "Emancipation Proclamation." After the Civil War, this emancipation was extended to the entire country and made law by the ratification of the 13th Amendment to the Constitution. Nowadays, emancipation refers to the point at which a child is free from parental control. It occurs when the child's parents no longer perform their parental duties and surrender their rights to the care, custody and earnings of their minor child. Emancipation may be the result of a voluntary agreement between the parents and child, or it may be implied from their acts and ongoing conduct. For example,

a child who leaves her parents' home and becomes entirely self-supporting without their objection is considered emancipated, while a child who goes to stay with a friend or relative and gets a part-time job is not. Emancipation may also occur when a minor child marries or enters the military.

emergency protective order

Any court-issued order meant to protect a person from harm or harassment. An emergency protective order is issued by the police, when court is out of session, to prevent domestic violence. An emergency protective order is a stop-gap measure, usually lasting only for a weekend or holiday, after which the abused person is expected to seek a temporary restraining order (TRO) from a court.

eminent domain

The power of the federal or state government to take private property for a public purpose, even if the property owner objects, provided that the property owner is compensated for the loss. The Fifth Amendment to the United States Constitution allows the government to take private property if the taking is for a public use and the owner is "justly compensated" (usually, paid fair market value) for his or her loss. A public use is virtually anything that is sanctioned by a federal or state legislative body, but such uses may include roads, parks, reservoirs, schools, hospitals or other public buildings. Sometimes called condemnation, taking or expropriation.

encroachment

The building of a structure entirely or partly on a neighbor's property. Encroachment may occur due to faulty surveying or sheer obstreperousness on the part of the builder. Solutions range from paying the rightful property owner for the use of the property to the court-ordered removal of the structure.

equitable distribution

A legal principle, followed by most states, under which assets and earnings acquired during marriage are divided equitably (fairly) at divorce. Typically this means a 50-50 split, but not always. In theory, equitable means equal, but in practice it often means that the higher wage earner gets two-thirds to the lower wage earner's one-third. If a spouse obtains a fault divorce, the "guilty" spouse may receive less than his equitable share upon divorce.

escheat

The forfeit of all property to the state when a person dies without heirs.

estate

Generally, all the property you own when you die. The term is also used when referring to a person's probate estate (the property actually passing through the probate process) and bankruptcy estate (the property subject to the bankruptcy court's jurisdiction)

estoppel

A legal principle that prevents a person from asserting or denying something in court that contradicts what has already been established as the truth. Types of estoppel include:

1. equitable estoppel

   A type of estoppel that bars a person from adopting a position in court that contradicts his or her past statements or actions when that contradictory stance would be unfair to another person who relied on the original position. For example, if a landlord agrees to allow a tenant to pay the rent ten days late for six months, it would be unfair to allow the landlord to bring a court action in the fourth month to evict the tenant for being a week late with the rent. The landlord would be estopped from asserting his right to evict the tenant for late payment of rent. Also known as estoppel in pais.

2. estoppel by deed

   A type of estoppel that prevents a person from denying the truth of anything that he or she stated in a deed, especially regarding who has valid ownership of the property. For example, someone who grants a deed to real estate before he actually owns the property can't later go back and undo the sale for that reason if, say, the new owner strikes oil in the backyard.

3. estoppel by silence

   A type of estoppel that prevents a person from asserting something when she had both the duty and the opportunity to speak up earlier, and her silence put another person at a disadvantage. For example, Edwards' Roofing Company has the wrong address and begins ripping the roof from Betty's house by mistake. If Betty sees this but remains silent, she cannot wait until the new roof is installed and then refuse to pay, asserting that the work was done without her agreement.

(4) promissory estoppel

    A. A type of estoppel that prevents a person who made a promise from reneging when someone else has reasonably relied on the promise and will suffer a loss if the promise is broken. For example, Forrest tells Antonio to go ahead and buy a boat without a motor, because he will sell Antonio an old boat motor at a very reasonable price. If Antonio relies on Forrest's promise and buys the motorless boat, Forrest cannot then deny his promise to sell John the motor at the agreed-upon price.

    B. A legal doctrine that prevents the relitigation of facts or issues that were previously resolved in court. For example, Alvin loses control of his car and accidentally sideswipes several parked cars. When the first car owner sues Alvin for damages, the court determines that Alvin was legally drunk at the time of the accident. Alvin will not be able to deny this fact in subsequent lawsuits against him. This type of estoppel is most commonly called collateral estoppel.

evidence

The many types of information presented to a judge or jury designed to convince them of the truth or falsity of key facts. Evidence typically includes testimony of witnesses, documents, photographs, items of damaged property, government records, videos and laboratory reports. Rules that are as strict as they are quirky and technical govern what types of evidence can be properly admitted as part of a trial. For example, the hearsay rule purports to prevent secondhand testimony of the "he said, she said" variety, but the existence of dozens of exceptions often means that hairsplitting lawyers can find a way to introduce such testimony into evidence. See also *admissible evidence, inadmissible evidence.*

exclusionary rule

A rule of evidence that disallows the use of illegally obtained evidence in criminal trials. For example, the exclusionary rule would prevent a prosecutor from introducing at trial evidence seized during an illegal search.

executive privilege

The privilege that allows the president and other high officials of the executive branch to keep certain communications private if disclosing those communications would disrupt the functions or decision-making processes of the executive branch. As demonstrated by the Watergate hearings, this privilege does not extend to information germane to a criminal investigation.

executor

The person named in a will to handle the property of someone who has died. The executor must collect and manage the property, pay debts and taxes, and then distribute what's left as specified in the will. In addition, the executor handles any probate court proceedings (with the help of a lawyer, if necessary) and takes care of day-to-day tasks—for example, terminating leases and credit cards, and notifying people and organizations of the death. Executors are also called personal representatives.

express warranty

A guarantee about the quality of goods or services made by a seller, such as, "This item is guaranteed against defects in construction for one year." Most express warranties come directly from the manufacturer or are included in the sales contract. If you want to hold the seller to an oral guarantee, it's best to get it in writing or have witnesses to the guarantee so that it doesn't come down to your word against the seller's if a problem arises.

expunge

To intentionally destroy, obliterate or strike out records or information in files, computers and other depositories. For example, state law may allow the criminal records of a juvenile offender to be expunged when he reaches the age of majority to allow him to begin his adult life with a clean record. Or, a company or government agency may routinely expunge out-of-date records to save storage space.

failure of consideration

The refusal or inability of a contracting party to perform its side of a bargain.

failure of issue

A situation in which a person dies without children who could have inherited her property.

fair use rule

A law that authorizes the use of copyrighted materials for certain purposes without the copyright owner's permission. Generally, uses intended to further scholarship, education

or an informed public are considered fair use, but recent years have seen severe limits placed on the amount of a work that can be reproduced under the fair use rule.

false imprisonment

Intentionally restraining another person's freedom of movement without having the legal right to do so. It's not necessary that physical force be used; threats or a show of apparent authority are sufficient. False imprisonment is a misdemeanor and a tort (a civil wrong). If the perpetrator confines the victim for a substantial period of time (or moves him a significant distance) in order to commit a felony, the false imprisonment may become a kidnapping. People who are arrested and get the charges dropped, or are later acquitted, often think that they can sue the arresting officer for false imprisonment (also known as false arrest). These lawsuits rarely succeed: As long as the officer had probable cause to arrest the person, the officer will not be liable for a false arrest, even if it turns out later that the information the officer relied upon was incorrect.

family court

A separate court, or more likely a separate division of the regular state trial court, that considers only cases involving divorce (dissolution of marriage), child custody and support, guardianship, adoption, and other cases having to do with family-related issues, including the issuance of restraining orders in domestic violence cases.

fault divorce

A tradition that required one spouse to prove that the other spouse was legally at fault, to obtain a divorce. The "innocent" spouse was then granted the divorce from the "guilty" spouse. Today, 35 states still allow a spouse to allege fault in obtaining a divorce. The traditional fault grounds for divorce are adultery, cruelty, desertion, confinement in prison, physical incapacity and incurable insanity. These grounds are also generally referred to as marital misconduct.

federal court

A branch of the United States government with power derived directly from the U.S. Constitution. Federal courts decide cases involving the U.S. Constitution, federal law— for example, patents, federal taxes, labor law and federal crimes, such as robbing a federally-chartered bank—and

cases where the parties are from different states and are involved in a dispute for $75,000 or more.

felony

A serious crime (contrasted with misdemeanors and infractions, less serious crimes), usually punishable by a prison term of more than one year or, in some cases, by death. For example, murder, extortion and kidnapping are felonies; a minor fist fight is usually charged as a misdemeanor, and a speeding ticket is generally an infraction.

Feres doctrine

A legal doctrine that prevents people who are injured as a result of military service from successfully suing the federal government under the Federal Tort Claims Act. The doctrine comes from the U.S. Supreme Court case *Feres v. United States*, in which servicemen who picked up highly radioactive weapons fragments from a crashed airplane were not permitted to recover damages from the government. Also known as the Feres-Stencel doctrine or the Feres rule.

fictitious name

Any name a person uses that is not his or her real name. Fictitious names are often used in conducting a business. (See *doing business as.*) They may also be used when filing a lawsuit against a party whose real name is unknown or when, with the consent of the court, it is appropriate to conceal the true name of the party. John Doe is often used for an unknown male and Jane Roe is used for an unknown female. For example, the most well-known use of a fictitious name in a court case is *Roe v. Wade*, the case that established a woman's right to have an abortion without undue interference from the government. Jane Roe was a fictitious name for the plaintiff in that case.

fieri facias

Latin for "that you cause to be done." This is a court document that instructs a sheriff to seize and sell a defendant's property in order to satisfy a monetary judgment against the defendant.

final beneficiary

The person or institution designated to receive trust property upon the death of a life beneficiary. For example,

Jim creates a trust through which his wife, Jane, receives income for the duration of her life. Their daughter, the final beneficiary, receives the trust principal after Jane's death.

forbearance

Voluntarily refraining from doing something, such as asserting a legal right. For example, a creditor may forbear on its right to collect a debt by temporarily postponing or reducing the borrower's payments.

foreclosure

The forced sale of real estate to pay off a loan on which the owner of the property has defaulted.

forfeiture

The loss of property or a privilege due to breaking a law. For example, a landlord may forfeit his or her property to the federal or state government if the landlord knows it is a drug-dealing site but fails to stop the illegal activity. Or, you may have to forfeit your driver's license if you commit too many moving violations or are convicted of driving under the influence of alcohol or drugs.

form interrogatories

Preprinted or "canned" sets of questions that one party in a lawsuit asks an opposing party. Form interrogatories cover the issues commonly encountered in the kind of lawsuit at hand. For example, lawyers' form books have sets of interrogatories designed for contract disputes, landlord-tenant cases and many others. Form interrogatories are often supplemented by questions written by the lawyers and designed for the particular issues in the case.

forum

Refers to the court in which a lawsuit is filed or in which a hearing or trial is conducted.

forum nonconveniens

Latin for "inconvenient court." Because these days strict written rules of jurisdiction and venue are used to decide where a case can and cannot be properly filed, this term has largely lost any real meaning, except as yet another example of a confusing Latin term that lawyers take pleasure in using.

forum shopping

The process by which a plaintiff chooses among two or more courts that have the power—technically, the correct jurisdiction and venue—to consider his case. This decision is based on which court is likely to consider the case most favorably. In some instances, a case can properly be filed in two or more federal district courts as well as in the trial courts of several states—and this makes forum shopping a complicated business. It often involves weighing a number of factors, including proximity to the court, the reputation of the judge in the particular legal area, the likely type of available jurors and subtle differences in governing law and procedure.

fraud

Intentionally deceiving another person and causing her to suffer a loss. Fraud includes lies and half-truths, such as selling a lemon and claiming "she runs like a dream."

future interest

A right to property that cannot be enforced in the present, but only at some time in the future. For example, John's will leaves his house to his sister Marian, but only after the death of his wife, Hillary. Marian has a future interest in the house.

garnishment

A court-ordered process that takes property from a person to satisfy a debt. For example, a person who owes money to a creditor may have her wages garnished if she loses a lawsuit filed by the creditor. Up to 25% of her wages can be deducted from her check to pay the debt before she ever sees her check on payday.

general partner

A person who joins together with at least one other to own and operate a business for profit—and who, unlike the owners of a corporation, is personally liable for all the business's debts. In addition to being responsible for all partnership debts and obligations, a general partner can take actions that legally bind the entire business. That means, for example, that if one partner signs a contract on behalf of the partnership, it will be fully enforceable against the partnership and each individual partner, even if the other partners weren't consulted in advance and didn't approve the contract. In contrast, a limited partner is

liable only to the extent of the capital he or she has invested in the business. The term general partner may also refer to the managing partner of a limited partnership who is responsible for partnership debts over and above his or her individual investment in the partnership. See also *partnership, limited partnership*.

general power of attorney

See *power of attorney*.

grand jury

In criminal cases, a group (usually between 17 and 23 persons) that decides whether there is enough evidence to justify an indictment (formal felony charges) and a trial. A grand jury indictment is the first step, after arrest, in any formal prosecution of a felony.

grandfather clause

A provision in a new law that limits its application to people who are new to the system; people already in the system are exempt from the new regulation. For example, when Washington, D.C., raised its drinking age from 18 to 21, people between those ages, who could drink under the old law, were allowed to retain the right to legally consume alcohol under a grandfather clause.

grant deed

A deed containing an implied promise that the person transferring the property actually owns the title and that it is not encumbered in any way, except as described in the deed. This is the most commonly used type of deed. Compare *quitclaim deed*.

gravamen

The essential element of a lawsuit. For example, the gravamen of a lawsuit involving a car accident might be the careless driving of the defendant.

gross lease

A commercial real estate lease in which the tenant pays a fixed amount of rent per month or year, regardless of the landlord's operating costs, such as maintenance, taxes and insurance. A gross lease closely resembles the typical residential lease. The tenant may agree to a "gross lease with stops," meaning that the tenant will pitch in if the landlord's operating costs rise above a certain level. In real estate lingo, the point when the tenant starts to contribute is called the "stop level," because that's where the landlord's share of the costs stops.

guarantor

A person who makes a legally binding promise to either pay another person's debt or perform another person's duty if that person defaults or fails to perform. The guarantor gives a "guaranty," which is an assurance that the debt or other obligation will be fulfilled.

guaranty

When used as a verb, to agree to pay another person's debt or perform another person's duty, if that person fails to come through. As a noun, the written document in which this assurance is made. For example, if you cosign a loan, you have made a guaranty and will be legally responsible for the debt if the borrower fails to repay the money as promised. The person who makes a guaranty is called the guarantor. Also known as a guarantee or warranty.

guardian

An adult who has been given the legal right by a court to control and care for a minor or (in some states) an incapacitated adult, and her property. Someone who looks after a child's property is called a "guardian of the estate." An adult who has legal authority to make personal decisions for the child, including responsibility for his physical, medical and educational needs, is called a "guardian of the person." Sometimes just one person will be named to take care of all these tasks. An individual appointed by a court to look after an incapacitated adult may also be known as a guardian, but is more frequently called a conservator.

guardian *ad litem*

A person, not necessarily a lawyer, who is appointed by a court to represent and protect the interests of a child or an incapacitated adult during a lawsuit. For example, a guardian *ad litem* (GAL) may be appointed to represent the interests of a child whose parents are locked in a contentious battle for custody, or to protect a child's interests in a lawsuit where there are allegations of child abuse. The GAL may conduct interviews and investigations, make reports to the court and participate in court hearings or mediation sessions. Sometimes called court-appointed special advocates (CASAs).

guardianship

A legal relationship created by a court between a guardian and his ward—either a minor child or an incapacitated adult. The guardian has a legal right and duty to care for the ward. This may involve making personal decisions on his or her behalf, managing property or both. Guardianships of incapacitated adults are more typically called conservatorships.

habeas corpus

Latin for "You have the body." A prisoner files a petition for writ of *habeas corpus* in order to challenge the authority of the prison or jail warden to continue to hold him. If the judge orders a hearing after reading the writ, the prisoner gets to argue that his confinement is illegal. These writs are frequently filed by convicted prisoners who challenge their conviction on the grounds that the trial attorney failed to prepare the defense and was incompetent. Prisoners sentenced to death also file *habeas* petitions challenging the constitutionality of the state death penalty law. *Habeas* writs are different from and do not replace appeals, which are arguments for reversal of a conviction based on claims that the judge conducted the trial improperly. Often, convicted prisoners file both.

hearing

In the trial court context, a legal proceeding (other than a full-scale trial) held before a judge. During a hearing, evidence and arguments are presented in an effort to resolve a disputed factual or legal issue. Hearings typically, but by no means always, occur prior to trial when a party asks the judge to decide a specific issue—often on an interim basis—such as whether a temporary restraining order or preliminary injunction should be issued, or temporary child custody or child support awarded. In the administrative or agency law context, a hearing is usually a proceeding before an administrative hearing officer or judge representing an agency that has the power to regulate a particular field or oversee a governmental benefit program. For example, the Federal Aviation Board has the authority to hold hearings on airline safety, and a state Worker's Compensation Appeals Board has the power to rule on the appeals of people whose applications for benefits have been denied.

hearsay rule

A rule of evidence that prohibits the consideration of secondhand testimony at a trial. For example, if an eyewitness to an accident later tells another person what she saw, the second person's testimony would normally be excluded from a trial by the hearsay rule. The major reason for this rule is that secondhand testimony is thought to be inherently unreliable in large part because the opposing party has no ability to confront and cross-examine the person who has firsthand knowledge of the event. However, there are a great many exceptions to the hearsay rule in situations where courts have concluded that a particular type of hearsay is likely to be reliable. These exceptions include statements by an opposing party that contradict what she has said in court (called "admissions against interest"), government records, the statements of dying people, spontaneous statements (something a person blurts out when excited or startled) and statements about a person's state of mind or future intentions, to name just a few. One important feature of alternative dispute resolution proceedings such as arbitration and mediation is that statements that would be barred from being introduced in court as hearsay are allowed.

heir

One who receives property from someone who has died. While the traditional meaning includes only those who had a legal right to the deceased person's property, modern usage includes anyone who receives property from the estate of a deceased person.

heir apparent

One who expects to be receive property from the estate of a family member, as long as she outlives that person.

heir at law

A person entitled to inherit property under intestate succession laws.

hold harmless

In a contract, a promise by one party not to hold the other party responsible if the other party carries out the contract in a way that causes damage to the first party. For example, many leases include a hold harmless clause in which the tenant agrees not to sue the landlord if the tenant is injured due to the landlord's failure to maintain the premises. In

most states, these clauses are illegal in residential tenancies, but may be upheld in commercial settings.

holographic will

A will that is completely handwritten, dated and signed by the person making it. Holographic wills are generally not witnessed. Although it's legal in many states, making a holographic will is never advised except as a last resort.

homestead

(1) The house in which a family lives, plus any adjoining land and other buildings on that land. (2) Real estate that is not subject to the claims of creditors as long as it is occupied as a home by the head of the household. After the head of the family dies, homestead laws often allow the surviving spouse or minor children to live on the property for as long as they choose. (3) Land acquired out of the public lands of the United States. The term "homesteaders" refers to people who got their land by settling it and making it productive, rather than purchasing it outright.

homestead declaration

A form filed with the county recorder's office to put on record your right to a homestead exemption. In most states, the homestead exemption is automatic—that is, you are not required to record a homestead declaration in order to claim the homestead exemption. A few states do require such a recording, however.

homicide

The killing of one human being by the act or omission of another. The term applies to all such killings, whether criminal or not. Homicide is considered noncriminal in a number of situations, including deaths as the result of war and putting someone to death by the valid sentence of a court. Killing may also be legally justified or excused, as it is in cases of self-defense or when someone is killed by another person who is attempting to prevent a violent felony. Criminal homicide occurs when a person purposely, knowingly, recklessly or negligently causes the death of another. Murder and manslaughter are both examples of criminal homicide.

hung jury

A jury unable to come to a final decision, resulting in a mistrial. Judges do their best to avoid hung juries, typically sending juries back into deliberations with an assurance (sometimes known as a "dynamite charge") that they will be able to reach a decision if they try harder. If a mistrial is declared, the case is tried again unless the parties settle the case (in a civil case) or the prosecution dismisses the charges or offers a plea bargain (in a criminal case).

illusory promise

A promise that pledges nothing, because it is vague or because the promisor can choose whether or not to honor it. Such promises are not legally binding. For example, if you get a new job and promise to work for three years, unless you resign sooner, you haven't made a valid contract and can resign or be fired at any time.

impeach

(1) To discredit. To impeach a witness's credibility, for example, is to show that the witness is not believable. A witness may be impeached by showing that he has made statements that are inconsistent with his present testimony, or that he has a reputation for not being a truthful person. (2) The process of charging a public official, such as the president or a federal judge, with a crime or misconduct and removing the official from office.

implied warranty

A guarantee about the quality of goods or services purchased that is not written down or explicitly spoken. Virtually everything you buy comes with two implied warranties, one for "merchantability" and one for "fitness." The implied warranty of merchantability is an assurance that a new item will work for its specified purpose. The item doesn't have to work wonderfully, and if you use it for something it wasn't designed for, say trimming shrubs with an electric carving knife, the warranty doesn't apply. The implied warranty of fitness applies when you buy an item for a specific purpose. If you notified the seller of your specific needs, the item is guaranteed to meet them. For example, if you buy new tires for your bicycle after telling the store clerk that you plan to use them for mountain cycling and the tires puncture when you pass over a small rock, the tires don't conform to the warranty of fitness.

implied warranty of habitability

A legal doctrine that requires landlords to offer and maintain livable premises for their tenants. If a landlord

fails to provide habitable housing, tenants in most states may legally withhold rent or take other measures, including hiring someone to fix the problem or moving out. See *constructive eviction.*

in camera

Latin for "in chambers." A legal proceeding is *in camera* when a hearing is held before the judge in her private chambers or when the public is excluded from the courtroom. Proceedings are often held *in camera* to protect victims and witnesses from public exposure, especially if the victim or witness is a child. There is still, however, a record made of the proceeding, typically by a court stenographer. The judge may decide to seal this record if the material is extremely sensitive or likely to prejudice one side or the other.

in terrorem

Latin meaning "in fear." This phrase is used to describe provisions in contracts or wills meant to scare a person into complying with the terms of the agreement. For example, a will might state that an heir will forfeit her inheritance if she challenges the validity of the will. Of course, if the will is challenged and found to be invalid, then the clause itself is also invalid and the heir takes whatever she would have inherited if there were no will.

in toto

Latin for "in its entirety" or "completely." For example, if a judge accepts a lawyer's argument *in toto*, it means that he's bought the whole thing, hook, line and sinker.

inadmissible evidence

Testimony or other evidence that fails to meet state or federal court rules governing the types of evidence that can be presented to a judge or jury. The main reason that evidence is ruled inadmissible is because it falls into a category deemed so unreliable that a court should not consider it as part of a deciding a case—for example, hearsay evidence, or an expert's opinion that is not based on facts generally accepted in the field. Evidence will also be declared inadmissible if it suffers from some other defect—for example, as compared to its value, it will take too long to present or risks enflaming the jury, as might be the case with graphic pictures of a homicide victim. In addition, in criminal cases, evidence that is gathered using illegal methods is commonly ruled inadmissible. Because the rules of evidence are so complicated (and because contesting lawyers waste so much time arguing over them), there is a strong trend towards using mediation or arbitration to resolve civil disputes. In mediation and arbitration, virtually all evidence can be considered. See *evidence, admissible evidence.*

incapacity

(1) A lack of physical or mental abilities that results in a person's inability to manage his or her own personal care, property or finances. (2) A lack of ability to understand one's actions when making a will or other legal document. (3) The inability of an injured worker to perform his or her job. This may qualify the worker for disability benefits or workers' compensation.

indispensable party

A person or entity (such as a corporation) that must be included in a lawsuit in order for the court to render a final judgment that will be just to everyone concerned. For example, if a person sues his neighbors to force them to prune a tree that poses a danger to his house, he must name all owners of the neighboring property in the suit.

information

The name of the document, sometimes called a criminal complaint or petition, in which a prosecutor charges a criminal defendant with a crime, either a felony or a misdemeanor. The information tells the defendant what crime he is charged with, against whom and when the offense allegedly occurred, but the prosecutor is not obliged to go into great detail. If the defendant wants more specifics, he must ask for it by way of a discovery request. Compare *indictment.*

informed consent

An agreement to do something or to allow something to happen, made with complete knowledge of all relevant facts, such as the risks involved or any available alternatives. For example, a patient may give informed consent to medical treatment only after the health care professional has disclosed all possible risks involved in accepting or rejecting the treatment. A health care provider or facility may be held responsible for an injury caused by an undisclosed risk. In another context, a person accused

of committing a crime cannot give up his constitutional rights—for example, to remain silent or to talk with an attorney—unless and until he has been informed of those rights, usually via the well-known *Miranda* warnings.

infraction

A minor violation of the law that is punishable only by a fine—for example, a traffic or parking ticket. Not all vehicle-related violations are infractions, however—refusing to identify oneself when involved in an accident is a misdemeanor in some states.

injunction

A court decision that is intended to prevent harm—often irreparable harm—as distinguished from most court decisions, which are designed to provide a remedy for harm that has already occurred. Injunctions are orders that one side refrain from or stop certain actions, such as an order that an abusive spouse stay away from the other spouse or that a logging company not cut down first-growth trees. Injunctions can be temporary, pending a consideration of the issue later at trial (these are called interlocutory decrees or preliminary injunctions). Judges can also issue permanent injunctions at the end of trials, in which a party may be permanently prohibited from engaging in some conduct—for example, infringing a copyright or trademark or making use of illegally obtained trade secrets. Although most injunctions order a party not to do something, occasionally a court will issue a "mandatory injunction" to order a party to carry out a positive act—for example, return stolen computer code.

injunctive relief

A situation in which a court grants an order, called an injunction, telling a party to refrain from doing something—or in the case of a mandatory injunction, to carry out a particular action. Usually injunctive relief is granted only after a hearing at which both sides have an opportunity to present testimony and legal arguments.

intangible property

Personal property that has no physical existence, such as stocks, bonds, bank notes, trade secrets, patents, copyrights and trademarks. Such "untouchable" items may be represented by a certificate or license that fixes or approximates the value, but others (such as the goodwill or reputation of a business) are not easily valued or embodied in any instrument. Compare *tangible property*.

intellectual property (IP) law

The area of law that regulates the ownership and use of creative works, including patent, copyright and trademark law.

intentional tort

A deliberate act that causes harm to another, for which the victim may sue the wrongdoer for damages. Examples of intentional torts include assault, battery, libel and intentional infliction of emotional distress. Acts of domestic violence, such as assault and battery, are intentional torts (as well as crimes).

inter vivos trust

The Latin name, favored by some lawyers, for a living trust. *Inter vivos* is Latin for "between the living."

interlocutory decree

A court judgment that is not final until the judge decides other matters in the case or until enough time has passed to see if the interim decision is working. In the past, interlocutory decrees were most often used in divorces. The terms of the divorce were set out in an interlocutory decree, which would become final only after a waiting period. The purpose of the waiting period was to allow the couple time to reconcile. They rarely did, however, so most states no longer use interlocutory decrees of divorce.

interrogatory

Written questions designed to discover key facts about an opposing party's case that a party to a lawsuit asks an opposing party (but not a nonparty witness, who can only be questioned in person at a deposition). Interrogatories are part of the pretrial discovery stage of a lawsuit, and must be answered under penalty of perjury. Court rules tightly regulate how, when and how many interrogatories can be asked. Lawyers can write their own sets of questions, or can use form interrogatories, designed to cover typical issues in common lawsuits.

intestate

The condition of dying without a valid will. The probate court appoints an administrator to distribute the deceased person's property according to state law.

intestate succession

The method by which property is distributed when a person dies without a valid will. Each state's law provides that the property be distributed to the closest surviving relatives. In most states, the surviving spouse, children, parents, siblings, nieces and nephews, and next of kin inherit, in that order.

inure

To take effect, or to benefit someone. In property law, the term means "to vest." For example, Jim buys a beach house that includes the right to travel across the neighbor's property to get to the water. That right of way is said, cryptically, "to inure to the benefit of Jim."

invitee

A business guest, or someone who enters property held open to members of the public, such as a visitor to a museum. Property owners must protect invitees from dangers on the property. In an example of the perversion of legalese, social guests that you invite into your home are called "licensees."

ipse dixit

Latin for "he himself said it." The term labels something that is asserted but unproved.

ipso facto

Latin for "by the fact itself." This term is used by Latin-addicted lawyers when something is so obvious that it needs no elaboration or further explanation. For example, it might be said that a blind person, *ipso facto*, is not qualified to obtain to a driver's license.

irrevocable trust

A permanent trust. Once you create it, it cannot be revoked, amended or changed in any way unless a court finds that a change is necessary for the trust to serve the purpose for which it was created.

issue

A term generally meaning all your children and their children down through the generations, including grandchildren, great-grandchildren, and so on. Also called "lineal descendants."

JNOV

See *judgment notwithstanding the verdict.*

joint tenancy

A way for two or more people to share ownership of real estate or other property. When two or more people own property as joint tenants and one owner dies, the other owners automatically own the deceased owner's share. For example, if a parent and child own a house as joint tenants and the parent dies, the child automatically becomes full owner. Because of this right of survivorship, no will is required to transfer the property; it goes directly to the surviving joint tenants without the delay and costs of probate.

judgment

A final court ruling resolving the key questions in a lawsuit and determining the rights and obligations of the opposing parties. For example, after a trial involving a vehicle accident, a court will issue a judgment determining which party was at fault—or most at fault—and how much money that party must pay the other. Most judgments can be appealed by the losing party, except judgments issued by default (the defendant doesn't show up), which normally require that the defendant first promptly move to vacate (set aside) the default and reopen the case.

judgment notwithstanding the verdict (JNOV)

Reversal of a jury's verdict by a judge when the judge believes that there were insufficient facts on which to base the jury's verdict, or that the verdict did not correctly apply the law. This procedure is similar to a situation in which a judge orders a jury to arrive at a particular verdict, called a directed verdict. In fact, a judgment notwithstanding the verdict is occasionally made when a jury refuses to follow a judge's instruction to arrive at a certain verdict. Incidentally, for those of a scholarly bent, this term has its roots in the Latin *non obstante verdicto*, meaning notwithstanding the verdict.

jurisdiction

The authority of a court to hear and decide a case. To make a legally-valid decision in a case, a court must have both "subject matter jurisdiction" (power to hear the type of case in question, which is granted by the state legislatures and Congress) and "personal jurisdiction" (power to make a

decision affecting the parties involved in the lawsuit, which a court gets as a result of the parties' actions). For example, state court's subject matter jurisdiction includes the civil and criminal laws that the state legislature has passed, but does not include the right to hear patent disputes or immigration violations, which Congress has decided may only be heard in federal courts. And no court can entertain a case unless the parties agree to be there or live in the state (or federal district) where the court sits, or have enough contacts with the state or district that it's fair to make them answer to that court. (Doing business in a state, owning property there or driving on its highways will usually be enough to allow the court to hear the case.) The term jurisdiction is also commonly used to define the amount of money a court has the power to award. For example, small claims courts have jurisdiction only to hear cases up to a relatively low monetary amount—depending on the state, typically in the range of $2,000 to $10,000. If a court doesn't have personal jurisdiction over all the parties and the subject matter involved, it "lacks jurisdiction," which means it doesn't have the power to render a decision.

jury nullification

A decision by the jury to acquit a defendant who has violated a law that the jury believes is unjust or wrong. Jury nullification has always been an option for juries in England and the United States, although judges will prevent a defense lawyer from urging the jury to acquit on this basis. Nullification was evident during the Vietnam war (when selective service protesters were acquitted by juries opposed to the war) and currently appears in criminal cases when the jury disagrees with the punishment—for example, in "three strikes" cases when the jury realizes that conviction of a relatively minor offense will result in lifetime imprisonment.

jus naturale

Latin for "natural law." This is a system of legal principles ostensibly derived from universal divine truths.

kindred

Under some state's probate codes, all relatives of a deceased person.

larceny

Another term for theft. Although the definition of this term differs from state to state, it typically means taking property belonging to another with the intent to permanently deprive the owner of the property. If the taking is non-forceful, it is larceny; if it is accompanied by force or fear directed against a person, it is robbery, a much more serious offense.

lawful issue

Formerly, statutes governing wills used this phrase to specify children born to married parents, and to exclude those born out of wedlock. Now, the phrase means the same as issue and "lineal descendant."

lease

An oral or written agreement (a contract) between two people concerning the use by one of the property of the other. A person can lease real estate (such as an apartment or business property) or personal property (such as a car or a boat). A lease should cover basic issues such as when the lease will begin and end, the rent or other costs, how payments should be made, and any restrictions on the use of the property. The property owner is often called the "lessor," and the person using the property is called the "lessee."

legacy

An outdated legal word meaning personal property left by a will. The more common term for this type of property is bequest. Compare *devise.*

legislative immunity

A legal doctrine that prevents legislators from being sued for actions performed and decisions made in the course of serving in government. This doctrine does not protect legislators from criminal prosecution, nor does it relieve them from responsibility for actions outside the scope of their office, such as the nefarious activities of former Senator Bob Packwood.

letters testamentary

The document given to an executor by the probate court authorizing the executor to settle the estate according to either a will or the state's intestate succession laws.

lex loci

Latin for the "law of the place." It means local law.

liability

1. The state of being liable—that is, legally responsible for an act or omission.

   Example: Peri hires Paul to fix a broken pipe in her bathroom, but the new pipe bursts the day after Paul installs it, ruining the bathroom floor. This raises the issue of liability: Who is responsible for the damage? Peri claims that Paul is responsible, and sues him for the cost of hiring another plumber to fix the pipe and replacing the floor. Paul, in turn, claims that the pipe manufacturer is responsible, because they supplied him with faulty materials. Both Peri and Paul must prove their claims in court; if Paul and/or the manufacturer is found liable, one or both will have to pay damages to Peri.

2. Something for which a person is liable. For example, a debt is often called a liability.

libel

An untruthful statement about a person, published in writing or through broadcast media, that injures the person's reputation or standing in the community. Because libel is a tort (a civil wrong), the injured person can bring a lawsuit against the person who made the false statement. Libel is a form of defamation, as is slander (an untruthful statement that is spoken, but not published in writing or broadcast through the media).

lien

The right of a secured creditor to grab a specific item of property if you don't pay a debt. Liens can also be created by court judgments (judgment liens) and by claims asserted by those who work to improve a person's real estate (mechanic's liens). Liens to which you agree are called security interests, and include mortgages, home equity loans, car loans and personal loans for which you pledge property to guarantee repayment. Liens created without your consent are called nonconsensual liens, and include judgment liens (liens filed by a creditor who has sued you and obtained a judgment), tax liens and mechanics liens (liens filed by a contractor who worked on your house but wasn't paid).

life beneficiary

A person who receives benefits, under a trust or by will, for his or her lifetime.

limited liability

The maximum amount a business owner can lose if the business is subject to debts, claims or other liabilities. An owner of a limited liability company or a person who invests in a corporation (a shareholder) generally stands to lose only the amount of money invested in the business. This means that if the limited liability company or corporation folds, creditors cannot seize or sell an owner's home, car or other personal assets. (This is known as "limited personal liability.") By contrast, owners of a sole proprietorship or general partnership have unlimited liability for business debts, as do the general partners in a limited partnership and limited partners who take part in managing the business.

limited liability company (LLC)

A relatively new and flexible business ownership structure. Particularly popular with small businesses, the LLC offers its owners the advantage of limited personal liability (like a corporation) and a choice of how the business will be taxed. Partners can choose for the LLC to be taxed as a separate entity (again, like a corporation) or as a partnership-like entity in which profits are passed through to partners and taxed on their personal income tax returns. Although state laws governing creation of LLCs and IRS regulations controlling their federal tax status are still evolving, because of their flexibility LLCs are increasingly regarded as the small business legal entity of choice.

limited liability partnership (LLP)

A type of partnership recognized in a majority of states that protects a partner from personal liability for negligent acts committed by other partners or by employees not under his or her direct control. Many states restrict this type partnership to professionals, such as lawyers, accountants, architects and health care providers.

limited partnership

A business structure that allows one or more partners (called limited partners) to enjoy limited personal liability for partnership debts while another partner or partners (called general partners) have unlimited personal liability. The key difference between a general and limited partner concerns management decision-making—general partners run the business, and limited partners, who are usually passive investors, are not allowed to make day-to-day

business decisions. If they do, they risk being treated as general partners with unlimited personal liability.

lis pendens

Latin for "a suit pending." (1) The term may refer to any pending lawsuit. (2) A written notice that a lawsuit has been filed concerning real estate, involving either the title to the property or a claimed ownership interest in it. The notice is usually filed in the county land records office. Recording a *lis pendens* against a piece of property alerts a potential purchaser or lender that the property's title is in question, which makes the property less attractive to a buyer or lender. After the notice is filed, anyone who nevertheless purchases the land or property described in the notice is subject to the ultimate decision of the lawsuit.

living trust

A trust you can set up during your life. Living trusts are an excellent way to avoid the cost and hassle of probate because, after death of the founder of the trust, the property you transfer into the trust during your life passes directly to the trust beneficiaries after you die, without court involvement. The successor trustee—the person you appoint to handle the trust after your death—simply transfers ownership to the beneficiaries you named in the trust. Living trusts are also called "*inter vivos* trusts."

living will

A legal document in which you state your wishes about certain kinds of medical treatments and life-prolonging procedures. The document takes effect if you can't communicate your own health care decisions at the time they have to be made. A living will may also be called a health care directive, advance directive or directive to physicians.

malfeasance

Doing something that is illegal. This term is often used when a professional or public official commits an illegal act that interferes with the performance of his or her duties. For example, an elected official who accepts a bribe in exchange for political favors has committed malfeasance. Compare *misfeasance.*

malpractice

The delivery of substandard care or services by a lawyer, doctor, dentist, accountant or other professional. Generally, malpractice occurs when a professional fails to provide the quality of care that should reasonably be expected in the circumstances, with the result that her patient or client is harmed. In the area of legal malpractice, you need to prove two things to show that you were harmed: first, that your lawyer screwed up; and second, that if the lawyer had handled the work properly, you would have won your original case.

mandamus

Latin for "we command." A writ of mandamus is a court order that requires another court, government official, public body, corporation or individual to perform a certain act. For example, after a hearing, a court might issue a writ of *mandamus* forcing a public school to admit certain students on the grounds that the school illegally discriminated against them when it denied them admission. A writ of *mandamus* is the opposite of an order to cease and desist, or stop doing something. Also called a "writ of mandate."

marital property

Most of the property accumulated by spouses during a marriage, called community property in some states. States differ as to exactly what is included in marital property; some states include all property and earnings during the marriage, while others exclude gifts and inheritances.

mechanic's lien

A legal claim placed on real estate by someone who is owed money for labor, services or supplies contributed to the property for the purpose of improving it. Typical lien claimants are general contractors, subcontractors and suppliers of building materials. A mechanic's lien claimant can sue to have the real estate sold at auction and recover the debt from the proceeds. Because property with a lien on it cannot be easily sold until the lien is satisfied (paid off), owners have a great incentive to pay their bills.

mediation

A dispute resolution method designed to help warring parties resolve their own dispute without going to court. In mediation, a neutral third party (the mediator) meets with

the opposing sides to help them find a mutually satisfactory solution. Unlike a judge in her courtroom or an arbitrator conducting a binding arbitration, the mediator has no power to impose a solution. No formal rules of evidence or procedure control mediation; the mediator and the parties usually agree on their own informal ways to proceed.

mens rea

The mental component of criminal liability. To be guilty of most crimes, a defendant must have committed the criminal act (the *actus reus*) in a certain mental state (the *mens rea*). The *mens rea* of robbery, for example, is the intent to permanently deprive the owner of his property.

minimum contacts

A requirement that must be satisfied before a defendant can be sued in a particular state. In order for the suit to go forward in the chosen state, the defendant must have some connections with that state. For example, advertising or having business offices within a state may provide minimum contacts between a company and the state.

minor

In most states, any person under 18 years of age. All minors must be under the care of a competent adult (parent or guardian) unless they are "emancipated"—in the military, married or living independently with court permission. Property left to a minor must be handled by an adult until the minor becomes an adult under the laws of the state where he or she lives.

Miranda warning

A warning that the police must give to a suspect before conducting an interrogation; otherwise, the suspect's answers may not be used as evidence in a trial. The *Miranda* warning requires that the suspect be told that he has the right to remain silent, the right to have an attorney present when being questioned, the right to a court appointed attorney if a private attorney is unaffordable, and the fact that any statements made by the suspect can be used against him in court. Giving the *Miranda* warning is also known as "reading a suspect his rights."

misdemeanor

A crime, less serious than a felony, punishable by no more than one year in jail. Petty theft (of articles worth less than

a certain amount), first-time drunk driving and leaving the scene of an accident are all common misdemeanors.

misfeasance

Performing a legal action in an improper way. This term is frequently used when a professional or public official does his job in a way that is not technically illegal, but is nevertheless mistaken or wrong. Here are some examples of misfeasance in a professional context: a lawyer who is mistaken about a deadline and files an important legal document too late, an accountant who makes unintentional errors on a client's tax return or a doctor who writes a prescription and accidentally includes the wrong dosage. Compare *malfeasance*.

mistrial

A trial that ends prematurely and without a judgment, due either to a mistake that jeopardizes a party's right to a fair trial or to a jury that can't agree on a verdict (a hung jury). If a judge declares a mistrial in a civil case, he or she will direct that the case be set for a new trial at a future date. Mistrials in criminal cases can result in a retrial, a plea bargain or a dismissal of the charges.

motion

During a lawsuit, a request to the judge for a decision—called an order or ruling—to resolve procedural or other issues that come up during litigation. For example, after receiving hundreds of irrelevant interrogatories, a party might file a motion asking that the other side be ordered to stop engaging in unduly burdensome discovery. A motion can be made before, during or after trial. Typically, one party submits a written motion to the court, at which point the other party has the opportunity to file a written response. The court then often schedules a hearing at which each side delivers a short oral argument. The court then approves or denies the motion. Most motions cannot be appealed until the case is over.

motion in limine

A request submitted to the court before trial in an attempt to exclude evidence from the proceedings. A motion in limine is usually made by a party when simply the mention of the evidence would prejudice the jury against that party, even if the judge later instructed the jury to disregard the evidence. For example, if a defendant in a criminal

trial were questioned and confessed to the crime without having been read his *Miranda* rights, his lawyer would file a motion in limine to keep evidence of the confession out of the trial.

natural person

A living, breathing human being, as opposed to a legal entity such as a corporation. Different rules and protections apply to natural persons and corporations, such as the Fifth Amendment right against self-incrimination, which applies only to natural persons.

naturalization

The process by which a foreign person becomes a U.S. citizen. Almost everyone who goes through naturalization must first have held a green card for several years. A naturalized U.S. citizen has virtually the same rights as a native-born American citizen.

negotiable instrument

A written document that represents an unconditional promise to pay a specified amount of money upon the demand of its owner. Examples include checks and promissory notes. Negotiable instruments can be transferred from one person to another, as when you write "pay to the order of" on the back of a check and turn it over to someone else.

net lease

A commercial real estate lease in which the tenant regularly pays not only for the space (as he does with a gross lease) but for a portion of the landlord's operating costs as well. When all three of the usual costs—taxes, maintenance and insurance—are passed on, the arrangement is known as a "triple net lease." Because these costs are variable and almost never decrease, a net lease favors the landlord. Accordingly, it may be possible for a tenant to bargain for a net lease with caps or ceilings, which limits the amount of rent the tenant must pay. For example, a net lease with caps may specify that an increase in taxes beyond a certain point (or any new taxes) will be paid by the landlord. The same kind of protection can be designed to cover increased insurance premiums and maintenance expenses.

no-fault divorce

Any divorce in which the spouse who wants to split up does not have to accuse the other of wrongdoing, but can simply state that the couple no longer gets along sufficiently. Until no-fault divorce arrived in the 1970s, the only way a person could get a divorce was to prove that the other spouse was at fault for the marriage not working. No-fault divorces are usually granted for reasons such as incompatibility, irreconcilable differences, or irretrievable or irremediable breakdown of the marriage. Also, some states allow incurable insanity as a basis for a no-fault divorce. Compare *fault divorce*.

nolle prosequi

Latin for "we shall no longer prosecute." At trial, this is an entry made on the record by a prosecutor in a criminal case stating that he will no longer pursue the matter. An entry of *nolle prosequi* may be made at any time after charges are brought and before a verdict is returned or a plea entered. Essentially, it is an admission on the part of the prosecution that some aspect of its case against the defendant has fallen apart. Abbreviated "nol. pros." or "nol-pros." Most of the time, prosecutors need a judge's permission to "nol-pros" a case. (See *Federal Rule of Criminal Procedure* 48a.)

nolo contendere

Latin for "I will not defend it." A plea entered by the defendant in response to being charged with a crime. If a defendant pleads *nolo contendere*, she neither admits nor denies that she committed the crime, but agrees to a punishment (usually a fine or jail time) as if guilty. Usually, this type of plea typically is entered because it can't be used as an admission of guilt if a civil suit against the defendant is possible. By not admitting guilt during the criminal trial, the defendant can defend the civil case without having to explain such an admission.

nondischargeable debts

Debts that cannot be erased by filing for bankruptcy. If you file for Chapter 7 bankruptcy, these debts will remain when your case is over. If you file for Chapter 13 bankruptcy, the nondischargeable debts will have to be paid in full during your plan or you will have a balance at the end of your case. Examples of nondischargeable debts include alimony and child support, most income tax debts, many student loans and debts for personal injury or death caused by drunk driving. Compare *dischargeable debts*.

nondisclosure agreement

A legally binding contract in which a person or business promises to treat specific information as a trade secret and not disclose it to others without proper authorization. Nondisclosure agreements are often used when a business discloses a trade secret to another person or business for such purposes as development, marketing, evaluation or securing financial backing. Although nondisclosure agreements are usually in the form of written contracts, they may also be implied if the context of a business relationship suggests that the parties intended to make an agreement. For example, a business that conducts patent searches for inventors is expected to keep information about the invention secret, even if no written agreement is signed, because the nature of the business is to deal in confidential information.

nonprofit corporation

A legal structure authorized by state law allowing people to come together to either benefit members of an organization (a club, or mutual benefit society) or for some public purpose (such as a hospital, environmental organization or literary society). Nonprofit corporations, despite the name, can make a profit, but the business cannot be designed primarily for profit-making purposes, and the profits must be used for the benefit of the organization or purpose the corporation was created to help. When a nonprofit corporation dissolves, any remaining assets must be distributed to another nonprofit, not to board members. As with for-profit corporations, directors of nonprofit corporations are normally shielded from personal liability for the organization's debts. Some nonprofit corporations qualify for a federal tax exemption under Section 501(c)(3) of the Internal Revenue Code, with the result that contributions to the nonprofit are tax deductible by their donors.

novation

The substitution of a new contract for an old one. A novation may change one of the parties to the contract or the duties that must be performed by the original parties.

nuisance

Something that interferes with the use of property by being irritating, offensive, obstructive or dangerous. Nuisances include a wide range of conditions, everything from a chemical plant's noxious odors to a neighbor's dog barking. The former would be a "public nuisance," one affecting many people, while the other would be a "private nuisance," limited to making your life difficult, unless the dog was bothering others. Lawsuits may be brought to abate (remove or reduce) a nuisance. See *quiet enjoyment*, *attractive nuisance*.

nulla bona

Latin for "no goods." This is what the sheriff writes when she can find no property to seize in order to pay off a court judgment.

oath

An attestation that one will tell the truth, or a promise to fulfill a pledge, often calling upon God as a witness. The best known oath is probably the witness's pledge "to tell the truth, the whole truth, and nothing but the truth" during a legal proceeding. In another context, a public official usually takes an "oath of office" before assuming her position, in which she declares that she will faithfully perform her duties.

offer of proof

At trial, a party's explanation to a judge as to how a proposed line of questioning, or a certain item of physical evidence, would be relevant to its case and admissible under the rules of evidence. Offers of proof arise when a party begins a line of questioning that the other side objects to as calling for irrelevant or inadmissible information. If the judge thinks that the questions might lead to proper evidence, the judge will stop the trial, ask the parties to "approach the bench," and give the questioner a chance to show how, if allowed, the expected answers will be both relevant and admissible. This explanation is usually presented out of the jury's hearing, but it does become part of the trial record. If the matter is later heard on appeal, the appellate court will use the record to decide whether the judge's ruling was correct.

opening statement

A statement made by an attorney or self-represented party at the beginning of a trial before evidence is introduced. The opening statement outlines the party's legal position and previews the evidence that will be introduced later. The purpose of an opening statement is to familiarize the jury with what it will hear—and why it will hear it—not

to present an argument as to why the speaker's side should win (that comes after all evidence is presented as part of the closing argument).

order

A decision issued by a court. It can be a simple command—for example, ordering a recalcitrant witness to answer a proper question—or it can be a complicated and reasoned decision made after a hearing, directing that a party either do or refrain from some act. For example, following a hearing, the court may order that evidence gathered by the police not be introduced at trial; or a judge may issue a temporary restraining order. This term usually does not describe the final decision in a case, which most often is called a judgment.

order to show cause

An order from a judge that directs a party to come to court and convince the judge why she shouldn't grant an action proposed by the other side or by the judge on her own (*sua sponte*). For example, in a divorce, at the request of one parent a judge might issue an order directing the other parent to appear in court on a particular date and time to show cause why the first parent should not be given sole physical custody of the children. Although it would seem that the person receiving an order to show cause is at a procedural disadvantage—she, after all, is the one who is told to come up with a convincing reason why the judge shouldn't order something—both sides normally have an equal chance to convince the judge to rule in their favor.

ordinance

A law adopted by a town or city council, county board of supervisors or other municipal governing board. Typically, local governments issue ordinances establishing zoning and parking rules and regulating noise, garbage removal, and the operation of parks and other areas that affect people who live or do business within the locality's borders.

own recognizance (OR)

A way the defendant can get out of jail, without paying bail, by promising to appear in court when next required to be there. Sometimes called "personal recognizance." Only those with strong ties to the community, such as a steady job, local family and no history of failing to appear in court, are good candidates for "OR" release. If the charge is very serious, however, OR may not be an option.

palimony

A nonlegal term coined by journalists to describe the division of property or alimony-like support given by one member of an unmarried couple to the other after they break up.

par value

The face value of a stock, assigned by a corporation at the time the stock is issued. The par value is often printed on the stock certificate, but the market value of the stock may be much more or much less than par.

partnership

When used without a qualifier such as "limited" or "limited liability," usually refers to a legal structure called a general partnership. This is a business owned by two or more people (called partners or general partners) who are personally liable for all business debts. To form a partnership, each partner normally contributes money, valuable property or labor in exchange for a partnership share, which reflects the amount contributed. Partnerships are easy to form since no registration is required with any governmental agency (although tax registration and other requirements to conduct business may still apply). Although not required, it is an excellent idea to prepare a written partnership agreement between the partners to define items such as ownership percentages, how profits and losses will be divided and what happens if a partner dies or becomes disabled. Partnerships themselves do not pay federal or state income taxes; rather, profits are passed through to partners who report and pay income taxes on their personal returns. See also *limited partnership, limited liability partnership*.

party

A person, corporation or other legal entity that files a lawsuit (the plaintiff or petitioner) or defends against one (the defendant or respondent).

pendente lite

Latin for "while the action is pending." This phrase is used to describe matters that are contingent upon the outcome of a lawsuit. For example, money may be deposited by the defendant with the court *pendente lite* in order to compensate the plaintiff if the defendant loses the case. If the defendant wins, she gets her money back.

per stirpes

Latin for "by right of representation." Under a will, a method of determining who inherits property when a joint beneficiary has died before the willmaker, leaving living children of his or her own. For example, Fred leaves his house jointly to his son Alan and his daughter Julie. But Alan dies before Fred, leaving two young children. If Fred's will states that heirs of a deceased beneficiary are to receive the property "per stirpes," Julie will receive one-half of the property, and Alan's two children will share his half in equal shares (through Alan by right of representation). If, on the other hand, Fred's will states that the property is to be divided per capita, Julie and the two grandchildren will each take a third.

peremptory challenge

During jury selection, an opportunity for a party to a lawsuit to dismiss or excuse a potential juror without having to give a valid reason, as would be the case when a juror is challenged for cause. Depending on court rules, each party typically gets to make from five to 15 peremptory challenges. Although parties may generally use their peremptory challenges as they see fit, the U.S. Constitution has been interpreted to prohibit their use to eliminate all jurors of a particular race or gender from a jury.

personal injury

An injury not to property, but to your body, mind or emotions. For example, if you slip and fall on a banana peel in the grocery store, personal injury covers any actual physical harm (broken leg and bruises) you suffered in the fall as well as the humiliation of falling in public, but not the harm of shattering your watch.

petition

A formal written request made to a court, asking for an order or ruling on a particular matter. For example, if you want to be appointed conservator for an elderly relative, you must file a petition with a court. See also *complaint*.

piercing the veil

A judicial doctrine that allows a plaintiff to hold otherwise immune corporate officers and directors personally liable for damages caused by a corporation under their control. The veil is pierced when officers have acted intentionally and illegally, or when their actions exceeded the power given them by the company's articles of incorporation.

plaintiff

The person, corporation or other legal entity that initiates a lawsuit. In certain states and for some types of lawsuits, the term petitioner is used instead of plaintiff. Compare *defendant, respondent*.

plea

The defendant's formal answer to criminal charges. Typically defendants enter one of the following pleas: guilty, not guilty or *nolo contendere*. A plea is usually entered when charges are formally brought (at arraignment).

plea bargain

A negotiation between the defense and prosecution (and sometimes the judge) that settles a criminal case. The defendant typically pleads guilty to a lesser crime (or fewer charges) than originally charged, in exchange for a guaranteed sentence that is shorter than what the defendant could face if convicted at trial. The prosecution gets the certainty of a conviction and a known sentence; the defendant avoids the risk of a higher sentence; and the judge gets to move on to other cases.

pleading

A statement of the plaintiff's case or the defendant's defense, set out in generally-accepted legal language and format. Today, in many states, the need to plead a case by drafting legal jargon—or borrowing from a legal form book—and printing it on numbered legal paper has been replaced by the use of preprinted forms. In this case, creating a proper pleading consists principally of checking the correct boxes and filling in the requested information.

post hoc

Part of the Latin phrase *post hoc, ergo propter hoc*, which means "after this, therefore because of this." The phrase represents the faulty logic of assuming that one thing was caused by another merely because it followed that event in time.

pot trust

A trust for children in which the trustee decides how to spend money on each child, taking money out of the trust to meet each child's specific needs. One important advantage of a pot trust over separate trusts is that it allows the trustee to provide for one child's unforeseen need, such

as a medical emergency. But a pot trust can also make the trustee's life difficult by requiring choices about disbursing funds to the various children. A pot trust ends when the youngest child reaches a certain age, usually 18 or 21.

pour-over will

A will that "pours over" property into a trust when the will-maker dies. Property left through the will must go through probate before it goes into the trust.

power of appointment

The legal authority to decide who will receive someone else's property, usually property held in a trust. Most trustees can distribute the income from a trust only according to the terms of the trust, but a trustee with a power of appointment can choose the beneficiaries, sometimes from a list of candidates specified by the grantor. For example, Karin creates a trust with power of appointment to benefit either the local art museum, symphony, library or park, depending on the trustee's assessment of need.

power of attorney

A document that gives another person legal authority to act on your behalf. If you create such a document, you are called the principal and the person to whom you give this authority is called your attorney-in-fact. A power of attorney may be "general," which gives your attorney-in-fact extensive powers over your affairs. Or it may be "limited" or "special," giving your attorney-in-fact permission to handle a specifically defined task. If you make a durable power of attorney, the document will continue in effect even if you become incapacitated. For examples, see *durable power of attorney for finances, durable power of attorney for health care.*

prayer for relief

What the plaintiff asks of the court—for example, the plaintiff may ask for an award of monetary damages, an injunction to make the defendant stop a certain activity, or both.

precedent

A legal principle or rule created by one or more decisions of a state or federal appellate court. These rules provide a point of reference or authority for judges deciding similar issues in later cases. Lower courts must apply these rules when faced with similar legal issues. For example, if the

Montana Supreme Court decides that a certain type of employment contract overly restricts the right of the employee to quit and get another job, all other Montana courts must apply this same rule.

presumption of innocence

One of the most sacred principles in the American criminal justice system, holding that a defendant is innocent until proven guilty. In other words, the prosecution must prove, beyond a reasonable doubt, each element of the crime charged.

pretermitted heir

A child or spouse who is not mentioned in a will and whom the court believes was accidentally overlooked by the person who made the will. For example, a child born or adopted after the will is made may be deemed a pretermitted heir. If the court determines that an heir was accidentally omitted, that heir is entitled to receive the same share of the estate as she would have if the deceased had died without a will. A pretermitted heir is sometimes called an "omitted heir."

prima facie

Latin for "on its face." A *prima facie* case is one that at first glance presents sufficient evidence for the plaintiff to win. Such a case must be refuted in some way by the defendant for him to have a chance of prevailing at trial. For example, if you can show that someone intentionally touched you in a harmful or offensive way and caused some injury to you, you have established a *prima facie* case of battery. However, this does not mean that you automatically win your case. The defendant would win if he could show that you consented to the harmful or offensive touching.

principal

(1) When creating a power of attorney or other legal document, the person who appoints an attorney-in-fact or agent to act on his or her behalf. (2) In criminal law, the main perpetrator of a crime. (3) In commercial law, the total amount of a loan, not including any capitalized fees or interest. (4) In the law of trusts, the property of the trust, as opposed to the income generated by that property. The principal is also known as the trust *corpus* (Latin for "body.") For example, Arthur establishes a new trust with $100,000, with interest and other income payable to Merlin; the $100,000 is the trust principal or *corpus.*

pro hac vice

Latin meaning "for this one particular occasion." The phrase usually refers to an out-of-state lawyer who has been granted special permission to participate in a particular case, even though the lawyer is not licensed to practice in the state where the case is being tried.

pro per

A term derived from the Latin *in propria*, meaning "for one's self," used in some states to describe a person who handles her own case without a lawyer. In other states, the term *pro se* is used. When a nonlawyer files his own legal papers, he is expected to write "*in pro per*" at the bottom of the heading on the first page.

pro se

A Latin phrase meaning "for himself" or "in one's own behalf." This term denotes a person who represents herself in court. It is used in some states in place of "*in pro per*" and has the same meaning.

probable cause

The amount and quality of information a judge must have before she will sign a search warrant allowing the police to conduct a search or arrest a suspect. If the police have presented reliable information that convinces the judge that it's more likely than not that a crime has occurred and the suspect is involved, the judge will conclude that there is "probable cause" and will issue the warrant. Police also need probable cause to conduct a warrantless search or seizure. When the police do not have time to go to a judge for a warrant (such as when they are in hot pursuit of a suspect), they still must have probable cause before they can arrest or search.

probate

The court process following a person's death that includes:

- proving the authenticity of the deceased person's will appointing someone to handle the deceased person's affairs;
- identifying and inventorying the deceased person's property;
- paying debts and taxes;
- identifying heirs; and
- distributing the deceased person's property according to the will or, if there is no will, according to state law.

Formal court-supervised probate is a costly, time-consuming process—a windfall for lawyers—which is best avoided if possible.

probate court

A specialized court or division of a state trial court that considers only cases concerning the distribution of deceased persons' estates. Called "surrogate court" in New York and several other states, this court normally examines the authenticity of a will—or, if a person dies intestate, figures out who receives her property under state law. It then oversees a procedure to pay the deceased person's debts and to distribute her assets to the proper inheritors. See *probate.*

prosecute

When a local District Attorney, state Attorney General or federal United States Attorney brings a criminal case against a defendant.

prosecutor

A lawyer who works for the local, state or federal government to bring and litigate criminal cases.

public defender

A lawyer appointed by the court and paid by the county, state, or federal government to represent clients who are charged with violations of criminal law and are unable to pay for their own defense.

pur autre vie

Legal French meaning "for another's life." It is a phrase used to describe the duration of a property interest. For example, if Bob is given use of the family house for as long as his mother lives, he has possession of the house *pur autre vie.*

quantum meruit

Latin for "as much as is deserved." The reasonable value of services provided, which a winning party may be able to recover from an opponent who broke a contract.

quasi-community property

A form of property owned by a married couple. If a couple moves to a community property state from a non-community property state, property they acquired together in the non-community property state may be considered quasi-community property. Quasi-community property is

treated just like community property when one spouse dies or if the couple divorces.

quiet enjoyment

The right of a property owner or tenant to enjoy his or her property without interference. Disruption of quiet enjoyment may constitute a nuisance. Leases and rental agreements often contain a "covenant of quiet enjoyment," expressly obligating the landlord to see that tenants have the opportunity to live undisturbed.

quitclaim deed

A deed that transfers whatever ownership interest the transferor has in a particular property. For example, a divorcing husband may quitclaim his interest in certain real estate to his ex-wife, officially giving up any legal interest in the property. The deed does not guarantee anything about what is being transferred, however. Compare *grant deed*.

real property

Another term for real estate. It includes land and things permanently attached to the land, such as trees, buildings, and stationary mobile homes. Anything that is not real property is termed personal property.

recording

The process of filing a copy of a deed or other document concerning real estate with the land records office for the county in which the land is located. Recording creates a public record of changes in ownership of all property in the state.

recusal

A situation in which a judge or prosecutor is removed or steps down from a case. This often happens when the judge or prosecutor has a conflict of interest—for example, a prior relationship with one of the parties.

red herring

A legal or factual issue that is irrelevant to the case at hand.

reformation

The act of changing a written contract when one of the parties can prove that the actual agreement was different than what's written down. The changes are usually made by a court when both parties overlooked a mistake in the document, or when one party has deceived the other.

remainderman

Someone who will inherit property in the future. For instance, if someone dies and leaves his home "to Alma for life, and then to Barry," Barry is a remainderman because he will inherit the home in the future, after Alma dies.

replevin

A type of legal action where the owner of movable goods is given the right to recover them from someone who shouldn't have them. Replevin is often used in disputes between buyers and sellers—for example, a seller might bring a replevin action to reclaim goods from a buyer who failed to pay for them.

request for admission

A discovery procedure, authorized by the Federal Rules of Civil Procedure and the court rules of many states, in which one party asks an opposing party to admit that certain facts are true. If the opponent admits the facts or fails to respond in a timely manner, the facts will be deemed true for purposes of trial. A request for admission is called a "request to admit" in many states.

res ipsa loquitur

A Latin term meaning "the thing speaks for itself." *Res ipsa loquitur* is a legal doctrine or rule of evidence that creates a presumption that a defendant acted negligently simply because a harmful accident occurred. The presumption arises only if (1) the thing that caused the accident was under the defendant's control, (2) the accident could happen only as a result of a careless act and, (3) the plaintiff's behavior did not contribute to the accident. Lawyers often refer to this doctrine as "*res ips*" or "*res ipsa*."

res nova

Latin for "a new thing," used by courts to describe an issue of law or case that has not previously been decided.

residuary beneficiary

A person who receives any property by a will or trust that is not specifically left to another designated beneficiary. For example, if Antonio makes a will leaving his home to Edwina and the remainder of his property to Elmo, then Elmo is the residuary beneficiary.

residuary estate

The property that remains in a deceased person's estate after all specific gifts are made, and all debts, taxes, administrative fees, probate costs, and court costs are paid. The residuary estate also includes any gifts under a will that fail or lapse. For example, Connie's will leaves her house and all its furnishings to Andrew, her VW bug to her friend Carl, and the remainder of her property (the residuary estate) to her sister, Sara. She doesn't name any alternate beneficiaries. Carl dies before Connie. The VW bug becomes part of the residuary estate and passes to Sara, along with all of Connie's property other than the house and furnishings. Also called the residual estate or residue.

respondent

A term used instead of defendant or appellee in some states—especially for divorce and other family law cases—to identify the party who is sued and must respond to the petitioner's complaint.

restraining order

An order from a court directing one person not to do something, such as make contact with another person, enter the family home or remove a child from the state. Restraining orders are typically issued in cases in which spousal abuse or stalking is feared—or has occurred—in an attempt to ensure the victim's safety. Restraining orders are also commonly issued to cool down ugly disputes between neighbors.

restraint on alienation

A provision in a deed or will that attempts to restrict ownership of the property—for example, selling your house to your daughter with the provision that it never be sold to anyone outside the family. These provisions are generally unenforceable.

right of survivorship

The right of a surviving joint tenant to take ownership of a deceased joint tenant's share of the property. See *joint tenancy*.

rule against perpetuities

An exceedingly complex legal doctrine that limits the amount of time that property can be controlled after death by a person's instructions in a will. For example, a person would not be allowed to leave property to her husband for his life, then to her children for their lives, then to her grandchildren. The gift would potentially go to the grandchildren at a point too remote in time.

ruling

Any decision a judge makes during the course of a lawsuit.

running with the land

A phrase used in property law to describe a right or duty that remains with a piece of property no matter who owns it. For example, the duty to allow a public beach access path across waterfront property would most likely pass from one owner of the property to the next.

S corporation

A term that describes a profit-making corporation organized under state law whose shareholders have applied for and received subchapter S corporation status from the Internal Revenue Service. Electing to do business as an S corporation lets shareholders enjoy limited liability status, as would be true of any corporation, but be taxed like a partnership or sole proprietor. That is, instead of being taxed as a separate entity (as would be the case with a regular or C corporation), an S corporation is a pass-through tax entity: income taxes are reported and paid by the shareholders, not the S corporation. To qualify as an S corporation a number of IRS rules must be met, such as a limit of 75 shareholders and citizenship requirements.

search warrant

An order signed by a judge that directs owners of private property to allow the police to enter and search for items named in the warrant. The judge won't issue the warrant unless she has been convinced that there is probable cause for the search—that reliable evidence shows that it's more likely than not that a crime has occurred and that the items sought by the police are connected with it and will be found at the location named in the warrant. In limited situations, the police may search without a warrant, but they cannot use what they find at trial if the defense can show that there was no probable cause for the search.

secured debt

A debt on which a creditor has a lien. The creditor can institute a foreclosure or repossession to take the property identified by the lien, called the collateral, to satisfy the debt if you default. Compare *unsecured debt*.

self-incrimination

The making of statements that might expose you to criminal prosecution, either now or in the future. The Fifth Amendment of the U.S. Constitution prohibits the government from forcing you to provide evidence (as in answering questions) that would or might lead to your prosecution for a crime.

self-proving will

A will that is created in a way that allows a probate court to easily accept it as the true will of the person who has died. In most states, a will is self-proving when two witnesses sign under penalty of perjury that they observed the willmaker sign it, he told them it was his will and that the willmaker appeared to be of sound mind and proper age to make a will. If no one contests the validity of the will, the probate court will accept the will without hearing the testimony of the witnesses or other evidence. To make a self-proving will in other states, the willmaker and one or more witnesses must sign an affidavit (sworn statement) before a notary public certifying that the will is genuine and that all willmaking formalities have been observed.

sentence

Punishment in a criminal case. A sentence can range from a fine and community service to life imprisonment or death. For most crimes, the sentence is chosen by the trial judge, who is limited by law to a narrow range of options—for example, burglary might be punishable by three, five or seven years in prison. Some crimes in some states, however, carry an indeterminate sentence—for example, "20 years to life" for first-degree murder. (The state's parole board decides when, if ever, the defendant should be paroled after he has served the 20-year minimum.) The jury chooses the sentence only in a capital case, when it must choose between life in prison without parole and death.

separate property

In community property states, property owned and controlled entirely by one spouse in a marriage. In community property states, property acquired by a spouse before the marriage or after separation is typically that spouse's separate property, as is a gift or inheritance received solely by that spouse. In other states, a spouse's separate property is property owned or acquired before the marriage or after separation, and all property to which title is held in that spouse's name. At divorce, separate property is not divided under the state's property division laws, but is kept by the spouse who owns it. Separate property includes all property that a spouse obtained before marriage, through inheritance or as a gift. It also includes any property that is traceable to separate property—for example, cash from the sale of a vintage car owned by one spouse before marriage and any property that the spouses agree is separate property. Compare *community property* and *equitable distribution*.

servient tenement

Property that is subject to use by another for a specific purpose. For example, a beachfront house that has a public walkway to the beach on its premises would be a servient tenement.

setback

The distance between a property boundary and a building. A minimum setback is usually required by law.

setoff

A claim made by someone who allegedly owes money, that the amount should be reduced because the other person owes him money. This is often raised in a counterclaim filed by a defendant in a lawsuit. Banks may try to exercise a setoff by taking money out of a deposit account to satisfy past due payments on a loan or credit card bill. Such an act is illegal under most circumstances.

severability clause

A provision in a contract that preserves the rest of the contract if a portion of it is invalidated by a court. Without a severability clause, a decision by the court finding one part of the contract unenforceable would invalidate the entire document.

shareholder

An owner of a corporation whose ownership interest is represented by shares of stock in the corporation. A shareholder—also called a stockholder—has rights conferred by state law, by the bylaws of the corporation and, if one has been adopted, by a shareholder's agreement (often called a buy-sell agreement). These include the right to be notified of annual shareholders' meetings, to elect directors, and to receive an appropriate share of any dividends. In large corporations, shareholders are usually investors whose shares are held in the name of their broker. On the other hand, in incorporated small businesses, owners often wear many hats—shareholder, director, officer and employee—with the result that distinctions between these legal categories become fuzzy.

slander

A type of defamation. Slander is an untruthful oral (spoken) statement about a person that harms the person's reputation or standing in the community. Because slander is a tort (a civil wrong), the injured person can bring a lawsuit against the person who made the false statement. If the statement is made via broadcast media—for example, over the radio or on TV—it is considered libel, rather than slander, because the statement has the potential to reach a very wide audience.

small claims court

A state court that resolves disputes involving relatively small amounts of money—usually between $2,000 and $10,000, depending on the state. Adversaries usually appear without lawyers—in fact, some states forbid lawyers in small claims court—and recount their side of the dispute in plain English. Evidence, including the testimony of eye witnesses and expert witnesses, is relatively easy to present because small claims courts do not follow the formal rules of evidence that govern regular trial cases. A small claims judgment has the same force as does the judgment of any other state court, meaning that if the loser—now called the "judgment debtor"—fails to pay the judgment voluntarily, it can be collected using normal collection techniques, such as property liens and wage garnishments.

sole proprietorship

A business owned and managed by one person (or for tax purposes, a husband and wife). For IRS purposes, a sole proprietor and her business are one tax entity, meaning that business profits are reported and taxed on the owner's personal tax return. Setting up a sole proprietorship is cheap and easy since no legal formation documents need be filed with any governmental agency (although tax registration and other permit and license requirements may still apply). Once you file a fictitious name statement (assuming you don't use your own name) and obtain any required basic tax permits and business licenses, you'll be in business. The main downside of a sole proprietorship is that its owner is personally liable for all business debts.

specific bequest

A specific item of property that is left to a named beneficiary under a will. If the person who made the will no longer owns the property when he dies, the bequest fails. In other words, the beneficiary cannot substitute a similar item in the estate. Example: If John leaves his 1954 Mercedes to Patti, and when John dies the 1954 Mercedes is long gone, Patti doesn't receive John's current car or the cash equivalent of the Mercedes. See *ademption*.

specific intent

An intent to produce the precise consequences of the crime, including the intent to do the physical act that causes the consequences. For example, the crime of larceny is the taking of the personal property of another with the intent to permanently deprive the other person of the property. A person is not guilty of larceny just because he took someone else's property; it must be proven that he took it with the purpose of keeping it permanently.

specific performance

A remedy provided by a court that orders the losing side to perform its part of a contract rather than, or possibly in addition to, paying money damages to the winner.

spendthrift trust

A trust created for a beneficiary the grantor considers irresponsible about money. The trustee keeps control of the trust income, doling out money to the beneficiary as needed, and sometimes paying third parties (creditors, for example) on the beneficiary's behalf, bypassing the

beneficiary completely. Spendthrift trusts typically contain a provision prohibiting creditors from seizing the trust fund to satisfy the beneficiary's debts. These trusts are legal in most states, even though creditors hate them.

stare decisis

Latin for "let the decision stand," a doctrine requiring that judges apply the same reasoning to lawsuits as has been used in prior similar cases.

state court

A court that decides cases involving state law or the state constitution. State courts have jurisdiction to consider disputes involving individual defendants who reside in that state or have minimum contacts with the state, such as using its highways, owning real property in the state or doing business in the state. State courts have very broad power to hear cases involving all subjects except those involving federal issues and laws, which are in the exclusive jurisdiction of the federal courts. State courts are often divided according to the dollar amount of the claims they can hear. Depending on the state, small claims, justice, municipal or city courts usually hear smaller cases, while district, circuit, superior or county courts (or in New York, supreme court) have jurisdiction over larger cases. Finally, state courts are also commonly divided according to subject matter, such as criminal court, family court and probate court.

statute of limitations

The legally-prescribed time limit in which a lawsuit must be filed. Statutes of limitation differ depending on the type of legal claim, and often the state. For example, many states require that a personal injury lawsuit be filed within one year from the date of injury—or in some instances, from the date when it should reasonably have been discovered—but some allow two years. Similarly, claims based on a written contract must be filed in court within four years from the date the contract was broken in some states and five years in others. Statute of limitations rules apply to cases filed in all courts, including federal court.

sua sponte

Latin for "on its own will or motion." This term is most commonly used to describe a decision or act that a judge decides upon without having been asked by either party.

subpena

The modern spelling of subpoena. A subpena is a court order issued at the request of a party requiring a witness to appear in court.

subpena duces tecum

A type of subpena, usually issued at the request of a party, by which a court orders a witness to produce certain documents at a deposition or trial. However, when one party wants an opposing party to produce documents, a different discovery device, called a Request for Production of Documents, is often used instead.

subrogation

A taking on of the legal rights of someone whose debts or expenses have been paid. For example, subrogation occurs when an insurance company that has paid off its injured claimant takes the legal rights the claimant has against a third party that caused the injury, and sues that third party.

substituted service

A method for the formal delivery of court papers that takes the place of personal service. Personal service means that the papers are placed directly into the hands of the person to be served. Substituted service, on the other hand, may be accomplished by leaving the documents with a designated agent, with another adult in the recipient's home, with the recipient's manager at work, or by posting a notice in a prominent place and then using certified mail to send copies of the documents to the recipient.

substitution of parties

A replacement of one of the sides in a lawsuit because of events that prevent the party from continuing with the trial. For example, substitution of parties may occur when one party dies or, in the case of a public official, when that public official is removed from office.

sui generis

Latin for "of its own kind," used to describe something that is unique or different.

summary adjudication of issues

A partial summary judgment motion, in which the judge is asked to decide only one or some of the legal issues in the case. For example, in a car accident case there might

be overwhelming and uncontradicted evidence of the defendant's carelessness, but conflicting evidence as to the extent of the plaintiff's injuries. The plaintiff might ask for summary adjudication on the issue of carelessness, but go to trial on the question of injuries.

summary judgment

A final decision by a judge that resolves a lawsuit in favor of one of the parties. A motion for summary judgment is made after discovery is completed but before the case goes to trial. The party making the motion marshals all the evidence in its favor, compares it to the other side's evidence, and argues that a reasonable jury looking at the same evidence could only decide the case one way—for the moving party. If the judge agrees, then a trial would be unnecessary and the judge enters judgment for the moving party.

summons

A paper prepared by the plaintiff and issued by a court that informs the defendant that she has been sued. The summons requires that the defendant file a response with the court—or in many small claims courts, simply appear in person on an appointed day—within a given time period or risk losing the case under the terms of a default judgment.

sunset law

A law that automatically terminates the agency or program it establishes unless it is expressly renewed. For example, a state law establishing and funding a new drug rehabilitation program within state prisons may provide that the program will shut down in two years unless it is reviewed and approved by the state legislature.

sunshine laws

Statutes that provide public access to governmental agency meetings and records.

superior court

The main county trial court in many states, mostly in the West. See *state court*.

Supremacy clause

Provision under Article IV, Section 2 of the U.S. Constitution, providing that federal law is superior to and overrides state law when they conflict.

Supreme Court

America's highest court, which has the final power to decide cases involving the interpretation of the U.S. Constitution, certain legal areas set forth in the Constitution (called federal questions), and federal laws. It can also make final decisions in certain lawsuits between parties in different states. The U.S. Supreme Court has nine justices—one of whom is the chief justice—who are appointed for life by the president and must be confirmed by the U.S. Senate. Most states also have a supreme court, which is the final arbiter of the state's constitution and state laws. However, in several states the highest state court uses a different name—most notably New York and Maryland, where it's called the "Court of Appeals," and Massachusetts, where it's called the "Supreme Judicial Court."

tangible personal property

Personal property that can be felt or touched. Examples include furniture, cars, jewelry and artwork. However, cash and checking accounts are not tangible personal property. The law is unsettled as to whether computer data is tangible personal property. Compare *intangible property*.

temporary restraining order (TRO)

An order that tells one person to stop harassing or harming another, issued after the aggrieved party appears before a judge. Once the TRO is issued, the court holds a second hearing where the other side can tell his story and the court can decide whether to make the TRO permanent by issuing an injunction. Although a TRO will often not stop an enraged spouse from acting violently, the police are more willing to intervene if the abused spouse has a TRO.

tenancy by the entirety

A special kind of property ownership that's only for married couples. Both spouses have the right to enjoy the entire property, and when one spouse dies, the surviving spouse gets title to the property (called a right of survivorship). It is similar to joint tenancy, but it is available in only about half the states.

tenancy in common

A way two or more people can own property together. Each can leave his or her interest upon death to beneficiaries of his choosing instead of to the other owners, as is required with joint tenancy. Also, unlike joint tenancy, the ownership

shares need not be equal. In most states, each tenant in common may encumber only his share of the property, so that the other share is debt-free. In some states, two people are presumed to own property as tenants in common unless they've agreed otherwise in writing.

testate

The circumstance of dying after making a valid will. A person who dies with a will is said to have died "testate." Compare *intestate*.

testify

To provide oral evidence under oath at a trial or at a deposition.

tort

An injury to one person for which the person who caused the injury is legally responsible. A tort can be intentional—for example, an angry punch in the nose—but is far more likely to result from carelessness (called "negligence"), such as riding your bicycle on the sidewalk and colliding with a pedestrian. While the injury that forms the basis of a tort is usually physical, this is not a requirement—libel, slander and the "intentional infliction of mental distress" are on a good-sized list of torts not based on a physical injury.

tortious interference

The causing of harm by disrupting something that belongs to someone else—for example, interfering with a contractual relationship so that one party fails to deliver goods on time.

trust corpus

Latin for "the body" of the trust. This term refers to all the property transferred to a trust. For example, if a trust is established (funded) with $250,000, that money is the corpus. Sometimes the trust corpus is known as the *res*, a Latin word meaning "thing."

trustee

The person who manages assets owned by a trust under the terms of the trust document. A trustee's purpose is to safeguard the trust and distribute trust income or principal as directed in the trust document. With a simple probate-avoidance living trust, the person who creates the trust is also the trustee.

ultra vires

Latin for "beyond powers." It refers to conduct by a corporation or its officers that exceeds the powers granted by law.

unclean hands

A legal doctrine that prevents a plaintiff who has acted unethically in relation to a lawsuit from winning the suit or from recovering as much money as she would have if she had behaved honorably. For example, if a contractor is suing a homeowner to recover the price of work he did on the home, his failure to perform the work as specified would leave him with unclean hands.

unconscionability

A seller's taking advantage of a buyer due to their unequal bargaining positions, perhaps because of the buyer's recent trauma, physical infirmity, ignorance, inability to read or inability to understand the language. The unfairness must be so severe that it is shocking to the average person. It usually includes the absence of any meaningful choice on the part of the buyer and contract terms so one-sided that they unreasonably favor the seller. A contract will be terminated if the buyer can prove unconscionability.

unjust enrichment

A legal doctrine stating that if a person receives money or other property through no effort of his own, at the expense of another, the recipient should return the property to the rightful owner, even if the property was not obtained illegally. Most courts will order that the property be returned if the party who has suffered the loss brings a lawsuit.

unsecured debt

A debt that is not tied to any item of property. A creditor doesn't have the right to grab property to satisfy the debt if you default. The creditor's only remedy is to sue you and get a judgment. Compare *secured debt*.

variance

An exception to a zoning ordinance, usually granted by a local government. For example, if you own an oddly-shaped lot that could not accommodate a home in accordance with your city's setback requirement, you could apply at the appropriate office for a variance allowing you to build closer to a boundary line.

venue

State laws or court rules that establish the proper court to hear a case, often based on the convenience of the defendant. Because state courts have jurisdiction to hear cases from a wide geographical area (for example, California courts have jurisdiction involving most disputes arising between California residents), additional rules, called rules of venue, have been developed to ensure that the defendant is not needlessly inconvenienced. For example, the correct venue for one Californian to sue another is usually limited to the court in the judicial district where the defendant lives, an accident occurred, or a contract was signed or to be carried out. Practically, venue rules mean that a defendant can't usually be sued far from where he lives or does business, if no key events happened at that location. Venue for a criminal case is normally the judicial district where the crime was committed.

vested remainder

An unconditional right to receive real property at some point in the future. A vested interest may be created by a deed or a will. For example, if Julie's will leaves her house to her daughter, but the daughter will gain possession only after Julie's husband dies, the daughter has a vested remainder in the house.

volenti non fit injuria

Latin for "to a willing person, no injury is done." This doctrine holds that a person who knowingly and willingly puts himself in a dangerous situation cannot sue for any resulting injuries.

with prejudice

A final and binding decision by a judge about a legal matter that prevents further pursuit of the same matter in any court. When a judge makes such a decision, he dismisses the matter "with prejudice."

witness

A person who testifies under oath at a deposition or trial, providing firsthand or expert evidence. In addition, the term also refers to someone who watches another person sign a document and then adds his name to confirm (called "attesting") that the signature is genuine.

wrongful death

A civil claim based upon a death caused by the fault of another. Examples of wrongful conduct that may lead to death include drinking and driving, manufacturing a deficient product, building an unstable structure or failing to diagnose a fatal disease.

zoning

The laws dividing cities into different areas according to use, from single-family residences to industrial plants. Zoning ordinances control the size, location and use of buildings within these different areas.

Index

M

Get the Latest in the Law

 Nolo's Legal Updater
We'll send you an email whenever a new edition of your book is published!
Sign up at **www.nolo.com/legalupdater**.

 Updates at Nolo.com
Check **www.nolo.com/update** to find recent changes in the law that
affect the current edition of your book.

 Nolo Customer Service
To make sure that this edition of the book is the most recent one, call us at
800-728-3555 and ask one of our friendly customer service representatives
(7:00 am to 6:00 pm PST, weekdays only). Or find out at **www.nolo.com**.

4 **Complete the Registration & Comment Card ...**
... and we'll do the work for you! Just indicate your preferences below:

Registration & Comment Card

NAME   DATE

ADDRESS

CITY   STATE   ZIP

PHONE   EMAIL

COMMENTS

WAS THIS BOOK EASY TO USE?   (VERY EASY)   5   4   3   2   1   (VERY DIFFICULT)

☐ Yes, you can quote me in future Nolo promotional materials. *Please include phone number above.*

☐ Yes, send me **Nolo's Legal Updater** via email when a new edition of this book is available.

Yes, I want to sign up for the following email newsletters:

   ☐ **NoloBriefs** (monthly)
   ☐ **Nolo's Special Offer** (monthly)
   ☐ **Nolo's BizBriefs** (monthly)
   ☐ **Every Landlord's Quarterly** (four times a year)

☐ Yes, you can give my contact info to carefully selected
partners whose products may be of interest to me.

NOLO

LRES 14.0

Nolo
950 Parker Street
Berkeley, CA 94710-9867
www.nolo.com